Macmillan
Teach Yourself
Personal Finance

in **24** hours

Pearson Education Macmillan USA
201 West 103rd Street
Indianapolis, IN 46290

Macmillan Teach Yourself Personal Finance in 24 Hours

International Standard Book Number: 0-02-863619-8
Library of Congress Catalog Card Number: Available upon request.

Printed in the United States of America

First printing: 2000

03   02   01   00   4   3   2   1

Note: This publication contains the opinions and ideas of its author. It is intended to provide helpful and informative material on the subject matter covered. It is sold with the understanding that the author and publisher are not engaged in rendering professional services in the book. If the reader requires personal assistance or advice, a competent professional should be consulted.

The author and publisher specifically disclaim any responsibility for any liability, loss, or risk, personal or otherwise, which is incurred as a consequence, directly or indirectly, of the use and application of any of the contents of this book.

Trademarks

SENIOR ACQUISITIONS EDITOR
Renee Wilmeth

DEVELOPMENT EDITOR
Nancy D. Warner

PRODUCTION EDITORS
Billy Fields
JoAnna Kremer
Christy Wagner

TECHNICAL EDITOR
Gail Perry

INDEXER
Angie Bess

PRODUCTION
Darin Crone
John Etchison

COVER DESIGNER
Aren Howell

BOOK DESIGNER
Gary Adair

MANAGING EDITOR
Cari Luna

PRODUCT MANAGER
Phil Kitchel

PUBLISHER
Marie Butler-Knight

Janet Bigham Bernstel dedicates this book to her beloved mother and father, Elizabeth and Harry Bigham, who taught her the true value of money.

Lea Saslav dedicates this book to her parents, Isidor and Ann Saslav, for their abundance of riches, both creative and financial; and to her Higher Power, which has shown her the financial serenity that comes from taking each day one day at a time.

Overview

Contents

Introduction

Congratulations! You've just taken the first step toward good financial health for the rest of your life. Keeping up with your financial fitness is just as important as the upkeep of any of your possessions, whether it be your body, car, home, or sailing yacht. Regular maintenance is going to leave you with a well-oiled machine that brings you pleasure and contentment. The best way for you to achieve that goal financially is to become an informed consumer and investor, and you are now well on your way to both.

We don't want to mislead you with the title. Sitting down with this book for the next 24 hours is probably not the best way to digest its contents. If you set aside a quiet time each day for the next 24 days and read an hour, however, we think you'll be able to absorb and understand a great deal about how to enrich your financial well-being.

WHAT YOU'LL FIND IN THIS BOOK

Personal finance isn't all about crunching numbers, and it doesn't have to be boring. Remember that we're talking about making, saving, and investing money for *you* and your healthy financial future.

Teach Yourself Personal Finance in 24 Hours is divided into five parts that will help you master the information in related segments. It's designed to gradually introduce you to the topic of personal finance by starting with a solid foundation and then building on it one hour at a time.

In **Part I, "Getting Up Close and Personal,"** we are going to focus on how you can become a better money manager by teaching you to check your financial pulse. Once you have a hold on your current financial health, we'll point you in the right direction for establishing good habits.

For example, we'll begin with financial goals. By the end of Hour 1, "Developing Your Financial Goals," you will have the tools to create a step-by-step plan for financial independence for you and your family far down the road of life.

Then it's time for some personal soul-searching. Even if you would rather talk about anything but money with your friends, we think that if you are open and honest in the upcoming hours, you'll learn a lot about yourself and your money habits. We may even help you cure some problems. There is such a thing as good health, but nothing is really terminal in finance, not even bankruptcy.

Part II, "Investment Methods," will help you learn about increasing your personal wealth through investments as simple as the company 401(k). Many people stumble through their lives worrying about how to pay the next bill, much less save for a comfortable retirement. Once you've read Hour 5, "Investing Basics," you'll wonder why you waited this long. Although building your own portfolio is not hard, getting started is—and you've already done that by purchasing this book.

Wherever possible, we try to give the reader Internet access. Millions of women and men are banking, investing, buying, and researching online, and few of us can afford to ignore it. In fact, a great deal of the research for this book was conducted on the Internet because the news is so instantaneous. Rates change, rules are reinterpreted, and we want to give you the most up-to-date personal finance information you can find anywhere … but we also give you the Web tools to find more.

Of course, you'll gain a lot from reading this book even if you open it on a sailboat in a remote lake. These hours were constructed to simplify the topic and make it easy for you to grasp. You don't need a computer to teach yourself personal finance, and in **Part III, "Tools,"** you'll discover all the tools you need to master your finances—online and off.

In **Part IV, "Long-Term Planning,"** you will get a better idea of how to plan for the future, including tax preparation, buying the right kind of insurance for you and your family, and what goes into buying a home and car. Also included is information on estate planning and will preparation.

Part V, "Life's Changes and Growth" will help you master your ongoing relationship with money. You will learn about changing goals as you age, as well as dealing with money on your own for the first time. In addition, you will learn more about potential financial pitfalls and how to avoid them. We've also included a chapter on finding a job online, to help you job-hunt well into the twenty-first century.

EXTRAS

At the end of each hour, you'll find a short quiz to help you support what you've learned. This is where you can pat yourself on the back for a job well done and know that you're ready for the next building block.

Take the quiz again the next time you sit down to read an hour. It will act as a refresher to help you remember what you've learned and to get your mind in gear for the next round of personal finance. You can also use the glossary in Appendix C as a quick reference guide for financial terms that you're not completely comfortable with yet.

We know you don't have a lot of extra time. You're a hard-working individual whose life is probably spent working for others, whether it's your boss or your family, and you want to do something for yourself. We've created this book for you, to make personal growth and personal financial health very manageable goals for your future.

Last, but not least, this book contains a lot of miscellaneous cross-references, tips, shortcuts, and warnings as sidebars from the regular text. These odds and ends are given particular names and here's how they stack up:

GO TO ▶
This sidebar cross-references you to another point in the book to learn more about a particular topic. For example, refer to Hour 12 to find out more about commodities.

JUST A MINUTE

 This sidebar offers advice or teaches an *easier* way to do something.

TIME SAVER

This sidebar offers a *faster* way to do something.

PROCEED WITH CAUTION

This sidebar is a warning. It advises you about potential problems and helps you steer clear of trouble. Generally, a **Time Out** has some ramifications/repercussions. If you don't heed the advice in this sidebar, you could lose money or waste time.

About the Authors

JANET BIGHAM BERNSTEL is the co-author of *The Complete Idiot's Guide to Making Money in the New Millennium*. She is an award-winning journalist who has been reporting for print and electronic broadcast for nearly two decades.

Bernstel is the creator of "Janet Talks Money," a syndicated weekly personal finance column distributed by Paradigm-TSA, and creates monthly special reports for the *Bank Marketing* magazine, an affiliate of the American Bankers Association. She also develops and instructs personal finance courses for the Ziff-Davis online learning community, SmartPlanet.com, including *Introduction to Personal Finance, Home Banking on the Web,* and *Making and Managing Money in 2000.*

Her writings are often featured in the Personal Finance area of America Online, where she was online managing editor and writer for the site MoneyWhiz. She helped develop MoneyWhiz into an independent Web site, theWhiz.com, which was launched in the summer of 1998. She recently created a comprehensive guide on starting and growing a small business for theWhiz's sister financial Web site, www.bankrate.com.

Bernstel's experience in television includes reports on CNN, ABC, and CBS. She was a member of the top-ranked ABC affiliate news team in Philadelphia, and a reporter and news anchor for an ABC affiliate in Florida. She also produced and anchored the nightly news for a CBS affiliate in the United States territory of the Virgin Islands.

LEA SASLAV, a graduate of Harvard University, began her career on the staff at *Esquire Magazine*. She was a long-time entertainment correspondent to the *USA Today* Life Section and has contributed articles and background research to *The New York Times, People* magazine, *The New York Times Syndicate,* the *Los Angeles Times Syndicate,* the *New York Post, TV Guide, Details* magazine, the *Houston Post,* the *Fort Worth Star-Telegram,* and *Hamptons* magazine.

She was also a contributor to the original "Parent Soup" Web site (now www.ivillage.com) and Disney/ABC's entertainment Web site (www. mrshowbiz.com). She will debut a column on www.msmoney.com in January 2000 dealing with issues of women, debt, and "financial decluttering."

Her interest in personal finance grew out of a two-year-plus membership in a nationally recognized 12-step program, "Debtors Anonymous," which deals with issues of debt, income growth, and general serenity issues around money.

She currently resides on New York City's Upper West Side.

Acknowledgments

Janet Bigham Bernstel would like to thank the people at Macmillan Reference who helped bring this book to print, including Development Editor Nancy Warner, who has offered much more than technical support on this and other books, and Gail Perry for her attention to factual details. She would especially like to thank Senior Acquisitions Editor Renee Wilmeth for charging onto the project like a white tornado, lifting spirits and energy.

Janet also thanks the many people willing to share their expertise on finance, including John Ventura, attorney and author of many bankruptcy books such as *The Bankruptcy Kit,* and his publicist, Mary Reed, for her generous donations; Irving Strauss, president emeritus of the 100 percent No-Load Mutual Fund Council; Richard McClintock of First Fidelity Federal Bank in Florida; Deborah Loehrke and the National Futures Association; and Don Johnson at sonic.net for his Discount Brokers rankings.

For supporting her career, Janet would like to thank Jennifer Golden at Ziff-Davis SmartPlanet.com; Jan Lindsey of Intelligent Life Corporation; freelance writer Lynn Vincent for the valuable exchanges and opportunities; and writer Lea Saslav and literary agent Sheree Bykofsky for including her on this exciting project.

Once again her heartfelt thanks go to her beloved husband, Maurice, and their dear children, Marissa and Connor, for the patience and the love that only they know how to provide.

Lea Saslav would like first and foremost to thank her literary agent, Sheree Bykofsky, who had the foresight to bring this book to her attention and consideration, and to Victoria Moran, who helped pave the way. Also, a great debt of gratitude to Janet Bigham Bernstel for coming up to the plate, eyeing the ball, and then hitting it out of the park in terms of her knowledge of finance, thoughtfulness, advice, and general all-around *Teach Yourself* camaraderie. Special thanks to the people at Macmillan Reference who helped bring this book to print, especially Development Editor Nancy Warner and Senior Acquisitions Editor Renee Wilmeth, who together formed a core team of *angels* in shepherding this book into print. Thanks also to Gail Perry for her attention to factual details.

Lea also thanks the many people willing to share their expertise and insight on finance, including Financial Planner Eileen Michaels, Legg Mason; Estate Planning Attorney Gerald Dunworth and his assistant Lori Martin; accountant Anita Katzen; money psychologist Judith Gruber; mortgage lender Micki Savant; Bankruptcy Attorney Mory Brenner, Esq.; Linda Barbanel, M.S.W., C.S.W.; Tiffany Bass, Founder of MsMoney.com; The American Academy of Estate Planning Attorneys; Jacqueline Gold, Librarian at the New York Public Library Science, Industry and Business Library; investment analyst Brad Bannon, John Konyak, tax consultant Jim Levett, Jerrold Mundis, Gary Susman, David Saslav, Larry Jasinover, and Matthew Weinberg.

Lea would also very much like to thank her personal *angels* for their support throughout the evolution of this project: Kathy Connolly, Corinna Lamb, Claire Riley, Scott Comin, Constance Gustke, Dennis Broe, Lois Schwartz, Todd and Theresa Parsons, Jeanne Lane, and "Ketul" Wayne Arnold, for his continuing wit and guidance.

In closing, a heartfelt thanks goes to Rick Shiels, whose patience, love, and kindness were a great and continuing support throughout the development and writing of this book.

PART I

Getting Up Close and Personal

HOUR 1

Developing Your Financial Goals

LESSON PLAN:

In this chapter you will learn the fundamentals of deciding upon your financial goals and ways to implement them. As your life changes, your financial goals will also change. You'll also learn how to:

- Complete a financial goals worksheet.
- Determine your net worth.
- Build a clear plan and put it in place.
- Research financial advice.

Congratulations. By picking up this book, *Macmillan Teach Yourself Personal Finance in 24 Hours,* you have made a commonsense commitment to yourself, your family, and your financial future. By thoroughly reading each chapter in this book and completing the "Hour's Up!" exercises after each chapter, you will learn more about strong financial techniques that, if implemented, can help you become much more firmly in control of your financial life. Using this book as a guide, you will have begun to open a door to a clearer and brighter financial future.

Over the next 24 reading hours you will learn much about yourself, how you relate to money, and how to improve upon your knowledge of personal finance. Whether you are planning short-term goals (such as saving to buy a new car) or are as forward-thinking as planning for retirement, you will find many of your answers within this book. With education prices looming larger and larger in the future, it is never too early to begin your larger financial plan.

Maybe you already have begun an investment portfolio but want to update it, *fine-tuning* its potential. Or perhaps you're considering buying a first home and aren't sure about mortgages and how to get one. Maybe you have older members of your family who have worries about insurance or just where they will end up and who will pay for their old-age care.

As you can see, the idea of "personal finance" can take on many perspectives and is as individualized as snowflake patterns. One person, single and earning a decent salary, has an inkling that he or she may want to begin a lifetime savings plan. A family of four will have different financial needs and goals and will hopefully begin a personal financial plan that will benefit the entire family. A person nearing retirement will have an entirely different set of financial goals.

ALLEVIATE YOUR MONEY WORRY

Without a doubt, most people would say that money—and making or getting more of it—leads their list of topics that cause worry. You may notice that several of the preceding paragraphs mention a lot about "worry" over money. Money tends to be what many people agonize over, day in and day out. But dealing with money doesn't have to be that way.

In fact, the more you can clarify your money issues, and the more you can understand and ask good questions about your money, the easier you can create a financial plan that works for you and your family. Investors say time and time again that good investing habits are all in the way you approach your money.

With that in mind, let's take a look at the concept of setting your financial goals.

DEVELOPING A FINANCIAL PLAN

Think back a minute to when you were in school. High school will do. Were you the kind of student who marked on your calendar when assignments were due? Did you make mental notes of upcoming tests? Perhaps you were the kind of person who would fly by the seat of your pants, say, studying for an exam—just enough, and usually at the last minute—knowing that you'd do "okay" but hoping you could get by on your charm and test-taking skills.

Unfortunately, the characteristics of the latter type of "student" won't do if you want to create a decent financial plan and stick to it in the future. Even if you were an "A" student in high school, if by the time your retirement rolls around you haven't saved a dime in any type of retirement account, well, let's just say that wouldn't be very practical—especially in this day and age when we know that no matter what benefits we get from Social Security, they won't meet all of our retirement needs.

The answer lies in financial planning. Everyone needs to plan for tomorrow. At every income level, there are steps you can take to make more efficient use of your assets and to ensure a secure financial future. It helps to develop well-defined goals and to map out appropriate strategies to turn your dreams into reality. The answer could be personal financial planning.

Let's Start with the Basics

For most people in the "baby boomer" age range, retirement looms large on the horizon. Will you have enough to retire comfortably when the time comes? Will you have enough for your family? Those in their 20s and 30s (who were born in the post-"boom" years, i.e., after 1964) are beginning to understand that perhaps Social Security will no longer be the *safety net* that so many previous generations have been able to rely on.

Another concern is whether your existing portfolio of investments is appropriate and how long it will last. According to one noted Manhattan-based financial planner, people in their 40s—or perhaps younger—want to be sure they have enough money to put their kids through school.

Even though inflation of education costs has moderated somewhat—it's not as bad as it used to be—education can still be incredibly expensive. Later in the book you will learn some terrific ways to begin saving for college costs, taking advantage of new Education IRAs, etc.

GO TO ▶
Refer to Hour 5, "Investing Basics," for more information on Education IRAs.

Another question arises from the "empty nesters." What should you do if you've owned a large home for most of your life because you had a family to raise, and suddenly they have moved out and you are left with too much house? Do you move? Do you buy a smaller house or condo?

Another consideration: Do you have enough life insurance to take of your family? A lot of people also are worried about long-term care. If you suddenly become sick, and you are in your 60s or 70s, do you have enough to pay medical costs and still have enough to live on down the road?

All of the preceding situations can cause panic and grief in many consumers, unless they have *planned ahead*. For this reason, we turn to goal setting and planning to ward off the worry that can come from no financial planning at all.

Short-Term vs. Long-Term Goals

By taking a look at both your short- and long-term financial goals, you will become clearer on what shape and form your financial life will take. In this section we will prepare a list of both kinds of financial goals and then rank them by importance.

Some of your goals could include …

- Adequate retirement income
- Loss of income protection
- Reduced taxes (income, inheritance, estate taxes)
- Vacations
- Buying a first home
- Starting a business
- Making college tuition payments for yourself
- Charitable donations
- Improved standard of living
- Catastrophic loss protection
- College education for children or grandchildren
- Disability protection
- Debt repayment
- Adding on to or improving your existing home
- Paying for a child's wedding

Or, for the long term, you might think of some of the following categories:

- Preparing for a secure retirement
- Planning for future college education for additional children
- Purchasing a second/summer home
- Estate planning
- Future planning of significant donations
- Long-term care for yourself or elderly relatives

Somehow, once your goals are down on paper, you will find it is easier to work toward them and finally achieve them.

FINANCIAL GOALS WORKSHEET

Let's take this one step further. By outlining an actual chart, you can help establish and prioritize your financial goals.

Short Term (One Year)

Goal:_____

Objective	Estimated Cost	Target Date	Weekly Amount
_____	$_____	_____	$_____
_____	$_____	_____	$_____
_____	$_____	_____	$_____
Total	$_____		$_____

Medium Term (Five Years)

Goal: _____

Objective	Estimated Cost	Target Date	Weekly Amount
_____	$_____	_____	$_____
_____	$_____	_____	$_____
_____	$_____	_____	$_____
Total	$_____		$_____

Long Term (More Than Five Years)

Goal: _____

Objective	Estimated Cost	Target Date	Weekly Amount
_____	$_____	_____	$_____
_____	$_____	_____	$_____
_____	$_____	_____	$_____
Total	$_____		$_____

Following is one example of a chart of an average investor with a family of two kids, a home, and thoughts of starting his own business in the future:

Goal	Amount Needed	When Needed	Amount Available	Earnings Rate
Financial independence	_____	_____	_____	_____
College education(s)	_____	_____	_____	_____
Debt repayment	_____	_____	_____	_____
Lifestyle desires:	_____	_____	_____	_____
Car	_____	_____	_____	_____
Home	_____	_____	_____	_____
Vacation	_____	_____	_____	_____
Other	_____	_____	_____	_____
Giving/tithing	_____	_____	_____	_____
Starting your own business	_____	_____	_____	_____

GO TO ▶
Refer to Hour 2, "Cleaning Up Clutter/Debt Repayment," if you find you are in severe financial debt. Once you are clear about debt, your life will change dramatically for the better.

As you create your own chart, keep in mind your financial needs (as opposed to financial wants) and see if you can determine a good plan of action that will over time incorporate all of the above.

FINANCIAL GOALS AND SAVINGS

When planning your financial future, it's important to begin setting up strategies to achieve your goals. By reading this sort of how-to book, you will begin to see more clearly how you spend money. Besides keeping tabs on your daily, weekly, monthly, and yearly spending, you will—if you budget properly—be able to determine how much money you can set aside for long-term savings or investments. Your budget will reflect the different times in your life when your ability to save or invest may change. As you grow in your career, your income capability will also grow, as will your expenditures and interests.

As you will see, different stories create different examples of budgeting. The couple who have young children and are paying off a mortgage, for instance, may not be able to save the same amount of money as a young, single working person who has only herself to take care of. Also, if you lose a job or go through a career transition, you may not be able to save with the regularity you did when you had a steady income every month.

As you begin to budget, keep the following tips in mind:

GO TO ▶
Refer to Hour 3, "Budgeting Your Way to the Future," for more tips on structuring a good budget for you.

- **Expect the unexpected.** Keep in mind that prices rise over time; give yourself more flexibility to accommodate these changes. Other unexpected obstacles might include the loss of a job, family illness, or the need for replacing a vehicle.

- **Start slow and build up.** If you start small with a weekly plan, you can give yourself a minimal structure with which to work. Thinking about how much you spend per year on gas, for example, might be more difficult than figuring out your gas expenditures per week.

- **Don't be hard on yourself.** For first-time budgeters, it's often not easy to get a handle on what you spend your money on. In addition, it can be an emotional issue. Take a few moments each week to sit down and plan where your money is going for that week. The more often you try to figure it out, the easier it will get.

JUST A MINUTE

Several financial software programs can help you plan your first budgets. Quicken and Microsoft Money are two excellent programs that can help create budgets from your ongoing financial activities.

- **Bring your family in on your financial plan.** Even if you don't think about it, your family plays a big role in where your money goes. If you have kids, for example, a large part of your budget might be going toward their clothes, toys, camps, school supplies, and so on. It is important to earmark a portion of your budget for their needs. In addition, you and your spouse may have large financial needs in other areas. Have a "business meeting" once a month with the entire family—if you can get them to sit down in one place together—to help plan allowances, future expenditures and so on.

- **Be realistic.** As we know, Rome wasn't built in a day—and neither will your complete budgeting and investing plans. Finding the right financial planner and building a structure for your financial life takes time. Know that in the end you are building clarity around an issue that can be known for its volatility. The more clear you are about your money, the more serene you will feel about it.

THOUGHTS AS YOU PRIORITIZE

Now that you have outlined some of your objectives, let's narrow things down. You want to be realistic as you frame your thoughts.

1. **Begin to narrow your objectives.** You'll learn over time that you won't be able to achieve every financial goal that you dream up. But, if you identify them clearly to yourself on paper and in your own mind, you will be able to achieve the most important ones on your priority list.

2. **Prioritize.** By focusing on the goals that matter most to you and your family, you may find that you need to put equally desirable but less-important goals on the back burner for a later time. With careful planning, you may be able to achieve all of your lifetime goals.

3. **Let time be on your side.** Let's face it: The only finite thing you have to count on is time. And the earlier you begin to prepare to meet your long-term goals—such as preparing for retirement—the better off you will be. Money that is invested gradually in mutual funds, stocks, or bonds can grow substantially to help meet your future goals and needs.

4. **Be prepared for conflicts.** Even worthy goals often conflict with one another. When faced with a conflict between goals of equal importance, you can sometimes choose by applying criteria such as: Will anyone's health be affected by my choice? Will one of the conflicting goals benefit more people than the other? Which goal will cause the greater harm if it is deferred?

GO TO ▶
Refer to Hours 5 through 9 on investing basics, stocks, mutual funds, bonds, and retirement planning for more information on objectives, prioritizing, and dealing with time.

DETERMINING YOUR NET WORTH

Only when you begin to be clear about how much you are worth can you accurately judge what some of your financial goals will be. Many people are surprised to find out how much they are really worth when they take a look at their assets.

The first step in determining your net worth is to take a look at the value of your assets. To some, owning your own home can turn into a nice nest egg that may have gone up in value since you last checked. There are many real estate professionals who can help you determine your home's worth.

Don't just throw bank and brokerage statements in the trash. Take a look at them. You might be surprised what you are worth in terms of IRAs, 401(k)s, or company savings. At the same time, list your liabilities such as mortgage, car loans, or credit card debt. Subtract your liabilities from your assets, and you will have a good estimate of net worth.

Following are two charts you can use to calculate your net worth. The first will explain your financial assets and the second your financial liabilities.

Financial Assets

Account	Value
Savings and investment accounts	_____
Retirement accounts	_____
Home value (mortgage-market value)	_____
Other assets (furniture, jewelry, collectibles, etc.)	_____
Total	_____

Benefits earned that pay a monthly retirement income:

Employer's pensions × life average (for example: 20 years × 12)	$_____/month
Total	_____
Total Financial Assets	_____

Financial Liabilities

Loan	Balance
Credit card	_____
Education (college)	_____
	_____
	_____
	_____
	_____
Total Financial Liabilities	_____

Your total net worth is equivalent to your total financial liabilities subtracted from your financial assets.

BUT WHAT HAPPENS IF I CAN'T SAVE ANYTHING?

This question will come up for you especially if you are going through a financial transition in your life. Try to create and stick with your budget. See if there are any categories where you can cut back in order to save.

GO TO ▶
Refer to Hour 3 for more tips on setting up a budget for your household, including setting up categories for you and your family.

GO TO ▶
Refer to Hour 2 to see where you can begin to save rather than spending all of your money on debt repayment.

GO TO ▶
Refer to Hour 15, "Insurance," for more ideas and information on picking the right insurance policies for you.

GO TO ▶
Refer to Hour 18, "Estate Planning," for more information on estate planning and wills.

It is hard to apply a rule of thumb on savings because it varies with age and income level. Ten percent is a good start. If that amount is too high for you, don't let that deter you. You can start by putting a little money aside each month and slowly increasing it.

INSURANCE NEEDS TO LAST A LIFETIME

Evaluating your insurance needs is part of personal financial planning. The insurance industry has changed a great deal over the past few years, and there is a wide array of new products. Some of them may be better options than your current coverage.

WHAT ABOUT A WILL? DO I NEED ONE?

Yes, it's true—everyone needs a will, including young people. Whether you are single or married, you need a will. No one but you knows how you want your estate divided after your death. If you have children, it is especially important that you have a will in place so that your assets will go to the people you love and want to have them. If you do not have a will and both you and your spouse die, the court will appoint a guardian for your children. Maybe you would have chosen someone else.

In addition, there are many reasons to build an estate plan. Estate plans are different than wills and can bring additional clarity to your financial planning. If you are nearing the age of retirement and still do not have a will or estate plan in place, now is the time to start.

WHAT ABOUT A FINANCIAL PLANNER?

It is not always easy to find a good, trustworthy financial planner, but in the end, doing something about your financial worth is better than doing nothing and hoping you are going to have enough when you retire.

Financial planners are often good at helping you identify your problems and goals, creating strategies to reach those goals, and helping you set priorities. At the same time, they can help in saving time with research, and in being a "sounding board" for investments you want to make sometime in the future. In addition, if you are in the midst of a divorce or other scenario where money is or will be an issue, having an objective party working with you can be a blessing.

On the other hand, you want to be sure to find a reputable financial planner (word of mouth works well here), and not someone who is out to gouge you on every single transaction. When you are considering working with a financial planner, you should find out how much that person will charge you before you begin working with him or her.

HOW OFTEN SHOULD I UPDATE MY FINANCIAL PLAN?

As with everything in life, financial needs can change. Knowing that nothing in life is certain can help you plan for a future with enough financial serenity to offset any possible changes. It is good to review your financial plan on a yearly basis, especially considering changes in goals and circumstances. Any significant life event such as marriage, birth, death, or divorce is good cause for again examining your financial plan.

RELOCATING OR STAYING PUT

Another important decision that affects many consumers is where to live after retirement. Perhaps you plan to relocate to a more favorable climate or to be near family. By researching the consequences of such a move in terms of the basic cost of living, access to health care, and state and federal tax obligations, you can make a much more clear decision. If you are considering the advantages and disadvantages of selling your home, whether or not you plan to relocate, these are some questions to ask:

- Can we afford monthly payments for mortgage, taxes, utilities, and maintenance?
- Will one or both of us be able and willing to take care of the house?
- Is the house a suitable place to live as we grow older and become less agile?
- Will we need to draw on our home equity as a source of income or credit, or would we have more options if we sold the home and invested the proceeds?

A financial planner and a real estate professional familiar with the area to which you would like to move can help you with these issues.

GO TO ▶
Refer to Hour 13, "Finding the Right Financial Advisor." Finding a financial advisor you feel comfortable with and who has your best interests at heart can be as important as finding a good doctor or therapist. Do as much research as you can, and then dive in!

GO TO ▶
Refer to Hour 19, "Changing Goals, as You Age," to find out more about life event changes such as marriage, birth, death, or divorce.

FINANCIAL ADVICE ON THE INTERNET

GO TO ▶
Refer to Hour 16, "Home Buying," for more advice on the advantages and disadvantages of buying and owning a home.

With the explosion of Internet sites devoted to financial news, planning, and research, you will find hundreds upon hundreds of Web sites that can help you. Following is a list of some that are extremely helpful and can point you in other directions in your search for financial security:

- **www.fool.com.** Known for its wit and brevity, this site has become popular with consumers for its breadth of knowledge about investing, the stock market, and thinking "long-term." Its "Fool's School" is a particularly fun way to learn more about finances while being able to chat online with other members of the "Motley Fool" about your financial portfolio.

- **www.thestreet.com.** Known for its insight and knowledge about the stock market, James J. Cramer's site has become a benchmark for financial know-how and planning.

- **www.quicken.com.** Originally begun for users of its "Quicken" software, www.quicken.com has quickly grown to encompass financial planning with topics such as "Making the Most of Your Money." It can also help you track the market and pick stocks, and has links to a host of other helpful financial-planning sites.

- **www.bloomberg.com.** Bloomberg continues to be a strong place to look for news on finance—this site links you to its various magazines including *Bloomberg Money, Bloomberg Personal Finance,* and *Bloomberg Wealth Manager.*

- **www.pueblo.gsa.gov/cic_text/money/financial-indepen/indepen.txt.** This was created in tandem by the American Express Consumer Affairs Office and IDS Financial Services in cooperation with the Consumer Information Center, U.S. Department of Agriculture Family Economics Research Group and Extension Service, American Association of Retired Persons, and National Foundation for Consumer Credit. This site helps you plan for continued financial independence into later life through assessing, planning, and managing your money.

- **www.financenter.com.** This is an excellent site with financial calculators for everything from buying a house to budgeting to investing and retirement plans. You can plug in your particular numbers to come up with an instant result in any step of your budgeting process. A wealth of information is available here.

- **www.yahoo.com, www.excite.com, www.altavista.com,** and **www. lycos.com.** All of these excellent search engines can point you in the right direction to finding good finance sites on the Web. Simply go to one and plug in the terms "personal finance," "finance," or "investing," and you will have a number of good sites to surf and experiment with.

THE KEY IS PLANNING

"If only I'd known then what I know now ...."

Looking to the future is key to financial planning at any age, but especially in the decade or so before retirement. For many households, retirement is a time to fulfill dreams and delayed ambitions. It also can be a time of anxiety if you postpone thinking realistically about the ways your financial identity will change—income, savings, investments, credit, insurance, job benefits, and perhaps living arrangements. Meeting the challenge of financial management will help remove uncertainty and increase your available options. Both partners need to be involved in retirement planning and may wish to discuss their plans with adult children.

Don't get caught short by not beginning your planning until it is too late. Whether you are 30, 40, 50, 60, 70, or 80, it is never too late to begin saving; however, the more time on your side, the greater the gains. Good luck!

HOUR'S UP!

The basics of financial planning can be confusing at first, but once grasped they go a long way to help you build a financial future. The following questions will test and strengthen what you've learned.

1. True or false: The sooner you begin creating a financial plan, the more money and financial security you can build for your future.

2. True or false: You should begin investing as soon as possible, even if you have outstanding bills and debt.

3. True or false: It is best to be foggy about your net worth; that way, you can never know how much you can really save.

4. True or false: People in their 20s, 30s, and 40s now can definitely count on Social Security for their complete retirement funds.

Quiz

5. Some of your financial goals could include …

   a. Adequate retirement income.

   b. Loss of income protection.

   c. Reduced taxes (income, estate taxes).

   d. Vacations.

   e. Buying a first home.

   f. All of the above.

6. A medium-term financial goal would happen between …

   a. One to two months.

   b. Two to twelve months.

   c. Three to five years.

7. True or false: You should bring in your family to discuss financial-planning decisions and budgeting.

8. True or false: You should try to create a budget weekly, then monthly, and then yearly.

9. The best time to begin thinking about saving is when you are in your …

   a. 20s.

   b. 30s.

   c. 40s.

   d. Now.

10. True or false: When you are considering working with a financial planner, you should find out how much that person will charge you before you begin working with him or her.

QUIZ

HOUR 2

Cleaning Up Clutter/Debt Repayment

CHAPTER SUMMARY

LESSON PLAN:

In this chapter you will learn the fundamentals of debt repayment, the differences between "unsecured" vs. "secured" debt, how to lower your credit card interest rates, and how to create a simple daily inventory system in order to record your daily spending habits. You'll also learn how to:

- Evaluate your current debt.
- Determine your monthly income.
- Reconcile your credit card debt.
- Keep a daily log and monthly spending record.

In Hour 2 we will begin to take a good, hard look at your basic finances. Are you clear as to where every penny in your pocket goes? Are you embarrassed that you never seem to have quite enough money to take your spouse to a nice, elegant restaurant, yet your credit card bills seem to keep piling up? Or, perhaps, are you beginning to realize that you pay with your credit card everywhere you go, and you can never really remember all your purchases by the end of the month? And, do you seem to never have the money at the end of the month to pay off your ever-growing balance?

Perhaps you are the type of consumer who is only able to pay the minimum payments on your credit cards, and you've been doing this for what seems like forever. You, like many other American consumers, may be crippling yourself by having too much consumer debt, which is keeping you from further investing, saving, or buying more of the things you want.

In order to truly conquer debt forever, you must make the commitment to not let your debt rule you ever again. Forever. The spending behavior that got you here, as you know, needs to be changed.

It is false to think that you must have credit cards or you're not going to be able to afford to buy what you want. Our consumer culture insists that we must have plastic to look good and buy nearly anything we want.

But savvy consumers are becoming more and more aware that using credit cards with 15, 18, and 21 percent interest rates not only isn't cool, it can put a drain on your ability to achieve financial independence, buy the home of your dreams, or save for a college education for you or your children.

By the end of this hour, you will have a good set of basic steps to take toward bringing down your debt forever and living a good life free from debt and the worry, anxiety, and fear it brings.

If you have moderate but controllable debt, be sure to keep up to date with your payments, possibly paying more than the minimums that the credit card companies want you to pay. Remember: the goal is to only charge what you can afford to pay out of your pocket.

A good rule of thumb: If you do use credit cards, be sure to pay off each purchase immediately by writing a check or money order to the company that day.

REALITY CHECK #1

Okay. Here goes. Take a deep breath. Let's take a look at Debt 101: your creditors.

Do you really know how much you owe your creditors? Not just a ballpark figure, but a real to-the-penny amount? For most people, getting clarity on the money they owe their creditors is a scary thought. It reaches deep into their psyches and dredges up some of the most chilling memories of money misused, credit cards maxed out, and bills unpaid. For many people, keeping within a nice, cheerful fog of "Oh, I really don't know how much I owe, but that's really okay—I'll take care of it someday!" keeps the financial wolves or fears at bay, allowing us to continue to function on a somewhat normal basis from day to day, yet pushing deeper the fears that we'll never get out of debt and that it will eat us alive. In the back of our minds, we know there is always that Big Bad Wolf of Debt right outside our front door.

For some of us, serious debting behavior has led to foreclosures on our houses, maxing out our credit cards, damaging our credit histories, and, quite simply, allowing a static lack of forward movement in our lives. In the same way that cleaning out the daily clutter of our bedrooms, offices, and inner spaces can create a serenity and open space needed to allow clarity and abundance in our lives, the sooner we get a financial "clarity," the sooner we can look into the eyes of this inner dragon and see that we can overcome it. We will be discussing serenity and money issues in Hour 23, "Financial

Serenity—It's Not All About the Money"; but for now, we will keep in mind that it's not punishment we're after, it's clarity and freedom!

The first thing you are going to have to do throughout this "24 Hour" tutorial on personal finance is to face up to the fact that cloudiness about your debt = lack of clarity = loss of potential earnings with your money. This is not the time to pass judgment on yourself, nor to be hard on yourself or your family. It's not about that extra pizza you ordered last week when you knew you had food at home. It's about taking the time to take a cold, hard look at past behaviors and to say to yourself that from this day forward you are going to begin to change the way you think about money in your life. If, in fact, you are the type of person who enjoys "living on the edge" from paycheck to paycheck or who doesn't mind that Timmy can't go to camp this summer because no money was saved up over the course of the year, then this chapter is not for you.

If, however, you are committed to finding a new way—a new pattern of living that knocks out debting behavior forever—then you have begun on the right road. This type of behavior does not have to continue.

Let's dig right in. We're going to use the best and most immediate tools out there: pen, paper, and in some cases, telephone. Let's get to work.

EVALUATING YOUR DEBT: THE DEBT REPAYMENT CHART

To begin, we are going to make a chart that will list everything you currently owe. It should look something like this:

Creditor	Amount Owed	Percentage	Time It Would Take to Pay Back Minimum Amount
_____	_____	_____	_____
_____	_____	_____	_____
_____	_____	_____	_____
_____	_____	_____	_____
_____	_____	_____	_____
_____	_____	_____	_____

Go on, list everything you owe. Don't worry—the first round will definitely feel the most painful, even miserable. Just begin by filling in the chart as best you can. Even though the process can be painful, the clarity you will achieve from knowing exactly what you owe to whom will far outweigh any of the emotions you may be experiencing from actually contacting the creditors to find out how much you owe.

If you do not have any up-to-date bills or letters from your creditors, this is the time to pick up the phone—as bad as that may sound—and call them individually, asking how much you owe to that particular company on that particular day. Add the information to your list. Eventually you will have a full list of the people, companies, or creditors you owe money to.

At the end of this process—which should not take more than a couple of hours to complete—you should have a list that looks something like the following chart. I've filled out one that closely resembles a past-history debting example.

Creditor	Amount Owed	Percentage	Time It Would Take to Pay Back Minimum Amount
Credit card	$1,000	21 percent	_____
Credit card	$700	15 percent	_____
Department store card	$800	18 percent	_____
Student loan	$8,000	10 percent	_____
Telephone company	$200	None/phone could be cut off	_____
Parents	$1,500	None/good faith loan	_____
Mortgage			
Car Payments			
Total	$12,200		

Doing the math, the total amount due is $12,200. To some this may sound huge, to others a drop in the bucket. Rest assured that if you're like millions of other Americans with debt, your chart will look something like this.

WHAT EXACTLY ARE CREDITORS, ANYWAY?

For the record, a "creditor," according to *Webster's Dictionary,* is "one who gives credit in business matters; *hence, one to whom money is due.*" (Italics are mine.)

For our purposes, a creditor is a person, business, or organization to whom you owe outstanding unsecured debt. The term "unsecured" is important here because it refers to debt that has been accrued without collateral being put up in case of a default. An excellent example of "unsecured debting" is credit card debt. Essentially, you have signed an agreement saying that you will pay back the bank or credit card company in charge of the card the loan money with interest without putting up any collateral in case you default on this loan.

The term "secured debt" is different. Secured debt is money loaned to you by a company, business, or person but for which you have given something of equal value back to that company in exchange. For example, say you need to borrow $20 from your best friend. But rather than accepting the money outright ("Oh, I'll pay you back someday!") you give your friend a watch worth the equivalent of $20.

In that case, if for some reason you default on this loan, your friend can take your watch and cash it in for $20, or a similar value. Or he may decide to wear the watch and "retire" the loan. Essentially, a car loan works on the same principle—if for some reason you default on a car loan, the bank or auto financing company can legally repossess the car; it becomes the bank's property—something you don't want to have happen to you, by the way!

GO TO ▶
Refer to Hour 17, "Buying a Car," for more on purchasing an automobile.

CREDIT CARDS

Thanks to endless credit card solicitations, toll-free numbers plastered on your television screen promising "low-interest rates!" if you call the number on your screen, and even student-rate credit card offers in the bottom of college students' book bags everywhere, you may think that credit card use is just fine and dandy. Everybody else is using one, so why shouldn't you? And it's fun to impress your friends by just "whipping out" the plastic and charging things. Right?

In this country, credit card companies have come up with the most ingenious ways of separating you from the good feeling that comes from buying a product or service and actually paying for it with cash or its equivalent. As Suze Orman says in her pioneer book, *The Courage to Be Rich* (Riverhead Books, 1999), "Our consumer culture makes us want things, and easy credit enables us to have them, long before we've paid for them. And the ease of use of that nice cold plastic in our hands makes it that much easier to forget this."

Yet your debt might just be a once-in-a-lifetime thing, an "oops" on your radar screen. If that's the case, writing out the preceding debting chart will also help you. Again, clarity is the key to understanding your financial profile.

DETERMINING YOUR MONTHLY INCOME

By clarifying your monthly income, you can better clarify your financial goals and money owed to creditors. One technique to do this is to take another sheet of paper and determine your monthly income. Using a similar chart as the preceding debting chart, begin to list your total monthly income, as in the following example:

Total Monthly Income	
Annual gross income	$21,000
Alimony or child support	$900
Social Security or government pay	_____
Interest/investment income	_____
Regular overtime (if guaranteed)	$300
Other income or support	_____
Total annual income	$22,200
Divided by 12	_____
Total Monthly Income	$1,850

Now, you will have a blueprint figure to use as you begin to figure out your monthly spreadsheets, which will be explained later in the chapter. For now, though, let's take a closer look at the nature of credit card debt and how to pay it off.

REVIEWING YOUR CREDIT CARD DEBT

Now that we've taken a cold, hard look at what you owe, let's investigate credit cards a bit more—what they are, what they represent, and ways of not going further into credit card "temptation."

Let's also look at a nation without credit cards. "But that's impossible!" you cry. "Everyone has debt! Everyone has credit cards! It's the American way!" Yes, it is true—our rate of consumer debt is quite high in this country—more so than in many other countries these days.

PAY BACK THE DEBT OR START INVESTING?

Here's a question. Let's say you have $1,000 to invest. On one hand, your broker is telling you about a really great mutual fund that has been paying an annual 18 percent rate. (Don't worry yet about mutual funds—we'll discuss them in Hour 7, "Mutual Funds.") On the other hand, you have nearly $1,000 on your Visa card, and Visa is charging you a 21 percent interest rate!

WHAT DO YOU DO?

This is a classic example of putting the cart before the horse. If you still have credit card debt at these high interest rates, it needs to be paid off first before you begin an investment plan. Pay off your credit card debt before you plan any other investments or savings plans. The money you save on late fees and interest can be greater than the amount you could earn investing.

If, for example, your credit card interest rate is 19 percent, you would have to find an investment that earned at least that amount, tax free. Even by finding such an investment, it's not guaranteed. Paying off debt is a sure thing.

The next step is to set your loan-payoff priorities. Refer again to your debt repayment chart. It might look easier to decrease your debt by paying off the largest loans first, but paying off the credit card and department store debts with the highest percentage rates, at 15, 18, and 21 percent, should become your first priority.

GO TO ▶
Refer to Hour 14, "Taxes: Time to Get Clarity," for more information on tax planning, or Hour 5, "Investing Basics," for other investment tips.

MAKING THE LISTS

You may ask yourself why you're making lists about what you owe. This was supposed to be a book about personal finance, right? Not a seminar on "communicating with creditors." You want to have more money, right now!

But, as you'll discover, financial abundance starts with making a personal decision not to increase your debt and coming to terms with the fact that you can live in this great country of ours without going into debt.

Think about it. You could take a friend out to dinner in 1996, pay for it by credit card, and still be paying for that dinner in 2010! Even if you pay the monthly minimum on your credit card debt, you could be paying off a debt of $1,000 for 15 years with the highest interest rates.

ONE CONSUMER'S EXPERIENCE

Here's a fun experiment one consumer tried while looking for clarity on her credit card debt. (The following amounts listed are approximate but can be used to make this point more clear.) When she called her credit card company regarding her one outstanding credit card, she began by asking the operator the following simple question:

> How long would it take to pay off my entire balance ($1,265) if I planned to only make minimum payments of $25 a month?
>
> Answer: 60 months, or five years.

> How about paying $50 a month (essentially doubling the minimum)?
>
> Answer: It would only take 31 months, or a little over two and a half years—cutting the time necessary for payback in half.

> And, finally, upping the ante to $100 a month (basically tripling the minimum payments)?
>
> Answer: A mere 12.6 months, and she's debt free!

Always pay at least double your minimum payments each month on your credit card bills if you are able to. If you are not accruing any new debt, you will wash away your debt that much more quickly!

PAYMENT OPTIONS

Well, then, speaking of payment options, just what are they?

First off, you can call your credit card companies and see if they can lower your interest rate. One consumer tried this during a late-night phone session with the 1-800 number on the back of her MasterCard, got a friendly operator on the phone, and because he was in a good mood (and she had been a good customer!), her rate was lowered from a very high 21 percent to a much more reasonable 15.4 percent.

In the end, credit card companies want your business—and want to keep your business with them. They want to keep you as a customer, especially if you threaten (in a nice way) that you will transfer your balance to a completely new credit card. If they won't budge, and if you have an okay credit history, you may be able to transfer the balance to a new credit card with a lower introductory rate.

PROCEED WITH CAUTION

Be warned, though, of low introductory credit card rate offers that seem to be too good to be true. Read the fine print, as many companies promise these low introductory rates in the beginning months but then often change to high non-introductory rates in the space of a few months or a year.

Whatever the case, pay off balances with the highest interest rates as soon as possible, since credit card balances grow fast with high interest rates. Only then can you turn around from being a "debtor" to an "investor."

If you feel that it's all hopeless and that you are so much in debt that you'll never dig yourself out of it, do not despair. There are ways out of what feels like this endless nightmare. Remember: You are not alone.

Also remember: You are not your debts. With a commitment to not spend irresponsibly and create more debt, you will pay off your bills one day at a time and live a much more fulfilling, serene life. Debtors Anonymous is an excellent 12-step program that exists to help the person who cannot get a handle on his or her personal spending habits. (To find a meeting of Debtors Anonymous near you, contact the General Service Board of D.A. at P.O. Box 20322, New York, NY 10025-9992; 212-969-8111). You can also access D.A. on the Web at www.debtorsanonymous.com.

By attending meetings, keeping a personal daily spending record, and having "pressure relief" meetings in the program, you will begin to carve a path out of debt and toward financial serenity.

In the breakthrough book of its kind, *How to Get Out of Debt, Stay Out of Debt and Live Prosperously* (Bantam Books, 1988), author Jerrold Mundis explores the genesis of why people compulsively spend money and get into or stay in debt, sometimes destroying their lives and self-esteem in the process. He has found that, over time, compulsive spenders and debtors can get into various financial "holes" in their lives. His first chapters deal with the many different types of debting, from anorexic debting to compulsive spending. For those who feel they may have this problem, this book is a must-read.

But, by doing the exercises mentioned in this chapter, most importantly non-debting one day at a time, doing a daily log, weekly log, and monthly spread-sheet, you will see your debting habits begin to decrease and a financial clarity taking their place.

In the next section you will learn how to keep logs and spreadsheets that will help you develop habits to decrease your spending and give you overall better control over your financial health and well-being.

REALITY CHECK #2

How, then, does this all fit into your day-to-day debt-repayment plan? We will return to your creditor payment chart shortly. For now, though, you are about to begin on a journey to find out exactly where your every penny goes on a daily basis—by using a spending record.

Again, you may hem and haw. "Nobody does this sort of thing! It's impossible!" You'd be surprised how many people of all walks of life would disagree. They have begun and have kept up the discipline of keeping in their purse or pocket a little notebook to write down absolutely everything they spend their money on.

So, it's time for another reality check. Take another deep breath, and let's go.

THE DAILY LOG BOOK

Beginning today, during your second hour of your "24 Hour" guide, go out and buy a small pocket notebook at your local drugstore. It doesn't need to be anything fancy, just small enough to be able to carry around with you at all times. Carry this notebook in your purse or pocket. (Some people buy purses or briefcases with a special pocket, just so they know where their notebook is at all times.)

This notebook is going to become your best financial friend because it will begin to "mirror" everything you spend your money on. But again, no judgments. This is just a way to continue getting clarity on your finances.

Turn to the first page of your notebook and date it with today's date. Then create two columns as shown in the following chart and write down how much you spent on the book.

Date

Item	Amount
Notebook	$1.99

That wasn't so bad, was it? Short and to the point. Now, keep writing down your entries during the day, jotting down each item you buy and how much you spend on it. One particular day could look like this:

Date

Item	Amount	
Notebook	$1.99	
Newspaper	$.50	
Coffee at corner stand	$1.50	
Lunch	$4.99	
Taxi	$7.00	
Groceries	$9.99	

There. That's it. You can take another deep breath. You've just started your first steps in a daily process of getting clarity about your money and your spending habits. After keeping your notebook for a while, not only will you know where every penny is going, you'll never be able to spend your money so quickly and "liquidly" without being able to account for it.

Remember, too, that this will only work if you commit to doing it on a daily basis. Keeping a spending notebook really won't help you in the long run if you decide to just jot down your purchases sporadically. You use money every day, as it constantly flows in and out of your life. Keeping track of all your spending—all of it—is the way to keep it straight at all times.

In the same way, too, if you write out a check to pay a bill or a company, and you log it in your checkbook, be sure to log it in your daily logbook as well. Your checks need to be fully noted in your logbook. A check acts like cash in the sense that once you write it you need to deduct that amount from your daily bank balance.

Now, once you've gotten used to this process, it's time to take the daily log one step further.

YOUR WEEKLY LOG

Now you've collected your spendings for a week. What do you do with them? You begin what's called a weekly record, using your numbers to get a clearer picture of your weekly spending habits.

Your weekly record might look like this:

June 1 Through June 7

Rent	$580.00
Groceries	$35.00
Clothes	$19.00
Entertainment	$25.00
Laundry	$10.00
Medical	$39.99
Telephone	$50.00
Transportation	$18.25
Total	$777.24

Everyone's weekly numbers chart will look different, but the preceding example will give you a general picture of how the weekly chart works. From there it is only one last step to the final chart—the monthly spending record.

MONTHLY SPENDING RECORD

The monthly spending record is a summary of your weekly expenses for the month. All you have to do is add up your weekly expenses in each category to arrive at the month's totals, as shown in the following chart:

Week	1	2	3	4	Total
Rent	$580.00				$580.00
Food	$35.00	$35.96	$14.00	$5.67	$90.63
Clothes	$19.00				$19.00
Entertainment	$25.00		$6.00	$10.00	$41.00
Gas and electric	$50.00				$50.00
Laundry	$10.00		$5.00		$15.00
Medical	$39.99				$39.99
Telephone	$50.00				$50.00
Transportation	$18.25	$17.50	$5.00	$10.00	$50.75
Total					$936.37

The monthly spending record is a record of what you are actually spending and where your money is actually going each month. Next, you will want to fine-tune your categories. Keep in mind that everyone's spending plan is as individual as their fingerprints.

Some possible categories can include:

- Alimony
- Books
- Cabs
- Cars
- Child support
- Clothes
- Cosmetics
- Dining/fast food
- Dry cleaning
- Education
- Entertainment: movies, videos, etc.
- Gas/electricity
- Gifts
- Groceries
- Hair care
- Health club
- Hobbies
- Home cleanings
- Home equipment (televisions, radios, dishes, pots and pans)
- Home furnishings (tables, chairs, wallpaper)
- Home repairs
- Home supplies
- Income taxes
- Investments
- Laundry
- Legal expenses
- Life insurance

- Magazines/newspapers
- Medical (doctors, prescriptions, glasses)
- Personal care (shampoo, soap, razors, toothbrushes, etc.)
- Pet costs (medicines, veterinarian visits, supplies, etc.)
- Property taxes
- Public transportation
- Restaurants
- Telephone
- Therapy
- Tuition
- Vacation/travel
- Yoga/meditation classes

As you can see, there are so many categories into which your spending habits can go. You will find the process gets easier as you keep your numbers, as you can more clearly earmark which categories apply to you. Again, there are no "right" or "wrong" categories. And the more you learn about your spending the more clarity you will achieve in your financial life.

OBTAINING A CREDIT REPORT

Along the way to financial clarity, it is important, too, to obtain a copy of your credit history. When applying for a car loan or a mortgage, it is important to have as strong a credit history as possible before applying. But, unfortunately, the credit rating system has its fallacies. There have been too many examples to count of consumers going to their banks, loan officers, etc., and being turned down for loans thanks to outdated or mistake-laden credit reports.

There are three major credit bureaus. Not all vendors and credit card companies obtain information from all three. That is why it is important that you have obtained an updated report from all three before applying for any credit.

When requesting information by mail, you will need to supply your full name, current and former addresses, Social Security number, and date of birth. Include a copy of your driver's license or a utility bill to confirm your address is correct.

The three credit bureaus are ...

Equifax
P.O. Box 105873
Atlanta, GA 30348
1-800-685-1111
Web site: www.equifax.com
Cost: $8

Experian
(formerly **TRW**)
1-800-682-7654
Web site: www.experian.com
Cost: $8

TransUnion
P.O. Box 390
Springfield, PA 19064-0390
1-800-888-4213
Cost: $8

All of the above credit report bureaus will issue a free credit report if you have been denied credit within the last 60 days. Keep the copy of the letter you receive from the company from which you have been denied credit and send to the above addresses. Within two to three weeks, you should receive a free credit report that will help you clarify your past credit record.

Another excellent resource to use in finding the lowest-rate credit cards to switch to is the Bankcard Holders of America (BHA). This national, non-profit, consumer education and advocacy organization offers a number of lists, including a list of low-rate cards ($4), Secured Cards ($4), and Rebate and Frequent Flyer Cards ($5). They also offer membership for $24, which includes a free copy of all of their publications. You can write to BHA at 524 Branch Drive, Salem, VA 24153; or call 540-389-5445.

COUNSELING

As we come to the end of our first hour on debt repayment and financial clarity, it is good to know there are several good counseling centers through-out the country that can also help you reconsolidate your debts into a realis-tic and doable monthly repayment plan. The one caveat to accepting these types of services is that the creditor companies are often paying the counseling services a fee, which means that they may want to please the counseling company first before working out a solvent payment plan for you. Be sure to ask up front what sort of payment the counseling center receives before beginning your credit counseling session.

The Consumer Credit Counseling Services offer inexpensive, confidential assistance for people having trouble managing or paying their bills. To find the office nearest you, call 1-800-388-2227.

The American Consumer Credit Counseling Service is a non-profit organization dedicated to helping people regain control of their financial direction by counseling consumers on issues of money and debt. They can be contacted at 24 Crescent Street, Waltham, MA, 02453 (1-800-769-3571), or on the Web at www.consumercredit.com.

Hour's Up!

Take a minute and take the "Hour's Up" on Debt Repayment to see what you have learned after reading this chapter. See if you can answer these without peeking back in the chapter! Good luck:

1. True or false: In the United States, it is mandatory that you use credit cards.

2. Some of the signs that you may have a problem with debt are …
   a. You are the type of person who enjoys living from paycheck to paycheck and "living on the edge."
   b. You "kite" or "bounce" checks with frequency.
   c. You pay more with credit cards than with cash.
   d. All of the above.

3. True or false: Secured debt is money loaned to you by a company, business, or person but for which you have given something of equal value back to that company in exchange.

4. True or false: A "creditor," accordingly to *Webster's Dictionary,* is "one who gives credit in business matters; *hence, one to whom money is due.*"

5. True or false: You don't need to "take down your numbers" every day; just guess what you spend each month and hope for the best when budgeting.

6. Categories in your personal spending plan could include …

   a. Rent.

   b. Clothing.

   c. Vacations.

   d. All of the above.

7. It doesn't matter how much interest your credit card companies are charging you per month; as long as you are getting in your payments on time, you're okay.

8. True or false: Credit reports are always accurate; there is no need to ever justify writing a letter to a credit bureau to protest an inaccuracy in your report.

9. True or false: One formula for looking at debt is: cloudiness about your debt = lack of clarity = loss of potential earnings with your money.

10. True or false: There are fifteen major credit bureaus.

Quiz

HOUR 3

Budgeting Your Way to the Future

CHAPTER SUMMARY

LESSON PLAN:

In this chapter you will learn how to manage your money more effectively by using a budget. You'll also learn how to:

- Organize your records for easy budget tracking.
- Create a monthly budget.
- Choose and evaluate budget tracking software.
- Save for school or a car.

Taking care of your financial health is as important as taking care of your physical health or the preservation of your home, car, or other possessions. The upkeep is similar, too. Regular maintenance gives you a well-oiled machine.

Keeping a budget is simply one part of that routine maintenance. Unfortunately, the word "budget" tends to conjure up torturous images of tightening belts and pinching pennies. But budgeting doesn't have to be painful. Budgets are meant to perform many functions, and none of them should hurt. We'll take a look at some of those functions, such as organizing your cash flow, helping you to pay off debt in a timely manner, and tracking spending habits.

A budget is really a tool for organizing expenses. It's something tangible that you can look at, analyze, and act on. It helps you view past spending and forecast future wealth.

As a money-tracker, a budget can help you pinpoint where you spend all your hard-earned cash. As an investment tool, it can help you stockpile some cash to spend on products that make you more money, such as securities and real estate.

As a worksheet, a budget can help you fine-tune your monthly or annual cash flow. It can even be fun if you rearrange numbers and play the "what if" game. What if you stopped paying for cable TV and invested that $40 a month instead? What if you took full advantage of your company 401(k)? What if you stopped buying vending machine sodas or brought your lunch to work instead of ordering out? The dollars can quickly add up in your favor. Use your budget, and the money you save, to plan for future expenses.

No amount of money earned can make up for bad budgeting or no budget at all. Unless you know where your money is going, you'll have a difficult time saving it for investments and building wealth. If you want to eliminate debt *and* build wealth, you need a budget.

GETTING STARTED

Sometimes the hardest part of a new routine is taking the first step, because it signals commitment. These first steps toward building a budget are very simple and don't take much time. Don't skip them, though, because they're essential to a good budget.

1. FILING

Budgeting involves organizing the paperwork. If you keep bills, passbooks, and receipts in file folders and clearly label all your files, collecting the paperwork should be the easiest step in the budget process. If you throw them all in a shoebox and sort through them once a year, you'll obviously try to avoid the task of managing your finances.

The purpose of gathering these bills is to establish the average monthly expenditure on each budget item, such as utilities or telephone. The key element in this collection step is to know what you should keep and what you can throw out. Despite popular forecasting, computers have not yet reduced the paperwork we wade through on a daily basis. Monthly billing statements, receipts, and warranties are still a necessary part of the commerce process.

If you establish a filing system, bills, receipts, and other paperwork can be put away or thrown away as soon as you receive them and have taken care of whatever you're required to do.

2. WHAT YOU CAN KEEP

Make sure to review all credit card statements as soon as they arrive, since you have 60 days to dispute a charge. You may want to keep them for a year or two because problems could crop up with a purchase or you may even be billed twice for the same item.

Keep any receipts that are related to a tax-deductible expense. Keep these and tax returns for at least three years, because that's the amount of time the Internal Revenue Service has to audit you under normal circumstances. If you failed to report more than 25 percent of your gross income, the government has six years to collect the tax or to start legal proceedings. There are no time limitations if you filed a fraudulent return or if you failed to file a return.

Medical bills can be kept for a year if you think you'll qualify for a tax deduction or if you have a medical reimbursement account through your office and are due monies. Home-improvement receipts should also be filed for insurance and appraisal purposes.

GO TO ▶ Refer to Hour 2, "Cleaning Up Clutter/Debt Repayment," for more information on clearing up the clutter of credit and debt.

PROCEED WITH CAUTION

It's easier to find things if you go through your files periodically and toss out expired guaranties, loan payment books, warranties, and owner's manuals. Credit card statements past the three-year mark can also go. Don't keep pay stubs, bank deposits, or old ATM receipts.

3. STORING

Searching for the right documents when it comes time to pay bills or file taxes can be frustrating. It's also counter-productive. It's critical to success to dedicate a space for budget supplies such as stamps, envelopes, and folders. Reserve a shelf in your bedroom closet or the corner in the kitchen, but make it clear to yourself and other household members that these supplies are for budget use only.

Make sure you file records and the budget itself in an easily accessible place, either on the home computer or in a clearly marked file folder. You should be able to pull out your budget at any time and know where you stand financially. You can color-code file tabs or file boxes each year to keep your accounts separate come tax time.

GO TO ▶ Refer to Hour 14, "Taxes: Time to Get Clarity," for more information on clarifying your taxes.

4. TRACKING

If you want to become financially independent, you'll have to become better informed about your own money habits. Are you a spender or a saver? Do you know how much money you have in the bank right now? Do you have a lot of credit card debt?

Before you can create a realistic budget for yourself, you need to find out where your money is going right now. A year's worth of credit card receipts can help you categorize your expenses. You can also look at your outstanding loans, such as auto, home, and school loans, to examine your own past credit history. Then review at least six months' to a year's worth of bills for utilities, gas receipts, rent, etc., to establish an average amount for your budget line items. If you have personal finance software, you can easily track what goes out from the data you've input.

You also need to track the other sources of outflow, your spending money. One exercise that surprises many people with its outcome is to track daily expenditures for a month. Hold on to all receipts and keep a notebook handy to write down miscellaneous items for which there are no receipts, such as vending machines. Total up the expenses in categories such as clothing, toiletries, snacks, entertainment, etc.

If you have done all of the above, you should have some very realistic numbers to use in your budget, and you may just open your own eyes to how much you really spend on unnecessary items. You won't have to repeat the money-tracking exercise every month, but keep it in mind whenever you reach for your wallet.

5. SCHEDULING

A simple and easily understood budget you review a set time each week will bring you more chance of success with your budget than a complicated plan that takes a lot of time and that you never want to look at. Like that shoebox full of bills and receipts, a desk full of paperwork will loom larger than life, and you'll tend to avoid it. So set aside a certain time each week when you can review bills, receipts, and other finance-related obligations.

With a half-hour or so a week spent on managing your finances, you can stay on top of your budget instead of the other way around. Enter data into your ledgers or financial software, pay bills on time to avoid late fees, and balance your accounts. Add your credit balances (expenses), and likewise add up your debits (income). If the total credits equal the total debits, the accounts balance. If you have more credits than debits, you have debt; conversely, a debit surplus leaves you with extra cash to put into savings and investment products.

PROCEED WITH CAUTION

A budget should remain flexible, so you don't feel constricted by your own cash crunch. Remember that you're not punishing yourself, but liberating your cash for better things, such as saving and investing. Don't change your master plan, but you may have a one-month emergency, for example, and will need to find an area of discretionary spending that you can cut back on. Above all, strive to save.

They say old habits die hard, and certainly changing spending habits can be difficult, but in the end a budget will save you a great deal of stress and anxiety. If you want to create a healthy budget, you'll have to get organized.

CREATING THE BUDGET

In Hour 1, "Developing Your Financial Goals," you set some short- and long-term financial goals and outlined your current financial assets and liabilities in the net worth charts. Now is the time to build your budget to reflect those savings goals.

Budgets are broken into two sections, income and expenses.

Income is usually a fixed item. Unless you're self-employed or a contract laborer, you should have a good idea of what your net income will be each month. If your pay varies greatly from month to month, as it can when you're self-employed, go over your income from the previous year and try to come up with a monthly average. Do the same for any interest income, dividends, or other miscellaneous income.

There are also fixed expenses, such as your car payment, rent or mortgage, and insurance costs. Variable expenses include groceries, clothing, and other expenses that can be adjusted each month. While you can cut back on your fixed expenses, such as reducing rent by moving to a smaller place or sharing an apartment, it might be easier to save money by trimming a variable expense such as the food bill.

Here is a basic budget worksheet to get you started in the right direction. You may have more or fewer categories than the ones listed here, but the goal is to get an idea of how much money you have and how much you spend.

Family Budget Worksheet—Monthly

Income

#1 net income _____

#2 net income _____

Dividends and interest (investments) _____

Other (rental property, second job) _____

Total income _____

Fixed Expenses

Auto payment _____

Insurance (homeowners, health, disability, life) _____

Mortgage or rent _____

Taxes _____

Debt repayment _____

Flexible Expenses

Childcare _____

Clothing _____

Entertainment (movies, dining out) _____

Food _____

Gas (auto, boat) _____

Gifts (holidays, birthdays) _____

Home repairs (general upkeep) _____

Savings (401[k], goals) _____

Telephone (home, cellular) _____

Utilities (water, electric) _____

Vacations _____

Other _____

Total expenses _____

Bottom line + or − _____

You may have noticed that there is only one line item for saving or investing in this budget. That's a good place to start in this very basic budget. Then it's important to analyze the bottom line.

If you break even when you subtract expenses from income, you're not going to have any cash for investing. If you're in the negative, you clearly need to find balance through spending cuts or by adding extra income. Any excess cash can be labeled "Investments," and fitted into your financial goals worksheets from Hour 1.

Before you can save money for goals, though, you should budget for the unexpected. This is called risk management and includes purchasing life insurance, if someone would suffer financially from your death, and disability insurance, to cover loss of income in case you are injured and can't work.

Some life insurance policies combine tax-deferred savings with the death benefit. If you give up the policy, you get some cash back, called the cash surrender value.

Term life insurance policies are less expensive than cash value polices, still provide valuable death benefits, but offer no cash surrender value.

GO TO ▶
Refer to Hour 15, "Insurance," for details on determining the best insurance for you.

Most financial planners also recommend a three- to six-month liquid cash reserve for emergency expenses as discussed in Hour 2, "Cleaning Up Clutter/Debt Repayment." These funds can be invested in short-term, interest-bearing accounts such as money-market funds and CDs.

E-Budgets

Free budget calculators, interactive worksheets, and reasonably priced software for managing money pepper the Internet. We'll show you some of the online resources for creating and keeping a healthy budget, and you'll no doubt discover some of your own once you get into the saving habit.

Interactive Worksheets

It's not necessary to keep your budget with pen and paper. Try some of these online worksheets and budget makers to get a handle on your saving and spending. You can always print out a copy of the ones that work best for you or combine the best features and make your own personalized budget.

Keepin' Up with Jones

www.keepingupwithjones.com

Want to know what the Joneses are paying for their mortgage, taxes, and meals out? Look at the budgets at the Keeping Up with Jones Web site, created by Search Technologies and based on statistics gathered by the Department of Labor. You can plug in your own basic statistics and find out what others in your range are budgeting for expenses.

MONEY.COM INSTANT BUDGET MAKER

www.pathfinder.com/money/101/lessons/2/intro.html

How do your spending habits measure up to the average American household? You can analyze your spending here and go on to read Money 101's lessons on Making a Budget.

IDEA CAFÉ'S INSTANT ALL-IN-ONE FIRST-YEAR BUDGET WORKSHEET

www.ideacafe.com/getmoney/fgr_budget.html

Starting a business? Want to create a personal budget? You can do either one or both with this interactive worksheet.

MONEYMINDED BUDGET WORKSHEET

www.moneyminded.com/incomego/start/a7budw15.htm

Fill in the blanks and submit the worksheet on this Web site for a personalized budget analysis. Savings are definitely a part of this budget!

CALCULATORS

Saving for financial goals often leaves you wondering just how much you should budget for that car, your insurance, or your perfect retirement home. These online calculators can relieve you of some of the guesswork.

FINANCENTER.COM

www.financenter.com

This Web site gives over 100 calculators in 12 areas of personal finance that present graphs and charts for illustration. Click on Budgeting and explore the Clickcalcs to answer questions such as "What is it worth to reduce my spending?" and "Should I pay off debt or invest in savings?" You may be surprised that even the slightest spending cutback can dramatically affect your budget's bottom line.

LabPuppy

www.labpuppy.com/tools.htm

A Web directory of the top online financial planning calculators are available at this Web site. Many of these calculators can help you work through your budget in other sections of this book as well.

Quicken

www.quicken.com

Quicken is referred to frequently in this book because of its extensive personal finance advice and tools. Quicken offers an array of calculators worth exploring when it comes to figuring your budget.

Personal-Finance Software

Today's personal-finance software makes it easy to manage a budget and forecast long-term goals. Of course, the software will only keep track of the data you enter, unless you use a program that will download your banking information into your register (for example, Quicken).

If you're using tax-preparation software, you'll need to purchase a new version each year, but money management packages can be used continuously. You may want to check each year's upgrade, though, to see if there are new features that can make managing your money easier, online and off. Two of the top personal-finance software programs are Quicken and Microsoft Money, both of which are upgraded every year. See the following sections for more information on both of these software programs.

Quicken

www.quicken.com

At this Web site, you can download Quicken from the section marked Quicken Solutions. With the basic version, you can pay bills and balance your checkbook and create reports. You can also download online banking and trading data. Quicken Deluxe allows you to track investments and do some future-casting, and also features Quicken Quick Entry, which lets you streamline data entry. Log on to see a comprehensive features comparison chart and check out free trial offers.

GO TO ▶
Refer to Hour 4,
"How Can I Keep
Track?" for more
details on how
personal-finance
software can help
you keep track of
your financial life.

MICROSOFT MONEY

www.microsoft.com/money/

Microsoft offers standard, deluxe, and suite versions of its Money 2000 software, which can help you can set up and manage your personal finances. Balance your checkbook, pay bills, bank online, create a budget, reduce debt, and even access your finances online from any computer. Log on for a five-minute online tour of the software and download a free 90-day trial of the deluxe version.

MAKE IT A HABIT

A budget, like a promise, is only as good as the person who makes it. Take a look at how you spend your money now. Every month you pay bills and write checks, maybe sometimes hoping you'll have enough cash to cover expenses. If your time is spent simply making money to cover expenses, it could be that your energy is not focused in the right place.

You've probably created simple budgets before—saving to buy a car or planning a wedding, for example. Any event that involves making a financial decision is a good time to begin your budget habit. Here are some events that may be coming up in your life that you can use as an excuse to begin budgeting, along with the Web sites to help you get started.

SAVING FOR SCHOOL

The number-one concern for most Americans used to be whether they would have enough money saved for their retirement. According to the College Savings Plans Network, an affiliate of the National Association of State Treasurers, that question is being replaced with "How will I be able to afford a college education for my children?"

In 1998, the College Board reported that the national average expense for one year at a public school, including room, board, and tuition, was $7,472. Private school expenses ran to $19,213. What will it cost when your baby wants to go to college?

PARENTTIME

protected.pathfinder.com/ParentTime/workfamily/collsave.html

Use this College Savings Calculator to see what it will cost to send Junior to college and how much you'll have to put away to reach that goal.

FASTWEB FREE SCHOLARSHIP SEARCH

www.fastweb.com

FastWeb offers a college directory of more than 4,000 schools with information on admissions, financial aid, and other general information on schools. An online survey helps FastWeb automatically match each student's background with eligibility requirements for scholarships from around the country and advises students about scholarship opportunities tailored to them.

FastWeb also offers many free tools, such as calendars, e-mail, and cost calculators to help students succeed once they get to school.

FINAID.ORG

www.finaid.org

Information about loans, financial aid, scholarships, and more is given at the Findaid.org Web site. The information given here is a must for every student-to-be—or the parent of one. Get personalized help from the "Ask the Advisor" section.

COLLEGE IS POSSIBLE

www.collegeispossible.org/paying/paying.htm

College Is Possible is a Web site maintained by the American Council on Education. It's a guide to the resources most admissions and financial aid professionals find helpful.

THINK COLLEGE EARLY

www.ed.gov/thinkcollege/early/tce_home.htm

Think College Early is a Web site designed by the U.S. Department of Education that includes Q&As, calculators, and financial-aid guides.

Your First Home

You can research and buy and sell properties in your own hometown or across the nation with online access. But knowing just how much house you can afford is important. If your mortgage is too large, you'll feel suffocated by monthly payments. It's better to buy a little less house and have a lot more flexibility in your budget.

GetSmart.com Mortgage Finder

www.getsmartinc.com/mortgage/HomeBanner?BANNERNAME=www.getsmartinc.com/mgotokwbuyingahome

Find a home loan that fits you or refinance an existing home with the right loan with the information available at the GetSmart.com Mortgage Finder Web site.

American Relocation Center

www.buyingrealestate.com

Click on the First Time Buyer Service or How to Save Money links on the American Relocation Center Web site before deciding how much home you can afford.

Yahoo! Real Estate

realestate.yahoo.com/realestate/calculators/

At the Yahoo! Real Estate Web site, you can choose from calculators that help you calculate your mortgage payments, decide whether to rent or own, figure out how much you'll pay in interest, and add up how much goes toward the principal amount.

A New Car

What will you have to pay for a new car? How much will you pay for a used car? The following Web sites can help you target the costs and the real value of a new set of wheels.

Autoweb.com

www.autoweb.com

Autoweb.com offers a network of over 4,000 new- and used-car dealers. Submit a request, and you can expect to hear from a dealer within one day. This is a good resource for anyone hoping to buy, sell, or finance an automobile.

CarsDirect.com

www.carsdirect.com

At CarsDirect.com, you can choose from a complete selection of makes and models, pick out options, obtain financing, and actually order your car—online—from where you're sitting right now. A no-pressure shopping environment and low, no-mystery prices makes it easy.

GO TO ▶
Refer to Hour 17, "Buying a Car," for more detailed information on purchasing an automobile.

GetSmart

www.getsmart.com

Insurance quotes, discount loans, and consumer reviews are just a few features of the GetSmart Web site.

CarFinance.com

www.carfinance.com

Instant rate payments and analysis for auto loans are available at the CarFinance.com Web site.

Edmunds.com

www.edmunds.com

Edmunds.com is a great site for comprehensive consumer information on buying a car. It includes buying tips, strategies, and pricing information.

Carpoint

www.carpoint.msn.com

Microsoft's Carpoint has over 100,000 used-car classifieds that are updated daily.

Tying the Knot

Just thinking about the expense of a wedding can cause you and your intended to decide to elope. With the help of experts at the following wedding Web sites, the cost of the nuptial dinner may not give you heartburn.

Modern Bride

www.modernbride.com/weddingplanning/whopays.cfm

Weddings can get so personal, especially when it comes time to divide the bills. Don't assume that the bride's family pays for everything. Find out who pays for what, and get started on a newlywed household budget in the "Legal and Money Talk" section.

WedNet

www.wednet.com/wedsense/wedsense.asp

Tips on general budgeting for a wedding—small or large—are available at the WedNet Web site.

Wedding Budget

www.geocities.com/SouthBeach/Marina/5714/ourwedding/budget.html

Print out the wedding budget grid available at this Web site and leave out any last-minute expense surprises.

Wedding Budget Tips

www.rocdjs.com/wedguide/

Whether you have $1,000 or $10,000 to spend, the budget example at this Web site is broken down by percentages. For example, according to this budget, only 2 percent of your money should be spent on the wedding cake.

MetLife

www.metlife.com/Lifeadvice/Family/Docs/getmarriedintro.html

Wedding costs and wedding worksheets at this Web site help ease your way into the special day.

BRINGING UP BABY

A new baby can be welcome news, but the accompanying bills, from hospital rooms to disposable diapers, can be a shock. Plan ahead with some input from the experts at the following Web sites.

QUICKEN'S LIFE EVENTS

www.quicken.com/life_events/parenting

Advice and calculators for baby budgets are given at the Quicken Life Events Web site. With the information at this site, you may be surprised to discover that you or your spouse can afford to stay at home and tend to the toddler while the other one works.

KIPLINGER

www.kiplinger.com/kids

A financial planning center, the Kiplinger Web site comes complete with a kids and money forum.

MSN MONEYCENTRAL

moneycentral.msn.com/articles/family/kids/contents.asp?p=2

Want to know what it will cost you to raise a child and pay for expenses? Find out at MoneyCentral and view strategies and tips to cut child-rearing costs while you're there.

BUILDING A NEST EGG

Company pension plans are quickly being replaced with 401(k) plans and IRAs. But are you ready to self-direct your investments? Up-to-date online information can help you be an effective money manager.

QUICKEN

quicken.com/retirement/qanda

Custom calculators can answer questions such as "How should I invest my retirement savings?" and "How much do I need to retire?" You can then plug those answers directly into your custom budget.

ABOUT.COM

retireplan.about.com/mbody.htm?COB=home&PID=2714&PM=66_815_T

A full guide to tax planning, investment strategies, and advice about retirement living, as well as important links to other retirement resources, are available at About.com.

ADMINISTRATION ON AGING

www.aoa.dhhs.gov/aoa/pages/finplan.html

General and financial planning for the retirement years is available from the U.S. Department of Health and Human Services office on aging at the Administration on Aging Web site.

TIME SAVER

Anything that can be done can be done even cheaper if you know where to look. Try the Dollar Stretcher Web site at www.stretcher.com. The site's motto is "living better ... for less." The information on the site is updated weekly.

KEEPING UP

Your budget should be easier to maintain than it was to create. That means everyone involved in the decisions about the household money management should be able to understand and follow it. Check your budget against actual figures on a monthly basis. If conditions have changed, such as a promotion or job loss, reflect those changes in a revised budget. Tracking your actual expenditures and comparing them with your budgeted expenses will give you a clearer idea on where your money is going, and why.

Try to keep your spending in line with goals you set, and avoid purchases that take you away from those long-range goals.

You don't have to give up the good life to keep a solid budget, you just have to conserve cash. Keep in mind your goal of having money left over in that bottom line to invest. That ultimately means more wealth for you, not eliminating it.

TIME SAVER

Feeling like a debt-head? The National Center for Financial Education at www.ncfe.org/index.htm has tips on how to avoid getting into debt, how to get out of debt, and how to shop smart.

Being frugal doesn't mean being stingy either. Here are some commonsense habits to work into your lifestyle that should help you keep up with your budget goals.

PAY OFF HIGH-RATE DEBT FIRST

Before you can begin to invest your money, you need to be debt-free. A stock or mutual fund that's paying a 10 percent return does little good when you're paying 12 percent on your credit card balance. To pay off your debt, begin with these steps:

- Set realistic goals to avoid getting discouraged and giving up on saving. You may only be able to sock away a few dollars a month at first, but it's a start.
- Pay yourself first. Take 10 percent out of your paycheck every month to save and invest.
- Shop with a list and thwart those Madison Avenue ad executives who try to lure you into impulse buys with shiny packages and loud headlines.
- Reward yourself on occasion, especially if you've reached a financial goal. For example, if you love shrimp, but it's not in your weekly food budget, treat yourself to a pound or two. It's less expensive to buy and cook them at home, and you'll still feel pampered.

TIME SAVER

Want to squeeze pennies from stones? Visit Julie's Frugal Tips at www.brightok. net/~neilmayo/index.html for a Tip of the Week. She is also very generous with her list of frugal links.

USING ONLINE CALENDARS

Another way to keep up with your budget is to use online calendars. These free interactive calendars will pop up and remind you to make appointments, gather data, file taxes, pay your housekeeper—whatever it is you need to remind you to keep your finances in order!

- **www.when.com.** Set up group calendars and track local events.
- **Jump!** at **www.jump.com.** Personal and group reminders in a full calendar service. In beta testing at this writing.

- **ScheduleOnline** at **www2.scheduleonline.com/login.html.** Schedule your budget meetings with your CPA or even your spouse, and check your To-Do list in your virtual office.

HOUR'S UP!

As you know, a budget doesn't have to hurt, but it does have to be taken seriously if you plan to conserve cash for investing. Take this short quiz to reinforce the new budgeting skills you've mastered in this hour.

1. A budget should be thought of as a tool to …
   a. Track spending.
   b. Save for future goals.
   c. Fine-tune cash flow.
   d. All of the above.

2. The best first step in creating a budget is to …
   a. Get a pen and paper.
   b. Buy personal-finance software.
   c. Get your paperwork organized.

3. You should keep tax returns and tax-related receipts for three years because …
   a. The Internal Revenue Service has three years in which to audit federal income tax returns.
   b. You never know when you need to amend a return.
   c. You might want to look at those receipts again.

4. Before you can decide where to trim expenses you have to …
   a. File your paperwork.
   b. Log on to the Internet.
   c. Track down where your money goes now.

5. To turn budgeting into a habit, you should …
   a. Remind yourself to check your budget periodically.
   b. Schedule the same time each week for reviewing financial paperwork, paying bills, etc.
   c. Tell all your friends.

6. True or false: Budgeting can be broken down into two parts: income and expenses.

7. A basic risk-management plan should include …

    a. Preparing for the unexpected.

    b. A three- to six-month's cash buffer for emergency expenses.

    c. Basic insurance coverage.

    d. All of the above.

8. True or false: Online interactive worksheets can help you …

    a. Create a budget.

    b. Analyze a basic budget.

    c. Compare your budget to the average American household.

    d. All of the above.

9. A good time to start budgeting is …

    a. Now.

    b. Any time there are major financial decisions to be made.

    c. When planning for a big event such as a wedding or birth.

    d. All of the above.

10. Living frugally means …

    a. Being stingy.

    b. Denying yourself the good things in life.

    c. Setting realistic spending goals.

Quiz

HOUR 4

How Can I Keep Track?

CHAPTER SUMMARY

LESSON PLAN:

In this chapter you will learn how to keep track of the financial plans you put in place. You'll discover the benefits of computer software for storing and organizing your data. You'll also learn how to:

- Keep the right records.
- Manage use of credit and debit cards.
- Use personal finance software and tracking.

Before you begin tracking your personal financial life, you need a sound financial plan. If you scatter your vegetable seeds to the wind, you won't be able to weed and nurture your garden. Throwing your money in too many directions will produce the same results. You have to hunt for your records when you need them, your accounts might have suffered from lack of attention, and in the long run, you go hungry!

THE BIG PICTURE

If you are working with a financial advisor, you know that part of his or her job is to help you stay on track. An advisor will assist you in creating a customized financial plan and offer ongoing advice.

Perhaps you only used an advisor's help to get started and then opted to carry out the plan on your own. Whether you're managing your finances alone or with professional help, in order to keep track, you first need to understand your present financial position including:

- **Protection.** What would happen to your financial position if you became disabled for several months? Will your family be financially devastated if you die? Insuring yourself and your family for the unexpected should be a major part of any personal-finance plan. Insurance needs will change with life events, such as marriages, births, and home ownership, and it's important to update your protection.

GO TO ▶
Refer to Hour 5, "Investing Basics," for more information on the power of compounding that can make your savings grow faster.

- **Investments.** How are your investments performing? Savings accounts will barely keep up with inflation, so if you want to see your money really grow, you'll need to choose an investment vehicle and track it. Stock portfolios outside of retirement accounts must be monitored for income tax purposes, as well as growth. In these days of self-directed retirement plans such as IRAs, 401(k)s, and 403(b)s, it's up to the individual to continually evaluate performance, asset allocation, and investment risk levels.

- **Income tax.** Keeping accurate tax records year-round can insure that you're set up for painless income tax return preparation. It can also help you to reduce taxes by taking advantage of all the deductions available to you.

GO TO ▶
Refer to Hour 12, "Online Money Management," for more information on what to do if you find an error on your credit card statement.

- **Personal spending.** Tracking where your own money goes can be an eye-opening experience. So much can be lost simply in bank account fees and credit card interest. Bank account and credit card statements provide detailed information on your money habits. Budgets can help you hold on to more of your money and plan for future growth.

- **News and events.** It's almost a fact of life that individual financial health is tied to the rest of the nation's economy. At the heart of the economy is the Federal Reserve System, commonly called the "Fed." Created by Congress in 1913 to serve as the central bank of the United States, the Fed controls the nation's flow of money and credit and their price—interest rates. This in turn influences employment, output, and the general level of prices.

In an effort to control economic stability, the Fed bases its monetary policy initially on the supply and demand of reserves for banks and other depository institutions. All depository institutions—banks, savings and loans, credit unions, and so on—are required by law to keep a certain amount of deposits as reserves. The Fed supplies reserves to the banking system in two ways: borrowed and non-borrowed reserves. The smaller portion of the reserve supply comes from lending through the Fed discount window, known as *borrowed reserve.* The Fed adjusts its supply of non-borrowed reserves by buying or selling securities in the open market, known as *open market operations.*

Active trading of reserves held at the Fed occurs among banks and depository institutions, usually overnight. The short-term interest rate they pay on these funds is called the federal funds rate and any change in this rate affects the market conditions for reserves and eventually, the economy. The resulting chain of events touches other short-term interest rates, foreign exchange rates, long-term interest rates, and back to the availability of money and credit in the economy.

For example, say the Fed reduces the supply of reserves. The federal fund rate increases as a result, spreading to other short-term rates, which can send the people toward higher yields on their money, possibly in the form of Treasury bills. So the money supply begins to drop as people pull it from banks. Banks may then have less money to lend, leading to higher borrowing costs and stricter lending policies. This rise in short-term rates can also lead to an increase in the long-term interest rates on other financial instruments such as home mortgages.

So when there is a change in interest rates as dictated by the Fed and it's most important monetary policymaking body, the Federal Open Market Committee (FOMC), it's almost guaranteed to affect the financial markets. But a whispered word about a company's future, quite outside the government, can also send its stock soaring or plummeting. By keeping current with the news about business and finance, you'll be better prepared to manage your own affairs.

KEEPING RECORDS

One of the hardest things to track in your financial life is the outlay of cold, hard cash. It's just too easy to spend. And receipts, those little bits of paper that act as records, are just as easy to lose. While allowing yourself a certain amount of discretionary spending cash in your pocket can give you a feeling of freedom, too much cash on hand can lead to financial shipwreck. One of the best ways to keep track of where your money goes is to use some other method of payment.

CHECKING ACCOUNTS

There are many reasons for opening a bank account. Most important of all is that it's easier to keep track of your money. An account may also help you save money, simply because it's not as easy to spend, and it's often safer than carrying cash.

Features and costs of accounts can vary greatly, so you need to shop around and find the best one for you. Many banks offer basic accounts with a limited set of services for a low price. You should be able to find "no frills" savings and checking accounts.

A checking account is vital to record keeping, as a checkbook register can provide a very accurate chronicle of where the bulk of your cash is going. Even if you forget to record the transactions, your bank statement will provide you with an account of what check number you used, when you wrote it, and for what amount. Keeping cancelled checks helps to provide a trail of where your money went. If your bank doesn't return cancelled checks, you can usually request a printed copy or the checks themselves for a small fee.

DEBIT CARDS

Another alternative to cash is to use a debit card. According to the U.S. Consumer Information Center, over 60 million Americans carry debit cards with the logos of two major payment card companies: Visa and MasterCard. That logo is what sets them apart from the typical automated teller machine (ATM) card. These debit cards carry clout because you can use them not only to get cash from ATM machines, but to purchase goods wherever the logo is accepted. They're convenient, too—accepted by over 14 million merchants worldwide. Although, most car rental companies feel their risk of loss is greater with debit cards and still require a credit card to guarantee a rental.

You can use your debit card to buy gas, food, and other items where you might normally spend cash. When you buy something with your debit card, the money is taken, or debited, from your checking account. Unlike credit cards, debit cards involve the use of your money, so there are no interest or finance charges. All transactions are reported on your monthly bank account statement, including date, place, and amount. That sure makes it easy to keep track.

Most debit cards require you to choose a personal identification number (PIN) to protect your account should you lose your card. Even though the two major payment card companies, Visa and MasterCard, limit your liability to $50 should someone use your card without your permission, it could take time to get your money back. If you get your debit card from your banking institution, make sure you're clear on their theft and liability policies before you start to use your card.

PROCEED WITH CAUTION

Always keep the PIN to your debit card confidential and check the contents of your wallet regularly to make sure you still have your card. Report lost or stolen cards immediately. If someone depletes your bank account by withdrawing cash or purchasing goods, it could take several months before the debit card company reimburses you.

CREDIT CARDS

Credit cards can be a convenient alternative to carrying cash for purchases. Credit cards are also a great way to leverage your finances so that you can purchase necessities or cover emergencies. If used wisely, there is no problem with credit card debt.

The Federal Reserve System publishes a semi-annual report on the credit card terms offered by financial institutions. The terms include the *availability* of the card to consumers and the *type of pricing*—fixed or variable. It also notes the *index* on which variable rate plans are based as well as the *grace period* for payment without charges, if any.

Like debit cards, each transaction is reported on your monthly credit card statement. Of course, it's important to remember that you are actually borrowing the money from the credit card company. If you don't pay it back promptly, you have to pay finance charges.

Credit cards, however, can lead to pyramiding debt when used without careful consideration. Problems arise when you begin to focus on how you can afford the monthly payment rather than the affordability of the total purchase with finance charges added on.

PROCEED WITH CAUTION

Credit terms differ among issuers, so read them carefully. What's best depends on how you plan to use the card. If you pay off bills each month, the annual fee may be important. If you use the card to pay over time, the Annual Percentage Rate, or yearly cost of credit, could be more significant to you.

If you decide to use a credit card to keep track of your finances, here are some basic credit card facts to remember:

- Shop around for the best credit card terms. Card companies are always making new, attractive offers.
- Read the fine print on the back of the credit card application and be sure you understand the terms before you sign.
- Cross out any blank spaces above the total when you sign a receipt.
- Keep copies of sales receipts. When your statement arrives, compare the charges.
- Pay your credit card bills in full every month to avoid finance charges.

- Make a list of all your credit cards, their account numbers, and the telephone numbers of each card issuer. If your cards are lost or stolen, you can report it immediately.

Even with the help of those credit and debit card statements, and your checkbook register, it takes time to keep up. You need to total the transactions and enter them somewhere, usually in specialized books called journals and ledgers. You can buy simplified paper versions in office supply stores. The simplest bookkeeping system to maintain is the single-entry system, in which you record the movement of income and expenses.

Many people use their checkbook as their main source of daily expense transactions. By depositing all receipts into the checking account and writing checks for all expenses, you can keep very adequate daily transaction records. These records can be transferred to your journals.

Personal-finance software, such as Quicken and Microsoft Money, has made life a little bit easier when it comes to transcribing income and expenses. You enter the data and use the power of the program to create budgets, reports that show you your big financial picture and future scenarios on savings and also sort transactions. If you have Internet access, you may not even need to enter the data; the program can accept downloaded information from your bank or your credit card.

BACK IT UP

Safe-keeping of your financial information is as important as the tracking of it. If you use a journal, make copies of key documents and store them separately. If you use a computer, you should do regular backups every time you create new entries. Alternate between two backup disks each month, so you have one in your computer drive and one in another location. In a worst-case scenario, you have a backup that is only one month behind in entries. Safety deposit boxes are ideal for safe storage of small items such as disks and papers, and can be rented from your bank for a minimal monthly fee.

UNCLE SAM SAYS

Your relationship with the IRS should always be kept in mind when you're working on a budget and tracking, or record-keeping system. The IRS doesn't require you to track and keep records in any special way, as long as it's organized and serves to back up your claims on your tax return. A checkbook will do if you enter all income and expenses. But they will need to see certain basic records as follows. All records and documents should be kept for three years following the filing of the return, or for as long as they relate to future tax returns.

- **Income.** W-2s from employers, 1099s from independent labor
- **Expenses.** Sales slips, receipts, invoices, or other proof of payment
- **Home.** Mortgage records, proof of payment, or insurance records
- **Investment.** Brokerage and mutual fund statements, or Forms 1099 and 2439
- **Others:**

   Alimony. Keep a copy of your written separation agreement or the divorce, separate maintenance, or support decree. If you pay alimony, you need your former spouse's social security number.

   Business use of your home. Keep records to show that some of your home is used exclusively and regularly for business to qualify for a tax deduction.

   Casualty theft and loss. Keep records to prove theft or loss.

   Childcare credit. You must keep the name, address, and taxpayer ID for whoever provides the care for your child or dependents.

TRACK IT ALL WITH A PC

Telling yourself you're going to take control of finances is the first step; doing it takes a big jump. The technological revolution has changed the way we keep track and organize, so that access to a personal computer is almost a necessity. With computer software programs and Internet access, the hardest part for you is to learn the program and get started.

There are several types of personal-finance software available, each with different user-friendly attributes and navigation. What they all have in common, though, is the ability to help you "get a financial life." The software can do the math if you don't like it, and even if you do, the calculations may be more accurate. It can take the tedious, mundane tasks off your hands, such as scheduling repeat payments. Most software programs also offer some basic advice on topics that may be new to you.

SOFTWARE

Personal-finance software takes a bit of getting used to because the programs are very powerful and contain many features. It's worth the effort, though.

Basically, you can update bank records, make and track budgets, create and update investment portfolios, and plan for the future. All of your entries can be coded to make tax preparation a planned process rather than an annual panic. Most of these things can be done within the program.

GO TO ▶
Refer to Hour 3, "Budgeting Your Way to the Future," for more information on personal-finance software.

Software will only keep track of what you enter, though, unless you link your computer application to an online bank. Then the top applications will update and download the information onto your desktop for you. You can pay bills, access your accounts 24 hours a day, make transfers between accounts, and check on the status of your investments.

The top two competitors in the personal-finance software arena are Intuit, with its Quicken products, and Microsoft's Money. Each year the competitors issue upgrades, but it pays to read the reviews to see if you need to spend the extra money. Most recent upgrades have involved the Internet: it's accessibility and integration with the software.

QUICKEN PRODUCTS

The first version of Quicken was shipped in 1984, designed as a consumer-friendly program for people to manage their personal finances. Since then, the product line has expanded into small-business software, tax software, and more. Here are some of Quicken's basic products:

- **Quicken.** Basic, Deluxe, and Suite versions
- **Quicken Web Entry.** Access to your accounts from any computer
- **TurboTax and MacinTax.** Tax preparation and filing
- **QuickBooks.** Small-business money management

MICROSOFT PRODUCTS

Perhaps better known for its Windows operating system, Microsoft has been running a close race with Intuit's personal-finance software. In 1999, Microsoft finally announced, but as of this writing had not released, the integrated tax software that would bring it in line with Quicken and TurboTax.

- **Microsoft Money.** Standard, Deluxe, and Business and Personal
- **TaxSaver.** Newly announced, but not released, in 1999 with the updated Microsoft Money 2000. TaxSaver is the company's tax preparation software that will allow you to transfer financial information from Money 2000 Deluxe to the program for tax preparation and filing.

DISCOUNTS, FREEWARE, AND SHAREWARE

There are other software programs available for managing your money, lesser-known than the top competitors. Some even come as part of an online banking package. A regular search on the Internet can bring up a bounty of free software, discounted software, and even products that you can try before you buy, called *shareware*.

Many software applications are not as broad in scope as the top commercial packages, but may be just what you're looking for. Go to the site, check out the computer requirements and follow the directions to download the package onto your hard drive. Be forewarned, however, that the two masters of personal finance software, Quicken and Money, annually try to push technology to new limits of functionality.

Here are some good sites to check for free downloadable software:

- **Equity Analytics Ltd. at www.e-analytics.com/soft2.htm.** Free applications to aid in finance and investing, including bond analysis, futures, commodities, and budgeting.

- **MacUpdate at www.macupdate.com/subcategory/Personal.html.** Shareware, freeware, and demos for Mac users.

- **Jumbo! at www.jumbo.com/pages/business/sections.asp?x_sectionid=10681.** Over 300,000 shareware and freeware programs with many finance and business related applications.

- **Pine Grove Software at www.pine-grove.com/.** Loan and lease calculators, as well as many others, both shareware and freeware.

- **ZDNet at www.zdnet.com.** A good resource for financial software tips, ideas, and reviews by Ziff-Davis. You'll find reviews on the latest releases from the company's *PC* and *Computing* magazines. They also have price comparison guides where you can shop by category at computershopper.zdnet.com/. Check their software library for free downloads, although not all are finance-related. They also conduct auctions and highlight daily freebies.

DISCOUNTED SOFTWARE

Besides conducting a keyword search through a search engine for freeware or shareware, other discounted software can be found on the shopping Web site Beyond.com. The inventory changes regularly, so check back often. Some of the items are free after rebates and can be downloaded so there are no shipping charges involved.

Tracking Online

GO TO ▶
Refer to Hour 12
for more tips on
how to manage
your money online
safely.

While you can do a lot on your home computer, some of your financial upkeep will involve logging on to the Internet. Many details, such as news, appointments, and portfolio tracking, can be kept on top of solely through the Internet if you're willing to learn what's out there.

TIME SAVER

 Online banking can save you time and energy by balancing your checkbook and keeping track of your accounts.

Web Portals

A Web portal is a Web page or service that acts as your doorway onto the Internet. They usually offer a number of resources such as e-mail, search engines, and online shopping malls. Some of the first portals were full services such as AOL, which also provided Internet access. Now, many of the initial search engines, such as Yahoo! and Excite have turned into full-service portals in the struggle to keep up traffic. Since portals are free, they sell advertising banner space in exchange for promising that you and millions of other visitors will log on to their page first.

Some of these sites may overlap in terms of content or transactions they provide. For example, Quicken and SmartMoney are major content generators of articles and advice that portals use to fill up their pages. Many get their industry and financial news from the same sources such as Reuters or Morningstar, a mutual fund rating service.

It's up to you to find the portal or site you like best in terms of look, feel, and usability. You can personalize pages that will track your stocks and funds—even several different portfolios—customize your news, and more. Like new software, once you set it up and learn the features, you just click on and go.

Some of the major Web portals geared toward finance include:

ALTA VISTA

altavista.looksmart.com/eus1/eus65300/r?comefrom= avhome-e65300andizf

One of the largest search engines on the Web, Alta Vista's Business and Finance channel has several finance-related categories including news, data and statistics, investments, business, jobs, quotes, portfolio tracking, and more.

AOL

www.aol.com

AOL's Personal Finance channel on the Web is the mirror image of the Excite finance channel, due to branding. You will find possibilities to personalize news and stock portfolios.

EXCITE

www.excite.com/money/

Offers financial news, quotes, and company research. The site links to Quicken for advice and content as well as portfolio tracking. It links to Charles Schwab Company for market index data.

LYCOS

www.lycos.com/money/

Personal finance guide with links to SmartMoney.com content. Offers stock quotes and company news, calculators, personalized news pages, and more.

NETSCAPE CENTER

home.netscape.com/finance/help/index.html

Choose the Personal Finance channel and read Reuters, which supplies most of the real-time financial news, and Morningstar, which provides a great deal of the content. Like AOL, this search engine is a branded version of Excite. This generous portfolio tracker allows you to enter over 100 stocks per portfolio.

Snap

www.snap.com

Go to Snap's Business and Money channel and you can choose from a huge menu of financial tools and information. Portfolio tracking is offered from the main Business and Money page.

WebCrawler

quicken.webcrawler.com/

Money and Investing channel with content provided by Quicken.com. WebCrawler allows you personalize your news and portfolio tracking.

Yahoo! Finance

quote.yahoo.com/

A comprehensive financial site with customizable features. In 1999 Yahoo! announced new features such as Corporate Financials, which offers balance sheets, income statements, and cash filings of publicly traded companies. They also now offer daily editorial content, which provides the latest professional stock analysis, news, and commentary from the Individual Investor.

Online Calendars

Interactive online calendars will remind you to make appointments, gather data, file taxes, pay your housekeeper—whatever it is you need to remind you to keep your finances in order! Many will synchronize with other PIMs, or personal information managers, such as Outlook or Palm Pilot. Better yet, these Net-based calendars allow you to log on anywhere you can find a computer with Internet access, even a mall kiosk! If you forgot your to-do list while out running errands, find a PC, log on, and check your calendar. What you can forget is to buy calendar software—it's all online.

The programs are very powerful now, often allowing you to add local events, movie and TV listings, and plenty of other outside news sources to your personal calendar. Here is a partial list of the free Web calendars available. There are many more in the beta stages, and the competitive nature of these services means the consumer will continue to benefit in the years to come. The following calendars offer differing options, such as downloadable capabilities to PIMs, or access from many different locations, even group access.

- **AnyDay.com.** This free online Dayplanner combines an integrated calendar, address book, reminder service, and a task manager with an event directory.

- **The Daily Drill at www.dailydrill.com.** A free online calendar and appointment book. You can customize a calendar to remind you of official and/or religious holidays, birthdays, and special events. The Drill will notify you of upcoming dates with a Web page alarm, send you e-mail, or page you if your pager is equipped with text messaging— whatever you choose.

  At the bottom of each page in the Daily Drill is a to-do list. Fill it out, update it from anywhere, print it out, and carry it with you.

- **Daily Web Planner at www.dwp.net/.** A free, Web-based daily planner with a free e-mail account. It also contains features such as Instant Reminder Service, Calendar, where you can bookmark Web pages, and more. They are planning to include future features such as Instant Messaging, search engines, E-Commerce, E-Biz to earn income, people find, Bulletin Board, and Stock Quotes.

- **Excite Planner at planner.excite.com.** A free Web-portal offering of calendar and day planner. The service can send e-mail and pager reminders, and synchronizes with Palm devices and Microsoft Outlook. You can also get your own 1-800 number for voicemail and faxing.

- **MyEvents.Com at www.myevents.com.** Groups and individuals can create and share calendars, to-do lists, photo albums, and homepages. My Events.com is an easy-to-use virtual secretary.

- **Yahoo! Calendar at calendar.yahoo.com.** This free Web-portal calendar has Time Guides, a feature that automatically overlays events such as sports games, co-workers' calendars, and stock splits onto your own personal schedule. You can keep track of earnings release dates, stock splits, and board meeting dates for companies in your portfolio.

OTHER ONLINE INVESTMENT SUPPORT

Web portals offer a variety of features besides the financial news and interactive tools. But if you don't need the search engine capabilities or the e-mail accounts, you can go directly to some of the top financial sources on the Internet. This financial arena is expanding constantly, with new technology being added almost daily. So you can regularly monitor your financial pulse, whether it's your recent stock pick or your life insurance quotes.

THE WALL STREET JOURNAL INTERACTIVE EDITION

www.wsj.com/

The Wall Street Journal Interactive has a subscription rate of $59 a year; however, they do offer a free trial. If you're a serious investor, this site has powerful customization features.

You can also use *The Wall Street Journal* free Web site at Dowjones.com. You must register (for free) to use personalized features such as portfolios, industry news, or forums.

You can create up to 5 portfolios with 30 issues each once you've registered. At this writing, stock prices were 20 minutes delayed, and mutual fund and cash prices were updated at trading day end.

A snapshot of your portfolio that includes the last trade during trading hours and the change from the previous trade will then appear on the dowjones. com Main Page and on the Personal Finance and Markets pages.

AMERICAN EXPRESS FINANCIAL ADVISORS

www.americanexpress.com/advisors/tracker/

The American Express Fund Tracker is an interactive tool that allows you to enter stock or mutual fund information to get current price and overall value of your investments. The information is stored on your hard drive.

You can also get the latest news and editorials from CBS Market Watch, as well as access many other American Express Financial Advisor's personal-finance services such as planning tools, online banking, and trading.

MORNINGSTAR

www.morningstar.com/

Morningstar is the leading provider of mutual fund analysis, and also tracks the performance of variable annuities and variable life insurance products.

They offer two levels of service: free and premium for $9.95 a month. Free service gives you access to the Portfolio Manager, which allows you to track, manage, and analyze up to 10 portfolios with up to 50 securities in each. You can also use Portfolio X-Rays. The Asset Class X-Ray summarizes your true allocation among cash, bonds, and U.S. and foreign stocks, and shows which market risks you are exposed to. The Stock Stats X-Ray tells you if your portfolio is under- or overvalued. The Fees and Expenses X-Ray reveals just how much of your investment goes toward paying the investment managers.

Conversations is the online chat with investors and Morningstar analysts, and Informational E-mail gives you the option of periodic updates about new features, articles, and benefits posted to Morningstar.com.

Premium service offers all that plus Advanced Portfolio X-Rays—a screening tool that screens more than 15,000 funds and stocks—top shelf financial news, and in-depth financial analysis through Morningstar's QuickTake Reports.

BLOOMBERG ONLINE PORTFOLIO TRACKER

www.bloomberg.com/pfc/tools99.html

Keep track of 5 portfolios that can contain up to 100 stocks apiece. Bloomberg's Market Monitor will stay open on your desktop and update every few minutes while you're online. Track up to ten securities with Market Monitor. You can also take advantage of their advice on taxes, investing, loan financing, and retirement strategies.

SMARTMONEY

www.smartmoney.com/intro/tools/

Don't miss the powerful Stock Tools channel, which you can personalize and keep track of:

- The economy
- The Dow
- The sectors
- Bond analysis
- Asset allocation
- Mutual funds
- Investments
- Debt management
- Retirement vehicles
- Real estate
- Taxes

HOUR'S UP!

Don't get discouraged trying to track where your money is going and what you'll need for the future. You've learned a great deal in the past hour to help you stay current, and the following questions will test and strengthen your knowledge.

1. True or false: Tracking your personal finances is nearly impossible without having a sound financial plan to follow.

2. Understanding your present financial position includes a knowledge of …

   a. Your insurance coverage.

   b. Your retirement plans.

   c. Your spending habits.

   d. All of the above.

3. True or false: One of the hardest segments of your financial life to track is cash outflow.

4. True or false: Bank statements for credit cards, debit cards, and checking accounts can all help you keep track of your spending habits.

5. If you use a credit card to track spending, you should remember to …

   a. Keep copies of all receipts to compare with statements.

   b. Shop for the terms that suit you best.

   c. Read the fine print on the back of the application and make sure you understand the lending terms.

   d. All of the above.

6. Personal-finance software will help you …

   a. Create a budget.

   b. Balance accounts.

   c. Track your portfolio.

   d. All of the above.

7. True or false: Quicken and Microsoft Money are the top two commercial personal-finance software packages available today.

8. True or false: All personal-finance software programs are competitive in price.

9. Web portals are …

    a. Your doorway to the Internet.

    b. Windows in a boat.

    c. Internet software packages.

10. True or false: There are plenty of powerful tools and services on the Internet to aid in your financial planning that are free.

Quiz

PART II
Investment Methods

HOUR 5
Investing Basics

CHAPTER SUMMARY

LESSON PLAN:

In this chapter you will learn the true definition of investing. You'll learn what your investment options are and how to find them, and you'll discover how to set some investment goals. You'll also learn how to:

- Figure compound interest.
- Protect yourself and your family.
- Set investing goals.
- Examine investment risks.
- Determine an investment strategy.
- Select a broker.

Many people automatically think "stock market" when they hear the word "investing." That is where a great deal of fortunes have been made and lost to be sure, but investing really means putting your money to work to earn you more money.

While it may seem that all your income dollars are spent on consumables required for daily living, you should make a real effort to put a few dollars a month into investments that bring you a return with more long-term satisfaction. Investing your money can help increase your wealth for bigger-ticket items such as a home, a college education for your children, or a comfortable retirement.

SECURITIES

There are many forms of investments that can help you earn more for your money, but for the next few hours you will be concentrating on buying shares of financial assets, called *securities*. Each one of the following securities categories should be considered key parts of any balanced investment portfolio. You can invest in them individually or diversify through mutual funds.

- **Stocks.** Ownership shares in a business
- **Bonds.** IOUs from or loans to the government or a business with a fixed rate of return and specified time period
- **Cash.** Treasury bills, bank accounts, or certificates of deposit

JUST A MINUTE

"Securities" once stood for the "secure document," or written proof of owner-ship in an investment. In today's electronic marketplace, securities now repre-sent the computer record more than a piece of paper.

There are many other types of investments in the world, too. For example, you can invest in real estate, commodities, or precious metals, some of which will be discussed in the hour ahead. Assuming, though, that you are a new investor, it's best to start with those areas that are easier to understand and research, and are highly regulated.

JUST A MINUTE

Mutual funds are run by investment companies. They pool investors' cash and buy up a variety of securities for the fund's portfolio. Owning shares in a mu-tual fund helps you spread the risk of losing your money over several stocks instead of taking a chance on just one.

COMPOUND IT

What makes investing your money so attractive is the idea of the time value of money. Basically, a dollar earned today is worth much more in the future because it can earn interest until it's used. It gets even better. Once you have invested, your interest earns interest, a concept called *compounding.*

Compounding is when the interest earned in one period earns additional in-terest in each future time period. For example, you have $1,000 nestled into a savings account earning 5 percent interest. The first compounding period will net you $50 in interest. Now you have $1,050 earning 5 percent interest, so you earn $52.50 in interest the next period. Both the interest and the princi-pal are increasing.

Take a look at what happens to that $1,000 over time and with varying rates of return:

Compound Interest

Years/Rates	5 Percent	8 Percent	10 Percent	12 Percent
1	$1,050	$1,080	$1,100	$1,120
5	$1,276	$1,469	$1,611	$1,762
10	$1,629	$2,159	$2,594	$3,106
15	$2,079	$3,172	$4,177	$5,474
20	$2,653	$4,661	$6,727	$9,646

You can see that the longer you leave your investment alone, the more chance it has to snowball into a tidy sum of money.

While 5 percent interest accumulated over 20 years looks pretty good, there is another consideration—inflation. Inflation is defined as the rate at which the prices of goods and services rise over time. Inflation is why a loaf of bread purchased in 1989 for 72¢ cost about one dollar 10 years later.

Inflation has been growing, on average, between 3 to 4 percent per year in the past 50 years, so you're not going to do much to increase your spending power by leaving your cash in a savings account bearing 5 percent interest. Your dollars may be worth more in the future, but not much more. Of course, stashed under the mattress, your dollar would only be worth about 97¢ because it's been eaten up by inflation.

That's why it's imperative to find investments that will at the very least outpace the cost of living. You aren't going to make a fortune overnight, but few people do. Real wealth comes from patience and the power of compounding.

TIME SAVER

 Find out the current inflation rate by watching the Consumer Price Index. It's reported quarterly by the Bureau of Labor Statistics (BLS) and can be found in newspapers or the BLS Web site at stats.bls.gov/news.release/cpi.toc.htm.

PREPARE YOURSELF FOR INVESTING

Once you see the magic that compounding can perform on your investment portfolio, you begin to understand the importance of early and regular investing. Now consider the reverse effect on your money—that of compounding interest on debt. That's what happens when you leave an outstanding balance on your credit card. With most credit cards compounding monthly, your debt can mushroom quickly.

PAY DOWN HIGH-INTEREST DEBT

Before you can begin to invest your money and watch it grow, you should work toward becoming debt-free. What good is a stock or mutual fund paying a 10 percent return when you're paying 12 percent on the balance owed for your latest water-sports toy?

GO TO ▶
Refer to Hour 1, "Developing Your Financial Goals," to find out more about credit and debt.

Your first investment should be in yourself. Pay off high-interest debt, such as credit card or car loans, as soon as you can. Then you can look for other investments.

When you find yourself reaching for your credit card or wallet, think about the time value of your money, or what that dollar would be worth invested over the next 10 years.

PROTECT YOURSELF AND YOUR FAMILY

No one invests to lose money, but investing can carry some degree of uncertainty. Before you launch into any endeavor that involves placing your money at risk, no matter how small, it's important to make sure you have adequately protected yourself and your family first.

GO TO ▶
Refer to Hour 15, "Insurance," to find out more about how to determine the right insurance product for your needs.

Your risk coverage should include life insurance to protect loved ones who may suffer financially in the event of your death. Cash value life insurance policies combine tax-deferred savings with the death benefit and offer a cash surrender if you give up the policy. Carefully review them for fees and commissions before buying.

Term life insurance policies can provide valuable death benefits and are less expensive than cash value polices. But if you stop paying the premiums or the policy ends, there is no surrender value.

Along with life insurance, it's a good idea to carry disability insurance to cover loss of income in case you are injured and can't work.

Most financial advisors also recommend that you have a three- to six-month cash reserve for emergency expenses, as discussed in Hour 1. These funds should be invested in short-term savings products such as money market funds and CDs. Hour 3, "Budgeting Your Way to the Future," has more information on finding the best banking products available.

With those safety nets in place you can start to factor your personal circumstances into the investment equation. To even consider investing, you need something to invest. How much money you have saved, how much money you can spare on a regular basis, and how much risk you're willing to take all play a role in your investment decision-making.

TEN PERCENT TO YOURSELF

You have probably heard of the 10 percent rule by now, but it always bears repeating. At least 10 percent of your income should be set aside for saving and investing. It's easy enough to calculate: 10 percent of a $2,000 paycheck is $200.

If you use direct deposit or automatic savings account withdrawals, you don't even have to think about it. Many banks and investment firms offer automatic investment programs that will link to your checking or savings account. You choose the investment vehicle and the amount you can invest. They often have minimum monthly amounts, such as $50. In exchange, many will waive the normal initial investment requirements, which range from $1,000 and up. Many automatic investors choose mutual funds for their diversity.

Think of this "forced" savings as paying yourself, and always think of yourself first. It should actually be a line item on your family budget marked "Savings." Obviously, the more you can spare for yourself now the longer that money has to compound and grow. But even if you can only squeeze out a small percent at first, you should start the savings habit now.

There are places to find money, too. If you're serious about investing, you need to be serious about cutting back on spending. Every dollar spent in the vending machine at work or at the movie theater means a dollar short of one of your goals.

SET SOME GOALS

Telling yourself you want to make money on investments is not really enough. It's a little bit like saying you want to go on a vacation. Where do you want to go? How do you want to get there? How long can you stay? There are more decisions to make than just deciding you want to go on a vacation. It's the same with investing.

JUST A MINUTE

The ease with which your investment can be turned into cash determines how liquid it is. Bank accounts are very liquid and are easy to cash. Stocks, on the other hand, may be harder to convert because you have to sell them, then wait for cash. Investments such as fine art and collections are even less liquid because you have to find a buyer before you can sell them.

The first thing you should do is decide what you hope to accomplish with your investments, such as building your dream home or having a healthy nest egg for your retirement. Listing your goals and accomplishments should be fairly simple if you sketched out a financial goals plan in Hour 1. Take your goals and list them in order of priority.

Setting Goals

Financial Goals	Target Date	Amount Needed
_____	_____	$_____
_____	_____	$_____
_____	_____	$_____

WHAT'S THE TIME HORIZON?

Now determine how long it will take to reach those goals. When will you need that money? If you are going to need the money in three to five years for a down payment on a home, you want to be able to get it quickly, and you can't afford much investment risk.

Some investments are better suited to long-term goals, such as retirement, where they can ride out the ups and downs of the market. If you know approximately how long you have to reach your goals, you are better equipped for making a decision on the right investment vehicle. Write your target date in the second column.

HOW MUCH WILL YOU NEED?

How much money will it take for you to achieve those goals? You will need to do some researching and soul-searching to determine what you'll need for retirement or what a down payment on that dream home will cost. That amount goes into column three, and your paper should now look something like this:

Setting Goals Example

Goal	Target Date	Amount Needed
Home	5 years	$10,000
Kids' college	10 years	$16,000 a year for four years
Retirement	25 years	$60,000 a year for 25 years

TIME SAVER

Online calculators available at www.kiplinger.com and www.quicken.com are a great help for projecting the future cost of life's events, especially for those of you who hate to crunch numbers. You can even print out graphs and reports to refer back to when you're working on your investment portfolio.

Besides giving you some concrete goals to work toward, this exercise is crucial for determining what kind of investment choices you will eventually make.

EXAMINE THE RISKS AND REWARDS

So far you have discovered that time, inflation, interest rates, and the amount of money you put aside are important factors in how quickly you can build wealth.

Now it's time to talk about the risk involved in investing. Risk means you take the chance of losing your money, as well as making more, when you decide to invest. No investment is without some level of risk. How much risk you take depends on two things: your approach to investing and the investment vehicles you choose.

INVESTMENT APPROACHES

As previously mentioned, no investment is without risk, so you have to determine your personal level of risk comfort or tolerance. Investments can rise and fall in huge jumps all in one business day. If your money is riding the wave, the fluctuations in the market can be very disturbing. Maybe you know you won't need to touch that money for several years, so a day of market turmoil wouldn't phase you.

Risk tolerance is defined as either low, moderate, or high. The following quiz can help you determine your position:

	Important (10 points)	Mildly Important (20 points)	Not Important (30 points)
I want to keep my capital (money you have to invest) investment intact.	_____	_____	_____
I am interested in liquidity versus high rate of return.	_____	_____	_____
I prefer price stability over high returns.	_____	_____	_____
For long-term investing, I prefer the safety to aggressive growth and risk.	_____	_____	_____
Subtotals	_____	_____	_____
Total			_____

Add up the points to determine your score. A score between 40 to 60 points means you have a lower risk tolerance than someone in the moderate 70 to 90 point range. If you scored over 100 points, you have a high risk tolerance.

Here's what those risk tolerance terms really mean for purposes of investing:

- **Low risk tolerance.** You don't want to be mired in the market's ups and down. Your primary concern is in preserving your capital.

- **Moderate risk tolerance.** You have more available income and are concerned about capital appreciation and growth.

- **High risk tolerance.** You have the time and money to invest and are concerned with maximum appreciation and growth of capital.

INVESTMENT CHOICES

Once you're clear on the amount of risk you're willing and able to take, you can start to look for suitable investments. The investment vehicles available to you are also rated by risk levels, from low to high.

JUST A MINUTE

The strength of the financial markets is the result of how well a range of different investments—not just one stock—perform over time.

Low-risk investments guarantee that you'll get your capital back plus interest, and include federally insured bank accounts, certificates of deposit, money-market funds, government treasury bonds, and bills.

Investments with limited to moderate risk include blue chip stocks and mutual funds. High-risk investing encompasses speculative stocks, commodities, and futures trading.

The types of investments you choose, most likely decided upon by your risk tolerance, will identify your investment strategy. If you take only limited risks with fixed-income investments such as bonds or secure liquid stocks, you would be considered a conservative investor. A moderate investment approach involves taking more risks in hopes of achieving a greater return. You might invest in more growth stocks or mutual funds. An aggressive approach to investing is taken by someone willing to take major risks on speculative investments in hopes of very high returns.

THE BEST APPROACH

There is no one best approach to investing, that's why you're advised to carefully consider your personal position before launching a plan. There are consequences in any level of risk-taking.

Taking no chances leaves you in the position of possibly running short of your goals. If you're saving for retirement through bank accounts, inflation may cause you to outlive your holdings. On the other hand, if you attempt to make huge profits quickly by investing in volatile stocks, you could lose your capital completely.

RETURN ON INVESTMENT

Many experts and experienced investors recommend a moderate approach to investing by balancing the type of securities you own. Of course only you know the long- or short-term goals that you hope to achieve, so you need to choose your investment products to mirror your risk category.

How do you choose? You look at the risk factor, which we discussed in the preceding section, "Investment Choices," and you look at a product's return. "Return" is the name given to the measurement of performance of investments. It tells you the change in the value of the investment over a period of time and gives you the real economic returns reaped by ownership.

PROCEED WITH CAUTION

Even a good return on investment looks lighter after taxes, called the after-tax return on investment. Here's a sample calculation for someone in a 28 percent tax bracket with a 10 percent pre-tax return:

Return (10) × your tax rate (.28) = 2.8.

Now subtract 2.8 from 10 percent for a realistic after-tax return of 7.2 percent.

There are several different ways to represent the return on an investment, but it's the total return that gives you the best overall picture of performance. The sum of both the product's change in price (up or down), and the amount of income derived from dividends, if any, are reflected in total return. To give the performance a time limit, total return is usually measured annually.

You can look to the history books to see how certain investment classes have performed over the years. According to Global Financial Data, long-term and current financial data specialists based in Los Angeles, in the past 100 years, stocks returned about 10 percent per year, bonds returned about 5 percent, while inflation averaged nearly 3 percent annually.

PROCEED WITH CAUTION

Pay attention to the type of performance information you're reading—the method of computing return can be misguiding. A *cumulative return* can look huge since it totals the annual return for a specified number of years. Divide the cumulative return by number of years for the *average annual return*. *Total return* is figured year by year.

INVESTING STRATEGIES

What is important to note about the historical data of market returns is that in any chosen time period, the total returns could have been way up. Or take the case of stocks in the decade between 1930 and 1939, when the returns were abysmal, but bonds had average returns of over 4 percent. Stock returns for the following decade reached to nearly 10 percent, and bonds fell to 2 percent in the 1940s.

So there are no guarantees on the returns on your investments. But long-term investing, to ride out the market bumps, is one strategy that works toward risk protection. Diversification is another.

DIVERSIFY

Diversification involves spreading your money around to different investments to lower the chances of having all your money, invested in only one vehicle, take a dive at one time.

With a diversified portfolio, you can take some risks for high returns, while keeping part of your investment in safer, more moderate investments. The simplest way to diversify your portfolio is to follow the analogy of the investment pyramid recommended by many financial experts.

THE INVESTMENT PYRAMID

If you divide up your investment choices according to the investment pyramid, you would start with a strong base of low-risk and secure liquid assets, such as Treasury bills, government bond funds, and money-market funds. The purpose here is to preserve your capital, such as your three- to six-month emergency fund, and look for small returns.

The second level looks to maximize income on investments while still taking moderate risks. This level along with next level, or growth level, should form the bulk of the pyramid. Your final category would involve aggressive growth investments with no guarantees but the potential to make large sums of money.

The Investment Pyramid

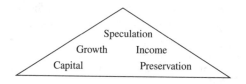

You will want to mix up your investment portfolio depending on your personal profile with regards to age, time horizon, and the amount of risk you're willing to take. There are other influences to consider, too, such as market conditions and tax laws, but the formula you choose to spread your money around is called *asset allocation*. Most experts agree that how you split your investments among the three categories of stocks, bonds, and cash is more important than the actual funds you choose.

GO TO ▶
Refer to Hour 14, "Taxes: Time to Get Clarity," for more information on how taxes can influence your investment decisions.

Asset Allocation

There are many different asset allocation models, and while experts don't all agree on what's right for the "average" investor, they do agree that the mix should shift around with each life stage.

For example, if you are approaching retirement, you might choose an asset allocation mix of 40 percent stocks, 50 percent bond funds, and about 10 percent in cash or money markets.

PROCEED WITH CAUTION

Decide whether you want to be an owner, a creditor, or both. Equity securities such as stock give you part ownership in a company you hope will rise in value. Debt securities such as bonds, CDs, and Treasury bills are loans that the invested-in organization promises to pay back with interest and the principal intact.

A young investor might split the pie into a more aggressive, wealth-building mix just the reverse of the retiree, with 60 to 70 percent allocated to stocks (divided up between blue chip and high-risk), 15 to 20 percent in bonds, and a minimal amount of liquid cash.

Devise your own asset allocation mix, or ask for recommendations from a financial advisor who is familiar with your personal profile. Most investment firms have sample models, and companies like Fidelity Investments at personal100.fidelity.com/planning/investment/content/peterlynch/strategy/ even have online questionnaires to help you build an investment strategy.

One thing almost all financial advisors do agree on is that everyone should have some exposure to the long-term growth potential of stocks. Just remember that some financial advisors may have a financial interest in the products they recommend. Of course you don't have to buy from them, but you can get a good feel for your personal portfolio mix.

You can take advantage of the markets' ups and downs by using a common investment strategy called *dollar cost averaging*. By regularly investing a fixed dollar amount into a certain investment you lessen the risk of investing a big sum into one investment at the wrong time. Your average cost per share is smaller over time. Some investment firms, banks, and brokerages offer automatic services.

Dollar Cost Averaging Example

	Monthly investment	Price per share	Shares Purchased
	$300	$5	60
	$300	$10	30
	$300	$15	20
Totals	$900	$8.18	110

Therefore, what you paid on average per share ($900 ÷ 110) is more like $8.18. The average share price over the same time period ($30 ÷ 3 months) = $10.

MAKING THE DECISION

Potential investors need to spend some time studying and tracking a company before purchasing stock. Here are some final items to consider while contemplating your investment decisions in a particular company, as recommended by the securities industry regulators:

- The higher the anticipated return, the greater the risk.
- Investing in unknown companies can be very risky.

- Securities investments are not federally insured against loss of market value.

- Your ownership share in a company can be affected by mergers, reorganizations, or third-party actions, so you should monitor information sent to you and public announcements.

- Past performance does not guarantee future success.

- Some investments are harder to convert to cash than others, and some carry penalties if sold before the maturity date.

SELECTING A BROKER

With the exception of a company retirement account, before you can make any securities investments, you'll need a broker or brokerage firm. Don't let the terms "brokers," "stock brokers," "account executives," or "registered representatives" confuse you. These people all work for full-service brokerage firms and do basically the same job—sell investments.

There are two types of stockbrokers: full-service and discount. Both have their pros and cons. A full-service brokerage house can give you product recommendations and investment advice, offer research services, and also execute the orders. All of those services carry a fee, of course—usually a commission fee based on the volume of business you do. While advice can be worth the money, remember that the fee deducts from the return on your investment.

You may pay $100 or more to buy shares of stock and then pay the same fee when you sell your stock. Keep in mind that commission sales representatives get paid on the volume of trading you do, so they will encourage you to trade often. Most national brokerage firms have local offices that can be found in the Yellow Pages. Examples of full-service brokerage firms include:

- **Merrill Lynch.** www.ml.com
- **Paine Webber.** www.painewebber.com
- **Prudential Securities.** www.prusec.com
- **Salomon Smith Barney.** www.smithbarney.com

If you already have a good sense of your personal profile and know the investment products you want, you can use a discount brokerage firm. Discount brokers offer execution services only, not recommendations, meaning they will place the buy or sell order for you, but won't research the company or offer advice. Discount brokers charge anywhere from $10 for buying

GO TO ▶
Refer to Hour 13, "Finding the Right Financial Advisor," for advice on your overall financial plan. A stock broker performs investment transactions and may offer advice on buying and selling securities.

shares (deep-discount brokers) to $50 or more, depending on the number of shares. Examples of some discount brokerage firms include:

- **Charles E. Schwab.** www.schwab.com; 1-800-435-4000
- **Fidelity Investments.** www100.fidelity.com:80/; 1-800-544-8888
- **Quick and Reilly.** www.quick-reilly.com; 1-800-672-7220

GO TO ▶
Many brokerages offer online trading. Refer to Hour 12, "Online Money Management," for more information about online investing and online money management.

Talk with potential brokers or sales representatives at several firms before deciding on one. It's important for you to find out about their experience, background, and education. With the world of online investing expanding so quickly, not all the newly hired brokers are screened as closely as they should be. You can also check into any possibility of fraud or disciplinary actions filed against a firm or representative by calling the National Association of Securities Dealers, Inc., at 1-800-289-9999.

There are also ways to protect yourself against a brokerage firm that goes broke—for example, choose one who is a member of the Securities Investor Protection Corporation (SIPC). The National Association of Security Dealers requires all of their member brokers to have SIPC insurance. Don't hesitate to ask them if they have it, as well as any other insurance coverage beyond SIPC limits.

JUST A MINUTE

If you receive notice that your broker is in financial trouble and have questions about where to submit a claim form, you can contact the Securities Investor Protection Corporation (SIPC) at 202-371-8300.

A New Account Agreement

If and when you choose a brokerage, you'll be asked to sign a new account agreement. Make sure everything the representative tells you is in writing. Don't rely on verbal claims. When filling out these forms you'll have to get personal (and honest) with your information, including your income, net worth, and investment experience.

Before you can start to buy and sell stocks, you'll have to answer three important questions on the agreement:

- **Who decides to buy and sell?** You will be authorized to make all the investment decisions in your account unless you sign over *discretionary investing authority.* This requires a signed limited power of attorney from you, which allows the investment manager to carry out transactions for you, but does not allow them to transfer assets out of your account. In a family trust, for example, the parents may be unable or uninterested in managing the assets, so they appoint an outside trustee with a similar investment philosophy. Some executives who travel often will also choose to sign the investing authority over to a broker or manager. In any case, it is a good idea to carefully monitor the activities in your investment account, whether or not you sign over the investing authority.

- **What is your risk level?** If you came to the brokerage fully prepared, then you already have a personal profile established. If you feel your objectives reflect moderate risk, make that known on the application. Then carefully monitor the broker's recommendations to make sure the products offered are in your risk range.

- **How will you pay?** You will probably be required to open and maintain a cash account to pay for your investment purchases. Find out the specifics of the account. If you decide to buy securities on *margin* (borrowing money from the firm to buy investments), you are giving the brokerage the right to sell any security in your account to cover a loss from those margin securities. The brokerage doesn't have to notify you when they sell those securities, either.

OTHER WAYS TO INVEST

There are other ways to purchase investment products besides going directly to a brokerage firm. A financial planner can purchase investment products for you for a fee on top of their service fees. You can also select from a range of products through an investment subsidiary employed by most banks. You still pay a commission fee, and it can be a pretty steep price for the convenience.

Company 401(k)s, or retirement plans, are an ideal investment forum that usually offer a choice of products. Most companies absorb the cost associated with managing the plan, with the exception of special requests such as early withdrawals or loans. You get the added benefit of growing your investments tax-deferred until you start withdrawing the money.

GO TO ▶
Refer to Hour 9, "Retirement Planning," for more information.

INVESTORS' BILL OF RIGHTS

When you sign an agreement with a broker, you are now both involved in a legal contract. The same goes for any security you purchase; you're not just a consumer, you're a person with rights and responsibilities. To make sure you understand those rights, the National Futures Organization collaborated with several investing and government agencies, as well as consumer organizations, to create the *Investors' Bill of Rights*.

Important especially for the new investor, a synopsis of this bill outlines certain truths about your rights as an investor. When you start to question what you can and can't do in the investment arena, always remember that you have the right to expect the features described in the following sections.

HONESTY IN ADVERTISING

Your first contact with an investment product may be through TV, newspaper, magazine, by mail, or online. Telemarketers also solicit business by phone. All of these sales approaches are considered a form of advertising and are regulated by law. False or misleading advertising is against the law in almost every area of investment activity and subject to penalties.

Just remember that advertising attempts to highlight the most attractive properties of a product and you are most likely getting limited information.

FULL AND ACCURATE INFORMATION

You have the right to obtain information about any investment before you buy. You also have the right to know about the people or the organization with which you will be doing business.

Get a copy of the prospectus, if there is one, and ask for any other literature available such as a copy of the latest annual report. If the rate of return is advertised, ask how it was calculated. You also have the right to know if the person or firm selling the product has a financial interest in the sale.

DISCLOSURE OF RISKS

You have the right to know the risks involved in making an investment. While it may be obvious that your stock value may decline or the business you invest in could fail, some risks are not so obvious. For instance, in some investments you can lose more than you initially invested, and you could owe more.

If there is no risk disclosure documentation, then ask for the risks to be explained in writing. Never buy an investment that you don't understand.

EXPLANATION OF OBLIGATIONS AND COSTS

There are many fees and obligations associated with some investments that you should know up front. You have the right to a full disclosure of costs including any commissions, sales charges (called *loads*), when you buy and sell, and penalties if certain actions aren't taken in a specific time period.

GO TO ▶
Refer to Hour 7, "Mutual Funds," to find out more about sales loads.

TIME TO CONSIDER

Never allow yourself to be pushed into an investment purchase. Any salesperson who tells you to buy "right now" should be viewed with suspicion. You have the right to make an informed decision, and you have the right to the time to decide for yourself.

RESPONSIBLE ADVICE

In the securities industry there are suitability rules that require investment advice be appropriate for the customer. In the commodity futures industry there is a "know your customer" rule that requires firms and brokers to be sure investors are informed of the risks.

You have the right to responsible advice, so beware of someone who knows nothing about you, yet insists a product is right for you.

BEST EFFORT MANAGEMENT

All firms that accept funds from the public have the legal and ethical obligation to manage those funds responsibly. Always check your brokerage statements to be sure there are no excess fees or unauthorized sales.

COMPLETE AND TRUTHFUL ACCOUNTING

Most firms prepare and send out periodic account statements. You have the right to expect that your statement be accurate and timely.

ACCESS TO YOUR FUNDS

You have the right to know about any restrictions on accessing your funds before you purchase the product. If there are no reasons why the investment can't be quickly converted to cash, you should be able to get your money back in a reasonable time frame.

RECOURSE, IF NECESSARY

If you think someone has handled your investment dishonestly, you have the right to seek help, whether it be through arbitration, mediation, or a court of law.

If you have questions or want to report investment fraud, contact the Securities and Exchange Commission Division of Enforcement at:

Enforcement Complaint Center
450 Fifth Street, N.W.
Washington, D.C. 20549-0710
E-mail: enforcement@sec.gov
Phone: 1-800-SEC-0330

HOUR'S UP!

The basics of investing can be confusing at first, but once you've grasped them they go a long way to help you build your financial future. The following questions will test and strengthen what you've learned.

1. True or false: Compounding is when the interest on your investment earns interest.

2. True or false: You should invest as soon as possible, even if you have outstanding bills and debt.

3. True or false: You are always guaranteed to get back at least the amount you put into any investment.

4. True or false: The moderate approach to investing recommended by financial experts involves a diversified portfolio.

5. You diversify a portfolio by …

    a. Asking advice from different sources.

    b. Buying products from different brokers.

    c. Dividing up your investments into different risk categories.

6. True or false: The term "return" is used to identify an investment performance.

7. True or false: The three things to consider when deciding your personal investment profile are your age, risk tolerance, and time horizon.

8. The investment pyramid is …

    a. A small monument in Egypt.

    b. A multi-level marketing scheme.

    c. A model for investment diversification.

9. The three major securities categories for any investment portfolio are …

    a. Age, time, and risk.

    b. Earth, wind, and fire.

    c. Stocks, bonds, and cash.

10. True or false: When you are considering purchasing an investment product, you have the right to know about the company, the person selling the product, and the risks involved in buying the product.

Quiz

HOUR 6

Stocks

LESSON PLAN:
In this chapter you will learn about investing in the stock market. You'll also learn how to:

- Make market forces work for you.
- Understand the types of stock.
- Buy and sell stock.
- Figure indexes and averages.
- Spot "get-rich-quick" scams.

Wall Street has long been the center for major trading transactions in the United States. In the 1700s, merchants and brokers were buying and selling shares of incoming ship's cargo on street corners, in markets, or anywhere people came together.

By 1790, the first financial assets were trading hands. The U.S. government sold war bonds to help pay off Revolutionary War debt, and the first shares of stock in a company were offered by the nation's first bank. But all of the transactions between brokers, merchants, and auctioneers were informal and the meetings haphazard.

It wasn't until 1792, when 24 brokers signed an agreement to trade exclusively among themselves, that the roots of today's modern stock market took hold. They called the document *The Buttonwood Agreement,* after the tree on Wall Street under which their unofficial meetings had taken place. The brokers would later name their organization the New York Stock Exchange (NYSE). The NYSE still resides on Wall Street in New York City, and by most measures is considered the largest equities market in the world.

JUST A MINUTE

When a company first offers to sell stock to the public, it's called an *initial public offering,* or *IPO.* Due to the lack of performance history of the company, investors in IPOs take great risks for the potential of great gains.

Working with the Stock Market

When a corporation wants to raise money for expansion or growth, it sells pieces of ownership in its assets and earnings called *stock*. *Shares* represent the amount of stock a company is willing to issue to the public.

A stock exchange is a public marketplace where shares of a company's stock are bought and sold. Because a company wants the stock to be available to the widest number of people, it applies to be listed with an exchange. The exchange measures the company by its own criteria, such as overall stability, the number of shares the company will sell, and the price of the shares. Once accepted, the company pays a fee to the exchange to get and remain listed.

JUST A MINUTE

The Securities and Exchange Commission (SEC) regulates all the market exchanges, public companies, investment firms, and brokers. The SEC is an independent agency responsible for ensuring that securities markets operate fairly and that investors have access to disclosure of all information concerning publicly traded securities.

Today there are over 10,000 publicly traded stocks to choose from and numerous exchanges worldwide, from Athens to Zimbabwe. You are probably most familiar with the big listed stock exchanges such as the New York Stock Exchange (NYSE) and the American Stock Exchange (AMEX), which has now combined with the National Association of Securities Dealers Automated Quotation System (NASDAQ) over-the-counter market to become NASDAQ-AMEX. (Public stock issues not traded on any domestic stock exchange are traded in the OTC market. The OTC is a negotiated market; most stock exchanges are auction markets.)

Some exchanges trade only stock; others, like the Chicago Board of Trade, provide a marketplace for trading futures and options. Options and futures differ from stocks in that an option is the right to buy or sell, whereas a futures contract is the promise to actually make a transaction.

For a fairly comprehensive listing of financial exchanges both domestic and global, go to InvestorLinks at www.investorlinks.com/exch.html.

Market Forces

Statistics have proven that over the long run, stocks have out-performed almost all other asset classes. While short-term investing in the stock market can be considered risky, it can also be very profitable. Buying and holding stocks is another strategy that has also worked well for many. Either approach can bring success. By taking advantage of the growth component of stocks, you're taking a chance that your initial investment will rise in value.

A stock's performance is affected in many ways. A number of forces cause the value to move up and down. Why and when it happens is always subject to huge debates and the *raison d'être* for stock analysts. As complex and mystical as these forces may seem, there are some solid reasons behind the market's movements.

SUPPLY AND DEMAND

Perhaps the simplest force to understand that drives the stock market is old-fashioned supply and demand. If people want stock, they'll pay for it. If XYZ company has announced a pill that will cure the common cold, everyone wants a piece of the company pie and the stock soars. It can even happen that the stock value moves up on just an announcement that the company *expects* to have the cure for the common cold soon.

There is only a limited amount of stock available, which makes it more valuable. Those who have some stock can hold on to it, and those who want to sell their stock can take advantage of the rising value.

Several things can happen at this point. Investors can decide the price is too high, so stock owners will have to accept a lower price if they want to encourage new investors. The value drops. Or if a stock price gets too high, a company may decide to do a stock split. For example, in a 2-for-1 split, the number of shares is doubled and the price is divided in half. As a shareholder, you have basically traded in a $10 bill for two $5 bills. If the stock's price goes up again, however, you have a lot more stock at a higher value. New investors may then feel the price is within their range.

Or maybe later it's discovered that XYZ falsified lab reports about the new cold-cure pill. People's perception of the company has changed for the worst, and with it, their desire to own the company stock.

JUST A MINUTE

There are two different methods that professional analysts use in predicting the direction of a stock. The *fundamental analyst* focuses on the company's financial situation, the management team, and industry position. The *technical analyst* looks at market and industry patterns and creates technical charts to predict price trends.

COMPANY PERFORMANCE

Investigating a company's past performance and future prospects is part of the fundamental analysis that goes into picking a good stock. It also helps determine what investors feel a stock is worth. Some items to consider are the strength of the management team, the management team's share of the industry market, and the amount of outstanding a debt a company is holding. Good news, such as a new product, makes the stock price rise. Bad news, such as a major lawsuit, makes the stock price fall.

INDUSTRY HEALTH

Some industries move in cycles, and those cycles have an impact on the value of their stock. The cycle can be seasonal or can be affected by the supply and demand of consumers. For example, people tend to spend more on travel and leisure in the summer, bringing greater wealth to those areas. Or the industry on the whole may be doing poorly, and even a strong company can't keep investors interested in the stock.

THE ECONOMY AND ITS INDICATORS

Changes in the economy have a direct effect on business performance and, consequently, on the direction of the stock market. Inflation, the country's budget deficit, and many other indicators can point to fluctuations in the economy. By carefully monitoring the leading economic indicators, you will have a better understanding of where the nation is headed and what that means for your investments.

GO TO ▶
Refer to Hour 4, "How Can I Keep Track?" for more information on the relationship between the economic indicators and the financial markets.

To keep up with the status of the economy, you can view the monthly leading index of economic indicators, computed by the Conference Board in New York, which can be viewed online at www.conference-board.org. The index is a summary of 10 individual indicators used to predict the waves of economic expansion and contraction known as the business cycle. A few of the components include manufacturers' orders, new building permits, stock prices, and an index of consumer expectations.

JUST A MINUTE

The economic news release you see printed monthly in the newspapers is called the LEI, which stands for the Leading Economic Indicators, and includes the leading index as well as the coincident and lagging indexes. Similar statistics are available for a subscriber fee from the Department of Commerce Web site, www.stat-usa.gov.

According to the Conference Board, the rule of thumb that three consecutive months of decline in the leading index is warning of a recession produces too many false signals. They claim that a more reliable indicator of a recession would be to look for a 1 percent decline in the leading index from its cyclical peak and simultaneous declines in at least half of the components.

NATIONAL AND GLOBAL EVENTS

Uncertainty about the economy or world events can cause investors to be more cautious about where they put their money. From war in the Middle East, which affects oil prices, to the swearing in of a new American president, people's perception of the future will directly affect the movement of the stock market.

THE MARKET ANIMALS

There is a name for an extended period of time in which stock prices are steadily climbing: It's called a *bull market*. When investors are confident and believe that stock prices will rise, they are said to be *bullish*.

The reverse is a *bear market*, or a prolonged period when stock prices are falling. Someone feeling *bearish* would believe that prices are generally on the downswing. The market can take a few dives without being termed a bear market, though, and it generally requires more than a 20 percent slide in prices to qualify.

For the most part, the stock market rises more than it falls. According to *The Wall Street Journal*, there have only been six bear markets between 1960 and 1996.

HOW YOU MAKE MONEY

There are two ways you make money with stocks: through dividends and capital gains.

By owning common stock, you own a piece of the company's assets and earnings. So you profit when they do well. Companies distribute this profit by paying a cash dividend. The amount of the dividend is based on the company earnings and is determined by the company board of directors. This share of the profits is distributed on a quarterly basis. The exception is preferred stock, explained in depth in the section "Types of Stock."

GO TO ▶
Refer to Hour 5, "Investing Basics," for more information on return on investment.

You also profit on the sale of your stock if it has risen in value. If you sell a stock and receive more than you paid for it, you've made a capital gain. No doubt you've heard the old phrase "buy low—sell high." That's the theory behind earning capital gains. Of course if you sell your stock for less than the purchase price, it's considered a capital loss.

DIVIDEND REINVESTMENT PLANS

Some companies offer special plans to shareholders called dividend reinvestment plans, commonly referred to as DRPs or DRIPs. These plans will reinvest your dividends to buy more shares of the company stock. They also give shareholders the option to buy more shares directly from the company. Both services allow shareholders to bypass brokerage commissions.

GO TO ▶
Refer to Hour 5 for an example of how dollar cost averaging works.

DRIP investing allows you to automatically *dollar cost average* the purchase of the stock. By regularly investing a fixed dollar amount into a certain investment, you lessen the risk of investing a big sum into one investment at the wrong time. Over time the average cost per share is smaller.

If you don't own stock with a DRIP plan, you can buy a number of shares through a broker to get started. Some companies only require you to own a single share registered in your name. The stock must be in your name, not the street name of the brokerage. There are a few drawbacks to DRIP plans; for example, some enrollment companies charge high fees so you lose the advantage of skipping the broker. For tax purposes, you also have to keep accurate records of the stocks you buy at intervals during the year that have different values.

Examples of companies that offer traditional dividend reinvestment plans are Coca Cola, Sara Lee, Wrigley, and Bell South.

ONLINE AND DAY TRADING

Online trading is an affordable and convenient way for investors to buy and sell stocks. Investors used to have to sign up with conventional brokerage firms that often charged high commissions and demanded large minimum investment amounts.

JUST A MINUTE

As an example of the growth in popularity of online trading, the research firm NFO Worldwide reported that there were over two million households with online trading accounts in December 1997. By April 1999, the number had exceeded six million. Jupiter Communications expects the number of online trading households to break the 20 million mark by the year 2003.

To trade online you have to find an online broker and set up a brokerage account. There are over 100 online brokerages to choose from, from discount to full-service, so research the brokerage firm as carefully as you would research a company you're considering investing in. One good source for broker information is Gomez Advisors, www.gomez.com, considered a leader in rating the performance of market trends and developments.

The speed of access of the Internet has also spurred a growth in the number of day-traders. The term *day trading* comes from the effort to make the most amount of money buying and selling stocks in the shortest time, usually in one day. Day trading is considered very risky and not for the inexperienced investor. For resources and links to day-trading brokers, try Internet Investing's Guide to Day Trading at www.afterhourstrading.com/daytrading.htm.

TAX ISSUES

The total return on your investment will be affected by the amount of tax you have to pay at year's end. Dividend distributions are taxed as income in the year you receive them unless they are purchased inside a tax-deferred retirement account.

When you sell your stock determines the amount of tax you pay. Short-term gains on stocks held for less than a year are taxed at your regular income rate. If you held your investment for more than a year and sold it at a gain, you'll be taxed at a maximum of 20 percent. Check the instructions on your tax return for the tax rate that applies to your sale.

TYPES OF STOCK

Stocks come in two main categories: common and preferred. Common stock is just that—the most common stock you will come across. As a common stockholder, you are part owner of the company, and you are tied directly to the financial ups and downs. You are the last to receive dividends, and in bad times, may not see any at all. But you also have the potential to make a lot more in dividends than other classes of stockholders in the prosperous times. Common stockholders can also play a roll in the company management by voting on corporate issues.

Preferred stock gets its name from the fact that preferred stockholders have first claim to the assets of the company should the company fail. Preferred

stockowners also come first when it comes to dividing up the company profits, or dividends. Like a mix of an equity security and a debt security, preferred stockholders receive a predetermined amount of dividends that doesn't
change regardless of how well or poorly the company does. So the potential
for appreciation is less than with common stock. The preferred stockholders
have no voting rights.

Preferred stock can also comes in classes, often marked A, B, and C. These
classes each have a different structure of pricing, dividend payments, and
restrictions.

JUST A MINUTE

Investment banks can help companies get ready to go public by underwriting
the sale of the securities, among many other services. They also act as inter-
mediaries who expedite corporate mergers and reorganizations, as well as act
as brokers.

There are several different varieties of stocks to choose from. You can narrow down your investment choices by knowing how they differ and understanding what kind of returns you can expect, whether it be income from
dividends or appreciation in price of the stock through growth or both. The
different types of stocks are listed in the following sections.

INCOME STOCKS

Income stocks get their name from the income they provide through regular
dividends. Many investors want income from their portfolio without having
to sell a stock and select stock in companies that have a history of paying
steady dividends. Utility stocks are an example of income stocks.

JUST A MINUTE

A company trying to raise money will sell off pieces of ownership in the form
of stocks. They used to be called *stock certificates* due to the actual document
that was handed over to the owner. Don't be surprised if you never see a
certificate—these days stocks are most often records in a computer rather than
on paper.

GROWTH STOCKS

Investors buy growth stocks because they expect them to outpace other companies in earnings growth and therefore rise in price. Investors buy and hold

growth stocks for the long-term. Growth stocks usually offer little or no dividends because the profits are plowed back into the company to continue expansion. Usually issued by new companies with little history and unknown stability, growth stocks can be very risky—but also very profitable.

CYCLICAL STOCKS

Cyclical stocks are affected by economic trends. The prices of these stocks rise and fall depending on economic conditions. If bought or sold at the right time, the gains from cyclical stocks can be favorable. Examples of industries with cyclical stocks are the construction industry and utilities.

DEFENSIVE STOCKS

Defensive stocks tend to retain their value in times of recession because they are based in industries that produce the staples of daily life. Stock in companies that produce products with constant demand such as food, drugs, and health care are considered to be in the defensive stock category.

PENNY STOCKS

Considered the lowest level of stocks issued, penny stocks generally cost about $5 or less a share. Penny stock companies are small companies that may never make it anywhere, but if they do, the stock can really escalate in value.

BLUE CHIP STOCKS

The most valuable chip at the poker table is the blue chip, and so it goes for stocks. The older, established companies such as IBM, AT&T, and Coca Cola are blue chips and considered a safe investment. Blue chip stocks are usually slow but predictable in their rate of income and growth.

VALUE STOCKS

A value stock is one whose price is low for some basic reason; maybe the company has just been erroneously undervalued or it has made a large investment in new equipment, research, or development. A value investor expects the price to rise and catch up to other stocks in its group.

Stock Valuation

Now that you know the categories to choose from, how do you know if the stock is worth the price? The answer takes research and analysis. At the root of the analysis is the concept that you want to buy a stock worth more than you pay for, either now or over time, otherwise known as valuing stock.

There are many approaches to valuing stocks, but a common method of determining the value of a company is to look at its earnings per share (EPS) and price/earnings ratio (P/E).

One way to estimate the company's earnings per share is to perform this simple calculation, but the actual calculation is much more intricate. Divide the dollar amount of earnings by the shares of outstanding stock. For example, if a company has $10,000 in earnings and 10,000 shares of stock for a period of 12 months, the EPS is $1.

The P/E shows the relationship between earnings and the current stock price. You divide the price per share by the EPS. If the company whose stock had an EPS of $1 a share was trading at $20 a share, the P/E would be 20. While a low P/E could mean a bargain stock, most experts recommend looking at the long-term growth prospects before making a decision.

Other methods of value investing include …

- **Book value.** This is a balance sheet look at the difference between a company's assets and liabilities. Figure the value per share by dividing by the number of shares. This is not necessarily what the company is worth, only what it paid for its assets and how much it borrowed against them. One way people evaluate the value of companies is by comparing the book value from one year to the next.

- **Dividend yields.** Divide the annual dividend by the current price of the stock. Income investors look for high yield.

- **Market capitalization.** Company stock performs differently depending on market cap size. Morningstar.com, a mutual fund rating service, says small-company stocks are those with less than $1 billion in market cap; mid-cap stocks are companies with $1 billion to $5 billion; large-cap stocks are companies with $5 billion and up.

BUYING STOCKS

As an investor, you can only buy stocks in a publicly held company.

JUST A MINUTE

The growing demands of an ever-increasing number of investors have prompted several exchanges and brokerages to extend trading hours beyond the traditional 9:30 A.M. to 4:30 P.M.

Privately held or closely held corporations are owned by small groups of private individuals, often family members, employees, or friends. These companies don't trade on a stock exchange, so you have no way to buy them.

You purchase publicly traded stocks through a broker. Once you have done your research and know what you want, you tell your broker to place your order with the firm's floor broker at the exchange. This action is called placing a *market order*. Stocks are usually bought and sold in *lots,* or groups. A hundred shares is called a *round lot;* less than 100 shares is known as an *odd lot*. There are several pieces of information you'll need to have ready before you place the order, such as …

- Money in your brokerage account for the stock and the commission.
- The ticker symbol of the stock, usually three or four letters, and the exchange (for example, AMEX). Several Web sites, such as www. Morningstar.com, an independent provider of mutual fund, stock, and variable-annuity investment information, and Quicken.com, can help you sift through the thousands of public companies. You can enter the company name and get the ticker symbol as well as price, changes, and volume of recent trading.
- The volume of shares you want to buy and the top price you are willing to pay for them.
- The time limit for your order. Do you want the order good for that day only or for a week?

The floor broker is the person who holds the place, or the seat, on the exchange. They hammer out the price of your shares with another floor broker specializing in that stock. If you had placed a *limit order,* the broker would know to trade only at the price you requested or lower.

Part of the trading game is to remember that at any one time there will be several orders to buy (bid) and sell (ask) stock that come to the floor of the exchange. Before placing an order, you can view current stock quotes in the newspaper and online to get an idea of the price range of the stock you're interested in. Since a stock is really only worth what someone will pay for it, and respectively, what someone will sell it for, stock quotes only list the highest bid price and the lowest ask price.

TIME SAVER

 When you are discussing a company's value on Wall Street, you are talking about *market capitalization*. Calculate market cap by multiplying the number of shares issued by the price per share. A company with 10,000 shares of stock priced at $15 a share has a market cap of $150,000.

According to the "best price" priority on the trading floor, the highest-priced stock orders will get filled first. Your stock order will be filled only after the higher-priced orders have been executed. If several trades come in at the same price and the same time, the orders are executed as they are received.

An order is executed once the two floor brokers agree on a price. The firm's broker then reports the executed trade back to the brokerage, who keeps a computer record of your stock. You receive a confirmation statement of the transaction rather than an actual certificate.

SELLING STOCKS

The process of selling a stock is basically the reverse of buying a stock. Your broker has the record of ownership, so you call and place a sell order. As with buying stock, you must be ready with the ticker symbol, the exchange name, the number of shares you want to sell, and the price you are willing to sell for.

PROCEED WITH CAUTION

 Stock exchanges make money on transaction fees. However, technology is taking a toll on the traditional stock exchanges as ECNs (electronic communication networks) enable buyers and sellers to get together without the exchanges. In July 1999, Morningstar reported that the NYSE lost 5 percent of volume and the NASDAQ lost 30 percent to ECNs.

As with orders to purchase stock, if orders to sell a stock come in at the same time with a similar price, they are sold in the order they were received.

UNFILLED ORDERS

Just as in the local grocery store there are days of light and heavy traffic, there are times of light and heavy action on the stock market exchanges. If you have placed an order on a day of light trading, your broker will let you know if the shares didn't trade at the price you specified. Since there was no transaction, you pay no fee.

There is the possibility of getting only a partial order after a day of trading. If you asked for 2,000 shares of IBM but only got 500, it's because there were only 500 shares available at the price you specified during the time limit you set. Partial fills can happen in both buying and selling transactions.

GO TO ▶
Refer to Hour 11, "Guide to Online Research," for more information on research, and Hour 12, "Online Money Management," for tips on online investing.

People who watch the markets closely can respond to this by constantly adjusting the price of their order. If you place an order with a time limit of several days, however, your broker will charge you for each day they fill part of the order.

You can cancel and change your order, but make sure you are clear on those conditions with your broker before you place an order.

TRACKING PERFORMANCE

Once you've purchased a stock, you'll want to track its performance. Your brokerage statement should break down the investments by categories, such as stocks, bonds, and mutual funds. You should compare the cash and securities value in your account monthly and annually to see what type of returns you're getting.

For a daily view, all you have to do is look at the stock tables published on the financial pages of almost every newspaper, or look up the stock by symbol online. Stock tables sum up what happened in the market. You can track stocks you own and look for trends in portfolio potentials. But you have to know what the raw data stands for.

Here is a list of what you'll find in a stock table in the order they're printed:

- **52 Weeks Hi/Lo.** The highest and lowest prices for the past 52 weeks help to measure a stock's volatility. Volatility is a risk indicator, so the greater the difference between the two numbers, the greater the potential to win or lose on your investment.

- **Stock.** The company name, usually abbreviated and listed alphabetically.

- **Sym.** Each publicly traded company is assigned a trading symbol, usually closely related to the company name. Preferred stocks symbols are followed by a **pf.**

- **Div.** Listed in dollar format, this field displays the dividend, or amount of anticipated annual profit distributions a company pays per share.

- **Yld %.** This field tells you the percentage of the stock's price that's paid out as a dividend, or it's rate of return on the investment.

- **PE.** The price/earnings ratio is the relationship between a stock's price and the annual earnings of a company.

- **Vol 100s.** The volume of shares traded the day before, shown in hundreds. Multiply the field number by 100 to get the actual number of shares traded.

- **Hi-Lo-Close.** This indicates the previous day's fluctuations by showing the stock's highest, lowest, and closing price.

- **Net Chg.** This compares the day's closing price with the price from the day before.

GO TO ▶
Refer to Hour 11 for more detail on how to research company information.

Company information can come from something as simple as observing the growth of a firm in your own town to reading *The Wall Street Journal* for a daily dose of business news.

INDEXES AND AVERAGES

You can also evaluate your portfolio performance by using over 20 indexes and averages for comparison. Any newspaper or online investing Web site will list the major indexes. These indexes are basically a bundle of stocks, bonds, or mutual funds that measure the ups and downs of the market. The indexes are a benchmark for comparing how well your personal portfolio is doing, such as the Dow Jones Industrial Average (DJIA), which represents blue chip stocks. If you were heavily invested in gas and telephone companies, for example, you would follow the Dow Jones Utility Average. Or you can follow an index geared toward other securities such as:

- Dow Jones Indexes at averages.dowjones.com.

- Nasdaq at www.nasdaq.com. The Nasdaq 100 lists stocks by market capitalization.

- Standard & Poor's Indexes at www.spglobal.com/ssindexmain.html, includes the S&P 500 and 100 Indexes, which measure large company U.S. stock performances, as well as mid- and small-cap and global indexes.

- The Russell Indexes, at www.russell.com, from the Frank Russell investment management and consulting firm, reports on the performance of domestic and global stocks.

- The Wilshire Indexes at www.wilshire.com, including the Wilshire 5,000 and 4,500, which measure the performance of a broad variety of investment styles.

- The Target Indexes, which track style-oriented investment products.

- Specialty Indexes, which measure specific industries such as Internet and real estate.

- Thirty-year Treasury-bond indexes.

SWINDLERS AND SCHEMERS

Whenever there is a venue where a great deal of money is changing hands, you can bet there will be some people trying to make an illegal dollar—or at least skirting the edge of the law to make a profit.

As an investor, you already know the basic "bill of rights" discussed in Hour 5. But it's also important to know what to look out for. Even seasoned traders have been stung by clever investing schemes.

There are a number of investment scams that continue to circulate. How do they succeed if people know about them? Not all people do know about the various schemes and scams. There will always be new investors, and there will always be investors hoping to make a fast buck.

The National Futures Association estimates that nearly $10 billion a year is lost to investment fraud. To help educate the public against these losses, they've compiled three of the top schemes that con artists use to win the trust of their victims—the names used are fictitious.

THE PONZI SCHEME

The Ponzi scheme has become one of the oldest and most often employed investment schemes because it's proven to be one of the most lucrative. While there are innumerable variations, here is how one person—let's call him Frank—practiced it.

At the outset, Frank approached a relatively small number of influential persons in the community and offered them the opportunity to invest—with a guaranteed high return—in a computer-generated program of arbitrage in foreign currency fluctuations.

It sounded high-tech and sophisticated, but Frank had his eye on sophisticated and well-heeled victims. Within a short period of time, he approached and sold the scheme to still other investors—then promptly used a portion of the money invested by these persons to pay large profits to the original group of investors.

As word spread of Frank's genius for making money and paying profits, even more would-be investors eagerly put up even larger sums of money. Frank used some of their money to recycle the fictitious profit payments, and, like a pebble in the water, the word of fast and fabulous rewards produced an ever-widening circle of eager investors. More money poured in.

And Frank left town a wealthy man.

THE INFALLIBLE FORECASTER

One scam artist, let's call him Jim, had a full-time job by day. With assets that consisted only of a phone, patience, and smooth talking, Jim managed to parlay a nighttime sideline into an ill-gotten fortune.

The routine went like this:

Jim would phone someone, say a Mrs. Smith, and quickly assure her that, "No," he didn't want her to invest a single cent. "Never invest with someone you don't know," he preached. But he said he would like to demonstrate his firm's "research skill" by sharing with her the forecast that so-and-so commodity was about to experience a significant price increase. Sure enough, the price soon went up.

A second phone call didn't solicit an investment either. Jim simply wanted to share with Mrs. Smith a prediction that the price of another so-and-so commodity was about to go down. "Our forecasts will help you decide whether ours is the kind of firm you might someday want to invest with," he added. As predicted, the price of the commodity subsequently declined.

By the time Mrs. Smith received Jim's third call, she was a believer. She not only wanted to invest, but she insisted on it—with a big enough investment to make up for the opportunities she had already missed out on.

Mrs. Smith had no way of knowing that Jim had begun his scam by calling a list of 200 persons. In the first call, he told 100 that the price of so-and-so commodity would go up, and he told the other 100 it would go down. When it went up, he made a second call to the 100 who had been given the "correct forecast." Of these, 50 were told the next price move would be up, and 50 were told it would be down.

The end result: Once the predicted price decline occurred, Jim had a list of 50 persons eager to invest. After all, how could they go wrong with someone so obviously infallible in forecasting prices?

ALL THAT GLITTERS

Two brothers had their own company in a fancy office building with their company name on it. The investment offer seemed sound and straight-forward.

Instead of buying gold outright and holding it for appreciation, they would suggest that investors make a small down payment for the firm to use to secure financing for a much larger quantity of gold to be bought and held for the investor's account. That way, when the price of gold rose—as was "sure to happen"—investors stood to realize highly leveraged profits.

JUST A MINUTE

Time value of money is the process of calculating the value of an asset in the past, present, or future. It is based on the concept that the principal will increase in value, with interest, over time. Essentially, $1 invested today should be worth more than $1 tomorrow.

The company provided storage vaults where investors could view the wall-to-wall stacks of glittering bullion. By the time authorities caught wind of the scheme's suspicious smell and looked for themselves, it turned out the only thing gold was the color of the paint on the cardboard used to construct look-alike bars of bullion.

The counterfeit gold, however, proved far easier to find than the millions of dollars of investors' money. Most of that is still missing.

STOP A SCAM

How can you tell if the offer you've heard on the phone or received in the mail is legitimate? The best way to defend yourself against investment fraud is to ask questions. A reputable firm will encourage questions—they want you to obtain the information necessary to make a good investment decision. A scam artist only wants your money—and prefers that you ask no questions.

Here are some questions that can help separate the good offers from the bad:

- **Where did you get my name?** If the response is that your name was chosen from a select list of prudent investors, be wary. This list could be anything from the telephone book to a purchased list of persons who've bought certain books or magazines.

- **What risks are involved in the proposed investment?** Almost all investments involve some degree of risk, with the exception of some U.S. Treasury obligations. Don't believe a "no-risk" sales pitch.

- **Can you send me a written explanation of your investment so I can consider it at my leisure?** No scam artist wants to put anything in writing, and they don't want victims to have time to think about an investment. Be wary of "act-now-or-lose-out" deals.

- **Would you mind explaining your investment proposal to a third party, such as my accountant, banker, or attorney?** If the salesperson tells you that normally they would be happy to but there just isn't time, you have a solid clue as to the fraudulent nature of the call.

HOUR'S UP!

That's a lot of new information to assimilate in one hour, but the following questions will help you review what you've read.

1. Who decides whether or not to pay a dividend?

    a. Shareholders

    b. The company president

    c. The board of directors

2. From a stock table you can determine …

    a. The most recent market activity of a traded company.

    b. Stock market trends.

    c. Preferred stock.

    d. All of the above.

3. True or false: A stock's yield will tell you the rate of return on investment.

4. True or false: Once a company signs up with a stock market exchange, the exchange has total control over a company portfolio.

5. A privately held company is different from a publicly held company in that it …

    a. Is the broker's biggest secret of the day.

    b. Trades on its own private stock exchange.

    c. Is controlled by private individuals, not the public.

6. There are three things you should have ready when you call your broker when you are buying or selling a stock. They are …

    a. Name, rank, and serial number.

    b. Phone number, tax ID, and tax bracket.

    c. Stock ticker symbol, stock market exchange name, and number of shares you want to buy or sell.

7. The following indicate a bull market, except …

    a. Steady rise in stock prices.

    b. Feelings that the stock prices will continue to rise.

    c. A drop in stock prices of at least 15 percent.

8. True or false: Three things that can affect the price of a stock are: the company's financial health, publicity on a new product, and a pending lawsuit.

9. To buy a stock, you would place a call to your broker and ask for a …

    a. Fund prospectus.

    b. Market order.

    c. Stock table.

10. True or false: The price-per-earnings ratio is a way to determine if a stock is over- or under-priced.

Quiz

Hour 7

Mutual Funds

LESSON PLAN:

In this chapter you'll learn about the different types of mutual funds available and which one suits your personal investing profile. You'll also learn how to:

- Make mutual funds work for you.
- Buy and sell mutual funds.
- Research companies, funds, and fund managers.
- Figure fee effect on returns.

At this point in the book you have an idea that the best way to get your money to produce more money is to invest it. At the very least, you want a safe place to put your nest egg where it won't be eroded by inflation.

The stock market has typically had a higher rate of return than most other investments in the last 100 years. But picking the right stock can be time-consuming and challenging for the new or busy investor. And there are so many types of stocks to choose from: income or growth, penny or blue chip, defensive or cyclical.

While the rewards of stock ownership can be tremendous, it's also a little risky. It's generally not a good idea to put all your nest eggs into one stock because you could lose them. The process of placing those eggs in more than one basket is called diversification.

One option is to put some of that money into lower-risk investments such as government or corporate bonds where you know the exact interest rate you will receive. You also know the exact date, called the maturity date, on which you will get that money back.

JUST A MINUTE

Mutual funds are not an asset class on their own like stocks, bonds, and cash, but they can contain investments from one class or some of each.

Or you can invest in CDs or money-market deposit accounts at your bank, which earn just slightly more than the traditional savings account and are FDIC-insured.

Each one of these investments has its advantages and a place in your portfolio, so how do you collect them all? You can go to your stockbroker or banker and buy them one at a time, paying a commission fee on each trade. Or you can follow your financial goals and asset allocation model a lot easier by investing in mutual funds. A mutual fund enables you to invest a small share in many companies that would cost a fortune in commissions if you were to do it on your own.

How Mutual Funds Work

A mutual fund is run by an investment company. The company pools the cash from many investors and uses it to buy a variety of different securities. Often a company will have more than one fund, with each one focusing on a different investment objective or asset class, such as a bond fund or a stock fund.

You buy shares of a mutual fund just like you would buy shares of a stock. By purchasing a share of a mutual fund, though, your portfolio is immediately diversified by the number of different securities in the fund.

Professional Management

When you buy shares of a mutual fund, you become a shareholder in a company with voting rights proportionate to your investment. The fund hires an investment advisor, or advisory firm, to manage the portfolio of securities.

Not only is your risk spread out among the fund's investments, but you have access to professional management and some securities you might not have been able to afford on your own. An investment fund manager watches the market and buys and sells huge amounts of securities at a time. They pay reduced commission rates, and the value is passed on to the investors.

As a shareholder, you hand over all the investment decision-making to the fund advisor, who observes market trends and makes investment choices for you and the other investors. This can be considered one of the advantages of a mutual fund, but at times it may seem like a disadvantage as well.

JUST A MINUTE

Mutual funds pay a professional manager or advisors to research, buy, and sell investments keeping with the fund's objectives. The terms *portfolio manager* and *investment advisor* are also used to describe this position.

Unlike the situation with personal stock picking, you have no say in how the mutual fund is managed or the investments that are chosen. The portfolio manager's background and experience are important to the success of the fund. The portfolio manager is bound by the fund's objectives and risks, however, and he or she answers to the board of directors, who keep a close eye on the performance of the investments.

PROCEED WITH CAUTION

Mutual funds are well regulated by the Securities and Exchange Commission and state regulators, but they are *not* federally insured. Even if you buy a money-market fund through your bank, it is not an insured bank deposit. Money-market funds are mutual funds. There is always an element of risk with investments in mutual funds.

OPEN OR CLOSED?

There are two different types of mutual funds: open-end and closed-end. Most people are familiar with the open-end funds (OEF), which allow any investor to buy into a fund providing they have the money. New shares are created as investors join the fund, so the number of outstanding shares is constantly changing.

Closed-end funds (CEF) are similar to open-end funds in that they pool cash from investors, offer diversification, and are managed by professionals. But the similarities end there. A CEF acts more like a stock. The company issues a fixed number of shares at the initial public offering, or IPO, just like a stock, and then buys securities for the fund portfolio. The CEF is listed and traded on a stock exchange and shares must be purchased through a broker.

For the remainder of this hour, you will be learning about open-end mutual funds unless otherwise specified.

HOW TO BUY AND SELL MUTUAL FUNDS

You can buy open-end mutual funds by contacting the company directly. There are a number of companies that offer information on their Web sites, or you can call them and ask for a fund prospectus. One reason to purchase mutual funds directly is to avoid sales charges, called loads (explained later in this hour).

Other funds are sold through full-service or discount brokers, banks, financial planners, and insurance agents. The shares are paid for either through your cash account with the brokerage or by check to the mutual fund company. You will normally pay a commission fee.

The initial investment into mutual funds can be relatively small in comparison to individual stocks, which you have to buy in lots. Each fund has a minimum investment amount, which can range anywhere from $100 up.

Banks and investment firms often offer automatic investment programs for mutual funds, which can lower the initial amount of investment required. You choose the fund and the amount you can invest, which is electronically deducted from your checking or savings account on a regular basis. There is normally a minimum monthly requirement, such as $50.

JUST A MINUTE

It's best to avoid buying mutual funds just before they make their annual income and capital gains distribution. The price is recalculated after the distribution and shares cost less.

Mutual fund shares are very liquid. By law the fund is required to buy back, or redeem, your shares whenever you ask them to. Your money must be refunded within seven days of redemption.

How You Make Money

There are three basic ways to make money from your investments:

1. **Dividends.** Mutual funds earn money from dividends and interest on the investments in their portfolio. They distribute the income to shareholders through dividends.

2. **Capital gains.** You may also receive capital gains if the fund sells off securities that have risen in value. Capital gains are normally distributed to shareholders at the end of the year.

3. **Rise in securities value.** Your shares could be worth more due to a rise in the value of the securities the fund is holding. If you sell those shares, you realize a capital gain.

Any of the money you earn through your fund can be sent directly to you in a check, or you can elect to have the money reinvested into more fund shares.

WHAT SHARES ARE WORTH

When you buy a share of a mutual fund, the current net asset value (NAV) determines the price you pay. The NAV represents the cost of one fund share. To calculate the NAV of a fund, you take the total assets minus total liabilities, divided by outstanding shares.

Both the fund's assets and outstanding shares are constantly changing, so the NAV will fluctuate as well. Following the closing bell each market day, most mutual funds will total up the new NAV and make it available within a few hours. When you buy or sell shares of the fund, your price is not normally the one quoted you, but the next NAV calculated at day's end.

For example, if you decided to invest $5,000 in a fund with a NAV of $10 per share, you could purchase 500 shares. But what if the funds portfolio value dropped to a NAV of $9 the day you bought? You would end up with 555.55 shares for your money. You can use the NAV to track your fund's performance by checking the daily financial pages or looking at the company Web site.

TIME SAVER

Mutual funds are priced by their net asset value (NAV). Closed-end funds are influenced by supply and demand as well as net asset value, so the shares may trade at above or below the NAV.

LOAD OR NO-LOAD?

The net asset value may not be all you pay for your fund's shares. Some funds also carry sales charges, called *loads*. The funds that don't have a sales charge are called *no-load* funds.

Mutual funds tack on sales loads primarily to cover broker commissions. Essentially what you are paying for is the advice and service of a broker, not necessarily premium fund performance. Historically, load funds have not outperformed no-load funds, according to Morningstar, a mutual fund rating service.

FRONT- AND BACK-END LOADS

GO TO ▶
Refer to Hour 12, "Online Money Management," for information on where to start investing online.

There are different types of loads, too. The *front-end* load is a straight-forward sales charge on the shares you buy. By law the load can be no higher than 8.5 percent, typically ranging from 3 to 6 percent. So if you invested $5,000 in a load fund with a 5 percent front-end load, $250 would go to the broker and $4,750 would go toward your investment.

Back-end loads, also known as *deferred* loads, are the sales charges you pay when you redeem your shares. Generally set on a sliding scale, the load gets smaller each year until finally there is no load to pay when you sell shares. Back-end load funds attempt to discourage market-timing investors from jumping fund to fund.

PROCEED WITH CAUTION

Market timing is an investment strategy generally discouraged by financial experts due to the associated risks and costs. A market timer changes his or her investment mix in response to short-term market forecasts. For example, an investor may carry 80 percent stocks one month and 10 percent stocks the next.

Funds with an annual 12b-1 distribution fee of .25 percent may legally call themselves no-load. A 100-percent no-load fund, though, does not charge fees.

All of the above-mentioned fees are normally outlined in the fund's prospectus.

THE PROSPECTUS

The prospectus is the most important piece of information you can read about a particular mutual fund. Before you buy one share in a mutual fund, ask the fund's investor information department or your financial planner to send you a copy of the mutual fund's prospectus. Most mutual funds won't let you buy a share until they have sent you this document.

The prospectus is the selling tool for the mutual fund, but it's also full of substantial information about the fund's fees, past performance, risks, and objectives. Prospectuses are not always easy to read, but there are key areas that spotlight the facts you need to know.

INVESTMENT RISKS

The securities held in a mutual fund portfolio go up and down in value. You take the risk of losing some, or all, of your principal when you invest. That goes for any investment.

You should pay particular attention to the risk disclosure in your mutual fund prospectus, because every mutual fund has different investment objectives. The prospectus should describe the type of investments the fund buys, such as small-cap stocks or Treasury bills, and their inherent risks.

Some specific risk areas to look for are …

- **Inflation.** Will the investment value decrease as inflation rates rise?
- **Interest rates.** Will the value of your investment decrease as interest rates rise?
- **Credit.** If the fund buys debt securities, what is the risk that debts won't be paid?
- **Currency.** If the fund invests internationally, what is the risk in the currency rate of exchange?
- **Politics.** If the fund invests internationally, how stable is the political climate?

If you don't understand the risks outlined in the prospectus, ask the fund's investor information department.

TIME SAVER

Try the online Mutual Fund Cost Calculator from the SEC Web site at www.sec. gov/mfcc/mfcc-int.htm. The Calculator helps you quickly and easily determine the cost of mutual fund ownership, including sales loads, operating expenses, and foregone earnings, or earnings you might have had if those fees were invested rather than spent.

INVESTMENT OBJECTIVES

There are several different types of mutual funds, which will be discussed later in this hour. Each fund has its risks and rewards, and, as with most investments, the higher the risk, the higher the potential for return.

A prospectus should clearly outline the fund's basic objectives, whether it be to maximize income and growth or preserve capital. The objectives should also identify how the fund expects to achieve those goals.

INVESTMENT POLICIES

What type of investments does the fund plan to buy? The investment policies of the prospectus section should describe the securities the fund is allowed to buy and those it can't, according to the fund's policies. You should be informed of the percentage of allowable investments, especially with regard to more speculative securities, such as derivatives.

PROCEED WITH CAUTION

Some mutual funds invest in derivatives, which leads to special risks. Derivatives are contracts, such as options and futures, whose price is derived from the price of the asset underlying the contract. Derivatives are very speculative since they can be affected by the slightest move in the stock market.

MANAGEMENT

The management section of the prospectus is where you learn who will be working to fulfill the fund's objectives. Consider the experience of the present management team and whether the fund's present record was accomplished by them or another team. A constant change in fund managers may adversely affect the return of the portfolio.

PROCEED WITH CAUTION

Due to fees involved, owning too many mutual funds can be detrimental to your long-term investment plan. Mutual funds were designed to provide portfolio diversification. If you have carefully researched funds' investments and know they meet your personal profile, you could have one fund for each category, such as market capitalization, growth, income, and an international fund.

Costs

Every mutual fund shareholder pays some expenses for either buying or holding fund shares—or sometimes both. A mutual fund's expenses are divided into two categories: shareholder transaction fees and fund operating expenses.

Each prospectus has a fee table that outlines the costs of the fund. The SEC has standardized the information that must be revealed in a fee table, so it's fairly easy to read. The categories should contain the following headings:

1. **Shareholder Fees.** These fees are taken directly from your investment and can include ...

   - *Maximum Sales Charge Imposed on Purchases.* This refers to the front-end load, a one-time fee deducted when you first buy your shares.

   - *Maximum Deferred Sales Charge.* This is the back-end load, deducted when you sell your fund shares. The sliding fee decreases with each year you hold your shares until there is no fee.

   - *Maximum Sales Charge Imposed on Reinvested Dividends.* Some funds charge a fee if you elect to reinvest your profit distributions into more fund shares.

TIME SAVER

To find out about pure no-load mutual funds—those that don't charge 12b-1 distribution fees—contact the 100% No-Load Mutual Fund Council at 630-305-4600 or visit their Web site at www.100noload.com and ask for their *100% No Load Mutual Fund Investment Guide.*

   - *Redemption Fee.* Some funds charge a fee when you sell your fund shares.

   - *Exchange Fee.* If the mutual fund is part of a fund family, you can switch your investments among the funds. You may have to pay a fee to the fund for this service.

   - *Maximum Account Fee.* These are usually account maintenance fees.

2. **Annual Fund Operating Expenses.** These fees are deducted from the fund's assets before earnings are distributed or performance is calculated and include …

- *Management Fees.* Actively managed funds tend to carry costly management fees, which affect the fund's total returns. These are apt to be the highest expense in the fund and can run up to 2 percent or more of the fund's total assets.

- *12b-1 Fees or Distribution Fees.* 12b-1 fees stem from the SEC rule that allows funds to charge up to 1 percent of the fund's assets to promote the fund. The revenues from this fee go to brokers, salespersons, and advertising expenses.

- *Other Expenses.* This section covers administrative fees for fund services such as record keeping, legal fees, and generating reports.

- *Total Annual Fund Operating Expenses.* A fund's total operating expenses are expressed as a percentage of average net assets and are also known as the fund's expense ratio. Many top no-load funds don't charge for reinvesting or exchanges and waive the redemption fee after a short time period.

PROCEED WITH CAUTION

 The SEC suggests that most of the 77 million mutual fund investors in the United States don't know how much they're paying in mutual fund expenses. Fewer than one in five surveyed could estimate expenses, and fewer than one in six understood that higher expenses lead to lower yields.

The fee table in the prospectus should also detail ongoing expenses, as discussed in the following sections.

FINANCIAL PERFORMANCE

The Financial Highlights section is close to the front of the prospectus and shows the yearly total return for the past 10 years. The prospectus should also carry the fund's financial statements.

ADDITIONAL

If you want more details on the fund's operations, ask for the Statement of Additional Information (SAI). Also called Part B of the prospectus, all funds are required to prepare this statement.

Mutual funds also prepare annual and semi-annual reports, which are sent to shareholders. If you are investigating a fund, ask for a copy of the previous reports, for the past ten years if available, but five years should suffice. As any financial planner will tell you, an informed investor is a secure investor.

IN PLAIN ENGLISH

To help investors become better informed, the SEC adopted the "Plain English" rule for mutual fund disclosures. The rule requires that the cover page, summary, and risk sections of the prospectus to be written in plain English.

A *Plain English Handbook* was developed to give issuers detailed guidance on how to make the prospectus clear, concise, and understandable. Some of the provisions of the rule include making the document visually inviting, using short sentences and bulleted lists, and avoiding legal and highly technical terms.

FEE EFFECT ON RETURNS

Keep in mind that a fund's total expenses can make a dramatic difference on the total return on your investments. Shareholders' expenses impact the buying power of your initial investment, and operating expenses take a toll on the fund's overall performance.

According to the Investment Company Institute, in 1997 investors with a stock load fund paid an annual 2.11 percent of their investments in fees. Ownership costs for no-load investors averaged .89 percent.

Some funds have such a high return that the expenses may be worth it. The prospectus and fund performance will provide most of the information you need to make the decision.

You can track your mutual fund's performance in the newspaper. *The Wall Street Journal* publishes quotations daily, along with best performers and several indexes to use as a comparison.

The mutual fund listings include …

- **Fund name.** The company name first, followed by its funds listed alphabetically.
- **NAV.** Net asset value, or the dollar value per share.
- **Net chg.** The NAV change from the previous day's trading.

- **Total return.** The percentage of gain or loss on the fund; the year to date (YTD) return.
- **Inv Obj.** The investment objective of the fund expressed in two-letter codes.
- **Max. Init chrg.** The maximum initial charge indicates the sales charge fee (load).

RESEARCH AND INFORMATION

There are many other ways to research a mutual fund besides the prospectus. All mutual funds issue quarterly and annual reports that can give solid clues as to the fund's performance and objectives.

PRESS CLIPPINGS

Newspapers and magazines also carry information on the financial pages regarding industry trends, expense ratios, yields, and fund profiles.

JUST A MINUTE

A mutual fund's yield is expressed as a percentage of current net asset value (NAV). Calculating yield is a way to measure what kind of money you can make through stock dividend income, bond interest income, and capital gains. For example, an annual 70¢ dividend on a stock with a $10 NAV equals a 7 percent yield (.7 ÷ 10 = 7 percent).

INTERNET ACCESS

Access to a computer is ideal for today's investor. Most mutual fund companies and investment firms have Web sites. There are also numerous Internet sites that provide valuable investor information and educational material.

You can also talk to other investors online through bulletin boards. One of the most popular is Morningstar's Socialize (www.morningstar.com), which is actually several bulletin boards with topics ranging from retirement investing to specific fund groups.

THE LIBRARY

There are several mutual fund reporting services that measure fund perfomances. Their reports can be found in your local library; some are available on the Internet, but not all. Some reports are by ...

- **Morningstar Mutual Funds.** www.morningstar.com.
- **Value Line Mutual Fund Survey.** www.valueline.com.
- **Standard & Poor's/Lipper Mutual Fund Profiles.** www.standardpoor.com
- **CDA/Weisenberger Mutual Funds Panorama.** Check the Business Reference area of your library

INVESTMENT CLUBS

If you want mutual fund advice and information but don't want to pay a financial advisor, you can try an investment club. Investment clubs are groups of 12 to 20 people who get together to share ideas and pool funds for investing. They even have online groups. According to the National Association of Investors Corporation (NAIC), a not-for-profit organization dedicated to investment education, investment clubs have been thriving since 1900.

NAIC offers dozens of aids, tools, and programs for the individual investor and those hoping to start or join a group. Most of their tools are based on four fundamental investment principles:

GO TO ▶
Refer to Hour 11, "Guide to Online Research," for more information on researching investments and finding the best places for fund investing.

- Invest a set sum regularly over a long period of time (dollar cost averaging).
- Reinvest earnings and dividends.
- Learn how to select companies that have a reasonable prospect of being worth substantially more in five years.
- Diversify your investments.

To find out more about becoming a member of an investment club, contact NAIC toll-free at 877-275-6242 or find them online at www.better-investing.org/index.html.

TAXES

Mutual funds buy and sell securities, frequently turning over their holdings. A high turnover rate can mean higher costs for the funds due to fees and commissions. That's just one reason to look for a fund with lower turnover rates. Another reason is capital gains tax.

If you are investing in mutual funds outside a tax-exempt or tax-advantaged retirement account, you will have to pay capital gains tax on investments the fund sold at a gain and tax on investment dividends the fund held. Reinvested dividends are still subject to ordinary income tax.

There are tax-managed and tax-exempt mutual funds that can save shareholders some money.

OBJECTIVE CATEGORIES

Mutual funds can be geared to a specific industry or toward investing strategies such as income and growth or long-term growth. Whatever your investment interests may be, there is likely to be a mutual fund to suit you.

In terms of sheer numbers, choosing a mutual fund may not be any simpler than choosing a stock since there are over 8,000 funds available. The alphabet soup of mutual fund objective categories runs from AA, asset allocation, to TxMMN, tax money-market nongovernmental.

The main categories include stock funds, bond funds, and money-market funds, but there are assorted funds within each. We'll learn the basic categories in the following sections.

TIME SAVER

For complete directories of open- and closed-end mutual funds along with contact information, go to the Investment Company Institute Web site and download the annual updates at www.ici.org/aboutfunds/98dofmf_toc.html.

STOCK FUNDS

Also known as equity funds, stock funds have a higher risk than bond or money-market funds. They can also offer the highest returns. Stock funds historically outperform other investments in the long term.

For the past 10 years, individual investors have continued to shift from owning individual stocks to holding stock funds.

The funds offer varying levels of risk for investors and are generally categorized, such as growth and income.

GROWTH FUNDS

Growth funds invest in stocks they believe will increase in terms of share price. The emphasis is on long-term growth of capital. Growth funds can be split into categories, too, depending on risk.

- **Aggressive growth funds** look for quick gains and are the most speculative.
- **Small cap stock funds** invest in new companies with unknown histories but with the potential to grow fast.
- **Sector funds** invest in specialty areas such as technology or precious metals. The risk with sector funds is the lack of diversification.

INCOME FUNDS

Income funds invest in stocks that pay out dividends. Total returns may be lower with income funds, but the investment objective is the regular income from dividends.

- **Equity income funds** can be less risky than other stock funds because they invest in fewer growth stocks.
- **Growth and income funds** try to invest in strong stocks, such as blue chips, that pay dividends. While appreciation of capital is a priority, they tend to balance the risk of full-fledged stock growth funds with a steady income of dividends.

JUST A MINUTE

Want to know the largest fund sector? According to a study conducted by the Investment Company Institute, the combined assets of the nation's mutual funds totaled more than $6 trillion in June 1999—nearly $3.5 trillion of which belonged to stock funds.

MONEY-MARKET FUNDS

Money-market funds lend short-term to banks, the U.S. government, and companies. The borrowers pay back the loan in three years or less. Considered the least risky of the three main fund categories, money-market funds invest in high-quality investments that still occasionally show poor performance.

Individual investors have turned to these funds because they pay slightly higher returns than a bank savings account. Money market funds usually buy and sell for $1 per share, so your original investment is considered secure. Even though they are just as liquid as a bank account, and often sold by banks, it's important to remember that money-market funds are not federally insured.

Tax-exempt money-market funds invest in short-term municipal bonds. The dividends paid to shareholders are tax-exempt but must be reported on annual returns.

Bond Funds

Bonds are securities that act like loans. The borrower promises to pay back the principal at a future date, as well as periodic interest. Also known as fixed-income funds, bond funds have higher risks but often greater yields than money-market funds.

Bond funds are tied to interest rates, so their returns are varied. Like the opposite ends of a seesaw, when interest rates go up, the value of bonds goes down. Bonds also carry a credit risk, or a possibility that the loans won't be paid. Treasury bonds don't carry the credit risk, but they can be affected by interest rates.

Tax-exempt bond funds can help defray what you pay the IRS on your dividends. Dividends from municipal bonds are exempt from federal income tax and, in certain cases, from state and local tax. The dividends must still be reported on your tax return. Consult with a tax professional regarding your tax liabilities.

Hybrid Funds

Hybrid funds invest in a mix of bonds and stocks. Balanced funds split the investments between the two.

More Funds

As previously mentioned, there are over 8,000 mutual funds to choose from, depending on your personal investment goals and the fund's objective. Besides the investment mix of stocks, bonds, and cash, there are—among others—political, ethical, and geographical approaches to investing.

- **International funds** invest worldwide, outside the United States. Currency rates and politics, as well as taxes, figure into the risk factors. Generally, taxes for the foreign countries are deducted from your dividends, which you must try to recoup on your U.S. income tax return.
- **Global funds** invest worldwide, both inside and outside the United States. Currency rates and politics should be considered among the risks.

- **Index funds** mirror the performance of a broad-based market index, such as the S&P 500. These passively managed funds are popular among investors due to high performance and lower management fees.

- **Socially responsible funds,** or **green funds,** have screens for companies that produce products that don't meet their social commitments. They might exclude investments in tobacco, alcohol, or nuclear energy. Different funds have different screens.

PROCEED WITH CAUTION

The three main categories of stock funds, bond funds, and money-market funds offer enormous variety within each fund. Pricing, objectives, and management style of funds vary, too, so it's important to read the prospectus before purchasing mutual fund shares.

PORTFOLIO TIPS

Even with the help of professional fund managers and a clear set of investment objectives, experts advise you to review your portfolio on a regular basis. Investments grow differently, and lifestyles change.

Perhaps you've changed jobs, moved, or gotten married in the past year. All of these personal changes can mean a different allocation of investments. Every financial planner could probably recommend a different mix, but there are some principles of investing that all tend to agree on, and you may find the following helpful when reviewing your portfolio:

- Rebalance your asset mix periodically, especially at different stages of your life.

- A mix of stocks, bonds, and cash gives your portfolio stability.

- Invest for the long-term—the longer the term, the more stocks you should own.

- Diversify the stock styles in your portfolio, such as growth and value stocks.

- Past performance doesn't guarantee future success. Look for strength rather than fast returns in the company you buy.

- Avoid short-term market timing. It can be risky and detrimental to your long-term plan.

- Global and international stocks represent investment opportunities. Emerging markets are more of a risk.

HOUR'S UP!

Mutual funds come in all shapes and sizes, so it's important to know what you want before you buy. A fund prospectus is brimming with vital company information, but it helps to know what the terms mean before you read one. Let's test your knowledge now:

1. A mutual fund is …
    a. A group of bankers with like interests.
    b. An investment company that buys numerous securities.
    c. A retirement plan.

2. True or false: Mutual fund investors can choose which companies they want the fund to invest in.

3. The price you pay when you buy into a mutual fund will usually be …
    a. The price you were quoted.
    b. The next price calculated at the end of the market day.
    c. A percentage of the cost of maintaining the fund.

4. Load funds have …
    a. Historically outperformed no-load funds.
    b. Higher-quality investments than no-load funds.
    c. A sales charge.

5. If you are investing in a mutual fund for long-term retirement goals, which type of fund would you choose?
    a. Stock fund
    b. Bond fund
    c. Money-market fund

6. True or false: If you want to receive fixed regular income from your mutual fund investments you should invest in a bond fund.

7. True or false: Mutual funds help reduce your exposure to risk, offering almost instant diversification.

8. A fund's expense ratio is …
    a. A measure of how much the fund can spend on any one type of security according to fund objectives.
    b. The fund's operating expenses and management fees expressed as a percent of fund assets.
    c. The amount you pay in sales charges, expressed as a percentage of your investment.

9. True or false: Components of the mutual fund prospectus fee table are standardized by law.

10. True or false: You can buy a no-load mutual fund from a broker, but it defeats the cost-saving advantage of buying direct from the company.

Quiz

HOUR 8
Bonds

CHAPTER SUMMARY

LESSON PLAN:

In this chapter you'll learn about the different types of bonds and how to value them. You'll also learn how to:

- Figure date, value, and rate for bonds.
- Calculate interest payments.
- Understand the different types of government bonds.
- Evaluate fixed-income bonds.
- Read the rating system.

Bonds are loan agreements made between you and a business or a government organization. Basically IOUs, the borrower issues a certificate promising to pay the loan back by a particular date. The borrower also agrees to make regular interest payments of a predetermined amount.

Bonds do not represent any ownership rights, but they are legally enforceable loans, which makes the bondholder a creditor.

How Bonds Work

When a company needs money for growth, they have a few options. If they don't have the profits to plow back into the business, they can sell off portions of ownership through stock. Or they can borrow money.

Borrowing money from a bank is one possibility, but banks are cautious lenders. They have stringent guidelines on the amount of money that can be borrowed and when it needs to be paid back.

JUST A MINUTE

The difference between owning stocks and bonds is the difference between lending and buying. Bonds are debt securities, which makes the bondholder a creditor. Stocks are equity securities, which makes the stockholder a partial owner in the company.

Borrowing from the public can help the company raise more money than it might be able to from a bank, without having to lose control of ownership. So they borrow from individual investors by issuing *bonds*. Once a bond is issued and sold, it can be traded like any other security.

WHY INVEST IN BONDS?

People buy bonds for three basic reasons: safety, income, and diversification.

SAFETY

Bonds are generally thought to be safe investments, and buyers expect to get their principal back intact. But with the exception of Treasury bonds, all bonds carry some risk. The investment risk depends a great deal on the financial strength of the issuer, as well as current market conditions.

From "high-quality" all the way down to "not desirable," bonds are rated for their level of risk, which you will read more about later in this hour. Some high-quality bonds are thought to be safer than other types of securities and can be used for long-term capital preservation by reinvesting the interest payments.

INCOME

Due to the steady income that comes from a bond's interest payments, they are called fixed-income securities. The income is set at the time of issue, so no matter who holds the bond, the money it pays out stays the same. Since you know exactly how much you'll earn, bonds are good investment products for budgeting and planning.

DIVERSIFICATION

Purchasing bonds is also a way to balance out the cash portion of a portfolio. Investors who are looking for income from their holdings buy bonds because the interest rates can be higher than money-market funds or CDs.

PROCEED WITH CAUTION

 Depending on who is issuing the bonds and what the rating is, bonds can be a very safe investment—or extremely risky.

DATE, VALUE, AND RATE

In order to compare bonds to other investments and understand what you're buying, you need to know three things: the maturity date, the par value, and the coupon rate.

MATURITY DATE

Unlike equity securities, which can be held indefinitely, bonds have a fixed life span. When a bond is first issued, there is a date set for when it must be paid back, called the *maturity date*. In most cases, the longer the maturity, the more money you can make on the bond.

An issuer can set the payback date for as little as one year or less. These bonds are referred to as short-term bonds. A short-term bond has a lower risk level because the principal is tied up for a shorter period of time. Short-term bonds also have lower interest payments.

An intermediate maturity date can fall anywhere from 2 to 10 years. A long-term date ranges from 10 to 30 years. Long-term bonds carry more risk and, consequently, offer a higher interest rate.

JUST A MINUTE

You don't have to buy a bond when it's first issued. After issue, it can be bought and sold through a broker on what is known as the *resale*, or *secondary, market*.

Owning a bond doesn't mean you have to keep it until it matures. You can sell it and receive the current market price, or the issuer may pay it back early. When the issuer pays the bond debt off before maturity, it's known as *calling* a bond. Callable bonds leave the investor in the position of having to reinvest the money somewhere else and losing expected income; therefore, callable bonds are not considered attractive. For that reason, callable bonds usually have specified terms regarding how soon they can be called.

PAR VALUE

Once a bond matures, the borrower is expected to pay back the exact amount they borrowed, called the *par value* or *face value* of the bond.

COUPON RATE

The *coupon rate* is what the investor will receive in interest payments. The coupon rate is set by the issuer of the bond. The coupon rate is expressed as a percentage of the par value. For example, if you bought a bond from XYZ Company when it was first issued with a par value of $1,000 and a coupon rate of 9 percent, your interest income would be $90 per year.

If you bought the bond when it was first issued, your return on investment, or the yield of your bond, will also be 9 percent.

JUST A MINUTE

Coupon rate payment terms will also indicate when the interest will be paid, such as monthly, quarterly, semi-annually, or annually.

Once set, the coupon rate stays the same until the bond's maturity. At that time, the issuer pays the loan back in full and no longer has an obligation to make interest payments.

THE PRICE YOU PAY

Bond issuers want to make the investment attractive to lenders. So when they set the terms for the coupon rate, they try to be competitive with other income investments of the day. They look at the market conditions and the current yields on bank accounts, money-market funds, and CDs.

UNDER AND OVER PAR

If a bond is traded rather than held until maturity, its price will change, based on current market conditions and the interest rate of the bond. A bond that pays a higher interest rate than similar new bonds is worth more to the investor, so it will cost more than its par value. If your bond rate is lower than similar bonds, your bond is worth less, and it will most likely sell for less than its face value.

For example, imagine that you bought the $1,000 XYZ Company bond in 1980 with a 9 percent coupon rate and a long-term maturity date of 30 years. You receive interest payments of $90 a year as explained in the preceding "Coupon Rate" section.

Now imagine that by 1990, interest rates had dropped to 6 percent. New bonds similar to XYZ Company bonds are being issued with a coupon rate near 6 percent. A $1,000 bond with a 6 percent interest rate will earn the investor $60 a year. If you want to sell your bond before it matures, an investor might be willing to pay you more than the $1,000 par value of the bond to get the higher annual payments.

INFLUENCE OF INTEREST RATES ON PRICE

Bond prices fluctuate with interest rates. Bonds and interest rates have an inverse relationship: As interest rates go up, bond prices go down. As interest prices go down, bond prices go up. Imagine a seesaw, with bond prices on one end and interest rates on the other.

Interest rates rise and fall depending on the state of the economy. The nation's money supply, ease of obtaining credit, and inflation expectations can all cause interest rates to fluctuate. So if interest rates drop to 6 percent, your bond issued in 1980 with a 9 percent coupon rate can be sold for a better price than if interest rates rose to 9.5 percent.

JUST A MINUTE

When you buy a bond through a broker on the secondary market, its price is tied to the interest rate of the bond. A bond that's selling for more than its par value will cost you more, called the *premium price*. If you buy a bond that's selling for less, it's called the *discount price*.

INFLUENCE OF PRICE ON YIELD

As an investor, you should be concerned about the return on your investment. Because a bond's market price is always changing, the current yield fluctuates as well. When looking at bonds in the secondary market, calculate current yield. While you will always get the same amount of interest payment, what you pay for the bond affects your year-end profits, or return on investment.

For example, if an investor were to purchase your XYZ bond, which has an annual interest payment of $90 and a current market price of $1,400, he would get a return on investment, or current yield, of 6 percent. Remember that the original buyer, you, had a 9 percent yield.

Annual Interest Payment

Current yield (percent) = Market value

The following chart illustrates how the purchase price of a bond affects the investor's current yield, using the (fictitious) XYZ Company bond mentioned.

Interest Payment

	Purchase Price	Based on Coupon Rate	Calculation	Yield
Par Value	$1,000	$90	90/1000	9%
Premium Price	$1,400	$90	90/1400	6.43%
Discount Price	$900	$90	90/900	10%

A rule of thumb to remember is that as the bond price goes up, the yield goes down and as the bond price goes down, the yield goes up—another seesaw.

YIELD TO MATURITY

Bonds purchased on the secondary market are also evaluated by their yield to maturity. Bonds can be purchased at any point before they mature, so yield to maturity includes the number of years you have left to collect interest payments as well as what you pay for the bond. The yield to maturity is complicated to calculate. You can ask your broker, or you can use math tables sold in bookstores.

TYPES OF BONDS

The four basic types of bonds available are categorized according to who is issuing the debt. For example …

- Bonds issued by the United States Treasury Department
- Bonds issued by other federal, state, and local government agencies, which carry a slightly higher risk level than Treasury bonds
- Corporate bonds sold by companies trying to raise money
- State and local government bonds called municipal bonds, or munis

U.S. GOVERNMENT BONDS

The United States government issues debt instruments to pay for its deficit spending, or the difference between what the government brings in and what they pay out. These securities are sold in the form of Treasury notes (T-notes), Treasury bills (T-bills), Treasury bonds (T-bonds), and inflation-indexed notes. You can also buy savings bonds.

Treasuries, as they're commonly known because they're sold by the Treasury Department, are backed by the full faith and credit of the federal government. Although not federally insured, the government promises to give you your money back.

Remembering that higher risks can bring potentially higher rewards, it stands to reason that the opposite is also true. The creditworthy reputation of the federal government means the return on your Treasury investments will be fairly low. Treasuries normally pay a lower interest rate than similar debt instruments issued by others.

JUST A MINUTE

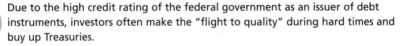

Due to the high credit rating of the federal government as an issuer of debt instruments, investors often make the "flight to quality" during hard times and buy up Treasuries.

Treasuries differ in the length of maturity, which will affect the return you get. Take a look at three different types of U.S. Treasuries:

	Maturity	Denomination	Minimum Purchase
T-Bill	13, 26, or 52 weeks	$1,000	$1,000
T-Note	2, 5, or 10 years	$1,000	$1,000
T-Bond	30 years	$1,000	$1,000

You can buy T-bills that mature in 13, 26, or 52 weeks. T-bills are sold differently than other Treasuries, on what's called a *discounted* basis. The real difference is in the interest payments.

T-notes and T-bonds are the most commonly purchased government debt securities. Sold as *coupon* securities, the Treasury makes semi-annual interest payments depending on the value and maturity date.

SECURITY AUCTIONS

Treasuries are sold at public auctions on a regular schedule. New T-bills are auctioned off every week to institutions such as pension funds, as well as banks and brokerages. Bid prices vary, depending on what the institutions are willing to spend and the quantity of Treasuries they ask for.

Individuals can buy Treasuries from brokerage firms and banks, who act as custodians for the investors. This means the bank or brokerage maintains the ownership records of the bonds. You can also purchase the bonds, bills, and notes directly from the U.S. Treasury Department called Treasury Direct on published auction dates.

JUST A MINUTE

Interest on Treasury securities has the added bonus of being exempt from state and local taxes.

TREASURY DIRECT

Treasury Direct is the easiest and least expensive way for individual investors to purchase government debt securities. If you have a Treasury Direct account, you can noncompetitively buy securities, schedule reinvestments, obtain account balances, and request account information. You can also perform basic administrative tasks such as changing the mailing address and phone number on your account.

To set up an account, you must first fill out and mail an application. You can order application forms on the Internet at www.publicdebt.treas.gov/sec/ sectrdir.htm or call any Federal Reserve Bank or branch.

When you buy from Treasury Direct you enter a noncompetitive bid, meaning you are willing to accept the price determined by the auction. You can only buy Treasuries direct at the time of auction. Auction dates are as follows:

- **Treasury bills.** Every Monday the Treasury auctions off the 13-week and 26-week bills. The 52-week bill is auctioned off monthly.

- **Treasury notes.** Two-year notes are auctioned every month. As of June 1998, five-year notes went from monthly auctions to mid-month auctions in February, May, August, and November. Ten-year notes are auctioned at the same time as five-year notes.

- **Treasury bonds.** T-bonds are auctioned with the 5- and 10-year T-notes, or every three months beginning in February. As of July 1999, 30-year bond auctions went from three times a year to only twice a year: February and August.

- **Inflation-index bonds and notes.** These pay a fixed yield plus the current rate of inflation. They are auctioned every three months and carry a maturity of 10 years. Interest is paid semi-annually.

For results of recent auctions, you can call the Kansas City Reserve information line at 1-800-333-2919. To find out about future auctions go the Bureau of Public Debt online at www.publicdebt.treas.gov/of/ofannpr.htm.

The Treasury doesn't keep records of the value of its securities in the secondary market, but you can get the daily Treasury report online from GovPX at www.govpx.com/mkting/go-start.htm. GovPx is the leading provider of real-time benchmark U.S. Treasury market prices and volume.

You can also find the quotes and yields in financial newspapers such as *The Wall Street Journal,* which lists them under "Treasury Bonds, Notes and Bills."

TIME SAVER

If you are interested in knowing the outstanding public debt total, go to the Bureau of Public Debt home page at www.publicdebt.treas.gov/spe/spe.htm. The public debt is calculated to the penny at the end of every day and posted on the Web site.

ABOUT CERTIFICATES AND RECORDS

Actual Treasury securities exist in the three following forms:

- **Book-entry bonds.** These are the most marketable Treasury securities. Once actual paper certificates, book-entry bonds now exist as ownership records on computer at the Treasury and with the banks and brokers who deal with government securities.

- **Bearer bonds.** There are still some bonds in existence called "bearer bonds." These are actual certificates that don't carry an owner's name or record of ownership. Instead, they have interest coupons attached that entitle the presenter to the interest and principal payments. There are no new bearer bonds; the Treasury stopped issuing them in 1982.

- **Registered bonds.** A very small percentage of outstanding Treasury securities exist in registered form. Up until 1986, the Treasury would put an owner's name on the face of a printed certificate. The Treasury maintains the ownership records and issues semi-annual interest payments. The owner can transfer the registered bond by filling out the assignment form on the back of the certificate, and the Treasury will adjust their records.

All new issues can be found only in the first form, book-entry bonds.

JUST A MINUTE

In January 2000, the Treasury issued the final rules for the unprecedented process of buying back bonds. Using reverse auctions, the Treasury will now accept offers from primary dealers on the securities that it wishes to buy back, such as bonds or bills. A booming economy has led to budget surpluses, enabling the U.S. government to reduce its public debt.

U.S. SAVINGS BONDS

United States savings bonds are issued by the Treasury Department but are different from T-bonds in that they are not normally transferable. If you want to get rid of a savings bond, you have to cash it in. Also, savings bonds mature in relation to interest rates, rather than a specified date.

There are three series of savings bonds: Series EE, Series HH, and I bonds. Savings bonds are popular because they can be purchased for small amounts of cash, from $25 to $15,000.

Bonds can be bought from the Treasury or through banks that act as Treasury agents. You receive your bonds in the mail a few weeks after buying them.

SERIES EE BONDS

Series EE bonds are an appreciation-type security, meaning that the value is increased as interest is added to the principal. They are bought at half their face value, so your minimum $25 investment would buy you a $50 bond. They earn market-based rates, based on the yields of actively traded Treasury securities, and change rates every six months.

Interest is accrued monthly and compounded twice a year. When the bonds reach face value depends on interest rates. For example, it would take a bond earning an average of 6 percent 12 years to reach full value.

You can redeem a bond after you've owned it for six months, but you will pay a 3 percent interest penalty for bonds redeemed within the first five years. If you cash in a bond after 18 months, for example, you will earn 15 months' worth of interest.

JUST A MINUTE

The Bureau of Public Debt issues, services, and redeems Treasury securities as part of its mission to finance and account for the public debt.

Interest earned on EE bonds is exempt from state and local income taxes, but the precise reporting of interest on the federal tax return is optional. You can elect to defer all interest until redemption, or you can report interest income as the interest is earned each year.

I Bonds

I bonds are so-named because they're indexed for inflation. You purchase I bonds at face value and accrue interest, as opposed to Series E bonds, which are issued at 50 percent face value. The interest the bonds earn is determined by the calculation of a fixed rate of return plus a semiannual inflation rate based on the Consumer Price Index.

Interest earned on I bonds is exempt from state and local income taxes, but the federal tax liability can be deferred until redeemed or reported as interest income as the interest is earned each year.

JUST A MINUTE

You may be able to exclude all or part of the interest you receive during the year from your gross income on the redemption of qualified U.S. savings bonds if you pay qualified higher educational expenses during the same year. See IRS Publication 970, Tax Benefits for Higher Education, Education Savings Bond Program, or go to the IRS Web site at www.irs.ustreas.gov/prod/forms_pubs/pubs/p97005.htm

Series HH

Series HH bonds are current income bonds that are only issued in exchange for accrual bonds such as EE bonds. You cannot buy HH bonds for cash. You can buy them in denominations of $500, $1,000, $5,000, and $10,000.

Series HH bonds pay interest semiannually at a fixed rate. Interest earned on HH bonds is exempt from state and local income taxes, but it is subject to annual federal income tax reporting.

Corporate Bonds

A major source of corporate borrowing is done through bonds. Bonds normally carry a higher interest rate than Treasury securities because they carry higher risk. The risk of bonds is that the company might default on its debts.

JUST A MINUTE

Some bonds have *puts* that allow the investor to demand that the issuer re-purchase the bonds at a specified time before maturity. An investor might use this option if they need cash if interest rates have risen since the bond issue, and they can then reinvest at a higher interest rate.

One drawback with corporate bonds is that many can be *called* by the issuer. When interest rates drop, as happened in the latter part of the 1990s, companies pay back the bonds early and take out loans with lower interest rates.

Callable bonds are issued with call provisions. If your bond is held in a street name, your broker should notify you of any calls. Bearer bond holders must keep track themselves. Redemption notices are published weekly in *The Wall Street Journal*.

TIME SAVER

Debentures are corporate bonds backed by the credit of the company. *Asset-backed bonds* are backed by company property or equipment. *Convertible bonds* can be traded in for ownership or equity in the company.

Corporate bonds can be bought through a broker and typically have a par value of $1,000. Very high-yield corporate bonds are known as *junk bonds,* because the issuer has a below-grade credit rating. High-quality corporate bonds are considered safe investments.

MUNICIPAL BONDS

When a city government wants to build a new bridge or school, it has to find large sums of money to finance the work, so it issues municipal bonds that try to be competitive with corporate bonds. Rather than raising taxes for these government projects, the federal government allows local governments to sell bonds whose interest rates are exempt from federal income tax. This way they don't have to pay out as much in interest but can still compete with corporate bond rates.

Municipal bonds are sold through brokers and are not considered as safe as federal bonds.

AGENCY BONDS

Some government agencies sell bonds that are backed by the full faith and credit of the federal government for special purposes. The most common purpose is to provide funding to the housing market.

The Government National Mortgage Association (Ginnie Mae), the Federal Home Loan Mortgage Corporation (Freddie Mac), and the Federal National Mortgage Association (Fannie Mae) are three agencies that issue bonds in this *mortgage-backed security* market. Mortgage-backed securities are based on a pool of individual mortgages.

These bonds can be purchased through a broker and are considered to carry a slightly higher risk than Treasury securities.

FIXED-INCOME BOND TYPES

There are a variety of other fixed-income instruments in the four basic bond categories available to you. Following are just a few.

ZERO-COUPON BONDS

Zero-coupon securities are deeply discounted bonds that pay no interest but allow the bondholder to redeem the full value at a specified future date. The price will depend on the years left to maturity, the current interest rates, and the credit risk of the issuer. Some investors like zero-coupon bonds because they can count on the payment at a future date and they work well in retirement portfolios. If you purchase a zero-coupon bond outside of a retirement plan, you have to pay income tax on the interest that accrues each year even though you don't receive periodic interest payments.

STRIPS

STRIPS stands for Separate Trading of Registered Interest and Principal Securities. These are Treasury securities that are sold in the marketplace as "Treasury zeros" or "Treasury zero coupons." They are called "zeros" because purchasers do not receive periodic interest payments. STRIPS work fine for the investor who is not concerned about current income but wants to preserve capital.

A stripped Treasury note or bond is separated into as many components as there are interest and principal payments remaining on the security. The minimum par value for a component is $1,000. For example, a 30-year bond, before the first interest payment, can be stripped into 61 separate securities, or 60 semiannual interest components and the principal component.

Stripped bonds can only be purchased through broker/dealers and depository institutions, as the Treasury does not issue or sell them. Your broker can give you current rates, or you can find quotes and ask yields for U.S. Treasury STRIPS in *The Wall Street Journal* under the table "Treasury Bonds, Notes and Bills."

JUST A MINUTE

When you buy a bond through a brokerage firm or bond dealer, it's not held in your name, but in the firm's name, otherwise known as the *street name*.

BOND FUNDS

GO TO ▶
Refer to Hour 7, "Mutual Funds," for more information on mutual funds, including bond funds.

Bond funds use pools of investors' money to buy bonds. Therefore, you do not have the rewards and risk of one bond, but many. Carefully examine the mix of bonds in a bond fund portfolio before investing.

RATINGS SERVICES

Credit rating agencies have taken on the task of researching the bond information made available to the public and assessing the risk involved. They assign grades to the issue and to the issuing company that reflect the ability of the company to meet the principal and interest payments.

Two of the best-known and most influential credit rating agencies are Moody's and Standard & Poor's. Both use a lettered rating system, but have slightly different definitions.

RATE THE ISSUER

Following is a listing of Standard & Poor's credit ratings of the bond issuers. For an idea of how the bond itself is rated, a listing of Moody's credit ratings for the bonds will follow.

- **Standard & Poor's Long-Term Issuer Credit Ratings.** A Standard & Poor's Issuer Credit Rating is a current opinion of an obligor's overall creditworthiness, or ability to pay its financial obligations.
- **AAA.** Extremely strong capacity to meet its financial commitments. "AAA" is the highest issuer credit rating assigned by Standard & Poor's.
- **AA.** Very strong capacity to meet its financial commitments. "AA" differs from the highest-rated obligors only in a small degree.

- **A.** Strong capacity to meet its financial commitments but is more susceptible to changes in circumstances and economic conditions.
- **BBB.** Adequate capacity to meet its financial commitments, but adverse economic conditions or changing circumstances are more likely to weaken BBB bonds capacity to pay.

JUST A MINUTE

"BB," "B," "CCC," and "CC" are regarded as having significant speculative characteristics. "BB" indicates the least degree of speculation and "CC" the highest.

- **BB.** Less vulnerable in the near term than other lower-rated obligors; however, major ongoing uncertainties could lead to an inability to meet its obligations.
- **B.** More vulnerable than the obligors rated "BB" but is still currently meeting financial obligations.
- **CCC.** Currently vulnerable and dependent upon favorable conditions to meet its financial commitments.
- **CC.** Currently highly vulnerable.

RATE THE BONDS

Moody's Bond Ratings illustrate the risk of holding a specific long-term bond. Their issuer ratings are identical. For example:

- **Aaa.** Bonds rated Aaa are judged to be of the best quality. They carry the smallest degree of investment risk and are generally referred to as "gilt edged." Interest payments are protected by a large or an exceptionally stable margin, and principal is secure.
- **Aa.** Bonds rated Aa are judged to be of high quality by all standards. Together with the Aaa group, they comprise what are generally known as high-grade bonds.
- **A.** Bonds rated A possess many favorable investment attributes and are considered as upper-medium-grade obligations. Factors giving security to principal and interest are considered adequate, but elements may be present that suggest a susceptibility to impairment some time in the future.
- **Baa.** Bonds rated Baa are considered medium-grade obligations (i.e., they are neither highly protected nor poorly secured). Interest payments

and principal security appear adequate for the present but certain protective elements may be lacking. Such bonds lack outstanding investment characteristics and in fact have speculative characteristics.

- **Ba.** Bonds rated Ba are judged to have speculative elements; their future cannot be considered as well-assured. Uncertainty of position characterizes bonds in this class.
- **B.** Bonds rated B generally lack characteristics of the desirable investment.
- **Caa.** Bonds rated Caa are of poor standing. Such issues may be in default, or there may be present elements of danger with respect to principal or interest.
- **Ca.** Bonds rated Ca represent obligations that are speculative in a high degree.
- **C.** Bonds rated C are the lowest-rated class of bonds, and issues so rated can be regarded as having extremely poor prospects of ever attaining any real investment standing.

More information on the subject of ratings can be obtained by contacting …

- **Moody's Investors Service.** 212-553-1658 or www.moodys.com/ratings/ratdefs.htm#lttaxable
- **Standard & Poor's New York Ratings Information Desk.** 212-438-2400 or www.standardandpoors.com/ratings/index.htm
- **Fitch Investors Service, L.P.** 1-800-75-FITCH or www.fitchibca.com
- **Duff & Phelps Credit Rating Co.** 312-368-3100 or www.dcrco.com

BOND FRAUD

Scam artists nationwide and abroad come up with some interesting bond fraud concepts. Unfortunately, many people are victims of bond fraud. The Treasury has noted several known security scams and warns the public not to purchase any of the following bonds.

LIMITED-EDITION TREASURY SECURITIES

The SEC is investigating foreign groups and individuals who have attempted to sell fictitious Treasury securities referred to as "Limited-Edition" Treasury securities.

FEDERAL NOTES AND TIGER ZEBRA BONDS

Samples of these bogus securities received by the Treasury proved to be combinations of old $100 bills that had been altered to read "One Hundred Million Dollars." Other bogus coupons were printed in a foreign language.

DE-FACTO TREASURY SECURITIES

This term usually appears in offers to assign, rent, or lease Treasury securities for a fee for a certain time period. There are no *de-facto* Treasury securities.

PHILIPPINE VICTORY NOTES

Philippine Treasury Certificates, Victory Series 66, commonly known as Philippine Victory Notes, were issued in 1944 by the Philippine government. At the time, the Philippines were a dependency of the United States, but the notes were obligations of the Philippine Treasury. All denominations were demonetized and withdrawn from circulation in 1957.

HISTORICAL BONDS

Historical bonds are becoming a favorite among scam artists. These bonds were once issued as real debt instruments by American companies who are no longer in existence. Though they currently have no value beyond that of collector's items, fraudulent artists are passing them off as valuable securities with inflated prices.

An example of historical bond fraud can be illustrated by the Chicago, Saginaw, and Canada Railroad bonds issued in 1873. CS&C went bankrupt in 1876, and its debts were settled in bankruptcy court. The bonds were later found in the basement of a federal building and eventually were sold off by a nearby museum as collector's items. Scam artists are claiming that they are payable by the Treasury in gold, which is untrue.

PROCEED WITH CAUTION

Many investors don't realize that they may have to pay *alternative minimum tax (ATM)*. ATM was designed to prevent taxpayers from taking advantage of deductions and other breaks to pay little or no federal income tax. Fill out IRS tax form 6251 to find out if you owe the tax. Otherwise you may be hit with expensive late fees and penalties.

HOUR'S UP!

Bonds can be good long-term investments, or they can be very risky. Once you know what to look for in a bond and how to determine its market value, you're on the right track to safe investing. Take this quiz to reinforce what you've learned.

1. A company issues bonds to …

   a. Lend money.

   b. Borrow money.

   c. Raise money by selling ownership of the company.

2. Which bond type is considered the safest investment?

   a. Municipal bonds

   b. Corporate bonds

   c. Treasury bonds

3. What is the yield on a $1,000 bond that earns $90 a year in interest?

   a. .9 percent

   b. 9 percent

   c. 90 percent

4. When an issuer calls its bond, it means they …

   a. Pay the debt off early.

   b. Pay a bonus to the bondholder.

   c. Check up on bondholder satisfaction.

5. A bond's coupon rate …

   a. Is competitive on first issue but can rise and fall in the secondary market.

   b. Is the same as its current yield.

   c. Can be negotiated.

6. The United States Bureau of Public Debt …

   a. Keeps track of credit ratings nationwide.

   b. Issues, services, and redeems Treasury securities as part of its mission to finance and account for the public debt.

   c. Provides housing loans for the underprivileged.

7. If a bond issuer receives a CCC rating from Standard & Poor's rating service, or a Caa from Moody's, it can be considered …

   a. In a very good position to meet financial obligations.

   b. Likely to meet financial obligations.

   c. Very vulnerable and unlikely to meet financial obligations.

8. Historical bonds are …

   a. Older and therefore more valuable.

   b. Good only as collector's items.

   c. Payable in gold by the Treasury.

9. If someone offers to sell you a Tiger Zebra bond, you should …

   a. Buy it because it's very rare.

   b. Hold it in your retirement account for the tax savings.

   c. Turn down the offer because it's a scam.

10. True or false: Investors don't pay tax on accruing interest with zero-coupon bonds.

HOUR 9
Retirement Planning

LESSON PLAN:

In this chapter you'll learn about The different types of retirement plans. You will learn about how your financial planning process affects how you achieve your financial goals for the future. You'll also learn how to:

- Determine social security eligibility.
- Figure how much money you'll need.
- Understand tax-deferred investment plans.
- Sort through IRAs, 401(k)s and pensions.

At the very beginning of this book, you learned that a financial plan is the most important roadmap you can have for reaching your life goals. To simplify even more, financial planning means translating your hopes and dreams for the future into real achievable numbers.

An important consideration in any financial plan is to ensure financial independence for your retirement years. Trying to plan for an event that may not happen for 30 or 40 years might seem unnecessary, especially when you're trying to meet daily bills today. But it's not. The earlier you begin to plan and save, the better your chances for a secure and comfortable retirement.

PROCEED WITH CAUTION

According to Senator William L. Armstrong, in 1950, there were 16 workers paying Social Security taxes for each one beneficiary. By 2025, there may be only two workers per one beneficiary. The result, according to Williams? A steeply rising burden on workers whose Social Security taxes keep the trust funds solvent.

As your life changes, so will your immediate financial needs. Whether you're paying off college loans or taking out a mortgage, you will probably have financial obligations. By identifying your specific needs early, you can create a flexible plan to help you attain a level of control as these events develop.

FINANCIAL PHASES

The years before retirement, while you are working and earning money, are considered to be the accumulation phase of your life. Retirement is the distribution phase. To make sure you accumulate enough to distribute takes planning and persistence in the accumulation phase.

The best place to start is to determine your retirement needs. Financial planners suggest that you define these needs in a real-life, measurable way. For example, do you want to retire at age 65 and maintain the same spending power you have now? Or do you plan to retire at age 60 and cut back on expenses and move to a lower-cost home?

JUST A MINUTE

According to the Consumer Information Center, the average American spends 18 years in retirement. Less than half of all Americans have put aside money specifically for retirement.

Most people use the age 65 as their retirement target date, mainly because for decades that was when you became eligible for full Social Security benefits. That changed beginning in 2000. For workers and spouses born in 1938 or later, the retirement age for Social Security benefits increases gradually from age 65 until it reaches age 67 in 2022. See the following table for more detail.

Age Eligibility for Full Social Security Benefits

If the birth date is ...	Then full retirement age is ...
1/2/38–1/1/39	65 years and 2 months
1/2/39–1/1/40	65 years and 4 months
1/2/40–1/1/41	65 years and 6 months
1/2/41–1/1/42	65 years and 8 months
1/2/42–1/1/43	65 years and 10 months
1/2/43–1/1/55	66 years
1/2/55–1/1/56	66 years and 2 months
1/2/56–1/1/57	66 years and 4 months
1/2/57–1/1/58	66 years and 6 months
1/2/58–1/1/59	66 years and 8 months

If the birth date is ...	Then full retirement age is ...
1/2/59–1/1/60	66 years and 10 months
1/2/60 and later	67 years

Source: Social Security Administration Handbook, 723; Reduction of Benefit Rate.

Following are some other critical dates in terms of benefits and penalties that you may want to factor into your retirement age decision.

- **59½.** The first chance you have to withdraw from your IRS-approved retirement savings plans without paying penalties.

- **62.** The earliest you can begin to collect Social Security benefits. Early acceptance, however, permanently reduces the benefit by 25 percent to 30 percent.

- **65.** The age at which you become eligible for Medicare benefits. Workers born between 1937 and 1943 become eligible for full Social Security Benefits at this age.

- **66–67.** The age at which workers born after 1943 start to become eligible for full Social Security benefits.

- **70½.** The age at which the IRS stipulates you must begin to make minimum withdrawals from tax-deferred investments, with the exception of Roth IRAs.

HOW MUCH WILL YOU NEED?

One thing that has become clear to most people not yet retired, and after a few decades in which others collected Social Security and pensions, is that they can't rely on someone else to support them in the golden years. While the financial-planning experts say that retirees will still receive Social Security payments, they're not counting on it as a significant part of retirement income. Retirement planning these days is up to the individual.

Once you've established a timeline for accumulating your cash, you have to realistically determine how much income you will need to live on. There are many interactive retirement calculators to be found on the Internet, such as the NationsBank Web site at www.bankofamerica.com/financialtools/, or the worksheet at the T. Rowe Price Web site at www.troweprice.com/retirement/retire.html.

Or you can work out your monthly numbers with plain old pencil and paper, using the following Cash Flow Worksheet as a guideline.

Cash Flow Worksheet for Retirement

Income

Social Security _____

IRA _____

Keogh/401(k) _____

Annuity _____

Pension _____

Your spouse's Social Security _____

Your spouse's IRA _____

Your spouse's Keogh/401(k) _____

Your spouse's annuity _____

Your spouse's pension _____

Income from business _____

Dividends _____

Interest _____

Rental income _____

Other _____

Total Annual Income _____

Expenses

Mortgage or rent _____

Electricity _____

Gas _____

Water and sewer _____

Telephone _____

Property taxes _____

Homeowner's insurance _____

Household help _____

Furniture _____

Home maintenance _____

Food and groceries _____

Clothing _____

Laundry _____

Toiletries _____

Cash Flow Worksheet for Retirement

Expenses

Gifts _____

Medical expenses _____

Dental expenses _____

Eye (glasses and exams) _____

Insurance (life, health, _____
dental, medical)

Other _____

Gasoline _____

Auto insurance _____

Auto maintenance _____

Auto payments _____

Other auto expense _____

Other travel expense _____

Other _____

Vacations _____

Movies and theater _____

Cable television _____

Magazines and books _____

Dining out _____

Club memberships _____

Educational expenses _____

Hobbies _____

Other _____

Taxes

Federal withheld _____

State withheld _____

Other _____

Total expenses _____

Total income _____

Minus total expenses _____

Positive or negative cash flow _____

A positive cash flow means you should be okay to meet the needs you projected for your retirement. A negative number suggests that you need to find ways to increase your income before you retire.

INFLATION EROSION

There are several possible sources of retirement income, some of which are listed in the Cash Flow Worksheet. It's important for you to understand how to maximize the benefits of the sources that you qualify to use. Perhaps the most important factor for you to understand is how quickly the power behind your money can dissipate when it loses the race with inflation.

Inflation is the continuing rise in the general price level of goods and services. It has been running at an average of 3 to 4 percent a year in the past 50 years. If you have your cash in a savings account earning 5 percent, you are keeping just ahead of inflation, but you're not doing much to increase your spending power. As an example, assuming an annual 4 percent rate of inflation consistent with historical statistics, take a look at how much you will need in the future to replace $1 today.

Year	4 Percent Inflation
1	$1.04
5	$1.22
10	$1.48
15	$1.80
20	$2.19
30	$3.24
40	$4.80

TAX TALK

One way to beat inflation is to put all the savings you can into tax-deferred accounts because they grow quickly. Over time the deferral of taxes and compounding interest can make a big difference in the amount of money you can accumulate.

Some financial experts recommend placing all you are allowed by law into tax-deferred accounts before investing for other big-ticket items such as a child's college savings plan. This is recommended for two reasons: Tax-deferred accounts grow faster, and financial aid consultants won't count tax-deferred accounts among your income and assets when figuring eligibility for college loans. Yet you can borrow from the plan if necessary for post-secondary education.

Each plan has its contribution limits, which can affect the amount you can contribute pre-tax to other plans. Check with your financial advisor or read up on current IRS rules to be sure.

You've seen what inflation can do to your spending power. Now take a look at what happens to $2,000 invested in an account that grows tax-free versus one that grows in a taxable account. For this illustration, assume an 8 percent return on investment and a 4 percent rate of inflation. Also note that state income tax has not been accounted for in the following illustration.

What $2000 Can Do

	Compounding Tax-Free	Compounding with Tax	Inflation Under the Mattress
1 year	$2,167	$2,120	$2,082
2 years	$2,347	$2,247	$2,167
5 years	$2,984	$2,676	$2,443
10 years	$4,451	$3,580	$2,984
15 years	$6,640	$4,790	$3,644
20 years	$9,906	$6,410	$4,451
30 years	$22,046	$11,476	$6,640
40 years	$49,065	$20,546	$9,906

If you are putting all the other bills ahead of retirement savings, consider how little you need to invest this year to make a substantial amount of cash for the future. Notice how leaving your money invested for the long term can nearly double its value every 10 years. In other words, waiting to save and invest will cost you.

RULE OF THUMB

Every financial planner has a different range of the percentage of income you'll need to retire on and hope for the same spending power you have today. The most conservative estimate is 60 percent. Still others say you may need the same amount, or 100 percent, depending on what you plan to do. If worldwide travel is your goal, you'll need a lot more cash than if you stayed home and tended the garden.

TAX-DEFERRED RETIREMENT INVESTMENT PLANS

There are a number of investments that make use of tax-free compounding. Some are even deductible from current taxable income. With tax-deferred plans, the money grows tax-free and you only pay tax on the income as you withdraw the money according to legal requirements. As previously mentioned, invest the maximum you can into each tax-deferred account for the greatest growth.

Financial advisors recommend investing a large portion of that long term retirement savings for growth. As you read in Hour 6, "Stocks," stocks typically provide the best return in the long run, so investing in stock funds will help to keep your investments far ahead of inflation. Reinvesting dividends will help that account grow, too, and you won't be taxed on the income as long as it exists inside a qualified retirement account. Bonds and other fixed-income securities may provide income, but won't help grow your money.

JUST A MINUTE

A qualified individual retirement account must meet IRS requirements. The account is defined as a trust or custodial account set up in the form of a written document in the United States for the exclusive benefit of you or your beneficiaries. The custodian must be a bank, a federally insured credit union, a savings and loan association, or an entity approved by the IRS to act as trustee or custodian.

INDIVIDUAL RETIREMENT ARRANGEMENTS

An individual retirement arrangement (IRA) is a personal savings plan that offers you tax advantages for setting aside retirement money. They were established to encourage people to save money before retirement. The main advantages to IRAs are that you may be able to deduct your contributions from your taxable income in whole or in part, depending on the type of IRA and your circumstances. Also, money in your IRA, including earnings and gains, is not generally taxed until distributed.

TRADITIONAL IRAs

Traditional IRAs, also known as deductible IRAs, are any IRAs besides the Roth IRA, SIMPLE IRA, or educational IRA. Anyone under the age of 70½ can open an IRA if they receive earned income. IRAs can be set up with a variety of organizations as long as they're approved as custodians by the IRS. Some common examples of custodians are banks and mutual fund or life insurance companies. You can also set one up through your stockbroker.

Any of these organizations can be used to manage your IRA, as long as they meet Internal Revenue Service code requirements. Some of the rules stipulate the amount of money they can accept, the form the contributions must take (they must be in cash, not property), and that the money can't be used for a life insurance policy or be shared with any other investment. IRAs can be invested in many diverse securities, including stocks, bonds, mutual funds, and certificates of deposit.

PROCEED WITH CAUTION

Ask your employer's benefit plan administrator about pass-through insurance on the plan's funds. Your retirement savings should be insured by the institution in which it's deposited, but may not be if the institution is considered by the federal government to be undercapitalized.

Contributions to IRAs cannot exceed $2,000 in one year. However, the custodian of your account can accept rollover contributions from other qualified retirement plans.

You can start to withdraw cash from your IRA when you reach age 59½, and you must start taking distributions by April 1 of the year following the year in which you reach age 70½. If you don't, you'll pay a 50 percent tax on any money you didn't take out but were supposed to. According to IRS rules, at age 70½, you have a life expectancy of 16 years, so you must withdraw ¹⁄₁₆ of your IRA each year after the age of 70½.

You must pay a 10 percent tax on early withdrawals, or those made before you are age 59½. This tax is in addition to any regular income tax you have to pay on the distribution. Some exceptions to the early withdrawal penalty include higher education expenses; qualified withdrawals for unreimbursed medical expenses that exceed 7.5 percent of your adjusted gross income; if you become disabled; if you buy, build, or rebuild a first home.

INDIVIDUAL RETIREMENT ANNUITY

You can set up an IRA as an individual retirement annuity by purchasing an annuity contract or an endowment contract from a life insurance company.

The annuity must be issued in your name as the owner, and only you or your beneficiaries can receive the benefits or payments. Unlike non-deductible annuities that you buy with taxable income, you cannot put more than $2,000 a year into the IRA annuity. If you are refunded any premiums, you must use them to buy more benefits or to pay for future premiums.

Simplified Employee Pension (SEP)

A simplified employee pension (SEP) is a written arrangement that allows your employer to make deductible contributions to an IRA that functions just like a traditional IRA. Because it's set up by your employer for you, though, it's called a SEP-IRA.

PROCEED WITH CAUTION

By law, your money is FDIC-insured up to $100,000 per account per bank. If you have a Roth IRA and a traditional IRA at the same bank, however, they may be considered as one account for insurance purposes. Check your account totals regularly, and move any money over the $100,000 threshold to another financial institution.

Self-employed individuals can also set up SEP plans. For SEP purposes, the self-employed person is both an employer and an employee, even if they're the only qualifying employee.

A SEP plan allows self-employed persons and employers to build up cash for retirement without becoming involved in more complex retirement plans. They just open an IRA with a qualified custodian and designate it as a SEP-IRA.

SEP holders can have a great deal more contributed than those using traditional IRAs. The $2000 IRA contribution limit does not apply to SEP-IRAs. An employer is allowed to contribute up to 15 percent of the employee's compensation or $30,000, whichever is less. These contributions are funded by the employer.

There are restrictions on who can qualify as an employee. To be considered an employee, one must meet all of the following conditions:

- Be at least 21 years old
- Work for the employer for three of the five years preceding the tax year
- Receive at least $400 in earnings in the tax year

Employees can also contribute to the SEP-IRA independently of the employer in the same way that other workers contribute to a traditional IRA outside an employer's retirement plan. The deductions may be reduced, though, because they are already covered by another retirement plan.

TIME SAVER

Financial advisors talk about the three-legged stool of retirement: how Social Security, pensions, and investment income supported retirees for generations. Many fear that Social Security may no longer hold up its share of the weight. You will have to reinforce your own stool with other income.

Self-employed persons have to figure their SEP deductions a little differently, mainly because for SEP purposes your compensation must take into account your deduction for contributions to your own SEP-IRA. Because your deduction amount and your earnings amount are each dependent on the other, the IRS has designed special worksheets. You can find these worksheets in Publication 590, Individual Retirement Arrangements; at your local IRS office, or online at the IRS Web site, The Digital Daily, at www.irs.treas.gov.

ROTH IRAs

Beginning in 1998, anyone, regardless of age, can make contributions to a Roth IRA. The Roth IRA is an individual retirement account that grows tax-deferred, and like traditional IRAs, has a $2,000 annual contribution limit.

Unlike the traditional IRA, contributions can be made to your Roth IRA after you reach age 70½ and left in the account as long as you live. However, to be fully eligible to contribute, your adjusted gross income must be $150,000 or less if you're married or $95,000 if you're single.

You cannot deduct contributions to a Roth IRA. But, if you satisfy the requirements, distributions are tax-free providing you leave the money in the account for at least five years after making your first contribution and are age 59½ before you take the first distribution.

EDUCATIONAL IRAs

Although educational IRAs are not a part of your retirement plan, they may be a consideration for any money you wish to invest once you've exhausted other tax-advantaged plans or are looking for a vehicle for tax-free saving for a college education.

With an education IRA, you may be able to contribute up to $500 each year for a child under age 18. Although these contributions are not deductible, they grow tax-free until distributed or the child reaches age 30. Anyone, even the child, can contribute to a child's education IRA if the individual's adjusted gross income is not more than $110,000 for an individual return or $160,000 for a joint return.

To keep the tax-free status, the money in the account must be used to cover qualifying expenses, which includes books, tuition, fees, supplies, and equipment for post-secondary education, and room and board for students enrolled at least half-time.

SIMPLE Retirement Plans

Called a salary reduction plan, a SIMPLE retirement plan is a tax-favored retirement plan that small employers and self-employed individuals can set up for the benefit of their employees (or themselves if self-employed).

JUST A MINUTE

SIMPLE and SEP plans are both tax-favored retirement plans that can be set up as IRAs.

In addition to salary reduction contributions, an employer must make matching contributions. The same distribution rules for other IRAs apply to contributions made to SIMPLE IRAs.

Keoghs

Keoghs are retirement plans for self-employed people and sole proprietors or partners in business. They are much more complicated than SEPs, IRAs, or 401(k)s. If you are considering setting up a Keogh plan, you should seek professional advice from a financial planner or accountant regarding taxation.

The main advantage to setting up a Keogh is the amount an individual may place in an account annually, which is the lesser of 25 percent or $30,000 of self-employment income. Self-employment income excludes dividends, interest, or capital gains from investments.

401(k) Plans

If you're eligible for one at work, the 401(k) plan may be the best retirement vehicle for you. 401(k)s are savings plans that allow you to contribute a percentage of your gross income. Gross income means the money is deducted from your paycheck before taxes. Any chance you have to contribute pre-tax income into a tax-deferred account should be taken. Here's an example of what you can save in taxes by contributing to your company 401(k) if you are married, filing jointly.

Here is your income without the benefit of a 401(k):

Pre-tax income:	$30,000
Tax bracket:	15 percent
Tax:	$4,500
Salary after taxes:	$25,500

Here is your income after a 401(k) maximum deduction of 15 percent:

Pre-tax income:	$30,000
401(k) contribution:	$4,500
Taxable income:	$25,500
Tax bracket:	15 percent
Tax:	$3,825
Salary after taxes:	$21,675

Conclusion: You paid $675 less in taxes and put $4,500 away in your retirement fund. Assuming an 8 percent return, in 20 years that $4,500 would be worth $22,289.

You are limited in the amount you are legally allowed to contribute: 15 percent of your income, or up to $9,500, periodically indexed for inflation.

JUST A MINUTE

A salary reduction plan is one where you agree to let your employer deduct part of your salary and place it in a retirement plan.

These managed plans usually offer a variety of investment options, from stocks, bonds, and cash to mutual funds. In most cases, you are responsible for examining and choosing your investment options according to your personal investment plan. Movement of your money within the plan does not usually incur charges, and the company typically takes on the costs associated with managing the plan.

Many companies will match the employee's contribution in either cash or company stock. For example, your employer may make a match of 10 percent on your total contributions or 50 percent on the first 5 percent of your gross income that you contribute. 401(k)s are worth taking advantage of.

PLAN DISTRIBUTION RULES AND REGULATIONS

In this age of constant career moves, you may not stay at a company for 30 years like your parents or grandparents did. If you leave the company in which you have a 401(k) investment before you retire, you have a few options.

First, you get to keep what you contributed along with its earnings. How much you get to keep of what the company contributed depends on how you're *vested*.

Vesting means entitlement. It is what gives an employee the right to share in the company plan, and is the amount you take with you when you leave. With 401(k)s, it usually refers to the matching contributions. All companies have different vesting structures. Some allow you to keep all the matching funds after the first year of employment, meaning you're 100 percent vested. Others use a gradual percentage increase over the years.

For example, after two to three years of employment you may be 20 to 50 percent vested, or entitled to 20 to 50 percent of what the company put into your account. Most nongovernment employers offer 100 percent vesting by the fifth year of employment.

The amount you're vested determines how much of your account you actually get to keep. What you do with your account depends on many things. Here are some 401(k) account options after you leave the company:

- Roll it over directly to another qualified IRA or employer-sponsored plan where it continues to grow tax-deferred.

- Keep the money for 60 days and then roll it over into another qualified plan. Caution: By law, your employer must hold 20 percent of it, and you have to replace the full 100 percent first from your sources. You get the 20 percent back from your employer at a later date.

- Leave it in the company plan to continue to grow, depending on the plan rules. Some companies allow investments of a certain dollar amount, say $3,500 to $5,000, to remain with the plan, although you cannot continue to contribute more money.

- Take the money and use it. If you're under $59\frac{1}{2}$ and can't prove a qualified hardship, you could pay substantial penalties for withdrawing the money. This option is generally not a good idea.

PENSION PLANS

GO TO ▶
Refer to Hour 5, "Investing Basics," for more information on asset allocation of your portfolio to maximize return and minimize risk.

The first private pension plan in America was established in 1875 by the American Express Company. It was soon followed by pensions offered by utility companies, banks, and manufacturing establishments. Most of the early pension plans paid workers a specific monthly benefit at retirement, called *defined benefit plans.*

Defined benefit (DB) pension plans are being gradually outnumbered by defined contribution (DC) plans such as the 401(k). But they are still a source of retirement income for many.

DB plan benefits are normally based on your salary and the number of years you worked for the company. With the exception of some government pensions, most monthly benefit payments are a fixed amount. This means they are not designed to adjust to any rise in inflation. Unless you are able to withdraw a lump sum and invest it, you will have to supplement your monthly pension money with savings and investments.

As you've seen from the examples in the preceding paragraphs, inflation cannot be ignored because in 20 years you'll need $2.25 to buy $1 worth of goods at today's prices.

There was no protection for pension plans until 1974, when Congress passed the Employee Retirement Income Security Act (ERISA). The ERISA set requirements for private pension plans and named the U.S. Department of Labor (DOL) as overseer of pension plans to make sure assets were properly managed.

The IRS is responsible for pension plan funding and vesting requirements and to make sure they comply with tax laws. ERISA also established the federal Pension Benefit Guaranty Corporation (PBGC) to insure the pensions of workers covered by private defined benefit pension plans.

ANNUITIES

An annuity is a contract that you arrange with a life insurance company to ensure that you don't outlive your money. Beginning on a specified date, the company pays you a monthly sum for the duration of your life.

With an annuity, you pay in a sum of money over time, called the *accumulation period*. The company invests that money, but an annuity is not a security, it's an insurance product. The company takes all the risk. You begin to collect payments in the *annuity period*.

With a fixed annuity, the amount of payment is predetermined. With a variable annuity, the payout depends on the performance of the portfolio. You can also opt for settlement options that allow for lump-sum payments or for a percentage of the annuity to pass on to a beneficiary you name.

JUST A MINUTE

There are retirement plans for nonprofit organizations like social service agencies, hospitals, or schools, called 403(b) tax sheltered annuities (TSAs). 403(b) TSAs are very similar to 401(k) plans. Generally, you can contribute the lesser of 15 percent or $9,500. As with 401(k) plans, the 59½ age limit for first distribution without penalties still applies.

Tax on annuities is deferred until you begin to receive payments. The age you receive payments is not regulated by law; you select the age. You can also surrender the annuity at any time and receive a lump sum.

LIFE INSURANCE

Life insurance policies may make a good addition to an overall retirement plan; however, they are not allowed in IRAs. There are no limits on the amount you can contribute to a life insurance policy, and the money accumulates tax-free. The contribution is not tax-deductible, though.

SOCIAL SECURITY

GO TO ▶
Refer to Hour 15, "Insurance," for more information on the types of insurance you should include in your financial plan.

There will be Social Security benefits when you retire; you'll just get them later, and you may receive less in comparison to what earlier generations received. To find out what benefits you qualify for based on projected future earnings, contact the Social Security Administration at www.ssa.gov or call 1-800-772-1213 and ask about your Personal Earnings and Benefits Estimate Statement (PEBES).

You need a certain number of credits to be eligible for Social Security benefits. The number of credits depends on your age and the type of benefit you're claiming. Most people need 40 credits to qualify for retirement benefits.

You can earn a maximum of four credits each year, and the qualifying amount of income changes. For 1998, you had to earn $700 of income to earn one credit; in 1999, that total increased to $740 of income for each credit.

You can continue to work and receive benefits with no penalties if you are over age 65 and your income doesn't exceed $15,500, as of 1999. For every $3 you earn over that limit, $1 is withheld. When you reach age 70, there is no limit on the amount you can earn and still receive full benefits.

JUST A MINUTE

In 1999, the average monthly Social Security payment was $500 for an individual and $751 for a couple.

BEFORE YOU RETIRE

Once you've established your long-term retirement goals and instituted a plan, you need to periodically check that your asset allocation is helping you achieve those goals. The more savings you accumulate, the more your portfolio within your retirement accounts should be weighted toward stocks. The closer you get to retirement, the less aggressive you may want to be with your approach.

The decade before you retire is a good time to take inventory of what you have and what you think you will need to fill the gaps, if there are any, you might encounter in retirement. A retirement gap is the shortfall you would have if your projected annual savings is less than your projected annual income.

If you do foresee a retirement gap, you can do a number of things:

- Review your retirement cash flow worksheet and make any possible adjustments.
- Delay your retirement date until your savings has increased.
- Change your portfolio investment mix to increase your return.
- Cut back on spending and save more now.

Repeat this exercise every five years until you retire. Several months before you retire, you should begin the process of applying for Social Security benefits. You will also have to decide the tax implications of receiving lump sum or periodic payments from your retirement accounts. Carefully monitor the progress of your investments and reallocate when necessary.

HOUR'S UP!

An informed investor is a secure investor, they say. Let's test your knowledge of retirement planning and retirement plans. After all, it's your future.

1. Most Americans spend how many years in retirement on average?
   a. Ten years
   b. Fifteen years
   c. Eighteen years

2. A ballpark estimate of how much money you'll need to retire is ...
   a. Fifty percent of your pre-retirement earnings to maintain your standard of living.
   b. Forty percent of your pre-retirement earnings to maintain your standard of living.
   c. Seventy to 100 percent of your pre-retirement earnings to maintain your standard of living.

3. To be sure your retirement income is inflation-proof, you should …

   a. Take advantage of a company retirement plan.

   b. Know how your pension and savings plan is invested.

   c. Both A and B.

4. You must wait to begin withdrawing portions of your employer-sponsored retirement accounts and IRAs until what age to avoid incurring penalties?

   a. $59\frac{1}{2}$

   b. 65

   c. $70\frac{1}{2}$

5. The main advantages to using employer-sponsored retirement plans to invest your money are …

   a. Deferred taxes and compounding interest.

   b. Your employer may add matching funds.

   c. There are usually a variety of investment options.

   d. All of the above.

6. Self-employed individuals can use which plans to maximize the amount they can contribute to their retirement accounts?

   a. Annuities and life insurance policies

   b. Keoghs and SEP-IRAs

   c. Roth IRAs and traditional IRAs

7. True or false: Employees cannot contribute their own funds to an employer-sponsored SEP-IRA.

8. True or false: You can estimate your projected Social Security benefits at any point in your working life by contacting the Social Security Administration.

9. True or false: In order to receive Social Security benefits, you have to have received taxable income that has earned you credits.

10. True or false: A life insurance policy is tax-deductible and grows tax-deferred.

PART III
Tools

Hour 10

Basic Banking

Chapter Summary

LESSON PLAN:

In this chapter you'll learn about the basics of banking, such as what banks have to offer and how to choose a bank. You'll discover ways to save money on the banking products you choose, as well as grow money in special bank accounts and products. You'll also learn how to:

- Examine your bank's financial services.
- Shop for and choose the right bank for your needs.
- Change your banking habits to fit your life.
- Know how your money is protected by banks today.

Personal finance is all about managing your money. The best way to manage your money is to keep track of its comings and goings. The most efficient way to do that is to have some type of bank account.

Keeping Records

Banks can take a lot of the pressure off the busy person in terms of record-keeping alone. When you have an account, you get monthly statements of account activity, or at the very minimum a passbook where deposits and withdrawals are entered. No need to remember when you paid a bill or dropped off your last paycheck—it's in the records. You can also keep track of how much you spend and what you spend it on for tighter control of your cash flow.

Safety

When you're not using your money, there are few places that can keep it as safe as a bank that's regulated by the government. Since 1933, the Federal Deposit Insurance Corporation (FDIC) has had the authority to provide deposit insurance to banks. That first year, the insurance covered deposits up to $5,000. Today your bank deposits are federally insured up to $100,000 per bank, per name. So you could also hold a joint account with your spouse that has its own $100,000 insured limit.

GO TO ▶

Refer to Hour 3, "Budgeting Your Way to the Future," for more information on budgeting.

Keeping your money at home under the mattress or hidden in a safe can be risky. The threat of fire or theft are bad enough. But you also lose out on some valuable services that can put money in your pocket.

INTEREST EARNINGS

Several types of bank accounts pay you a monthly sum of money depending on the amount of your deposit or your account balance. The payment is called interest, and it helps your money make more money. As was discussed in Hour 5, "Investing Basics," the power of compounding interest can nearly double your savings in the long-term. With compounding, the money that you save earns interest, which is added to the savings and earns interest as well.

Some accounts, such as passbook savings, offer you immediate access to your cash but also pay out lower interest rates. Other savings methods can bring in more in interest payments, but tie up your cash for specified periods—from months to years.

PROCEED WITH CAUTION

Look for the FDIC label before you deposit your money in a bank. Never bank in an unregulated bank, even if the name sounds familiar or trustworthy.

BANKING SERVICES

You can use a bank for much more than just storing your cash. For example, you can open a special account for writing checks to pay your bills conveniently. Or you can use banking machines, called automatic teller machines (ATMs), for banking outside normal business hours.

Banks also have customer service representatives who can help you with your money-management questions. Home banking is now widespread among traditional banks and can be done with a home personal computer either by a telephone dial-up connection or through the Internet.

CREDIT REFERENCE

At some point in your life, you may wish to apply for a loan or secure a mortgage to buy a home. If you have had a steady relationship with a bank, they can provide ready references on how well you manage your money and pay your bills.

Your bank can also supply you with a credit card that can help you build a credit history. Be careful to pay the credit card bills every month, or you will damage your credit record rather than prove your creditworthiness.

TYPES OF BANKS

There are several types of banks you can choose to do business with, each one offering a variety of services.

COMMERCIAL BANKS

For the most part, commercial banks are the megabanks that have offices, or branches, throughout the country. Most of the commercial banks also have locations worldwide. They tend to be convenient, often with several locations within the same town. Commercial banks offer a full range of banking services, but they generally charge the highest fees to use those services.

JUST A MINUTE

A survey taken in early 1999 by the American Bankers Association revealed that 56 percent of Americans pay $3 or less each month on bank services.

SAVINGS AND LOANS

Savings banks can be a little more personal than the larger commercial banks. However, they have fewer locations and may not be as convenient. Most are federally insured, but look for the FDIC label or ask the bank manager before you open an account.

CREDIT UNIONS

Credit unions are not-for-profit, so their fees and loan rates are normally lower than other, for-profit financial institutions. You have to become a member to enjoy the savings on service fees.

Organizations start credit unions to help their employees with savings and loans. If your or your spouse's place of work is affiliated with a credit union, or you belong to a club with credit union access, it pays to investigate the membership requirements and services.

INVESTMENT COMPANIES

Some mutual funds and brokerage firms offer limited banking services, usually check-writing privileges attached to money-market accounts. Investment banks are not federally insured, but should carry private SIPC insurance as described in Hour 5.

PRIVATE BANKS

Private banks offer personalized services, money management, financial advice, and investment services for high net worth clients. Private banks are often banks within banks. Chase Manhattan and Citibank, for example, both provide private banking. Their typical clients include entrepreneurs, businesspeople, and wealthy families from many countries interested in international business and finance.

Private banks are regularly examined by the Federal Reserve, which tries to assist them with guidelines to prevent illegal procedures such as money laundering.

Of course, having a relationship with a bank should be beneficial to you, not detrimental, so you need to understand fees and charges, as well as what you can and cannot do.

TIME SAVER

To find out if your bank is federally insured, go to the FDIC Web page *Is My Bank Insured?* at www2.fdic.gov/structur/search/findoneinst.cfm. You can type in the name of your bank, or if you don't remember the name, type in a city and state and get a listing of insured banks in your area. The list is updated every Monday.

BANKING FEES

Banks make money by charging interest on money loaned out. They have to earn enough money to pay out the interest income they distribute to depositors like you, as well as pay for salaries, rent, and equipment for the banking operations. In order to make money, the interest charged to borrowers is usually higher than that which is paid to savers.

Banks also cover expenses by charging fees for bank services. That's why it's important when choosing a financial institution to pay close attention to the charges levied on products and services, or you could wind up spending more than you save at the bank.

According to a survey done by *Consumer Reports* in 1996, banks charge fees for over 100 services, including balance inquiries, ATM usage, seeing a teller, per-check fees, flat monthly fees, insufficient funds fees, check stop payment fees, providing cancelled checks, and closing out accounts.

By law, all financial institutions must list their fees for insufficient funds, stop payment orders, certified checks, and wire transfers. They can't advertise free checking if minimum balances or hidden charges are attached.

They are also obligated to comply with the Truth in Savings Act, which means they have to disclose the annual percentage yield, or APY, on savings accounts. The APY will tell you how much you would earn if you kept $100 in the account for a year.

PROCEED WITH CAUTION

Unlike traditional bank deposit products, nondeposit investment products are not federally insured. Examples of uninsured investment products include annuities, mutual funds, stocks, bonds, government securities, municipal securities, and U.S. Treasury securities.

SHOPPING FOR A BANK

You should shop for a bank much like you shop for any other service. You interview the key people and compare prices—only with the bank, you're comparing fees. There are many Web sites that rate banks and fees, which you can find in Hour 11, "Guide to Online Research." For now, you can concentrate on the types of services you're going to need, which will affect the fees you incur.

One of the best ways to determine the bank services you'll need is to ask yourself what kind of banking you intend to do. The following questionnaire can help you get started.

Q: Do you only need occasional access to cash?

A: If that's the case, a savings account may be all you need. If you want to save some of your money for a special purpose, you should look for banks with good rates on certificates of deposits, high-yield savings accounts, or vacation club accounts.

Q: Do you want to write checks to pay bills? How many checks?

A: If you need check-writing privileges, you'll want to compare different checking options, such as the fee for limited check-writing privileges versus unlimited checking.

Q: Do you want mainly a savings account with occasional check-writing privileges?

A: You may need a savings account that charges a check-writing fee only when you use that feature.

Q: Do you need to keep your cancelled checks?

A: The bank will probably charge a few extra dollars a month for that service. Check "safekeeping," whereby the bank keeps your cancelled checks and sends you photocopies, or electronic copies called check images, are usually free.

Q: Do you plan to walk into the bank, or use an ATM and home banking?

A: Some banks have more ATMs and online access, while others have more local branch offices.

JUST A MINUTE

According to the American Bankers Association, in 1998, 44 percent of large banks offered dial-up personal-computer banking, and 32 percent of mid-size banks offered the service.

Q: How much money do you think you can maintain in your account at all times?

A: Banks usually require a minimum balance to keep the service charges lower. Generally, the larger the balance you keep in the account, the wider the range of services available to you.

WAYS TO BANK

Today there are many choices in how you use your bank. Decide which ones are important to you before you choose a bank.

BRANCH BANKING

Branch banking means going in person to talk to a bank representative. At the branch you can deposit money, withdraw cash, cash checks, and get drafts or money orders. You can also get special orders such as certified checks or traveler's checks. Make sure you understand the fee arrangement of seeing live tellers and conducting transactions.

ELECTRONIC BANKING

Technology is changing the way people bank. First ATMs were introduced and then came personal-computer banking and Internet banking (virtual banking). You really never have to set foot inside a bank again.

ATMs

ATMs offer a level of self-service banking. You can make deposits and withdraw cash, check account balances, transfer money, and even pay bills. Most banks with ATM services have convenient access locations such as shopping malls, gas stations, grocery stores, airports, and, of course, outside the bank.

JUST A MINUTE

According to the FDIC, as of the first quarter 1999, there were 8,721 insured commercial banks in the U.S.

ATMs are accessed with cards that have your account information stored electronically and a PIN, or personal identification number, unique to you. Many ATM cards also act as *debit cards,* so that when used in a store, the money is debited to your account like a check.

While everyone agrees that ATMs are convenient, not everyone agrees that ATM surcharge fees are fair. Surcharges are additional fees levied on consumers who use ATMs to withdraw cash. Banks usually charge this fee to customers of other banks who access their machines, but some ATM owners make everyone pay. Not all ATMs have surcharges, but it's difficult to find one that doesn't.

Here are some ways to reduce or eliminate ATM surcharges:

- Only use your bank's ATMs; note whether you have a limited number of transactions, after which fees will be charged.
- Look for ATMs that don't surcharge. Fees should be posted.
- Keep in mind that ATMs in convenience stores, hotels, and restaurants are likely to impose high surcharges.

- Plan your cash needs in advance.
- If you need cash while you're shopping, some merchants will add a cash withdrawal to a purchase without imposing a surcharge.
- Use traveler's checks, personal checks, or credit cards when you're away from home.
- Use Internet and personal computer banking.

By using telephone dial-up access or the Internet, bank customers can now do much of what they were able to do at a branch office from the comfort of home. With the exception of downloading cash through the computer, electronic bank services have few defined boundaries. Like ATMs, services are available 24 hours a day, seven days a week.

Most brick-and-mortar commercial banks offer some form of banking from home, whether it's direct dial-up to the bank using their proprietary software or through an Internet connection. Direct dial-up access is thought to be more secure, but banks stack up firewalls and encryption codes to keep possible computer hackers away from online customer accounts. With FDIC insurance, a possible cyber-stick-up of your account may mean that your personal information will be exposed, but your money will be covered.

GO TO ▶
Refer to Hour 12, "Online Money Management," for specifics on electronic banking and virtual banks.

Online access is free with most banks, but if you want to pay bills electronically, you'll probably incur a monthly fee. Electronic bill-payment means that you give the bank the billing information, usually through an online form, and they cut a check from your account and mail it to the designated party.

If the other party is set up to receive electronic payments, a check is never even processed; your account is debited, and they receive a credit. You can even have bills paid on a regular schedule, such as monthly rent or mortgage payments.

VIRTUAL BANKS

Virtual banks have no physical locations. You couldn't walk in to see a teller even if you wanted to. Virtual banks can be accessed only through the Internet.

The ranks of Internet banks are growing, and they offer an inexpensive alternative to traditional brick-and-mortar banks. Checking accounts and online bill-payment services are generally free. One drawback is access to cash.

Few virtual banks own their own ATM machines. Many are part of ATM networks, though, and they sometimes reimburse customers for a limited amount of surcharge fees they incur as outside customers.

OPENING AN ACCOUNT

No matter where you open an account, you will have to give personal information. They will ask to record your address and phone number, date of birth, and Social Security number. A copy of your signature will be kept on file for cash withdrawal purposes.

PROCEED WITH CAUTION

The Federal Deposit Insurance Corporation, or FDIC, was created by Congress in 1933 to protect depositors' funds in the event of the financial failure of their bank or savings institution. The FDIC does not protect against losses due to fire, theft, or fraud.

You may also need some identification:

- Photo identification such as a passport, driver's license, or student identification for brick-and-mortar banks.
- A document that verifies your address such as a phone bill or other utility bill.

After you've opened an account, you have many products and services available to choose from. As previously mentioned, each one has a corresponding fee, so choose wisely.

BASIC BANK SERVICES

There are two basic reasons people go to a bank: to store their money safely where it can earn interest, and to have a secure, convenient way to distribute it, such as a checking account.

CHECKING ACCOUNTS

A checking account is an easy way to pay for purchases without carrying around a lot of cash. Checkbooks come with ledgers where you can note the check number and amount, and who you made the check out to and when. This register will help you keep track of the amount of money in your account, as well as give you an idea of where your money is actually being spent.

The bank will send you monthly statements that are important records for keeping track of your finances. The statement will show your deposits and withdrawals, check activity, and service charges. If you have special accounts with the bank, such as CDs or savings accounts, you may receive a relationship statement that will also show the other account activity.

Before you open a checking account, get a listing of what it will cost you to obtain checks and the fees charged for writing and bouncing checks.

BALANCING THE CHECKBOOK

When you get a bank statement, you should check it against the entries in your checkbook ledger for accuracy. Chances are, the bank statement and your ledger amounts will differ because you probably didn't record bank service fees in your ledger. Record the fees and any transactions you may have forgotten to write down as soon as you get your statement.

PROCEED WITH CAUTION

While bank failures are not common, they do happen. One bank failed in the first quarter of 1999, and three FDIC-insured banks failed in 1998. Looking back through the 1990s, one bank failed in 1997, five in 1996, six in 1995, 11 in 1994, and 42 in 1993, according to the FDIC Banking Profiles.

Some experts advise rounding up the amounts of the checks you write to the nearest dollar when entering them in your ledger to cover the cost of the fees and avoid overdrafts. For example, if you write a check at the grocery store for $26.16, enter it in your ledger as $27. Just make a note to yourself of the exact amount if you need to discuss the check with the payee later.

Tally up the total in your ledger and compare it to the bank statement. This is called balancing your checkbook. The back of each statement has a worksheet that you can use for balancing your account. If there are any errors, notify your bank immediately.

HOLDS ON CHECKS

Checks from another source you deposit into your account may take a few days before they become available to you. Banks take three to five days on the average to clear paper checks, and they use that time to verify that the funds are available from the other source. ATM deposits take longer to clear.

The time between when the check is deposited into your account and when it clears is called the *float*. Banks publish their float times, so make sure any checks you write will clear the float, or you may have a check bounce back due to insufficient funds. For example, if you deposit your paycheck on the fifteenth of the month, you shouldn't try to pay bills on the funds until after the eighteenth. Your bank can refuse to honor a check you wrote on insufficient funds during the float and your payee will get the bad check returned to them. You will most likely pay a fee to your bank, and possibly a fee to the payee, for the bounced check.

OVERDRAFT PROTECTION

The best way to cover your account from bounced checks is to have overdraft protection. You may or may not have to apply for it, but once in place, your bank will automatically cover you when you write checks that exceed the amount in your account. Funds are usually taken from a separate savings account.

DIRECT DEPOSIT

One way to avoid the float time involved in paper check transactions is to have your paycheck or government check deposited directly into your account. With direct deposit, payments are credited to your account the day they are issued. Ask your employer about direct deposit. It saves time and can save you money.

Many banks will lower or eliminate check-writing fees for accounts that use direct deposit. Your employer will issue you a receipt telling you when the deposit was made and in what amount.

TYPES OF CHECKING ACCOUNTS AVAILABLE

You have several options when choosing the checking account you want. Banks have different names and interest charges for them, but they offer similar features to the ones listed in the following sections.

BASIC CHECKING

Basic checking accounts are for people who do minimal transactions and don't keep a high balance in their accounts.

Many banks offer a no-frills or Lifeline account to provide basic banking services for low-income customers. The fees on basic checking accounts can range from $0 to $6 and may require a minimum balance of only $1. A limited number of checks are allowed each month before more fees are incurred.

In order to give lower-income citizens access to banking services, states such as New York, Rhode Island, Illinois, Massachusetts, Minnesota, New Jersey, and Vermont require that banks that offer personal consumer transaction accounts must also provide basic banking accounts. Terms and conditions are also set by state law, not by the banks.

INTEREST ACCOUNT

Some accounts offer interest payments on the balance if a certain level is maintained. Levels between $1,500 and $10,000 may be required to earn interest. The average interest paid is just over 1 percent, according to the financial information Web site www.bankrate.com.

If account levels fall below the minimum, many interest-bearing checking accounts will charge fees well in excess of noninterest-bearing accounts. One example of these is Negotiable Order of Withdrawal, or NOW, accounts.

JOINT CHECKING

Most checking accounts allow joint access, where one or more people share the account. The signature of each participant must be on file at the bank to allow cash withdrawals.

EXPRESS CHECKING

The express checking account is for the person who does most of their banking through ATMs or home banking. The accounts usually offer unlimited checks and low monthly fees, but teller visits can cost up to $3.

AGE-RELATED ACCOUNTS

Students and seniors citizens can often receive discounts on checks, ATM usage, and other transactions with age-related accounts.

MONEY MARKET

Money-market accounts (MMAs) are fully insured bank products that combine savings and checking features. The bank invests your money while offering minimal check-writing privileges. The account minimum balance ranges from $1,000 to $10,000, and fees can be very high if you drop below the minimum. The average annual percentage yield, according to www. bankrate.com, is 3.5 percent.

Writing checks is a popular way to pay bills. The Board of Governors of the Federal Reserve System reported that in 1996, approximately 64 billion checks were written with a total value of $75 trillion.

SAVINGS ACCOUNTS

Bank savings accounts earn the lowest rate of interest of all bank savings products: only 2 percent on average. That kind of return won't keep up with inflation, but it will keep your money safe. Savings accounts are convenient for holding a sum of cash for the short-term, or to use as an overdraft-protection account that earns interest.

There are two types of basic savings accounts: passbook and statement. Passbook accounts were started in the 1920s when people carried ledgers to and from the bank to have entries recorded in ink. Today they are still carried to and from the bank, but the passbooks are processed electronically.

Statement savings accounts are computer-generated records that itemize account activity and are mailed out monthly. The interest on each type of account can be different, but it is usually very comparable.

CERTIFICATES OF DEPOSIT

Certificates of deposit, or CDs, are fully insured savings products that pay higher interest than regular savings accounts but will tie up your money for specific periods of time, such as three months, six months, and up to several years. The CD reaches maturity when the term expires. The longer the term, the higher the interest rate. Rates vary, but high-yield CDs can offer as much as 6 percent.

When a CD matures, you can take the money out or roll it over into another CD. The interest rates may be different at that point in time, so you should compare returns with similar investment. If you need your money before a CD matures, the bank charges a stiff penalty.

CREDIT CARDS

Banks also offer credit cards to customers, often with a line of credit for emergencies linked to your bank account.

Compare annual fees and interest charges on the bank's credit card with other credit card offers before accepting the terms. Also, if you have another account with the bank, you may have signed a statement giving the bank the right to take money from that account to cover credit card balances. If you don't want that to happen, keep your bank account and your credit card with separate banks.

INSURANCE PRODUCTS

Banks also offer a number of insurance products, according to a survey released in 1999 by the American Bankers Association Insurance Association. In addition to the credit-related insurance products that banks have sold for years, property and casualty products and life and health insurance are being added to the list.

For example, dental insurance is now sold by 5.3 percent of large banks, 16.7 percent of medium-sized banks, and 11 percent of small banks. Many banks are now offering homeowner's insurance and disability insurance, too.

ABOUT THE FDIC

The Federal Deposit Insurance Corporation was created in 1933 to provide insurance protection for depositors if their bank should fail. The FDIC has responded to thousands of bank failures, and it has now expanded its insurance protection to include accounts in savings and loan associations.

All insured depositors of failed banks and thrifts in the past have been protected by the FDIC. It doesn't matter what type of account you have—savings or checking account, certificate of deposit, money market, or retirement account—the FDIC protects up to $100,000 of your funds.

The FDIC does more than just clean up bank failures. They are also the federal bank regulator responsible for supervising certain savings banks and state-chartered banks that are not members of the Federal Reserve System.

As a regulator, the FDIC aims to prevent bank failures by monitoring the industry's performance and enforcing regulations to make sure financial institutions operate in a safe manner. But banking is a competitive business, and the FDIC attempts to balance regulation without stifling competition.

WHEN A BANK FAILS

When a banks fails, the FDIC staff goes on location and uses money from the FDIC insurance fund to promptly reimburse insured depositors. Later, the FDIC recovers a portion of this money by selling the failed financial institution's loans and other assets.

WHERE IS THE FDIC?

The FDIC's main office is in Washington, D.C. They also have regional offices in eight cities: Atlanta, Georgia; Boston, Massachusetts; Chicago, Illinois; Dallas, Texas; Kansas City, Missouri; Memphis, Tennessee; New York, New York; and San Francisco, California. More than 80 small field offices are scattered throughout the country.

ARE YOUR FUNDS INSURED?

The FDIC calculates deposit insurance based on the type of ownership at one FDIC-insured depository or bank location. All deposits, such as CDs, checking accounts, and savings accounts, are considered held in the same type of ownership if they're held in the same FDIC-insured financial institution. They are added together and insured up to $100,000. The different types of ownership funds can be held as individual, joint, trust, or retirement accounts and are separately insured up to $100,000 each.

JUST A MINUTE

Testamentary trust accounts, also called Payable-on-Death (POD) or In Trust For (ITF) accounts, are separately insured up to $100,000 if the beneficiary is the spouse, child, grandchild, sibling, or parent of the owner. Each owner can assign three beneficiaries. With two owners on one account—parents, for example—the funds are insured up to $600,000, even with identical beneficiaries.

Whenever there is a change in family relationships, such as a birth, death, or divorce, the deposit insurance coverage of your accounts may be affected. In addition, if your bank merges with another institution that you do business with, the insurance on your accounts may be affected. Contact your banker to be sure of your position.

FDIC BANK FRAUD WARNINGS

You should always be careful with the amount of personal information you give out. Always know who is asking and what they need it for.

Unfortunately, other people who have access to your information can be fooled into giving it out. The FDIC has noticed a rise in *pretext calling,* where people call the bank posing as the customer and obtain personal information. It's especially simple if they have found out the customer's Social Security number.

To help protect yourself against this possibility, you should …

- Ask your bank about its privacy policies and information practices.
- Find out about the types of security your bank uses to prevent the improper disclosure of their account information.
- Understand what types of personal information the bank will provide over the telephone and to whom it will provide that information. Also find out what forms of identification they will require from a caller before disclosing account information.

HOUR'S UP!

Banks are changing every day as technology provides new and faster ways for money to change hands. The fundamentals remain the same, though, and after you know the banking basics, you can test new products. First test yourself to see if you can remember what you read in this hour:

1. A good reason to keep your money in a bank is …
   a. For the variety of bank services.
   b. For the credit reference when you try to get a loan.
   c. For the interest you can earn that you don't find under the mattress.
   d. All of the above.

2. Credit unions …

    a. Are not-for-profit, membership-only financial institutions.

    b. Are not federally insured—any of them.

    c. Only provide credit cards and loans to customers.

3. True or false: All financial institutions are obligated to comply with the Truth in Savings Act.

4. The following are not federally insured:

    a. ATM machines and debit cards

    b. U.S. Treasury securities

    c. money-market accounts (MMAs)

5. Over the Internet, you can …

    a. Make deposits to your account.

    b. Transfer funds among your accounts within the same bank.

    c. Withdraw cash.

6. The following are ways to cut back on ATM surcharges:

    a. Avoid high-convenience hotel and restaurant ATMs

    b. Use only your bank's ATM

    c. Calculate your cash needs in advance

    d. All of the above

7. True or false: You can walk into a branch of your virtual bank any time you wish.

8. The float time on a check is …

    a. The time it takes to open an account.

    b. The time it takes to receive interest payments.

    c. The time between when a check is deposited and when it clears.

9. A certificate of deposit is …

    a. Not federally insured.

    b. A bank savings product.

    c. The receipt you get for opening an account.

10. When a bank fails, the FDIC …

    a. Sues the bank.

    b. Goes to the bank and reimburses depositors.

    c. Locks the doors of the bank and conducts an investigation before issuing any money.

Quiz

HOUR 11

Guide to Online Research

CHAPTER SUMMARY

LESSON PLAN:

In this chapter you'll learn how to chart your course for good personal financial health through effective research. You'll learn what the best research method is for you and how to achieve great results with reliable information. You'll also learn how to:

- Research your financial plan online.
- Find data on companies and potential investments.
- Evaluate what you find.
- Take advantage of online financial planners and services.

You are living in the Information Age. Print and electronic media demand your attention at every turn. It's easy to become overwhelmed with the amount of facts and advice you encounter just trying to perform common tasks such as balancing your budget or opening a bank account. To avoid becoming a casualty in this firestorm of data, you need to become a discriminating operative of information.

Looking for facts on a particular topic can make you feel like the last party back to base in a scavenger hunt. If you don't know where to start your search, you end up misinterpreting clues, following cold trails, and hitting dead ends. That's why it's important to begin your search with the right map coordinates that can take you from point A, your question, to point B, your answer.

INTERNET RESEARCH

Much of the information you need can now be found on the Internet. Today, most brick-and-mortar institutions have an online presence. You may never have to step foot in a library for research purposes again; and other organizations, such as government agencies, banks, investment firms, and real estate agents, allow you to access data and perform transactions online. Several valuable organizations exist for the consumer only in cyberspace, and you can lose out on their assistance if you can't log on.

PROCEED WITH CAUTION

URL stands for uniform resource locator, which is the term for Internet addresses that begin with "http://." You don't have to understand the coding, but you do have to have the *exact* configuration of letters, dots, and slashes to reach the site you want.

Of course, it's a good idea to be a bit skeptical, and don't believe everything you read on the Internet. No one person or organization controls or censors what appears on the Web, so it's up to you to weed out the facts from fiction and fantasy. As with any information, consider the source carefully before acting on the data. Remember, just because it's in print or on a Web site doesn't necessarily mean it's true.

TIME SAVER

Most Internet Web sites can be identified by their URL endings. Commercial Web sites (and many personal pages) end in .com. Government addresses end in .gov. Educational sites, such as those belonging to schools and universities, end in .edu. Organizations end with .org.

If you don't know much about computers, a basic computer or Internet access course at your local high school, college, library, or computer store will quickly bring you up to speed. Take one even if you don't own a computer. Most people can access a computer through a local library or community college. There are also office and computer centers that offer computer use and Internet access for a fee.

Internet research can save you a lot of time, but it's easy to waste hours in an online goose chase in search of the right Web site. Later in this hour you'll learn the specifics of Internet research. Armed with this book, which will give you many Internet addresses, you should be able to find the information you need quickly and efficiently. Limit your frustration by referring often to this chapter, which will suggest many helpful Internet sites as well as traditional methods of research.

STEPS TO SUCCESSFUL RESEARCH

Even with the wealth of information available, good research takes planning. Online or off, you have to outline your goals, target your information sources, and evaluate their levels of accuracy.

1. Define Your Goals

Conducting effective research starts with defining your need. Ask yourself exactly what it is you want to find out and what you hope to accomplish with the information. For example, if you want to learn about personal finance, be prepared to come upon information from a number of related areas, many of which are covered in this book (such as credit and debt, retirement planning, taxes, and insurance).

You see that the topic "personal finance" is fairly broad. But if you want to know how your tax bracket will be affected by your retirement, then you have narrowed the focus to retirement planning and taxes. You have pinpointed the question you need to answer.

2. Target Your Source

Starting a search for information can be the most daunting part of all. Again, with a goal in mind, you can focus the hunt on a less-broad topic.

JUST A MINUTE

Most of your research on personal finance will come from secondary sources, or those that are readily and easily available, as opposed to primary sources, which take a great deal more investigation. An example of a secondary source would be a monthly government report. A primary source would be a personal interview or personally conducted survey.

Here are some places you can look to narrow your search:

- **Books.** Search libraries and bookstores, both online and off. Look for publishers of reference guides in your particular area of focus.
- **Newspapers.** For the most current facts and information, check local and national newspapers. Daily stock quotes, currency rates, and financial news are examples of the advantages newspapers have over other print resources.

TIME SAVER

You can read the online version of almost any newspaper in the country. To find the Web site of a publication, or to search for a publication by category, go to Editor & Publisher's Media Links database in their Online Media Directory at emedia1.mediainfo.com/emedia/.

- **Magazines.** Magazines may not be as current as the daily paper, but they can afford to go more in-depth on popular topics. It's also easy to target your subject, such as *Better Homes and Garden's Family Money,* or *Kiplinger's Personal Finance Magazine.* Many magazines that exist in print can also be found online. One very comprehensive online magazine directory can be found at Yahoo!'s News and Media listing at dir.yahoo.com/news/magazines/.

- **Company and industry reports.** Most established companies compile balance sheets, annual income statements, earnings information, and more that can be found in the library or online. Ask your librarian for their best resource for company research, including economic, financial, and industrial statistics. Some possible titles when researching company information include …

  - *Barron's* weekly paper offers studies of selected industries. See *Barron's* online at www.barrons.com.

  - *Hoover's.* Gary Hoover published his first book on company information, *Hoover's Handbook 1991: Profiles of Over 500 Major Corporations,* in late 1990. Today, *Hoover's* covers nearly 14,000 public and private enterprises worldwide. Hoover's Online at www.hoovers.com also provides news, stock quotes, and other business information such as global industry overviews. Free basic information is offered on all 14,000 companies; paid subscribers can research in-depth information on 8,000.

TIME SAVER

For the quintessential directory on company research, go to www.quintcareers.com/researching_companies.html.

- **EDGAR.** This Securities and Exchange Commission database, which stands for Electronic Data Gathering, Analysis, and Retrieval system, contains most of the data that every public company in the United States is required to file. You can access this database online at www.edgar-online.com. Register for free as a visitor and get access to …

  - **Complete EDGAR** database to 1994.

  - **Today's Filings,** one full business day after filing date.

  - **EDGAR Online People** to search Proxy Filings by individual name.

- **Full Search** to access specific filings.
- **EDGAR Online Glimpse,** an extract of the Management Discussion and Analysis for an overview of the company's operating results.
- **Financial Data Schedule (FDS),** which will download a company's balance sheet and vital financial statistics into a spreadsheet.

- **Zacks Investment Research (www.zacks.com).** An investment research firm that compiles earnings estimates, research, and fundamental data from 235 Wall Street brokerage firms. This information is compiled, analyzed, and redistributed for over 6,000 public companies. Most company reports are free.

- **Market Guide.** Market Guide specializes in the compilation of a database of descriptive and analytic information on over 11,000 publicly traded domestic and foreign corporations. Try them online at www. marketguide.com. Some possible titles when researching industry information include …

  - **Industry Norms and Key Business Ratios,** published by Dun's Analytical Services. This annual report carries financial ratios of 800 different industries.
  - **Almanac of Business and Industrial Financial Ratios by Leo Troy.** Using current IRS data, this almanac provides performance data and industry profiles.
  - **Analyst's Handbook.** Standard & Poor's monthly updated statistics and ratios for the industries presented in their S&P 500 Index.
  - **Dun's Business Rankings** ranks more than 7,500 top U.S. companies by industry and by state.
  - **Standard & Poor's Industry Surveys.** Contains information on major industries and financial comparisons of leading companies in each industry.
  - **U.S. Industry and Trade Outlook.** Evaluations and projections of major industrial and commercial segments of the U.S. economy.

- **Professional and trade publications.** Professional organizations and trade associations often publish journals and magazines appropriate to their industry. You can find useful information, statistics, and support.

LIBRARIES ONLINE AND OFFLINE

Few people or computer programs can out-search a good reference librarian. But don't expect them to have all the answers. You can help them help you by having a specific question in mind, such as "Where can I find the past five years of financial statements for ABC Company?"

Once you have pinpointed the information you need, your local branch librarian can help you find it, whether it's a book, professional publication, academic paper, or industry journal.

Most main branch libraries will give you a tour of the reference section by appointment. Some major libraries, such as the New York Public Library's Research Library on Madison Avenue in New York City, have a full series of free public training classes on how to find what you need at the library, as well as more advanced research courses. It's worth the time spent to learn about the incredible amounts of data waiting to be tapped.

JUST A MINUTE

The New York Public Library posts an annual *Best of Reference* page that includes their chosen outstanding resources in both print and electronic versions. You can view current and top picks since 1995 at www.nypl.org/branch/ref/brefarch.html.

Just like in the physical world, there are libraries, media centers, and study areas on the Internet. While copyright law prohibits most books from being posted full-text on the Internet, there is a great deal of useful information online.

If you need a specialized library, you can find their physical locations and access some of their online databases and full-text articles on the Internet. For example, the Library of Congress online has the full-text versions of many of its bibliographies and guides, such as *The Entrepreneur's Reference Guide to Small Business Information* at lcweb.loc.gov/rr/business/guide2.html.

An excellent place to start an online search for a specific library is the Library Spot at www.libraryspot.com.

Virtual libraries select, evaluate, and organize Web resources. Some are maintained by librarians; others are maintained by computer programs. For example, the Internet Public Library (www.ipl.org) is based in the University of Michigan's School of Information and staffed by four full-time librarians.

Not only do they maintain a collection of online reference works, they respond to reference questions, create Web resources, and even arrange space for exhibitions.

USENET NEWSGROUPS

A newsgroup is a collection of messages posted online from people who share an interest in the same topic. You can find newsgroups on many topics—not all of them in good taste, so choose the topics carefully. Much like a traditional bulletin board, people post messages on newsgroups for others to read. Sometimes people respond and a back-and-forth discussion ensues. Just remember that any information you post will be online for the public to see.

Deja.com is an example of an online destination site that offers consumers free access to more than 40,000 discussion groups.

EVALUATE YOUR INFORMATION

You know what your questions are and found some pertinent resources, but can you trust them? One potential pitfall in this information revolution is that everyone is clamoring to be heard, read, and noticed.

There are many different ways to obtain information, including print and media broadcasts. Before you accept the final word of any one source, it's best to follow an evaluation checklist to determine how credible that information really is.

Your checklist should at minimum answer the following questions:

- ❑ Who is the author or originator of the data?
- ❑ What makes them an authority?
- ❑ Do they have a particular bias?

Printed materials should include the names of the author and publisher somewhere on the document. Internet materials should provide the same. This will help you weigh the importance of the document. For example, an online search for the top 10 hot stocks may come up with the address to someone's personal Web page describing their hot picks. Unless that person is the manager for a well-established mutual fund with solid returns or from an investment firm with a good track record, it should be viewed as the personal opinion of a novice investor and nothing more.

JUST A MINUTE

Not all Internet information is free. You don't usually have to pay to read data from local newspapers, professional organizations and associations, individual Web pages, and government Web sites. But there are sites that require service fees or paid subscriptions.

If you're reading an Internet resource, is there a link to a page about the parent company, such as "About Us"? They should list additional contact information beyond an e-mail address, such as phone numbers and physical addresses.

Continuing down your checklist, answer the following questions:

❑ What was the purpose for the document?

❑ Is it commercial, educational, professional, or generated as an opinion?

For example, many banks provide personal finance information in the form of brochures or Web site worksheets and calculators. The information may be very helpful and accurate; just keep in mind that a bank is a commercial venture in the business of making money.

❑ Is this information accurate?

Look for references within the content to outside sources, such as government reports or academic and professional papers that can help you verify the data. Internet reports often provide these references in the form of Web links.

Also, make sure the content is accurate in terms of grammar and spelling. Error-free copy is a sign that there are editors reviewing the information before it gets printed or posted on the Internet.

❑ Is this information timely?

Technology has changed the pace of the way we do business today, so advice that worked 10 years ago may not be helpful now. Check the publishing dates of printed materials. Internet articles should have posting dates. If the posting date is missing, you don't know if the data was correct two days or two years ago, so don't rely on it.

TIME SAVER

Need a statistic to back up your decision or fill in a line item on your budget? For example, did you know that middle-income families spend over $8,000 on their children each year? Don't waste time searching the world; try the University of Michigan's Statistical Resources on the Web listings at www.lib. umich.edu/libhome/Documents.center/stats.html.

Using the Internet Effectively

There is a lot of junk mixed in with the valuable stuff on the Internet. Unfortunately, wading through the mass of data can be time-consuming. There are a few ways to cut down on the unnecessary input, but for the most part it's up to you to know what you want and to learn to filter out what you don't want.

Search Engines

The main way to find information on the Internet is to use a search engine. Search engines are to the Internet what card catalogs (now computer-based) are to the library. They're indexing systems that catalog key words, phrases, and topics and contain the URLs and Web sites of the pages that match the information you entered a search for.

Enter a brief description of what you're looking for, and your results will appear in the form of a headline that links you to the sources and a brief description of the resulting Web sites. Sometimes those results are pages long and contain a lot of irrelevant sites. The descriptions can help you decide whether to click on the link or keep skimming headlines.

Many search engines bring you the results from other search engines as well, providing a powerful source of information retrieval.

Examples of existing search engines include …

- **Altavista.com.** Indexes Web pages, Usenet Newsgroups.

PROCEED WITH CAUTION

Just as information hits the Internet at lightning speed, so do information sources come and go. If you don't find a search engine tomorrow that you used today, go to the Search Engine Watch Web site at www.searchenginewatch.com to check on its status. You can also research search engine technology, tools, and usage tips while you're there.

- **AskJeeves.com.** You can enter a complete question rather than just key words.
- **Dogpile.com.** Uses 13 search engines in the hunt through the Web.
- **Excite.com.** Indexes Web pages, e-mail addresses, NewsTracker, Excite reviews, and Usenet Newsgroups. Has a directory.

TIME SAVER

Web directories organize Internet information into subject categories. Many search engines have directories, such as Infoseek and Lycos. Humans and computers do collection and organization. They are best used for browsing more generalized topics and will guide the user in an efficient manner. Many search engines have directories for accessing their databases.

- **Infoseek.com.** Indexes Web pages, FTP sites, gopher sites, Usenet Newsgroups, and e-mail addresses. Has a directory.
- **Lycos.com.** Indexes Web pages, FTP sites, gopher sites, and Usenet Newsgroups. Gives Web page abstracts. Has a directory.
- **Metacrawler.com.** Uses other search engines in the hunt. Also accessible at www.go2net.com/search.html.
- **WebCrawler.com.** Indexes Web pages, FTP sites, and gopher sites.

TIME SAVER

If you're new to the Internet, you can try The Info Service's supersite list of *Internet Beginner's Guides* at info-s.com/internet.html. You're certain to find an introduction that fits your style, from *All About the World Wide Web* to *Zen and the Art of the Internet*.

WEB SITES OF USE AND INTEREST

The following topics are indications of the types of financial information you can find on the Web. They will help get you started in your research, and you'll quickly find your own favorite sites and research methodology.

GOVERNMENT SITES

The U.S. government is a formidable supplier of information to its public.

- **Consumer Information Center (CIC)** at www.pueblo.gsa.gov. A part of the U.S. General Services Administration, the CIC has hundreds of free federal consumer publications available online.
- **FedWorld.gov.** A central access point for searching, locating, ordering, and acquiring government and business information. Includes full- and partial-text databases, Web searching, and bulletin boards.
- **FedLaw** at www.legal.gsa.gov. From federal laws and regulations to general reference on how to find people and things, the FedLaw site has an incredible number of Web site links.

- **Small Business Administration** at www.sba.gov. A comprehensive site on how to start and run a small business. Plenty of free worksheets, tutorials, and contact information.

- **Social Security Administration** at www.ssa.gov. Find out what your Social Security benefits will be by ordering a PEBES (Personal Earnings and Benefits Estimate Statement; remember that from Hour 9?), or check into the status of the Social Security Administration.

- **The Federal Reserve Board** at www.bog.frb.fed.us/default.htm. The Federal Reserve Board was set up to oversee the nation's monetary and financial systems. On its Web site you can find surveys and reports on finances, both commercial and consumer, as well as easy-to-read consumer advice.

FINANCIAL NEWS AND INFORMATION

There are several top personal finance and investment news sites to help keep you informed on the issues of the day.

Here are some financial glossaries:

- **Equity Analytics.** www.e-analytics.com/glossdir.htm
- **New York Stock Exchange.** www.nyse.com/public/glossary/09ix.htm
- **Inc. Online.** www.inc.com/finance/learn/glossaries.html

The following contain business and financial news:

- Businessweek.com
- BusinessWire.com
- CNN Financial Network (www.cnnfn.com)
- Forbes.com
- Kiplinger.com
- Money.com
- SmartMoney.com
- Worth.com
- ZDNet.com

Also look to the many online channels, including ZDTV's *The Money Machine,* which covers investing, personal finance, money tools, small business, home office, jobs, and careers.

FINANCIAL SERVICES AND PLANNING

GO TO ▶
Refer to Hour 12, "Online Money Management," for more information on business and financial news sources that offer interactive functions to help you manage your money.

Where do you go when you want to file a tax return, create a budget, and order a copy of your credit report? The following sites will steer you in the right direction.

For tax information:

- **The Internal Revenue Service.** www.irs.treas.gov
- **The Tax Library.** www.cyberhaven.com/taxlibrary/tablecont.html

For insurance information:

- insurance.yahoo.com

BUDGET MANAGEMENT

The following Web sites will help you squeeze pennies from stones to make that monthly paycheck hold out.

- **Cheapskate Monthly.** www.cheapskatemonthly.com
- **The Dollar Stretcher.** www.stretcher.com
- **Frugal Corner.** www.frugalcorner.com or www.best.com/~piner/index.html

CREDIT AND DEBT

GO TO ▶
For more information on credit and debt, refer to Hour 2, "Cleaning Up Clutter/Debt Repayment."

The following Web sites will help with your debt and building credit:

- **Nolo.com Law for All** at www.nolo.com/encyclopedia/dc_ency.html. Encyclopedia of credit and debt from the online self-help law center.
- **Debt Counselors of America** at www.dca.org. Information on getting out of debt and rebuilding credit.
- **National Foundation for Consumer Credit** at www.nfcc.org. A network of 1,450 nonprofit agencies that provide money-management education, counseling, and debt-repayment plans for individuals and families. Services are free or low-cost.

FINANCING

Finding money can be as easy as finding the right lender. Here are some Web sites that may end your search for treasure:

- **E-Loan.com.** Search top lenders to find the right mortgage for you.
- **Homeadvisor.msn.com.** Track rates and calculate an affordable monthly payment.
- **National Mortgage News** at www.nmnews.fgray.com. News and links geared toward the mortgage professional, but packed with useful information for anyone interested in real estate.
- **Quicken.com.** Apply for a mortgage approval online.
- **Yahoo! Broadcast Services—Education** at dir.yahoo.com/Education/ Financial_Aid. A directory of loans, grants, organizations, and scholarship programs.
- **The Foundation Center** at fdncenter.org. A source for grant-makers and grant-seekers alike.

ONLINE CALCULATORS

Is it better to rent versus buying a home? Do you understand how quickly your money grows with the power of compounding interest? Try these and other great free interactive calculators for the answers to many financial questions:

- **Financenter's Personal Finance and Calculators.** www.financenter.com
- **Free Finance.** weber.u.washington.edu/~simont/freefinance
- **Kiplinger.com Calculators.** www.kiplinger.com/calc/calchome.html
- **Economic indicators.** biz.yahoo.com/c/e.html

  Yahoo has taken the key indicators from several government areas and condensed them into an economic calendar. What makes this online calendar so distinctive is that it provides the links to the actual government report for those who want to read more.

INVESTING

The term "investing" encompasses such a broad topic that you can search for days to find what you need. The following are a few starting places by subject:

- **Online Investment Services** at www.sonic.net/donaldj. Discount stockbrokers ranked and updated monthly.
- **Gomez Advisors** at www.gomezadvisors.com. Gomez report on discounts of about 80 brokers.

- **Motley Fool** at www.fool.com/media/DiscountBrokerageCenter/ DiscountBrokerageCenter.htm. Discount brokerage rankings and bulletin boards.
- **CyberInvest.com** at www.cyberinvest. com/tooltips/tooltips.learn.htm. Free investing guides.
- **CyberInvest.com** at www.cyberinvest.com/guides/education. inv101.guide.html. List of investor education Web sites.
- **Securities Exchange Commission** at www.sec.gov/consumer/ toolkit.htm. Financial facts toolkit.

DIVIDEND REINVESTING

Dividend reinvestment plans, or DRIPs, are a good way to get started in investing with little money. Here are some information resources for DRIPs:

- **Moneypaper.com.** An introduction to DRIP investing.
- **Netstock Direct** at www.netstockdirect.com. An online channel that provides comprehensive information about Direct Stock Plans (DSPs), Dividend Reinvestment Plans (DRIPs), and direct investing.
- **The DRIP Advisor** at www.DRIPAdvisor.com. Information and advice on Dividend Reinvestment Plans.
- **StockPower** at www.stockpower.com. Home of StockClick, a product that allows investors to enroll in a direct stock purchase plan. You can also buy, sell, and manage company stock.

RETIREMENT PLANNING

Planning for retirement means different things to different people. Some folks are looking for a way to make ends meet and retire early. Others want to purchase a second home now to retire in later. Whatever your needs, here are a few Web sites to help you start your plan.

- **Administration on Aging** at www.aoa.dhhs.gov/aoa/pages/finplan. html. U.S. government site with links to government and Internet resources.
- **Equity Analytics** at www.e-analytics.com/insdir.htm. Insurance and retirement planning directory of information.
- **About.com** at retireplan.about.com/finance/retireplan. A complete listing of links and information on retirement planning from the Mining Co.

HOUR'S UP!

From the local library to the World Wide Web, you have a wealth of knowledge at your fingertips. The following questions will test and strengthen what you've learned in this hour about the fundamentals of research.

1. To take advantage of the Information Age, you have to …
   a. Read everything you see.
   b. Subscribe to as many print and electronic publications as you can afford.
   c. Become a discriminating operative of information.

2. True or false: Most companies, educational facilities, and government agencies have an online presence.

3. True or false: Uniform resource locators (URLs) are case-sensitive, so that mistyping a lowercase letter where a capital is required would result in an error message.

4. Internet Web sites can be identified by their URL endings. For example, a nonprofit organization URL address would end in …
   a. .com.
   b. .org.
   c. .edu.
   d. .gov.

5. Search engines work best if you …
   a. Enter a broad topic for your search.
   b. Narrow your topic to specific key words and phrases.
   c. Bypass them in favor of directories.

6. A virtual library is …
   a. An online collection of full-text books.
   b. An exact replica of a physical library.
   c. An online collection of Web resources organized either by computer or human.

7. True or false: Most Web resources can be considered very reliable.

8. Before acting on any information you read online or off, you should ask yourself:
   a. Who wrote the document?
   b. What was the purpose of the document?
   c. How timely is the information?
   d. All of the above

9. True or false: The U.S. government has a number of useful consumer information and investing Web pages.

10. Search engines find Internet Web pages and resources by …

    a. Searching the Web for key words and phrases.

    b. Searching other search engines.

    c. Both A and B.

HOUR 12

Online Money Management

CHAPTER SUMMARY

LESSON PLAN:

In this chapter you'll learn how to log on to the Internet to manage your personal finances. You'll learn how to get Web-ready to pay bills, purchase insurance, buy a home, plan for retirement, and even plan your day, without ever leaving your chair. You'll also learn how to:

- Protect yourself from online fraud.
- Take your investing plan to an online trading site.
- Make online banking work for you.
- Research tax information on the Web.

Technology can keep you in direct contact with your broker, banker, and even your insurance company—24 hours a day. With Internet access, this ability to stay in touch will continue to grow at hyper-speed, allowing you to assess and reach financial objectives like never before.

Many transactions can now be performed online, from paying your bills to buying a home. Here are just a few of the financial activities that can take place on the Internet:

- Investing
- Shopping
- Banking and bill-paying
- Making loan comparisons
- Browsing real estate price ranges
- Applying for a mortgage
- Planning for retirement
- Filing taxes
- Researching a company
- Getting real-time stock quotes
- Insurance comparison and purchase
- Managing risk

What used to require at least the physical act of travel can be done at home, in comfort and privacy. Or can it? The issue of privacy is not fully resolved when it comes to online transactions involving money, at least in the consumer's mind. One thing is certain: It pays to be cautious when stepping out online.

GET READY FOR THE WEB

GO TO ▶
Refer to Hour 11, "Guide to Online Research," for more information on where to find what you need to make your money management decisions.

There were over 100 million online users in 1999, according to Jupiter Communications, a new media research group. Of that number, 75 percent use the Internet to shop. While the online majority are just looking around, the constant focus on making commerce sites safe and user-friendly is rapidly changing the habits of browsers into buyers.

If you want to become a member of the online buyers group, you need to be Net-savvy and Web-ready. In the following sections are some ways to safely use the Internet to your financial advantage.

PROCEED WITH CAUTION

 It's nearly impossible to control fraud on the Internet. With the following concepts in mind, you will know how to protect yourself on the Net by learning to identify Internet fraud. You'll also learn how to avoid Internet fraud and report it if you find it.

STAY SECURE

When you make purchases online, your first thought should be to make sure your transactions are secure. That involves using a secure Web browser or software that scrambles the information you send over the Internet to shield your online transactions from would-be hackers.

Most computers have a secure browser installed, but if yours doesn't, you can download one from the Internet for free. ZDNet's PC Online at www.zdnet.com/pcmag/pcmag.htm has regular updates on browser downloads. Look for the latest in encryption technology when choosing a browser, and upgrade the one you have as technology advances.

KEEP RECORDS

Try to always keep an electronic and hard copy of your online transactions. Pay close attention to any e-mail that merchants send you regarding your purchases.

KNOW YOUR SOURCE

Don't get too personal with your personal information on the Internet unless you know who is collecting that information and how they plan to use it.

Many sites will ask for your name, address, telephone number, e-mail address, and even your Social Security number. Find out why they need it. They should post an explanation somewhere on the information page or in the site's policy statements.

By the same theory, don't give out payment information, such as credit card numbers or bank account data, to any company you don't know or are not confident about. When you do give information over the Internet, make sure it's in designated order forms.

READ THE POLICY STATEMENTS

Every Web site should have a statement on security of transactions you perform with them as well as status of the privacy of the information they collect. For example, do they sell contact lists to advertisers? There should also be some mention of their trade practices, such as a refund policy. Look in the "About Us" sections, or under "FAQs" or "Policies." A site with no policy is best avoided.

CHECK FRAUD WARNINGS

Be a fraud detective by always being on the lookout for scams and deceptions. The following sites list the top scams to look for; check them periodically to stay informed.

- **Internet Fraud Watch.** By the National Consumer's League at www.fraud.org

- **Internet Scams.** Developed for the Washington State Attorney General's Office at www.wa.gov/ago/youth/internet/page.html

- **Internet Scambusters.** By Audri and Jim Lanford of NETrageous, Inc., self-proclaimed leading experts on Internet scams at www. scambusters.com

- **U.S. Consumer Gateway.** Reports on Internet scams and what the FTC is doing about them at www.consumer.gov

JUST A MINUTE

The Internet Alliance is the leading association devoted to promoting and developing online and Internet services worldwide. Through public policy, advocacy, consumer outreach, and strategic alliances, the IA hopes to build the confidence and trust necessary for the Internet to become the global mass-market medium of the twenty-first century. You can find them at www. internetalliance.com or call them at 202-955-8091.

KEEP PERSONAL INFORMATION CONFIDENTIAL

Keep passwords and personal identification numbers, or PINs, private and confidential. When choosing a new password or PIN, use original combinations of numbers and letters. Even though they're easier to remember, avoid using the obvious ones such as birth dates, Social Security numbers, or addresses.

REVIEW STATEMENTS

Carefully review your monthly bank and credit card statements for any unauthorized purchases. If you think there are any errors, contact your credit card company or bank immediately.

PROCEED WITH CAUTION

 If you feel you've been the victim of Internet fraud, you can check out online fraud reports on the Internet Fraud Watch page at www.fraud.org, or call their toll-free number at 1-800-876-7060. You can also file a complaint online with the FTC at www.ftc.gov/ftc/complaint.htm. Although they can't resolve individual disputes, they can investigate a company with a pattern of violations.

WHAT TO DO IF YOU FIND AN ERROR

Consumers are protected against fraud, and there are procedures in place to resolve errors on credit accounts, bank accounts, and electronic fund transfers. However, those protections only apply if you are diligent. You have to catch the mistake and notify the financial institution in a timely manner in order to invoke your federal rights.

If a mistake appears in your records, contact the institution immediately. Follow up verbal reports with a written explanation sent by certified mail, return receipt requested, so that you have a copy for your records. You should notify your credit card company within 60 days of receiving the bill, according to the Fair Credit Billing Act explained later in this chapter.

CONSUMER PROTECTION

Both the Fair Credit Billing Act (FCBA) and the Electronic Fund Transfer Act (EFTA) offer some protection when you use a credit card or debit card for transactions.

Some of the procedures in place protect consumers against credit charges or electronic fund transfers that ...

- Were not authorized by you.
- Show transaction errors such as incorrect amount, date, or calculations.
- Reflect inaccurate payments, credits, or transfers.
- Result in billing statements not mailed to your current address, as long as you reported any address changes in writing to the creditor at least 20 days before the billing period ended.
- You thought might be in error and requested documentation to review.

CREDIT CARDS AND THE FCBA

By credit, the FCBA refers and applies to "open-end" credit accounts. These include credit cards that must be paid monthly, revolving charge accounts, and overdraft checking accounts. It does not pertain to loans that are paid on a fixed schedule such as a mortgage or auto loan.

PROCEED WITH CAUTION

Internet fraud complaints rose 600 percent between 1997 and the end of 1998, according to Internet Fraud Watch, operated by the National Consumers League. The number-one complaint involved online auction complaints, rising from 26 percent of fraud reported in 1997 to 68 percent in 1998.

Under the FCBA, if your credit card is lost or stolen and used without your authorization, you can be held liable for up to $50 per account. Report the loss of your card before it is used, and you're not liable for any unauthorized charges.

If you want to dispute a charge, you have 60 days after receiving a bill. First, you must send a letter explaining the disputed item to the creditor. It must be sent to the address on the statement for billing error notices. If you don't know the address, call the company's 800 number and get it.

Your letter must include your name, your account number, a statement explaining the error and the dollar amount involved, and the reasons you believe there is a mistake.

The creditor has 30 days to acknowledge your dispute in writing. They then have not more than 90 days to investigate and correct the mistake or explain why they think the bill was correct.

You can withhold payment of the dollar amount in dispute, as well as any finance charges, without concern for creditor collection action during the dispute.

Debit Cards and the EFTA

According to the EFTA, electronic fund transfers are transactions involving ATMs, debit cards and point-of-sale debit transactions (like swiping your card at a grocery store), and electronic banking transactions that could end up in cash being withdrawn from your account.

According to the Act, if your debit card is used without your permission for cash withdrawal or to make a retail purchase, you have 60 days after the statement was sent to notify your financial institution.

Once they've gotten notice of the error, the financial institution has up to 20 business days to investigate. By law, they must tell you the results within three business days of completing the investigation. They then have one business day to correct the error. If they need more time, they can take up to 90 days to finish the investigation, but they have to return the amount of money in dispute to you within 20 days of receiving the error notice.

The bottom line is that you can lose up to $500 if someone uses your debit card unauthorized. If you don't report an unauthorized transfer or withdrawal within 60 days, you could lose a great deal more. Some institutions will put a cap on the risk to equal that of credit card loss, about $50, so you should ask about your financial institution's liability limits.

With these safeguards in place and consumer rights backing you up, you can begin to take advantage of the Internet's many online financial tools—safely.

Cyber Shopping

The first step most people take when it comes to sending money into cyberspace is to buy something: a book, flowers, maybe a new computer. More than $3 billion worth of transactions took place during the 1998 holiday season alone. That's a lot of money being sent through cyberspace.

As of late 1999, almost half of all online users utilized the Internet to research the products they wanted to buy versus buying online outright, according to Jupiter Communications. The reason? Their past online buying experiences have been unsatisfactory, and they quickly abandon any Web site that offers poor performance either in ease of buying or in customer service. Instead, online users tap the vast resources of the Web to compare prices, features, and availability of products, and then make their purchases in a brick-and-mortar store.

User satisfaction is so critical to success for electronic commerce that Web merchants will undoubtedly continue to find ways to provide faster, more reliable services to shoppers.

One benefit of shopping online is lower pricing. For example, a study done by ZDNet found that 17 out of 21 times, the computer consumers were shopping for was cheaper online than in a brick-and-mortar store.

Online shopping can be very convenient, and you can still shop at the same stores you know and trust. Most department stores have an online presence that can usually be found by putting "www." before the name (or plugging the store name into a search engine to get their Web address). Online virtual malls and shopping guides at major portals such as Yahoo! and Excite can beat any real-world mall for variety. Browse through categories such as Home and Garden or Automobiles, or search by key word for an exact item. There's always plenty of parking at an online mall—and no crowds!

GO TO ▶
Refer to Hour 11 for in-depth details on how to search the Internet.

Practice keeping your money safe online by following the suggestions earlier in this Hour, and cyber shopping can save you time, money, and the hassles of fighting crowds and parking cars.

INVESTING ONLINE

Americans are taking their investment portfolios to the Internet in record numbers. Online trading is attractive to beginning and intermediate investors for two major reasons: It's convenient and affordable. Prior to the arrival of online brokerages and easy Internet access, investors had to sign up with conventional brokerage firms that often charged high commissions and demanded large minimum investment amounts. Not anymore.

GO TO ▶
Refer to Hour 5, "Investing Basics," to learn more about the basics of investing before you jump into online investing.

ONLINE TRADING BOOM

Employers no longer offer the pension plans that earlier generations of employees could rely on, and Social Security benefits distributions are being pushed back from mid to late 60s. Therefore, more people are taking responsibility for their own retirement plans, many of which involve investments.

As an example of the growth in popularity of online trading, research firm NFO Worldwide reports that there were over two million households with online trading accounts in December 1997. By April 1999, the number had exceeded six million. Jupiter Communications expects the number of online trading households to break the 20 million mark by the year 2003.

GETTING STARTED

To trade online you must have a brokerage account. Finding an online broker is not complicated, but it's a move that should be researched as carefully as you would research a company you're considering investing in. The largest number of complaints about online trading have been in the customer service area. Part of that problem has stemmed from the rapid growth in the industry that should level out as the market reaches its saturation point.

With over 100 online brokerages to choose from, the task of selecting a broker can be daunting. Fortunately, as with most investment information, there are plenty of Web sites offering current news and advice on brokers.

BROKER RANKINGS

Online investment firms are popping up like mushrooms on a spring lawn. So how do you know whom you can trust or who is the best? One good source for broker information is Gomez Advisors at www.gomez.com. Gomez is fast becoming a leader in rating the performance of Internet and e-commerce companies, market trends, and developments.

Their surveys for consumers include the Internet Broker Scorecard, Internet Banker Scorecard, and, as of summer 1999, an Internet Insurance Scorecard. For this hour, you can focus on the Internet Broker Scorecard, which ranks online investment brokers, to see which firm you might consider going to if you wanted to open an account.

The Internet Broker Scorecard ranks online investment brokers in respect to five key areas: ease of use, consumer confidence, onsite resources, relationship services, and overall cost. The brokers are also ranked according to the investor profile, such as *Hyper-Active Trader* or *Life Goal Planner*. You'll want to identify your profile by reading Gomez's online descriptions and then see what firms suit your style.

If you want to investigate the financial health of an online brokerage, take a look at Weiss Ratings at www.weissratings.com. For a fee, Weiss issues financial safety ratings on nearly 250 U.S. brokerage firms each year. Their ratings are based on analysts' reviews of publicly available information collected by the SEC. Verbal ratings are offered over the phone by calling 1-800-289-9222.

PROCEED WITH CAUTION

Less than 40 percent of Web sites offering financial services responded to customer inquiries within 24 hours, according to Jupiter Communications. Online trading leads the financial services in growth, but it falls behind other businesses when it comes to customer service.

WHAT TO ASK A BROKERAGE FIRM

Before choosing an online brokerage, you should interview the firm. You'll want to find out what services they offer, what kind of research they have available, and whether it will cost you to use the firm. The fee structure for placing orders should be clearly defined. For instance, many brokerages will charge a fee for broker services; in other words, it costs you more to speak to a broker.

The SEC has several Web pages devoted to the Internet and online trading at www.sec.gov/consumer/jneton.htm. Among other advice, the SEC recommends asking the following questions of the sellers before placing your money in any investment. Get the company phone number from the Web site and interview the firm before you sign up.

- Are you registered with the state securities regulator?
- Have you ever been disciplined by the SEC, a state regulator, or other organization?
- What training and experience do you have?
- How long have you been in the business?
- What is your investment philosophy?
- Can you provide any names and telephone numbers of your long-term clients?
- How do you get paid? By commission, amount of assets managed, or some other way?
- Are there any choices on how to pay you, such as by the transaction, or do you charge a flat fee regardless of the number of transactions?

- Do you make more if you sell this security rather than another? If you weren't making extra money, would your recommendation be the same?

- Where do you send orders to be executed? Is it possible to get a better price from another market?

Once you have asked the appropriate questions and have received satisfactory answers, you can open an account and start trading. If your brokerage offers free research, you can investigate a company before you buy. Or, you can use many of the free services that can be found on the Internet.

ONLINE COMPANY RESEARCH

GO TO ▶
Refer to Hour 5 for a comparison of full-service broker fees with discount broker fees.

One way to find out what a company is all about is to read their annual report. Most mid- to large-size firms have their reports posted on the Internet for the public to see. You can search a database of annual reports at www. annualreportservice.com.

Other investment data can be found on Web sites such as Marketguide.com, which offers both free and for-fee information on most publicly traded stocks.

GO TO ▶
For a complete listing of online investment research sites, refer to Hour 11.

Information on Market Guide, as well as Zacks, MarketSmart, and Invest-o-rama, can be found at most of the major search engine Web sites. For example, Yahoo's! Finance/Inside Yahoo section breaks down the research into Online Trading, Stock Market News, and more.

One truly comprehensive start page for company research is justQuotes.com, with a page of links to historical charts, price quotes, analyst advice, and more.

READ THE NEWS

Keeping up with the markets and the economics of what moves the markets can help you make good investment decisions. All of the national news organizations have online news channels. For a quick assembly of daily investment news, go to Cyberhaven's Newsletter round-up at www.cyberhaven.com and click on Daily Investment Newsletters.

JUST A MINUTE

For links to over 7,000 investor Web sites, go to InvestorGuide at www.investorguide.com. For definitions to over 4,000 investment terms, go to InvestorWords at www.investorwords.com.

ECONOMIC INDICATORS

Whenever the data for economic indicators is released, the stock market reacts—sometimes dramatically. In turn, so can the value of your investment portfolio. Economic calendars can be invaluable when it comes to understanding the impact of the economy on your investment strategy.

It's important to know the dates of market events and to understand the significance of these events. With an awareness of economic indicators, you can focus on what moves the market, analyze the data, and understand how the market has reacted in the past to these indicators.

Follow the events that move the markets by looking at economic indicators and economic calendars. Yahoo! has its own Economic and Treasury Calendar in its Economics/Calendars area, as well as links to other calendars.

The Dismal Scientist Web site at www.dismal.com/economy/releases/new_home.asp uses economic analyses and forecasts from both corporate and university-affiliated economists. Each major economic release in the calendar is accompanied by a hyperlink to a quick summary along with an economist's perspective on its implications.

PICK STOCKS

A few Web sites, such as www.Morningstar.com, an independent provider of mutual fund, stock, and variable-annuity investment information, and Quicken.com, have stock-picking tools to help you sift through the thousands of public companies. At this writing, Quicken.com offered a larger search selection.

GO TO ▶
Refer to Hour 6, "Stocks," for more information on market forces, how you make money, and different types of stock.

To pick a stock or mutual fund, you chose an industry and a screening method—for example, by price/earnings ratio—and then view results. Make sure to read up on the companies in your selected area, though, as one stock that showed up at the top of the list for P/E had recently filed for bankruptcy.

FINANCIAL PLANNING

Whether you're saving for your children's college or your own golden years, a good financial plan is indispensable. Logging on and checking out calculators is a big help in determining how much you'll need to achieve these life goals. The following Web sites offer the best in financial planning advice coupled with useful calculators:

- **Quicken.com.** From how to reduce debt to planning for a comfortable retirement and everything in between. Each question has an accompanying calculator, which makes it easy to transform advice into a real working plan.

GO TO ▶
Refer to Hour 4, "How Can I Keep Track?" for more information on the software available to help you manage your money and retirement accounts.

- **Kiplinger.com.** Known for their investment and personal finance magazines, Kiplinger's has plenty of calculators to help you with savings, retirement, purchasing a home, insurance and taxes, and much more. Read the topic-specific areas, or go directly to the calculator home page at www.kiplinger.com/calc/calchome.html.

- **Financenter.com.** Personal finance and calculators for all occasions: budgeting, saving, automobiles, and investing, to name a few. Log on and see how it all adds up.

- **www.Bloomberg.com.** Bloomberg's tools page offers not only calculators, but also a market monitor that updates while open on your computer desktop. They also have a portfolio tracker for up to five portfolios of 100 stocks each.

BANKING ONLINE

GO TO ▶
Refer to Hour 10, "Basic Banking," for more information on banking—online and off.

In September 1999, *The Online Banking Report* listed 498 true Internet banks in the United States. They define a true Internet bank as one that provides account balances and transaction details to retail customers on the Web.

Whether you call it electronic banking, PC banking, Internet banking, or online banking, banking from the comfort of your home (or office) computer is very convenient. You can do just about anything at your online bank that you can do in the brick-and-mortar version. For the moment, you may not actually be able to download cash onto your desktop, but you can download cash credits onto smart cards, which some merchants will accept as cash.

The variety of methods and banking transactions available are enormous. What you choose to do depends largely on what you want and what the bank offers. For example, many banks offer their own proprietary software, or personal finance managers (PFMs), for banking online. The PFMs have been customized to meet the bank's requirements, but they can be limited in helping you organize your overall finances.

Carefully examine the features of the PFM software offered by the bank you choose. Almost every bank that offers online banking has an online demonstration or tour that you can use to test-drive the ease of use and functionality. Check to make sure your bank can download any transaction information into your personal finance software, such as Quicken or Microsoft Money, if you use it. Essentially, you want to be able to do two main functions:

- **Check your account balances.** You want to know your account activity at your convenience. This will help you manage your money easier than waiting for the monthly statement to check for errors or inconsistencies.

- **Pay bills and transfer funds.** While online bill-paying most often involves an extra fee, it barely equals what you would pay in stamps. With bill-paying, the transaction time is cut in half. You can also set it up so that a regularly recurring bill, such as a monthly mortgage payment or insurance premium, is automatically paid each month or period.

TIME SAVER

 As if online banking wasn't convenient enough, Web-based banking is now being offered by Quicken. WebEntry allows you to perform transactions from any computer through a secure Web page. Once you're home, you can download that data from the Web into your personal software or bank register.

REAL ESTATE

Only about 40 percent of the American population own stocks. Over 70 percent have purchased homes. Why? Because there are so many financial advantages. And when it comes to the Internet, it's location, location, location. The Internet is the perfect place to start your research as a potential real estate investor.

Even if you're just contemplating buying a home, you can find out a lot by logging on. Calculate how much house you can afford, then look online for what's selling in your area.

You can research, buy, and sell properties in your own backyard or across continents. You don't have to speak with a realtor, but you can set up a search, enter your e-mail address, and get electronic notices of new listings sent to you. You'll have to contact a real estate agent for complete local listings, but here are some online services with limited versions of the Multiple Listing Service (MLS):

- **Cyberhomes.com.** Claims to offer the entire MLS database in your area, but also reports that agents and brokers may choose not to post some listings. Has interactive street-level mapping and homes by e-mail (a service that notifies you whenever a property meeting your housing preference comes on the market).

- **Homeadvisor.msn.com.** Check out the free Home Tracker e-mail service at homeadvisor.msn.com/ie/trackers/hometracker.asp for updates when homes match your saved criteria.

GO TO ▶

Refer to Hour 16, "Buying a Home," for more information on how to find and obtain financing for your new home.

- **Homeseekers.com.** Daily updates of listings of over 650,000 homes nationwide.

- **Realtor.com.** Over one million homes nationwide contributed by 516 MLSs.

Twenty percent of all mortgage loans are expected to originate on the Internet by the year 2003. Lenders are even trying to simplify the process so those loans can be approved in 30 minutes or less.

PROCEED WITH CAUTION

Be aware that all online loan applications will require a credit report, and the lending institution may charge you for it before they can process your request.

To find a loan online, or to calculate how much of a mortgage you can afford, try these Web sites:

- **E-loan.com.** Compare, apply for, and obtain loans from one of over 70 nationwide lenders. E-loan claims to save consumers an average of about $1,000 per loan.

- **Homeadvisor.msn.com.** Shop for loan rates, get pre-approved for a loan, and even investigate the neighborhood at this site.

- **Quicken.com.** For refinancing or a first-time mortgage, you can compare loans and get pre-approved online. Quicken periodically offers a rebate for online applications.

INSURANCE

The insurance industry has been slow to implement e-commerce strategies to advance online insurance shopping, but that position is changing. While few insurance companies offer the ability to purchase a policy online at this writing, many offer quotes, purchase registration, and claims information.

One of the best features the Web has to offer is one-stop shopping. Finding a Web site where you can compare real-time rates is the highlight of an online search. Insurance malls offer this prize to consumers seeking risk management through property and casualty, disability, health, life, auto, and other types of insurance.

The malls usually provide financial calculating tools and insurance company ratings information. Insurers partner with the mall and usually pay a fee to the mall for each policy sold. Two major insurance malls are Insweb.com and Quicken's InsureMarket.com.

TAXES

The best place to begin a tax tour of the Internet would be the Internal Revenue Service Web site at www.irs.treas.gov. Their Digital Daily is a tax publication with constantly updated news headlines from the IRS. It also has links to all the online federal tax forms and publications, taxpayer help and education, information for business and individuals, and electronic services. If you want to learn more about filing your tax returns electronically, this is the place to start. Over 20 million Americans used the e-file option in 1998, according to the IRS. The IRS claims that their e-file system is faster and more accurate than paper returns, and refunds are processed in half the time.

You can e-file your own tax return if you have a computer, modem and tax preparation software, such as Quicken TurboTax, that offers the IRS *e-file* option.

After the IRS checks the online return, they tell you whether it's been accepted or rejected. Once accepted, you mail Form 8453-OL, *U.S. Individual Income Tax Declaration for On-Line Filing,* and supporting documents to the appropriate service center. The IRS began experimenting with an entirely paperless return for the first time in 2000 for 1999 returns with select taxpayers. Go to the IRS e-file page www.irs.treas.gov/elec_svs/ol-txpyr.html for more information.

You can also e-file through a tax professional who is an authorized e-file provider. Refunds should be in your account within three weeks. Payments can also be made electronically through an appropriate credit card or direct transfer from your checking or savings account.

To look for an e-file provider near you, search the IRS database at www.irs.treas.gov/elec_svs/ero/indiv.html.

Here are examples of online tax sites that can help you prepare and file your federal and state returns:

- **Intuit, Inc.** You can go to Intuit's WebTurboTax.com to prepare and file your tax return electronically. The service costs a minimum of $9.95, but the e-file is free.
- **Kiplinger's TaxCut** at www.kiplinger.com/software/taxcut.htm. Use TaxCut 1040EZ Online to prepare and e-file your 1040EZ, for $9.95, or you can download Kiplinger TaxCut for federal and state tax returns.
- **H & R Block** at hrblock.com. You can file your own return online with their free-form tax preparation for $9.95.

GO TO ▶
Refer to Hour 14, "Taxes: Time to Get Clarity," for more information on taxes.

- **Jackson Hewitt** at JacksonHewitt.com. Has over 3,000 offices in 45 states. They offer a 20 percent discount tax-preparation coupon you can download and bring into a nearby office.

- **TaxWeb.com.** A consumer-oriented source for federal, state, and local tax-related developments. They provide answers to general tax questions plus hyperlinks to current federal- and state-sponsored tax sites that allow for a more detailed tax research.

Preparing your tax return may never be fun, but filing online can remove some of the tedium. Check back regularly to the IRS site for new developments in e-filing.

HOUR'S UP!

Sending your money into cyberspace can be dangerous—or it can be a time-saver. Take this quiz to reinforce what you've learned in this hour.

1. The Internet has transformed when and where we can perform financial activities such as …

   a. Applying for a mortgage.

   b. Planning for retirement.

   c. Filing taxes.

   d. All of the above.

2. True or false: The first thing you should do before attempting to perform any online financial activities is to make sure you have a secure browser.

3. Where should you look on a Web site to learn about the company's policies in regard to privacy and commerce?

   a. The "About Us" link

   b. The "Privacy Policy" link

   c. The "Policy Statements" link

   d. All of the above

4. The best action you can take to avoid Internet fraud is to …

   a. Stay off the Internet.

   b. Never perform online transactions that involve money.

   c. Become a fraud detective and be aware of scams.

5. Passwords and PINs should always be …

    a. An original combination of letters and numbers.

    b. Familiar numbers you can remember.

    c. Written down in an easily accessible place.

6. True or false: The Fair Credit Billing Act covers all credit, including installment loans such as mortgages and auto loans.

7. True or false: You have 60 days from receiving your billing statement to dispute a questionable charge on your credit card or debit card, but it must be made in writing.

8. True or false: The largest number of complaints about online trading have been in the customer service area.

9. The benefits of online shopping include …

    a. Comparison shopping and lower pricing.

    b. Convenience.

    c. Speed.

    d. All of the above.

10. Electronic filing of tax returns can be done …

    a. Individually from a home computer.

    b. Through an IRS-approved e-file provider.

    c. To cut the time it takes to receive a refund in half.

    d. All of the above.

HOUR 13

Finding the Right Financial Advisor

CHAPTER SUMMARY

LESSON PLAN:

In this chapter you will explore the ins and outs of finding the right financial advisor for you, and the right questions to ask any financial advisor before deciding on the one who can best help realize your financial goals. You'll also learn how to:

- Know what your advisor should share with you.
- Set goals for your financial future.
- Ask questions that get you the best results.

Finding the right financial advisor for you should not be difficult. Sometimes, though, people give more thought to their doctor, plumber, or therapist than they do to their financial planner—if they decide on one at all.

In a world crowded with new investments, changing tax laws, and rapidly evolving financial products, more people are looking for clearer direction in their financial lives. Good financial planning, as you will see, involves more than just managing and investing money. A good financial planner will help you take a look at all facets of your money intake and outflow, your dreams, and your realities when it comes to money.

DO YOU REALLY NEED A FINANCIAL PLANNER?

The selection of financial professionals is not one to take lightly. The first question you need to ask yourself is whether you *really* need a financial planner or financial advice in the first place. Could you make appropriate financial decisions without the help of a specialist?

Many everyday consumers have begun using the new information technology to their benefit. Financial seminars and classes have sprouted up across the country; many consumers are knowledgeable of the up-to-the-minute Internet sites with up-to-the-minute market quotes.

New and venerable newspapers and magazines are read widely for their financial information pages. Now more than ever, there seems to be an information overload and no end to the financial information available to eager and resourceful investors.

However, with this in mind, many consumers feel they need to select an advisor who can help guide them through the maze of finance. It is important to choose well and to do your research, because the advice your financial advisor gives can affect your future financial well-being.

There are many professionals out there who can offer financial advice, including the following:

- Attorneys
- Accountants
- Bank trust officers
- Brokers
- Credit counselors
- Insurance and real-estate agents
- Employee benefits staff
- Family members
- Financial planners

You can see that each of these people would obviously bring a certain expertise (or at least an opinion) to the table, and you may have full confidence in the people you have selected to help you with your financial needs. But because many people lack confidence in managing their money and their financial futures, they need an overall financial planner to help them in making financial decisions. Because many people do not have the time to manage their own accounts on a daily basis they, too, rely on financial advisors to help them chart their financial lives.

WHAT SAY THE EXPERTS?

John P. Leidy, a Manhattan-based financial advisor with one of the top-tier brokerage firms in the world, suggests that when choosing a financial advisor, you find someone who has experience doing what *you* want them to do.

For instance, if you want to do a lot of individual stock investing, "you want to have someone who has experience buying selling and picking individual stocks," says Leidy. "You wouldn't want someone with just a mutual fund background; you want to find someone with the particular area that you need representation."

More women today are also finding themselves in control of large sums of money, seeking to learn more about investing to keep that money growing and to plan for their financial futures. See Hour 20, "Financial Independence," for additional information.

Many investors, including most beginners, should be comfortable with a full-service broker who can help with all sorts of financial information from 401(k) choices, IRAs, and mutual funds.

But because there is so much financial information to sort through out there, let's take a look at the road map of planning that comes with a good financial advisor.

CATEGORIES TO CONSIDER

When considering a financial advisor, the following categories should be part of your planning. Although not all may apply at this juncture of your life, all will eventually make their way into your financial field of vision.

FINANCIAL INVENTORY

As you begin your journey down the road to financial health, you will want to begin taking a close look at your present financial situation. In Hour 2, "Cleaning Up Clutter/Debt Repayment," we took an inventory of any debt that you might still have outstanding. A good financial planner will help you detail your current assets, liabilities, sources of income, and expenditures, and should provide clear documentation of this information.

Because so much of everything that follows will flow out of this solid financial clarity, it is important that your inventory of information is collected in such a way by you and your advisor that it is clear to you both. Ask your financial planner for copies of any and all information printed out on your behalf during your appointment.

Eileen Michaels, a Certified Financial Planner at one of the top brokerage houses in New York and author of *When Are You Entitled to New Underwear and Other Major Financial Decisions?* (Scribner, 1997), started out in the health profession—as a nurse—before embarking on a financial advisory career. She likens the financial–inventory taking to seeing your medical doctor.

"When somebody comes into my office," says Michaels, "I'm trying to get them to tell me everything about their financial health. You have to be willing to get undressed financially, to get *naked*." Otherwise, she adds, the same people who are afraid of medical tests are also the type of consumers who will keep putting off scheduling a financial consultation for better financial health. (And, keep in mind, she sees this all the time!)

PROCEED WITH CAUTION

When seeing your financial advisor for the first time, be sure to bring any and all financial papers that can help clarify your current financial situation. Be sure to include past tax returns, pay slips, or invoices from past and current jobs, and any investments you may currently be holding.

CASH FLOW

It is important to figure out whether you are living above or beneath your means and to measure current cash flow against expense requirements and project these factors into the future. A good financial advisor can also help you with this step. Hour 2 on debt repayment and cleaning up your financial clutter can help you create an overall spending record that mirrors your current financial intake and outflow.

A good financial advisor will also help you take a good "pulse" of what your cash flow is and can help determine what steps should be taken in such areas as debt management, saving levels, and emergency reserve funds.

GOALS

GO TO ▶
Refer to Hour 1, "Developing Your Financial Goals," for developing and clarifying your financial goals.

Financial goals will change as your life changes. Working with your advisor/ guide, you need to establish definitive and realistic personal financial objectives. These could include education funds for your children or for yourself, support for elderly parents, buying a second home or vacation home, etc. Good financial advisors can help define objectives including necessary dollar amounts for your goals, a time frame to achieve them, and a priority ranking.

Every person's financial goals will be different; it is important to find an advisor who has a good background in helping many types of clients and who can help you, too.

INVESTMENTS

A coherent investment strategy will be a necessary part of a successful financial journey. Whether you decide to take risks or be more conservative in choosing a portfolio, a financial planner can be of enormous help. Your advisor can help determine your tolerance for investment risk, set a target rate of returns, and estimate the amount and timing of future contributions.

GO TO ▶
Refer to Hours 5 through 9 for more information on various investment methods, including investing basics, stocks, mutual funds, bonds, and other retirement plans.

PROTECTION

Your financial security could be destroyed due to a variety of unexpected catastrophes. The $150,000 home that you own with your spouse could be demolished by a hurricane in a matter of seconds. Your aging parent may need the help that only a long-term health-care facility can offer. If events such as these are not budgeted in, they could wipe you and your family out of your life savings.

In other words, the more you can protect yourself and your family through appropriate property, liability, and life and health insurance—including disability income and long-term care—the better off you will be. A good planner can help with purchasing various insurance products that are good for you.

GO TO ▶
Refer to Hour 15, "Insurance," to help focus on the types of insurance you may need down the road.

TAXES, RETIREMENT, AND ESTATE PLANNING

Although financial planners are not accountants (although many have backgrounds in accounting and estate planning), they can be very helpful in developing a logical approach to reduce and defer taxes for years to come. Such a strategy can involve the use of many techniques, addressing the federal and state systems of taxation as well as the specific types of levies (income, estate, gift, etc.) involved in them.

GO TO ▶
Refer to Hour 14, "Taxes: Time to Get Clarity," for more information on your taxes.

A good financial planner will be aware of various retirement goals and estate-planning options. See Hours 9, "Retirement Plans," and 18, "Estate Planning," on retirement goals and techniques for planning your estate needs.

QUESTIONS TO ASK A FINANCIAL ADVISOR

Now you've gotten a good picture of what a good financial advisor can do to help plot out your financial timeline. But are all financial planners equally qualified to handle your money?

First, let's start with some basic questions to ask a financial advisor. In a perfect world, you will be at the place in your life where you are comfortable discussing the details of your finances, goals, lifestyle, and financial status. The financial advisor you choose should be trustworthy, resourceful, knowledgeable, and creative in mapping out the right strategies for your financial future.

The Institute of Certified Financial Planners and the International Association for Financial Planning in Atlanta, Georgia, are two groups that offer referral services. They will send you a list of consultants in your area and background information on each advisor.

But because just about anyone can call himself an investment advisor, it is important to examine more closely their varying levels of experience and coursework. Here are some definitions of the various credentials you may find in your search for an investment advisor.

- **Certified Financial Planner (CFP).** This designates a professional who should have a broad knowledge of all aspects of financial planning. Subject areas studied include securities, estate planning, insurance, and taxes. The CFP is certified by the International Board of Standards and Practices of the Institute of Certified Financial Planners, in Denver, Colorado.

- **Registered Investment Advisors.** All financial planners and investment advisors are required to be registered with the Securities and Exchange Commission. But keep in mind that because this is only a paper registration process (and not an accredited one), not all Registered Investment Advisors may have gone through the more rigorous assessments as the advisors that follow in this list.

GO TO ▶
Refer to Hour 4, "How Can I Keep Track?" for a review of taxes and finding a good CPA/accountant.

- **Chartered Financial Analysts (CFA).** CFAs earn their designation by undergoing a three-year independent study course run by the Association of Investment Management and Research in Charlottesville, Virginia. Many CFAs work for pension funds, mutual fund companies, or institutional asset management organizations.

- **Chartered Investment Counselor (CIC).** The CIC program focuses on portfolio management and is offered through the Investment Counsel Association of America in New York.

- **Certified Public Accountant (CPA).** This more familiar designation is held by those who have completed a 150-hour program and passed a CPA exam. Because your CPA is involved in tax implications of your investment decisions, he or she can be vital to your financial preparations. The American Institute of Certified Public Accountants is the national association for CPAs.

FINDING AN ADVISOR

The following questions can help indicate how well a financial planner will be able to serve your needs:

- How long have you been providing financial-planning services? (Hint: They should answer from 5 to 10 years.)
- In what area(s) of financial planning do you specialize, if any?
- What is your educational background?

    ___ College degree

    Area of study _____

    ___ Graduate degree

    Area of study _____

- Do you have any additional financial-planning education or designations?
- How often have you performed similar services in the past? Can you provide the names of clients or colleagues I may contact?
- How are you compensated for your services?
- What type of financial-planning service do you think I need based on my concerns and goals?
- On average, how long have your financial-planning clients utilized your services?
- How do you intend to help me implement my financial plan?

FINANCIAL-PLANNING ASSOCIATIONS

Because just about anybody can put out a shingle advertising himself as a financial-planning expert, the National Association of Personal Financial Advisors (NAPFA) puts out a pamphlet to assist consumers in selecting a personal financial planner.

JUST A MINUTE

The Internet can be a vast source of information about financial-planning organizations and the professionals they represent. Try surfing the National Association of Personal Financial Advisors Web site at www.napfa.org and the Institute of Certified Financial Planners Web site at www.icfp.org for quick access to this information.

Here are some of the questions the National Association of Personal Financial Advisors suggests you ask:

- What is your financial-planning education and designation?

  ___ Certified Financial Planner (CFP)

  ___ Chartered Financial Consultant (ChFC)

  ___ CPA/PFS

- What continuing education in financial planning do you pursue?

  ___ One to 14 hours of professional education each year

  ___ Fifteen to 30 hours of professional education each year

  ___ At least 30 hours of professional education each year

- Are you a member of any professional financial-planning associations?

  ___ Institute of Certified Financial Planners (ICFP)

  ___ National Association of Personal Financial Advisors

  ___ International Association for Financial Planning (IAFP)

And maybe the most important questions to ask:

- Have you ever been cited by a professional or regulatory governing body for disciplinary reasons?

  ____ Yes____ No

- Will you or an associate work with me?

  ___ Advisor___ Associate

If the answer to this last question leans more toward an associate, you will want to ask of that person many, if not all, of the preceding questions as well.

BROKERS

With all of the advertising on TV and on the Internet, you've heard the hint to "call your broker" probably many times a day. Keep in mind that a stockbroker is really a salesperson. Most investors pay for the services of their broker based on a commission on each transaction.

But what do brokers do?

Basically, brokers represent investors in the purchase and sale of stocks and bonds. Many brokerage firms have satellite office locations in lobbies of banks, office buildings, and retail stores. You have probably seen one of these offices while commuting to work, catching a train, or driving by a mall.

But also remember that since different products can carry very different commissions, the type of arrangement that is the norm in the business (i.e., the broker suggesting you buy something and getting a commission out of it if you buy or sell) can influence the recommendation your broker makes. Don't confuse a sales pitch with impartial advice. Ask questions. Consider any recommendation to buy or sell stock just as you would any other commercial solicitation.

Keep in mind that a good stockbroker proposes investments that are tailored to your goals and financial position, not what will earn him the largest commission.

JUST A MINUTE

You can get a background check on a broker by calling the National Association of Securities Dealers Public Disclosure Hotline at 1-800-289-9999. The service is available weekdays from 8 A.M. to 6 P.M. EST.

Keep in mind that securities brokers are licensed in the state where their clients reside and are registered with the National Association of Securities Dealers (NASD). Futures brokers are licensed by and registered with the National Futures Association (NFA).

TYPES OF BROKERS

These days there are two types of brokers: discount and full-service. Discount brokers buy and sell stocks and bonds at lower rates than full-service brokers. These brokers are paid a salary or small commission.

Full-service brokers give investment advice as well as buy and sell securities. They are paid on a commission basis and can offer a range of advice to the consumer. The broker's commission for buying or selling securities or commodities is based on the dollar amount of the transaction. Before you buy or sell, ask the broker what the transaction costs will be.

Keep in mind that depending on the investment, there are up-front commissions, commissions spread out for as long as you hold the product, or both. Commissions paid at the time you invest are called "up-front fees" or "loads." Commissions paid when you take your money out of the investment are called "back-end fees" or "deferred loads."

PROCEED WITH CAUTION

Although many brokers can be knowledgeable about the big-picture event of investing, they might not be up to date on the microcosm of *your* investment portfolio. So, be careful: Brokers work on a commission basis, so what may be best for them may not be best for you.

What's It Going to Cost?

Now let's take a look at how much financial planners can cost. The range can vary widely; keep in mind that not all planners are alike in what they charge.

A financial planner's income can be obtained in one of three ways:

- A **fee-only planner** will charge on an hourly or flat-rate basis; normally, the rate is negotiated ahead of time between planner and client. The planner will provide advice but will not sell certain products to the client in hope of making a commission.

- A **fee-and-commission planner** will provide advice for a fee and can earn a commission on the financial products sold to the client. Some larger companies and brokerage firms can make big bucks this way.

- A **commission-only planner** earns money from the financial products sold and does not charge a fee for advice. Armed with this knowledge up front, a client can better understand what side of the "bread" the planner's "butter" is coming from!

According to a recent study by the Eastern Michigan University National Institute for Consumer Education, a recent *Wall Street Journal* article reported that comprehensive financial-planning services from fee-only planners can range from $100 to $250 an hour or more. The minimum amount of time spent is usually 10 to 15 hours, so the total bill for planning services could range from $1,000 to nearly $4,000. Under certain conditions, however, just a couple of hours' consultation with a competent financial planner could provide an answer to a sticky financial question and be well worth the cost.

The typical computerized financial analysis program can range from $200 to $2,000 or more. The individual investor may want to consider the cost of planning as a percentage of the total amount to be invested.

It is so very important to have worked out your fee-for-hire amount with your planner before beginning to work with him or her. You don't want any surprises when your bill arrives!

ONLINE BROKER WEB ADDRESSES

Because there are so many online brokers these days, we are including several here for your use. The following listings will provide contact information, Web site addresses, what types of commissions are charged, and whether the broker uses the Internet or software to execute trades.

- **Accutrade**
  4211 South 102nd Street
  Omaha, NE 68127
  Web address: www.accutrade.com
  Web-based trading? Yes
  E-mail: Info@accutrade.com
  Toll-free number: 1-800-228-3011

- **American Express Financial Direct**
  P.O. Box 59196
  Minneapolis, MN 55459-0196
  Web address: www.americanexpress.com/direct
  Web-based trading? Yes
  Toll-free number: 1-800-658-4677

- **Bull & Bear Securities**
  11 Hanover Square
  New York, NY 10005
  Web address: www.bullandbear.com
  Web-based trading? Yes
  E-mail address: bullbear@aol.com
  Toll-free number: 1-800-262-5800

- **Charles Schwab**
  101 Montgomery Street
  San Francisco, CA 94104
  Web address: www.schwab.com
  Web-based trading? Yes: www.eschwab.com
  Toll-free number: 1-800-435-4000

- **E*Trade**
  Four Embarcadero Place
  2400 Geng Road
  Palo Alto, CA 94303
  Web address: www.etrade.com
  Web-based trading? Yes
  E-mail address: service@etrade.com
  Toll-free number: 1-800-786-2575

- **Fidelity Investments**
  161 Devonshire Street
  Boston, MA 02110
  Web address: www.fid-inv.com
  Web-based trading? No
  Toll-free number: 1-800-544-8666

- **National Discount Brokers**
  50 Broadway, 18th Floor
  New York, NY 10004
  Web address: pawws.secapl.com/ndb
  Web-based trading: Yes
  E-mail address: ndb@secapl.com
  Toll-free number: 1-800-888-3999

- **Pacific Brokerage Services**
  5757 Wilshire Boulevard, Suite 3
  Los Angeles, CA 90036
  Web address: www.tradepbs.com
  Web-based trading? Yes
  E-mail address: tradepbs@interramp.com
  Toll-free number: 1-800-421-8395

- **Quick & Reilly**
  26 Broadway
  New York, NY 10004
  Web address: www.quick-reilly.com or through CompuServe (GO QWKI)
  Web-based trading? No
  E-mail address: peter_t@ix.netcom.com
  Toll-free number: 1-800-221-5220

- **T. Rowe Price Discount Brokerage**
  100 East Pratt Avenue
  Baltimore, MD 21202
  Web address: www.troweprice.com
  Web-based trading? No
  E-mail address: info@troweprice.com
  Toll-free number: 1-800-225-7720

- **The Vanguard Group**
  Vanguard Financial Center
  Valley Forge, PA 19496-9906

Web address: www.vanguard.com
Web-based trading? No
E-mail address: vgonline@aol.com
Toll-free number: 1-800-992-8327

- **The Wall Street Discount Corporation**
  100 Wall Street
  New York, NY 10005
  Web address: www.wsdc.com
  Web-based trading? Yes
  E-mail address: info@wsdc.com
  Toll-free number: 1-800-221-7870

- **Waterhouse Securities**
  100 Wall Street
  New York, NY 10005
  Web address: www.waterhouse.com
  Web-based trading? No
  Toll-free number: 1-800-934-4430

HOUR'S UP!

Remembering what you learned in this hour—without looking back—see
if you can answer the following questions about finding a good financial
advisor:

1. True or false: A financial advisor should have a broad knowledge in all
   aspects of financial planning, including securities, estate planning,
   insurance, and taxes.

2. A CFA is …

   a. A Common Financial Analyst.

   b. A Chartered Financial Analyst.

   c. A Corporate Financial Analyst.

   d. All of the above.

3. True or false: Working through a broker, commissions paid at the time
   you invest are called "back-end fees."

4. True or false: Commissions paid when you take your money out of the
   investment are called "up-front fees" or "loads."

5. True or false: When finding a good financial advisor, it is important to discuss your financial goals, including financial inventory, cash flow, and investment protection.

6. True or false: When you are considering purchasing an investment product, you have the right to know about the company, the person selling the product, and the risks involved in buying the product, including any commissions your broker might charge.

7. True or false: When selecting a financial advisor, it is important to ask whether he or she has ever been cited by a professional or regulatory governing body for disciplinary reasons.

8. Additional questions to ask your future advisor include …
    a. How long he or she has been in the business of advising.
    b. If he or she is a member of any financial-planning associations.
    c. What is his or her educational background.
    d. All of the above.

9. When is the right time to try and find a financial advisor?
    a. When you do not have the time to consciously work on your investments
    b. When you do not think you have a complete grasp of your investment choices
    c. When you would like a second opinion
    d. All of the above

10. True or false: The typical computerized financial analysis program can range from $200 to $2,000 or more.

PART IV
Long-Term Planning

HOUR 14

Taxes: Time to Get Clarity

CHAPTER SUMMARY

LESSON PLAN:

In this chapter, you will learn about how the IRS works, how to choose an accountant who's right for you, and what to bring to that first meeting with your accountant. You'll also learn how to:

- Sort out income, deductions, and credits.
- Reduce your income tax by investing.
- Understand deductions.
- Keep records for an easy audit.

As we discussed in Hour 2, "Cleaning Up Clutter/Debt Repayment," it is very important to be clear about your tax profile. If you think you might still owe back taxes to the IRS, it is important to contact them to work out a payment schedule. They won't exactly bite your head off, but they do tend to "growl" if you never contact them! (Not to mention that you will have to pay the accruing interest that will add up over the time you neglect to reestablish contact.) As we discovered in Hour 1, "Developing Your Financial Goals," old debts don't just go away because we wish them to.

THE IRS: THE BIG BAD WOLF?

Let's begin by taking a good look at the Internal Revenue Service. Many consumers consider the IRS to be the bane of their existence. Some people ask themselves, "Why do I have to pay taxes? What good does that do?" The realistic answer to this is, of course, that by being a citizen of the United States or a legal immigrant to this country, you have agreed to pay taxes, pure and simple. The tax revenue that the government collects goes to paying for our schools, roads, and a host of other benefits that come from living in a country such as ours.

Once you become a taxpayer, the more you understand where your taxes go, the more you can become an informed voter and citizen in the democratic process.

But if you're the kind of taxpayer who likes to sit back, fold your arms, and say, "Bah, humbug!" you'll be happy to know that according to a 1992 *Forbes* Magazine article, almost all the members of Congress who sit on the tax-writing committees—the Senate Finance Committee and the House Ways and Means Committee—hire tax help every year. That means that 11 of the 12 members of the tax-writing committees don't prepare their own tax returns!

So don't feel bad if you need to hire a tax advisor when April rolls around (actually, the best advice is to start getting your tax information to your accountant early in the year). The system keeps getting more and more complicated, and for that reason it is important to seek out sharp tax people to help you.

If you currently owe taxes and do not have the money to pay them, the IRS has made it relatively easy to obtain an installment agreement. Include Form 9465 with your tax return (the IRS usually sends this to you in the mail with your return or you may ask your accountant to obtain one for you), or call the IRS at 1-800-829-1040 and use the Touch Tone system to schedule your payments. Meet each payment on time, keep all other taxes current, and this will work for you.

CHOOSING AN ACCOUNTANT

Choosing an accountant or tax preparer can be a very important decision. The most important element in getting your taxes back in order to submit to the IRS is to find a good, decent, and, most important, reasonably priced accountant. Not all accountants are out to get your money, and in the end, your accountant can sometimes help you find clarity in other realms of your life, as well. You are not admitting defeat if you must rely on your accountant.

Most consumers breathe a sigh of relief when they find a good, clear-thinking accountant who can help straighten out their financial past history and future goals. Says Anita Katzen, CPA and partner at Ellenbogen, Rubenstein, Eisdorfer and Co., LLP, Certified Public Accountants in Manhattan, "Sometimes I not only serve as a client's tax accountant, but I end up acting as a client's 'money psychologist,' as well."

Katzen explains, "You have to ask the right questions. Was money talked about openly as a child, growing up? Was it a closed topic? I find that just talking about money can sometimes be the most sensitive button to push."

But not all accountants can be so caring about their clients. There are also differences between accountants and tax preparers. The widely popular tax-preparation centers of H&R Block, for example, offer tax-preparation services for a reasonable cost. It is important to note, however, that not all of their preparers are CPAs (Certified Public Accountants). Many are highly experienced tax preparers, but some consumers have a noteable preference for having a full-fledged CPA do their tax forms. If you do get audited (a possibility, but unlikely if you've followed the guidelines set by the IRS), it is sometimes better to have a CPA with you at the audit meeting.

FINDING A GOOD ACCOUNTANT

Word of mouth works best when you're trying to find a good accountant. Ask your friends, your colleagues at work, and perhaps parents at your children's school. Who do they go to? Have they had good experiences with their accountant? Again, this can be very subjective, and experiences can vary. But asking someone you trust can be very beneficial.

If, however, you still have no luck and need to find a good accountant, a good source of information is the American Institute of Certified Public Accountants (AICPA) at 212-596-6200. They can help you find an accountant in your area. In addition, they also have a relatively new accreditation, the Certified Public Accountant/Personal Financial Specialist (or CPA/PFS), a special niche for CPAs who want to help consumers plan their personal financial goals.

ACCREDITATIONS

The PFS accreditation was recently established for CPAs who specialize in personal financial planning and is awarded exclusively to AICPA members who have demonstrated considerable experience and expertise in that area. As of this writing, the AICPA has accredited approximately 2,500 CPA/PFSs.

A CPA must meet certain accreditation requirements before becoming a CPA/PFS and must continue to meet reaccreditation requirements every three years to maintain the accreditation.

KEEP YOUR ACCOUNTANT POSTED

One additional tip: If you have a large change in income or other lifestyle change (getting married, getting divorced, inheriting a large sum of money, etc.), tell your accountant about it as soon as possible. Anita Katzen remembers an experience of one of her clients—an entertainer—who hadn't earned a large income for several years. One year he was given a contract to perform at a very high salary level. It completely changed his income bracket, and he wisely made sure Katzen, his accountant, knew of the change to get ready for the following tax year, so he would not be penalized down the road.

DOING IT YOURSELF

For those readers who are convinced that filing their own tax returns is the way to go, the path can be treacherous but doable. Recheck your backup information such as sales and expense receipts, statements from banks and/or brokers, trade slips, etc., and recheck that your entries on your tax forms are correct. Many do-it-yourselfers have kept themselves from a larger refund check than they expected by not rechecking their information.

In most states you have to pay state income tax. The seven states that do not have a state income tax are Alaska, Florida, Nevada, South Dakota, Texas, Washington, and Wyoming. Florida does have an intangibles tax on the value of your investments. Again, it's best to check with the IRS about which tax would apply in your area.

Tax forms are supplied by the IRS, including the 1040, which is the most commonly used tax form. Forms can be obtained from the IRS, your local library or post office, some banks, or by calling 1-800-TAX-FORM (1-800-829-3676). The IRS also has an excellent Web site filled with updated information at www.irs.ustreas.gov. You can also get forms by fax, or check the tax booklet for the number of the form you need by calling 1-703-368-9694.

GETTING CLEAR ON YOUR INCOME

It's only after you find a good accountant or tax preparer that financial clarity can begin. Most good accountants will ask you some specific questions about income that you must answer. Think over your past year's income for a minute. How much did you actually earn during the past year? Let's get to it.

By the time you set up an appointment (most consumers do this in mid-spring, before the mandatory April 15 tax-filing deadline) you should have received a W-2 form or Form 1099 from your employer. These forms represent your income earned during the prior year.

TAXABLE INCOME

Think about where your money came from this past year. There are many categories of earned income; some of them include ...

- Wages.
- Commissions.
- Compensation for services.
- Bonuses.

In a word, earned income includes all the income and wages you get from working—even if it is not taxable.

There are two ways to get earned income:

- You work for someone who pays you.
- You work in a business you own.

Nontaxable earned income includes …

- Salary deferrals (example: 401[k] plan).
- Military combat zone pay.
- Basic housing and subsistence allowances and in-kind housing and subsistence for the U.S. Military.
- Value of meals or lodging provided by an employer for the convenience of the employer.
- Housing allowance or rental value of a parsonage for the clergy.

Excludable benefits are those provided by the employer, such as dependent care, educational benefits, adoption benefits, and salary reductions, such as under a cafeteria plan.

The following are not considered "earned" income:

- Interest.
- Dividends.
- Capital gains.
- Unemployment compensation.
- Alimony.
- Annuities.
- Royalties.
- Rent collected from owned property.
- Profits from self-employment or a partnership.
- Social Security.
- Pensions and income from other retirement plans.
- Gambling winnings.

THE EARNED INCOME TAX CREDIT—WHAT IS IT?

The earned income tax credit (ETIC) reduces the amount of tax you owe. The earned income tax credit is special credit for certain persons who work and is intended to offset some of the increases in living expenses and Social Security taxes. To claim the EITC you must meet all of the following rules:

- You must have earned income during the year.
- Your earned income and modified AGI (adjusted gross income) must each be less than ...
  - $10,030 if you have no qualifying children.
  - $26,473 if you have one qualifying child.
  - $30,095 if you have more than one qualifying child.
- Your investment income cannot be more than $2,300.
- Your filing status can be any filing status *except* married filing a separate return.
- You cannot be a qualifying child of another person. If you are filing a joint return, neither you nor your spouse can be a qualifying child of another person.
- Your qualifying child cannot be the qualifying child of another person whose modified AGI is more than yours.

Additionally, to claim the EITC, you must have a Social Security number (SSN) for you, your spouse (if filing a joint return), and your qualifying child(ren).

You cannot get the earned income tax credit if any SSN was issued solely for use in applying for or receiving federally funded benefits. Also, you cannot get the credit if, instead of a SSN, you, your spouse, or your qualifying child has ...

- An Individual Taxpayer Identification Number (ITIN), which is issued to a noncitizen who cannot get a SSN.
- An Adoption Taxpayer Identification Number (ATIN), which is issued for a child to adopting parents who cannot get a SSN for the child being adopted until the adoption is final.

QUALIFYING CHILDREN

You may be wondering exactly what a qualifying child is and how your child(ren) might qualify. Basically, a qualifying child is a child who is *all* of the following:

- Is your son, daughter, adopted child, grandchild, stepchild, or eligible foster child
- Was (at the end of the tax year) under age 19, under age 24 and a full-time student, or permanently and totally disabled at any age during the year
- Lived with you in the United States for more than half of the tax year (all of the tax year if the child is your eligible foster child)

If you have children who might be attending a college or university in the future, you might have to consider this: If my child is enrolled in a college or university, does she still have to file a tax return?

The answer: Whether she has to file a tax return depends on her filing status, age, and gross income. Assuming she is a U.S. citizen or resident alien, she must file a return if her unearned income was either more than $700 or $250 unearned and up to a total of $4,250 earned income—the applicable standard deduction.

Examples of unearned income are taxable interest, dividends, capital gains, and trust distributions. A dependent with earned income must file a return only if his income is more than his deduction amount. Examples of earned income are wages, tips, and salaries.

BACK TO FILLING OUT THE FORMS

When you get to this stage (and to be sure that your entries on your tax forms are correct), you need to compute your total income and your adjusted gross income (AGI), which is the number you will use most often while calculating itemized deductions. The AGI is calculated by deducting "above-the-line" expenses from your income. Some of the above-the-line expenses can include:

- Deductible IRA contributions
- Medical savings account deductions
- Moving expenses
- Half of your self-employment tax
- Your self-employed health insurance deduction
- Contributions to Keogh and self-employed SEP and SIMPLE plans
- Penalty paid on early withdrawal from savings accounts
- Alimony paid

GO TO ▶
Refer to Hour 9,
"Retirement Plan-
ning," for more
information on
deductible IRA
contributions.

Once the AGI has been calculated, it is up to you whether you want to take the standard deduction or your itemized deductions from Schedule A in your tax booklet. From the chart in your tax booklet, you can determine which method is in your favor.

For 1998, the standard deductions were, by category:

Single	$4,250
Married Filing Jointly	$7,100
Head of Household	$6,250
Married Filing Separately	$3,550

There is a greater standard deduction if you are 65 or older and/or blind. More specifics on standard deductions vs. itemizing will be discussed later in this hour.

REDUCING YOUR EMPLOYMENT INCOME TAX

Half the fun of dealing with the IRS is figuring out how to reduce your taxes every year—legally. There are three main ways of reducing your taxes:

- Minimize your gross annual income (GAI) by finding tax-free invest-ments in which to put your money.
- Take as many itemized deductions as allowable.
- Earn less money and fall into a lower tax bracket.

Even though the last item might seem strange, it makes sense. Imagine you are due to receive a large bonus or additional amount of ordinary income before the end of a calendar year, say, December 15. You may want to try to defer receiving that money until January 1 of the following year to keep it out of the current calendar year. This would help avoid running into a higher tax bracket.

RETIREMENT CONTRIBUTIONS

By now, many of you have heard of the terrific retirement contribution plans that many employers offer, such as 401(k)s. Using these plans are a great way to reduce your taxable employment income. And, of course, putting away savings in these plans works toward saving up a nest egg for your re-tirement.

Any money that you contribute to these employer-offered plans—or through 403(b)s, SEP IRAs, or Keoghs if you're self-employed—is deducted from your taxable income. Let's say you contribute $1,000 to your plan. Your combined federal and state tax rate is 22 percent, so you reduce your total taxes by $220.

If you contribute an additional $1,000, you reduce your taxes by another $220. The government wants you to save your money and has created some pretty nifty ways of helping you do so.

GO TO ▶
Refer to Hour 9 to find out more about IRAs and retirement planning.

401(k)s

Some people think "How can I even think of putting money into my company 401(k)? I can barely make it as it is" or "I'll just put in 3 percent of my paycheck. That's all I can afford." This can be more of a spending issue than a saving issue.

Don't put the minimum into your 401(k). Don't think that scraping a "little off the top" to put away for a rainy day will help you down the road of retirement. Put in the maximum allowed by your company.

Your company may match a percentage of whatever you decide to save out of your paycheck and funnel to your 401(k). You shouldn't pass up this benefit! By putting more into your 401(k) plan, you end up paying less taxes over the year, so it will cost you less than you think. If it means that you will have slightly less in your take-home paycheck, so be it. With a little planning and looking at your budget, you will eventually find a way to live with less so that you can eventually have more—much more—down the road.

Some employers do not offer this option of saving money through a retirement plan. If this is the case where you work, try to lobby for a retirement plan with the powers that be at your company. As we head into the next millennium, more and more employers are realizing what an incentive this savings opportunity can be for their employees and potential employees.

IRAs

IRAs may or may not be deductible, depending on whether you've chosen a traditional IRA or the newer Roth IRA (see Hour 9 for more information on IRAs). Depending on the plan, however, you may have to pay taxes when you withdraw money from your IRA. This isn't necessarily bad, since your income level during retirement may be less than it is now.

INVESTING IN TAX-FREE MONEY-MARKET FUNDS

GO TO ▶
Refer to Hour 8, "Bonds," for more information on bonds.

Some consumers fall in a high enough tax bracket that it's beneficial to consider investing in tax-free investments. Tax-free investments yield less than comparable investments that produce taxable earnings. But because of the large difference in taxes, the earnings from tax-free investments can end up being greater than what is left from taxable investments.

Tax-free money-market funds can be a better alternative to bank savings accounts that pay interest, which is subject to taxation. Likewise, tax-free bonds are longer-term investments that pay tax-free interest.

SELECTING OTHER TAX-FRIENDLY INVESTMENTS

It's a common mistake: focusing on past performance and rate of return, say, in a mutual fund, rather than zeroing in on the amount that you will actually get to keep. Choosing an investment with a reportedly high rate of return without considering tax consequences can be a big mistake.

MUTUAL FUNDS

GO TO ▶
Refer to Hour 7, "Mutual Funds," to find out more about mutual fund investing.

Mutual funds are an excellent example of an investment with a possible taxable consequence. Your broker may have urged you to begin investing in a mutual fund with, say, a 15 percent rate of return, which is a really good rate. What you may not have taken into account was the fact that the mutual fund could be taxed at the end of the year on dividends earned. You're only taxed on the gain when you sell.

So, in the end, your 15 percent fund really only yields 10 percent, whereas a more tax-friendly fund could bring in more *after taxes*.

It's important to check with both your broker and, if you still have questions, your accountant to find out the final yield of your investment.

JUST A MINUTE

If you hold on to a mutual fund for 10 years, add the dividends you reinvested to the base to determine your gain. You were taxed each prior year on the increases contributed by dividends.

REAL ESTATE

Because the government has set up ways to offer deductions for mortgage interest and property taxes, real estate can sometimes be a great investment. The IRS also allows depreciation on rental property in order to reduce your taxable income.

Keep in mind, though, if your rental property shows a loss for the year, you might not be able to take this loss on your tax return. If your adjusted gross income is less than $100,000, you are allowed to deduct up to $25,000 a year of your losses on operating rental real estate.

GO TO ▶
Refer to Hour 16, "Buying a Home," for more information on real estate/home buying.

Check with your accountant if you make more than $100,000 per year, because you start to lose these rental write-offs after that point. At an income of $150,000 or above, you cannot deduct rental real estate losses from your other income. These losses are recaptured when you sell the property.

QUARTERLY VS. YEARLY TAX PAYMENTS

You might think that the April 15 deadline for filing your tax return each year means that's the day taxes are due. Not true! April 15 is when the tax *return* is due. Many people fall into categories that would recommend filing taxes on a quarterly basis rather than an annual basis. The rule of thumb is that anyone who has money coming in (that would result in $1,000 or more in taxes) and does not have taxes taken out by their employer should pay quarterly estimated taxes. Otherwise they may end up paying interest and penalties.

A majority of people already have their taxes taken out by their employer. If you receive dividends, interest, capital gains, and other income, you should be paying estimated taxes.

According to CPA Anita Katzen, estimated taxes for the current year are often based on the actual taxes from the previous year, less the withholdings. For example, if you paid $16,000 in taxes last year, or $4,000 per quarter, and then you suddenly started making an extra $100,000 per year, you could still pay just the $4,000 per quarter in estimated taxes. You are protected from penalties by equaling or exceeding 100 percent of last year's taxes, but 90 percent of the current year's taxes are due by April 15 to avoid penalties. The payment must be 105 percent of prior year tax, or 90 percent of current year, if the income is over $150,000. This percentage will change each year until 2003.

Some consumers begin savings accounts to keep track of monies designated for their quarterly tax payments. Double-check with both your accountant and financial planner to see what is the best choice for you—and which method would yield the most in investment results.

If you are keeping a calendar with the requisite dates, keep in mind that quarterly estimated taxes are paid for the period ending March 31, with the tax payment due April 15; May 31, with the tax payment due June 15; August 31, with the tax payment due September 15; and December 31 with the tax payment due January 15.

When people forget to pay their quarterly taxes and save all their income taxes for the following April 15, they are usually surprised to find that they have incurred penalties for not paying on time.

ITEMIZING VS. STANDARD DEDUCTIONS

One of the more confusing sides of filling out yearly tax forms is the decision whether to choose the standard deduction or to itemize your expenses for the previous year. Many people elect to go with the standard deduction, since it requires no calculations or detailed work. If you are not earning a high income, rent your house or apartment, and lack unusually large expenses such as medical bills, state taxes and contributions, or loss due to theft, then the standard deduction is probably for you.

"Itemizing" is listing on the Schedule A of Form 1040 of all amounts you paid during the year for certain items such as medical and dental care, state and local income taxes, real estate taxes, home mortgage interest, and gifts to charity. For nonreimbursable business expenses, use Form 2106.

When you complete your spending list, you total the amount spent and compare the total with your standard deduction. The larger of the two deductions, standard or itemized, will be the deduction to choose, since it will lower the amount of federal income tax you owe. Keep in mind also that the deduction doesn't exactly lower the tax you owe—it lowers the income on which the tax is computed. It seems picky, but sometimes the income is low enough already that the deduction doesn't change the amount of tax.

GO TO ▶
Refer to Hour 4, "How Can I Keep Track?" for more on keeping track by using tax-oriented software.

Definitely verify with your accountant which type of deduction is right for you. There are a number of resources available to explain in detail what you can and cannot deduct on Schedule A, including IRS instructions, guide books, and software programs. TurboTax Software and Quicken, made by Intuit, are both recommended software programs. Both can help in organizing the structure of your expenses throughout the year.

SOME STRAIGHTFORWARD ITEMIZED DEDUCTIONS

Here are some items you may be able to deduct:

- State and local income taxes
- Property taxes
- Housing costs
- Donations to charities

Donations to charities, including donations of clothes, furniture, and household items to most churches, synagogues, educational organizations, and organizations such as Goodwill or the Salvation Army can be deducted. Check with the organization to make sure it is considered a "qualified tax-exempt organization" by the IRS, and be sure to get a receipt from the donation center once you have given over your items.

JUST A MINUTE

Keep in mind that any charitable contribution of cash—$250 or more—needs a receipt. Donated property of $5,000 or more needs an independent appraisal and Form 8283 signed by the organization.

TRICKIER ITEMIZED DEDUCTIONS

For items that fall under the miscellaneous heading, a good resource for information is available by calling 1-800-TAX-FORM (1-800-829-3676) and asking for Miscellaneous Deductions, Publication 529.

These miscellaneous deductions can include:

- Work-related home computers, cellular phones, and other equipment
- Job-search expenses
- Work-related educational expenses that gain you skills to improve your current profession, but not a new one
- Business travel and entertainment expenses
- Tax-preparation fees

Though the following deductions are not miscellaneous, they can be tricky to itemize:

- Medical expenses (You can deduct out-of-pocket medical and dental expenses that are greater than 7.5 percent of your adjusted gross income. Call 1-800-TAX-FORM [1-800-829-3676] for more info.)
- Losses due to theft and disaster greater than $100 and 10 percent of your AGI

EXTENSIONS

Yes, extensions are available if you do not get your forms in on time. But even though you can get a six-month extension of time to file, the taxes are still due—you're just asking for a delay in filing the return.

Unfortunately, as with debt repayment, some people think that just because they have filed an "extension" means that they don't have to pay any more attention to their taxes for the time being. Out of sight, out of mind, right? Wrong! Your taxes due are going to start accruing more penalties until your tax return is completely taken care of.

TIME SAVER

The IRS encourages consumers to file their tax returns through the Internet, cutting down on work and time. Electronically filed returns are up by 20 percent since 1997—but since mistakes can still be made, double-check your math before filing!

WHAT HAPPENS IF YOU GET AUDITED

It's safe to say that most people would rather have a root canal than get audited. It doesn't have to be that way. Upon first receiving word of an audit, many people panic, cursing the system—and maybe even their accountant—for getting them in this position.

The IRS frequently selects various random tax reports to audit to find areas of the tax return that tend to be difficult for people to fill out. Nearly 20 percent of audited returns are left unchanged by the audit. Sometimes money can actually be due back to the consumer after the audit!

You want to be sure to have everything ready for your tax audit when you sit down with the auditor (forms, receipts, returns, and so on). The IRS will inform you which sections of your return they will want to look at, so it's best to have these areas ready to go, including your list of expenses. The easier you make the audit for the auditor, the better things will turn out for you!

There are two schools of thought about whether or not to have your tax advisor with you when you meet with the IRS. On one hand, if you prepared the forms yourself and are fairly confident that you can answer any and all of the IRS's questions confidently, it's fine not to have your advisor with you. On the other hand, if you are unsure about any aspect of the IRS's audit letter and feel you need help, then it's time to bring in your tax preparer, CPA, or advisor.

If you used a tax preparer for your return, you should definitely bring the pre-parer with you to an audit. Problems with the return may be a preparer's errors and the preparer will be liable for penalties resulting from a change in the tax. Even if you prepared your return yourself, it is always wise to bring a tax pro with you.

Taking your advisor with you may cost a few bucks up front, but your advisor may be able to answer the auditor's questions easier than you, possibly saving you many bucks down the road. Go through your return with your tax advisor ahead of time so she can refresh her memory about its scope and what exactly the IRS wants to go over. This will save time at the actual audit.

Definitely *do not* ignore your audit request letter. Make a note of when the IRS wants to meet with you. Remember: It is not like an overdue notice for any other bill! You do not want to get on the IRS's bad side.

FURTHER TAX QUESTIONS

The IRS's Web site (www.irs.ustreas.gov) has an excellent FAQ section with frequently asked questions from consumers across the country. Following are a few questions to give you a sense of the scope of the site.

Medical Expenses

Q: My father is in a nursing home and I pay the entire cost. Can I deduct this on my tax return?

A: You may deduct qualified medical expenses you pay for yourself, your spouse, and your dependents, including a person you claim as a depen-dent under a Multiple Support Agreement. You can also deduct medical expenses you paid for someone who would have qualified as your de-pendent except that the person did not meet the gross income or joint return test.

Nursing-home expenses are allowable as medical expenses in certain instances. If you, your spouse, or your dependent is in a nursing home or home for the aged, and the primary reason for being there is for medical care, the entire cost, including meals and lodging, is a medical expense. If the individual is in the home mainly for personal reasons, then only the cost of the actual medical care is a medical expense, and the cost of the meals and lodging is not deductible.

Real Estate Tax

Q: I paid my mother's real estate taxes last year. Can I deduct this on my tax return?

A: Generally, you can deduct only taxes that are imposed on you.

Mortgage

Q: I refinanced my home last year and paid points. Are they all deductible this year?

A: No. Points paid solely to refinance your home mortgage cannot be deducted in the year paid. Instead, they must be deducted over the life of the loan.

Student Loans

Q: Can I take a deduction for the interest I paid on my student loan?

A: Beginning January 1, 1998, taxpayers who have taken loans to pay the cost of attending an eligible educational institution for themselves, their spouse, or their dependent generally may subtract from income the interest they pay on these student loans.

Again, the IRS's Web site is definitely worth a visit because it is filled with much good information, and a variety of questions can be answered electronically.

HOUR'S UP!

As a quiz on your newfound knowledge of taxes, try to answer the following questions without referring back to the chapter:

1. True or false: *Earned income* can contain some or all of the following categories: wages, commissions, compensation for services, bonuses.

2. A CPA/PFS is …

    a. An accountant with a Bachelors Degree.

    b. A Certified Public Accountant with special training and accreditation in personal-finance planning.

    c. A junior accountant.

3. If you have a major change or increase in income, you should …

   a. Tell your accountant as soon as possible.

   b. Tell your spouse.

   c. Feel good about yourself.

   d. All of the above.

4. The term "AGI" is a short form for …

   a. A Good Income.

   b. Adjusted Gross Income.

   c. A Giant Increase in Income.

5. True or false: There are two ways to get earned income:

   a. You work for someone who pays you.

   b. You work in a business you own.

6. True or false: Points paid solely to refinance your home mortgage cannot be deducted in the year paid. Instead, they must be deducted over the life of the loan.

7. True or false: The earned income tax credit actually increases the amount of tax you owe.

8. A qualifying child is a child who …

   a. Is your son, daughter, adopted child, grandchild, stepchild, or eligible foster child.

   b. Was (at the end of the tax year) under age 19 or under age 24 and a full-time student, or permanently and totally disabled at any age during the year.

   c. Lived with you in the United States for more than half of the tax year (all of the tax year if the child is your eligible foster child).

   d. All of the above.

9. True or false: If you are chosen by the IRS to be audited, it is best to have everything ready to show the auditor, including any adding machine tape of expenses, income, and other financial data you have gathered.

10. True or false: The IRS encourages consumers to file their tax forms electronically over the Internet to speed up the filing process.

Quiz

HOUR 15

Insurance

CHAPTER SUMMARY

LESSON PLAN:

In this chapter you will learn about the five main types of insurance (life, homeowner's, auto, health, and disability) and what to look for when researching the right policies for you. You'll also learn how to:

- Tell the difference between term, whole-life, and variable universal insurance.
- Best insure your home, valuables, and car.
- Decide which health insurance plan is best for you.

Let's face it: Insurance isn't exactly the *sexiest* of financial topics. As financial planning goes, life insurance lacks the glamour and the sizzle of most other investments you might make. Most people at a cocktail party will talk about stocks and the Standard & Poor's Index Fund before discussing their term life insurance policies stashed safely at home in their desk drawer.

But even though mutual funds, stocks, and bonds are the products that excite us, it's important to remember that almost nothing out there can bring in the return of a solid life insurance policy. You are essentially spending a few cents today to buy more than a few dollars for tomorrow's life crises.

A person can decide to buy insurance for a variety of reasons. A parent wants to provide for his or her loved ones. You might want to protect yourself from liability. Mortgage companies also take out their own brand of insurance in case of loan default.

When you consider how many times over your original insurance investment may be returned, it's hard to think of a mutual fund, stock, or bond that achieves as great a rate of return as the life insurance policy.

However, there are also numerous pitfalls to avoid when selecting the right insurance product for you, which we will explore later in the hour.

Your insurance choices should be the foundation for which you plan other investments and other parts of your life. Overall, there are five significant forms of insurance coverage to consider:

- Life insurance
- Health insurance
- Auto insurance
- Homeowner's insurance
- Disability coverage

Of course, there are all sorts of tangential forms of insurance (riders) that you may occasionally need, but these five categories will give you your most firm foundation.

JUST A MINUTE

Don't become a sucker for buying a lot of additional insurance for every little thing you can think of. Be sure to think carefully through the types of insurance you really need before taking the plunge.

RAISING THE BARN

Years ago, people as a community would get together to build a home for a newlywed couple or to build a barn (a barn raising). Or if there were, say, a fire, people would help get together to rebuild the lost structure. The people in the community lent materials and physical capital to help someone who had a personal tragedy or misfortune.

We don't have barn raising these days (unless you live on an Amish farm, perhaps!). Instead, we have created another way of essentially doing the same thing as the barn raising: insurance.

By buying insurance policies for their homes, cars, and their own lives (to be able to care for their families in case of their untimely death or disability), consumers essentially help each other by reassigning the risk to an insurance company, which then absorbs the cost of misfortunes that befall others.

Currently, there are thousands of types of insurance options covering everything from your life to your antique Barbie collection. Even though it takes time to sift through all the different company information and brochures, it's important not to just buy from the first broker who comes along. Doing some research will go a long way.

LIFE INSURANCE

What are the main reasons, then, for buying life insurance?

The main reason is to cover the cost of what a person would have earned over the course of his or her lifetime in case that earning power is taken away by death. Typically, people begin thinking about buying life insurance when they get married and have children.

While you're young, the cost of insurance is more reasonable. The older you get, the more expensive your insurance can become due to your health and other issues. It's best to start early thinking about what kind of insurance is right for you.

INCOME REPLACEMENT

The general rule for "How much insurance do I need?" falls normally between 5 and 10 times your annual income. So if you're making $50,000 a year, you should have at least a $500,000 policy. For example, a husband makes $50,000 a year for the next 10 years. His earning potential will equal the $500,000 of possible income over 10 years. If he has a wife and two kids and he passes away, where will they get the income to live on over the next 10 years?

If the wife were to receive the proceeds of a $500,000 life insurance policy should the husband pass away suddenly, and together they had had a mortgage on a $250,000 home, she could pay off the mortgage with the proceeds of the life insurance policy. She could continue to raise the kids. And she could still set up an education fund (especially if the kids are 5 to 10 years old) for their children to use to go to college 10 or 15 years later.

If the husband was making $50,000 a year, the resulting $500,000 from his policy could also then be invested at a 10 percent return, taking the place of his income. The wife doesn't have to touch the principal at $500,000. It's replacing his salary; it's enough to keep her going. The policy would be in an account for a foundation to protect future finances.

TERM VS. WHOLE-LIFE VS. VARIABLE UNIVERSAL

Term insurance is insurance you buy to cover a specific term, say 1, 2, 5, 10, or 20 years. Term life insurance covers you for a certain period of time—a term of one or more years. The death benefit will only be paid if you die within the term covered by the policy. Term insurance also offers coverage without the savings and investment features you'll find in whole- or universal-life coverage. Term insurance gets increasingly more expensive as you get older.

Premiums are generally lower for term insurance, allowing you to buy higher levels of coverage. Unlike other types of life insurance, you can drop coverage without penalty. If you choose to renew your term insurance at the end of the term or purchase a new term policy, however, premiums can increase dramatically.

IT'S LIKE "RENTING" YOUR INSURANCE

Term insurance can also be likened to "renting" a home. When you "rent," it's for a specific length of time: 1 year, 2 years, 5 years, maybe even 10 years. Term insurance follows the same concept: By buying term insurance, you are essentially renting the insurance. You have a locked-in rate for the length of time you have the policy.

But what usually happens when the lease is up? The landlord usually raises the rent. It's the same idea with term insurance. Your policy may and probably will change upon its next installation. Generally speaking, if you're looking for coverage for a short period of time, term life makes the most sense.

If you are looking to have a policy for the rest of your life or have certain investment goals that you want to accomplish, permanent insurance is a better fit.

TERM LIFE EXAMPLE

The normal term life coverage a person gets is a 20-year term. You choose either a 10-year or 20-year level term, for example, paying a level premium of $35 a month, for $100,000 worth of coverage. So for $35 a month, you're protecting yourself for $100,000 in case of your demise.

Let's say you buy a 10-year term insurance policy. After 10 years the term is up. If you renew your policy, you can bet on your rates going up. Since the rates are based on your age, they, too, go up. Let's say you're 45 years old now. You're nearer to the latter part of your life, and your rates will reflect that.

Obviously, rates vary due to the age, weight, height, smoking or nonsmoking, and so forth, of the policy holder. The healthier person is probably going to live longer and will be less of a risk; therefore, the insurance company is going to reward him with the more reasonable premium.

WHOLE-LIFE INSURANCE

Permanent or "whole-life" insurance covers you as long as you pay your premiums. The premiums are usually level, or increase at scheduled intervals, and do not increase dramatically in later years.

There are two types of permanent insurance: traditional, or "classic," and variable. Both types offer cash values and a guaranteed death benefit. However, traditional whole-life policies offer cash values that are a combination of guaranteed and nonguaranteed elements. The nonguaranteed elements usually include any dividends earned.

Because you bear the investment risk, variable universal life is considered a "security," subject to federal securities laws and protections, and is sold by prospectus.

PROCEED WITH CAUTION

Definitely read any prospectus carefully before you purchase a variable life insurance policy. With the various investment shifts involved with variable life, any loss of revenue could wind up being your responsibility.

Similar to yearly renewable term and convertible term, whole-life policies stretch the cost of insurance out over a longer period of time in order to level out the otherwise increasing cost of insurance. In this case, however, it is spread not over a few years but over your entire life. Your excess premium dollars are invested in the insurance company's general portfolio. Because you aren't personally managing that investment, your selection of an insurance company is vitally important.

With this type of policy, however, the inflexibility of premium payments could become a burden if your expenses increase or if you lose your job.

JUST A MINUTE

Keep in mind that all "cash value" insurance policies—those that result in your money being put into an investment or savings plan, like whole, universal, variable, etc.—are aggressively pushed by insurance salespeople because of the high commissions they earn from them. In many cases, a simple term plan may save money over a cash value plan in the long run.

UNIVERSAL LIFE

The universal life option offers greater flexibility than whole or term life. After your initial payment, you can reduce or increase the amount of your death benefit (most likely you will have to provide medical proof that you are still in good health). Also, after your initial payment, you can pay premiums any time in almost any amount within the policy's required minimums and maximums.

You will need to actively manage these policies to maintain sufficient funding, because the insurance company can increase charges (like mortality and expenses). Plus, part of your premium is invested by your insurance company, so you'll need to be careful when choosing a company.

JUST A MINUTE

Dividends can be derived from a return on investments that is higher than expected from your insurance company. They can also be derived from lower operating costs than anticipated at the beginning of the year.

VARIABLE LIFE

There are both universal and whole-life versions of variable life insurance. Variable life provides death benefits and cash values that fluctuate with the performance of the insurance company's portfolio of investments (you'll receive a prospectus along with your policy). The cash value is not guaranteed, but you get to choose where your premium dollars go among the variety of investments in the portfolio. Thus, while there is no guaranteed cash value, you have control over your money and can invest it according to your own tolerance for risk.

Variable universal life insurance is similar to buying a home versus renting a home. With variable life, the landlord isn't going to raise the rent on you, per se. You own it—as long as you keep paying the coupon to the bank or whomever owns the mortgage on it.

Whole-life generally will have a fixed or guaranteed return. Term insurance may cost $30 a month, while whole-life might cost $55 or $65 a month. A portion of that would be paid into the term to buy the insurance, and the rest of it would be invested. The company could invest it—for example, in CDs or fixed rate—and give you 4 percent as a dividend. It's a guaranteed rate fixed by the insurance company.

The variable insurance products will be put at the mercy of the market, but according to Roy Nazaroff, an insurance agent at one of the nation's largest insurance firms, "It's not like the money will be put into AOL or Yahoo! and let ride; it will be put into mutual funds. But, as there are hundreds of mutual funds to choose from, it's important to keep up with your specific policies."

Says Nazaroff, "Variable insurance is a savings plan, but people have misinterpreted it and insurance companies have sold it incorrectly in the past. Most of the time (and you have to be careful here), people get mixed up with [the question], is it insurance or an investment? We can't sell it as an investment, because it's not. It's insurance. But there's a savings side to it, a dividend that could be compounded.

For instance, you could throw in $100 the first year, and then $100 the second year. You would end up with, say, $220 with interest, tax-deferred that would grow. The next year, you add another $100, so you're up to $370, perhaps. And on it goes. It adds to the death benefit. You can borrow off of it, you can withdraw it. There are certain things you can do from an IRS standpoint that you can do without jeopardizing your insurance side of it."

JUST A MINUTE

Permanent insurance (traditional or variable) has the lowest degree of insurability risk because coverage can last for your whole life without you having to reapply (as long as you pay premiums when due). Buying insurance when you're young and healthy can lock in lower premiums for life.

THE RATINGS SYSTEM

Because life insurance policies are now available from hundreds of insurance companies in the United States, it's important to understand the financial strength of the companies behind the products. Essentially, before buying, you need to be sure the insurer is financially sound.

It's important to be sure that whichever company you choose will be in business when the time comes to redeem your policy. A ratings system was put in place to rate the solvency of various companies. Look for the best ratings of AAA, AA, or A++ when researching your insurance companies.

You could check with A.M. Best (908-439-2200; www.ambest.com), Duff & Phelps (312-368-3157; www.dcrco.com), Moody's Investors Service (212-553-0377; www.moodys.com), Standard & Poor's (212-438-2000; www.standardandpoors.com/ratings), or Weiss Group (800-289-9222).

Insure.com also carries company ratings from Standard & Poor's and Duff & Phelps to help you monitor the financial strength of individual insurers.

This is especially important when you're buying life insurance, because policies will probably pay out many years from now, maybe even decades from now. Therefore, you'll want to know whether the company you're buying from will be solvent down the road.

Is Online Insurance for You?

As with everything else in the 1990s, the explosion of online insurance companies with their own Web sites has caused insurance agents to sit up and take notice. According to one insurance agent, everyday consumers are definitely shopping around in very conscious ways.

"Years ago, you'd have people come in and say, 'Here's my money: buy me something,'" according to one agent. "People are becoming much more educated with the products, and the products are becoming much more competitive."

A recent *Business Week* article on online investing confirms this. Tracing the online research of a customer, a 45-year-old man in good health who wanted a 20-year, $1 million term policy with level premiums would have cost more than $1,800 a year, according to Moody's Investors Service. Today, with a bit of online research, that annual premium could be as little as $964.

TIME SAVER

 Try these online sites for insurance quotes and competitive bids: www. lifeinsurance.net, www.insurance.com, www.autoinsure.com, and www. homefair.com.

But be wary of just surfing and shopping the Web. Even if the online world has leveled the playing field by offering more competitive rates, the National Association of Insurance Commissioners has approved regulations requiring insurers to raise the reserves they set aside to cover claims. This, in turn, may jack up premiums and limit rate guarantees, which will most probably take effect by January 1, 2000.

JUST A MINUTE

Keep in mind that buying insurance online where companies may just list a 1-800 number may not be right for everyone. Because it can be an impersonal process, if you don't know exactly what you need, the person on the other end of the phone may not know either, and you may end up with a policy that is wrong for you.

Even though some people prefer to shop on the Web, buying their books or antiques that way, buying insurance may be a bit different. You may need someone more than an online representative to discuss what types of insurance you have in order to make changes to your policy. You may want a local contact—someone who can "hold your hand" through the process. The best insurance agents are the ones who can review what is truly the best insurance for you, based on your budget and your financial goals.

PROCEED WITH CAUTION

 To save money on excess premiums, some people choose to stop buying life insurance entirely once their kids are out of college and they are on their own. It's best to check with your financial advisor on this option to be sure your needs are appropriately covered.

HOMEOWNER'S INSURANCE

After life insurance, the most common need for consumers is to be sure they have enough insurance to cover their house in case of fire, hurricane, or other catastrophes. As you can understand, there are many variations on this theme, which we will explore in this section.

Factors can include the age of the home, its condition, its location, and whether or not you, as the homeowner, have kept appropriate safety requirements up to code. Obviously, the insurance coverage for a summer house on a beach that has seen recent tidal wave disaster will probably mean a higher rate than an inland home that hasn't ever seen an earthquake.

For the homeowner with a mortgage, the bank will require you to have homeowner's insurance to protect what is basically its asset during the life of the mortgage. In the case of fire, for instance, the bank wants to see that its asset is covered.

Homeowner's insurance covers the value of your home, if in case of catastrophe you have to rebuild from the ground up. For example, say you live in a factory town and have a $100,000 home. Because of lowering real estate costs you may only be able to sell the house for $50,000; but to replace this building after a catastrophe, this home—the bricks, mortar, and so on—would cost $100,000.

You would need to take out a similarly valued policy. The bank wants to be sure an insurance policy is taken out for the same amount as the mortgage.

Generally, policies also cover the land the house sits on and can include other structures such as garages, storage barns, and so on, that are not attached to the house.

One smart consumer, Lou, owns a split-level house valued at $175,000. Should his house be destroyed, it would cost him at least $140,000 in replacement costs to rebuild. So he insures his house for the complete $175,000. If your home needs to be rebuilt, most homeowner's policies will give you some money to pay for living offsite. Knowing this, Lou makes sure his policy would protect him and his family in case they have to live offsite for six months while their home is being rebuilt.

Homeowner's insurance should also include liability. This protects you, for example, in the case that a visiting child, swimming in your pool in the backyard, suddenly does a back-flip and hits his head on the diving board, suffering a catastrophic injury. You want to be protected from any legal liability if the family of the child decides to sue.

What about all of your personal belongings, or as comedian George Carlin puts it, your personal "stuff"? Most homeowner's policies cover these, usually up to 50 percent since most items—even new ones—depreciate over time. If something is included in your homeowner's policy, you are given a value on it, known as its *actual cash value*. You may also choose a policy giving you full replacement value of the item as though you were buying it brand new.

In Lou's case, he has nearly $100,000 worth of items such as electronics, computers, televisions, furniture, etc. in his home. He double-checked to make sure these items are covered in case of loss or theft by his homeowner's policy.

JUST A MINUTE

Take a day and videotape all of the valuables in your home you want to insure. Make a handwritten list as well. Take a copy of both the videotape and list and deposit them in your safety deposit box. That way, in case of emergency, you will have a record of what you really own.

PRIVATE MORTGAGE INSURANCE (PMI)

Private mortgage insurance (PMI) is insurance that some lenders may require to cover the lender in case you default on your mortgage payments. PMI is essentially coverage guaranteeing that the full cost of the loan will be paid.

If you make a down payment of 10 to 20 percent, you should not have to buy this insurance; it is more for the consumer who can only put down the initial 5 percent.

For example, say you are interested in buying a $200,000 house and take out a mortgage to cover it. But if you are only able to put down 5 percent on a $200,000 home, the bank, in the end, is lending you $190,000. Who has the greatest exposure to risk? The bank does, putting up the $190,000. PMI covers the lender in such cases.

If you're putting up more up front, say $50,000 toward the $200,000 home, the lender will be more comfortable in loaning you the money, and you will not have to take out a PMI policy.

RENTER'S INSURANCE

Because it protects the contents of the home, renter's insurance is similar to homeowner's insurance. In case of a burglary or a fire, the landlord of a property might have the insurance to cover repairs to the structure, but he may not have enough to cover the contents.

What happens if you have your silver collection or your antique penny collection in your rented apartment and it goes up in flames? It's best to have renter's insurance in advance. Again, you can usually choose between replacement cost coverage (covering items in full) and cash value coverage, which allows for depreciation.

AUTOMOBILE INSURANCE

Automobile insurance is required by state law in most states. But as with all insurance there are variations on this theme. What's good in Pennsylvania is not always the same as in New York or Florida. New Jersey has higher rates than New York, for example, which could be due to accidents, losses, and theft. Certain things are mandated per state, with minimum coverages.

In general, in case of an accident the vehicle owner has to have coverage to protect himself, his car in case of damage, and possible damage to the car or the health of the other driver.

There are three types of automobile insurance coverage: collision, comprehensive, and liability. Liability covers more bases than the others. You could risk losing the cost of your car without collision insurance, but if you don't have liability you could lose your home or other assets in resulting lawsuits if you're not properly covered.

Liability is set up to protect you against bodily injury or property damage caused by a third party in an accident. Check with your state department of insurance to verify the minimal levels of liability coverage that you must purchase. If you're in a higher income bracket, you might consider umbrella liability coverage to protect you against any accident for which you could be held responsible and risk losing much of your wealth or assets.

Collision insurance pays for damage to your vehicle. The maximum amount is limited to the depreciation value of your car, which is not the same as the car's replacement cost. Comprehensive insurance pays for noncollision expenses including theft, vandalism, and natural disasters.

THE COST OF INSURANCE

Some factors that will influence the cost of your auto insurance are …

- Your age.
- Your length of driving experience as well as your driving record.
- The town where you live and park your car.
- Use of your vehicle—how far you drive to work or school and whether you use your vehicle in your work.
- The type of coverage that you purchase.

The following sections discuss some of the insurance types to consider.

BODILY INJURY LIABILITY COVERAGE

Bodily injury coverage protects you if your vehicle causes physical harm and injury to other people and they decide to sue you. Defense and legal costs are also provided at no extra charge to protect you when you are sued for covered situations.

It is difficult to determine how much coverage you may need. It is not unusual for courts to award judgments in the hundreds of thousands of dollars. You must purchase at least the state minimum limit. You should purchase as much insurance as you can afford, and certainly consider an "umbrella" policy that will provide you with additional limits for an unpredictable catastrophe.

PROPERTY DAMAGE LIABILITY COVERAGE

Property damage coverage protects you when your vehicle causes physical damage and or loss of use to other people's property. Other property could include such items as vehicles, houses, fences, etc. Defense and legal costs are also provided under this coverage to protect you when you are sued for covered claims.

Again, it is difficult to determine just how much coverage you will need. Being responsible for a "total loss" to another car or causing structural damage to a building could be quite expensive. You must purchase at least the state minimum limit, and it would be wise to carry as much insurance as you can afford. Again, you should consider an umbrella policy to provide you with additional limits for the unpredictable disaster.

PERSONAL INJURY PROTECTION COVERAGE

Many states demand mandatory personal injury protection coverage (PIP). PIP provides coverage for you, members of your household, and all passengers when injured due to an auto accident. It can also pay for medical bills, lost wages, and replacement services incurred in a covered loss situation.

MEDICAL PAYMENTS COVERAGE

Medical payments coverage can provide first-dollar medical insurance for you and your passengers who do not have health insurance coverage. This coverage can be very helpful in filling in the "gaps" in health insurance co-payment requirements, deductibles, and restrictions. Check with your agent for the per-person limits available.

Buying medical payments coverage can still make good sense even though you may purchase personal injury protection. Your agent can explain the value to you.

UNINSURED MOTORIST COVERAGE

Uninsured motorist coverage protects you when you are injured in an accident caused by someone who does not have motor vehicle insurance. Even though motor vehicle insurance is generally required in every state, some people choose to break the law and not buy coverage. Uninsured motorist coverage helps you recover loss of income, medical bills, and "pain and suffering" caused by another who has no insurance to pay your losses. You should purchase uninsured motorist coverage limits equal to your bodily injury limits.

UNDERINSURED MOTORIST COVERAGE

Underinsured motorist coverage protects you when you are injured in an accident caused by someone else who has insurance … but not enough to pay for your injury. This coverage is so similar to the uninsured motorist coverage that most states combine uninsured and underinsured motorist coverage. Massachusetts keeps these coverages separate, though. You should consider purchasing the same limits as your bodily injury and uninsured motorist coverages.

COLLISION COVERAGE

Collision coverage pays for the damage to your vehicle caused when you hit another vehicle or object or another vehicle hits your vehicle. It covers you whether you are at fault or not. If you are not at fault, you could present a claim against the "guilty party," but submitting a claim to your own insurance carrier will often be easier. This coverage is always subject to a deductible. A deductible is that amount of a loss you must pay. Deductible options vary by state.

COMPREHENSIVE COVERAGE

Comprehensive coverage pays for the damage to your vehicle caused by situations other than collision. Some "usual" comprehensive losses are flood, fire, theft, and broken glass. In some states you can purchase first-dollar (no deductible) coverage. In other states if you purchase a deductible it applies to all losses, including glass.

SUBSTITUTE TRANSPORTATION/RENTAL REIMBURSEMENT

Substitute transportation/rental reimbursement coverage pays you a certain amount per day for a certain length of time for any rental car or alternate transportation necessary when your auto is inoperable due to a covered collision or comprehensive claim. Coverage is provided for the length of time your car cannot be driven up to a maximum of 30 days. Payment is also subject to a daily limit amount.

Again, as with all insurance, it's important to do the research and discuss your needs with a reputable agent. Keep in mind, though, that an agent's fees are derived from making a sale to you of their insurance products. But the serenity that comes from knowing you are "covered" in case of an emergency is a good feeling, indeed.

HEALTH INSURANCE

Health insurance may be *the* hot-button topic of the 1990s and beyond. Even in the late 1990s, many millions of Americans remain uninsured or underinsured.

People have a well-founded uneasy feeling about health insurance. The cost of health insurance continues to rise at a steady rate. Those people with full-time jobs that provide health benefits feel anxious about keeping their jobs in order to keep up coverage for themselves and their families. Those without full-time jobs or insurance know it's a matter of "biting the bullet" when it comes to paying out big premiums on individual policies.

No matter what, it is important to have health coverage. Let's take a look at some of the methods of insuring yourself and your family in the event of a health emergency.

EMPLOYER-BASED HEALTH INSURANCE

If your employer offers health insurance, you will probably be offered one of the two most common insurance offerings: a fee-for-service plan or the managed-care option. Some companies offer a "flexible benefits" plan, or a "cafeteria" plan, which means that employees can choose among many options that fit their needs. Most companies offer some combination of health benefits, life insurance, and disability.

Picking the fee-for-service option means that you can go to any doctor you choose. Depending on the policy, you may have to pay a high annual deductible for the privilege of choosing your own physician. Once the deductible is reached, the insurance company usually will reimburse up to 80 percent of the cost.

The second option available is managed care. This coverage costs less, but offers you less flexibility in your choice of doctors. The most universal type of managed-care program is the health maintenance organization (HMO). With an HMO, you are given a list of participating doctors from which you can pick your choice of care. You usually have to go to your primary care physician to get permission to see a specialist within the HMO network.

If you are self-employed and are not covered by an employer, your choices can be more limited and expensive. Even if you believe you don't need coverage or can get along without it, don't. Any catastrophic illness or accident has the potential of wiping your savings—or those of your family—completely out.

Check with any professional organizations or unions to which you may belong. They may provide inexpensive or cheaper coverage than going it alone. Several insurers, including Oxford Health Insurance, have coverage that individuals may purchase.

LONG-TERM CARE (LTC)

According to a 1997 *Consumer Reports* study, half of all women and a third of all men who are now age 65 will spend their last years in a nursing home at a cost of $40,000 a year. Medicaid will pay the bill for those willing to first "spend down" all their assets. Not surprisingly, however, many Americans balk at forfeiting a life's savings to qualify for Medicaid and living their last years in poverty. Others want to leave something for children or grandchildren. For them, long-term-care insurance is an option.

What often happens with couples is that one of them ends up in a nursing home, and it takes every dollar of income they both have coming in just to pay those nursing home bills. Many experts agree that long-term-care insurance is an excellent way of being sure you are covered down the road when and if your life takes this turn. Relying purely on Medicare would be a mistake. Medicare will only pay 100 percent for the first 20 days of a LTC stay and will pay only if the facility is a Medicare-approved skilled nursing home.

LTC can be very expensive and is not for everyone. *Consumer Reports* advises against it for those who qualify for Medicaid or will qualify soon after entering a nursing home. Nor is it for those who can afford to set aside roughly $160,000 for their care and still have enough left over to provide for their spouse. However, for the majority of nonrich, nonpoor Americans between these income extremes, long-term-care insurance is an option worth considering.

Most LTC policies are expensive since they contain many of the following features:

- **Inflation protection.** Compounded 5 percent inflation coverage is the single most important element any policy can offer, given inflation in nursing home costs—though it may increase the price by up to 70 percent at some ages.

- **An adequate daily benefit.** Daily benefits, varying from $20 to $300 per day, will determine your premium, and it is vital to choose a benefit at least as high as the average price of nursing homes in your area.

The daily benefit for home care is typically half that for nursing-home care, but policies vary.

- **An adequate benefit period.** Because you don't know how long a nursing-home stay will last, and because lifetime coverage is extravagantly expensive, you need to play the odds with a four-year benefit.

- **An affordable elimination period.** Long-term-care policies have "elimination periods"—the first 20 to 100 days of care you must pay for yourself. The longer the period, the lower the premium—but don't let a low premium tempt you into a policy with a long elimination period, or you may end up spending everything anyway.

- **Flexible benefits triggers.** Policies that require you to fail only one or two of a long list of "activities of daily living" to trigger benefits are better, especially if the list includes bathing, the activity a disabled person is most likely to need help with.

- **Flexibility of location.** A policy should provide coverage in a variety of care settings, either a nursing home or an assisted-living facility, a term defined differently from policy to policy.

Consumers considering LTC should purchase it at age 65, or sooner if a medical condition such as diabetes could worsen and make them uninsurable. Coverage is much more expensive after age 65.

Adequate long-term-care policies are so expensive that only about 10 to 20 percent of Americans can afford them. Based on its analysis, *Consumer Reports* concludes that policies costing the average 65-year-old couple about $3,500 annually (or 13 percent of the median income for elderly couples) are out of reach for many and no substitute for a national health-care policy that covers all Americans in their old age.

DISABILITY INSURANCE

In case of an accident causing a disability to you, you need enough disability coverage to provide you with a sufficient income to live on. Depending on whether or not you have enough money saved up, it is important to buy a policy that will cover your full income in the event that you are unable to earn your regular income. Again, your company may cover some or all of your disability insurance; check with your company for more details.

You also want to select the duration of time that you want a policy to pay you benefits, which could affect the amount needed in payments. If you need to purchase disability insurance, check with several wholesale insurance dealers, including Wholesale Insurance Network (1-800-808-5810), USAA (1-800-531-8000), and Direct Insurance Services (1-800-622-3699), which could bring down the price.

If you are buying disability insurance, you may also want to join a "list billing." With list billing, you and several others who are filing for disability at the same time can be invoiced together, save several dollars in the group process.

HOUR'S UP!

As a quiz on your newfound knowledge of insurance, try to answer the following questions without looking back at the chapter:

1. True or false: The general rule of thumb for the strongest life insurance policy reflecting income replacement is between five and ten times your annual income.

2. True or false: You should always buy the most expensive policy that your agent presents to you, because the "luxury" insurance policy is always the best.

3. True or false: Because variable universal life insurance is both insurance and an investment vehicle, it puts your money at a higher risk. Therefore, it is important to check the prospectus of your insurance company before buying the policy.

4. True or false: Term insurance gets increasingly less expensive as you get older.

5. The three main types of life insurance are …
   a. Young life, old life, and mid-life.
   b. Term, whole-life, and variable universal life.
   c. Universal, umbrella, and whole.

6. True or false: Private mortgage insurance (PMI) is insurance that some lenders may require to cover the lender in case you default on your mortgage payments.

7. True or false: The five things usually considered in an automobile insurance policy are: your age, your length of driving experience, your driving record, the town where you live and park your car, and the use of your vehicle.

8. The term "PIP" refers to …

   a. Personal Insurance Policy

   b. Personal injury protection coverage providing coverage for you, members of your household, and any passengers when injured due to an auto accident.

   c. Peoples' Insurance Policy

9. True or false: Long-term-care policies have "elimination periods," which are the equivalent of the first 20 to 100 days of care that you must pay for yourself.

10. The best age to begin to buy a LTC insurance policy is …

    a. 45.

    b. 55.

    c. 65.

HOUR 16

Buying a Home

CHAPTER SUMMARY

LESSON PLAN:
In this chapter you will be exploring the ins and outs of buying real estate. You will better understand the advantages of and reasons for investing in real estate, how to figure out how much you can afford to spend, tips on finding an agent, and where to get the best deals on loans. You'll also learn how to:

- Understand the types of loans for homeowners today.
- Decide if Fannie Mae, Freddie Mac, or Ginnie Mae loans are what you need.
- Refinance your home.
- Find a mortgage broker online.

Whether you're a Rockefeller or just someone contemplating becoming a first-time homeowner, buying your first home has the potential of being one of the largest—and probably most intimidating—purchases you'll ever make. You are going to have to find a lender, i.e., a bank or institution willing to loan you possibly more money than you've ever spent in your life, and sit down with a complete stranger—a loan officer—to discuss your mortgage options.

Many have likened the paperwork of getting a mortgage with its closing costs to getting a root canal (let's hope not!). The mortgage process really doesn't have to be that bad. There are many more resources available to the consumer regarding the purchase of a new home, including more and more the use of the Internet to get rates and information.

Some families are just too afraid that they can't afford a new home and will never be approved for a loan.

Most new homeowners have noted that the overall rewards of becoming a homeowner (despite the occasional headaches!) are worth it.

REASONS TO INVEST IN REAL ESTATE

Let's take a look at some of the elements that go into making the decision whether or not buying a home is right for you at this time.

If you are like most consumers, you either own your home or you rent. (Or maybe you live free with a generous relative!) In any case, you may have to ask yourself some or all of the following questions when deciding whether or not to make the transition from renting to owning:

- Do you see yourself staying put in one location for at least three years?
- Are you ready for the responsibility of becoming a landlord—to yourself? (Meaning no landlord to call about the leaky roof! You *are* the landlord.)
- How expensive of a home can you *really* afford?
- Are you considering buying real estate as an investment or as a resident? Or both?
- Do you have a growing family and need more space in the future?
- Are you really just buying a more expensive house/car/boat to "keep up with the Joneses"?

Only you can answer the preceding questions. Normally, you can do one of two things: You can rent or you can own your apartment or home. If you are presently renting, your monthly rent check usually covers the cost of living in your present space and sometimes even utilities such as heat, water, and electricity. Your landlord takes care of maintaining the property, and you are able to take your complaints to him or her.

JUST A MINUTE

If you think about it, people invest in a variety of areas: stocks, bonds, mutual funds, futures—you name it. But investing in stocks can be a wild, roller-coaster ride. For many, owning a home can be one of the most important investments they make. With only about 40 percent of the American population owning stocks, but over 70 percent purchasing homes, many consumers are taking advantage of the many tax breaks and other advantages that come from owning a home.

EQUITY

Making rent payments helps your landlord pay his mortgage, not your own. Buying your own property helps you establish *equity,* which is really the money value of a property over any debts that can be held against it. When you make mortgage payments, you're paying the principal on your mortgage plus interest.

In essence, equity represents a way for you to save toward the future. Any money you pay toward the principle of your mortgage can later be used toward home-equity loans on your house. It also represents the amount of capital you have built up when and if you decide to sell your house later.

Equity contributes to a person's net worth, whether they sell the home or not. Borrowing against equity can be a convenient and less expensive way to finance large purchases such as a second home, remodeling or expanding a home, a car or boat, a wedding, college tuition, vacation, or medical emergencies.

DEDUCTIBLE INTEREST

Interest is both the way your lender makes money off your mortgage and the way you can lower your taxable income. Mortgage interest payments on both first and second homes can be deducted from gross income. Also deductible are certain property or real estate taxes (such as those levied by state and local government to pay for public services). Certain loan fees, points, and pre-payment penalties can all be deducted from your gross income.

Check with a tax consultant or CPA about the tax deductions available to you as you consider the purchase of a house or property.

JUST A MINUTE

If you are thinking about buying a home in a specific area, contact a local real estate broker to ask about various prices and taxes on recently sold homes in the price range you are considering.

HOW MUCH OF A HOME CAN I AFFORD?

Before you start looking at homes, you need to have some idea of what you can afford. Don't submit yourself to the heartbreak of choosing a home only to find you can't afford it. Be realistic, and buy what you can handle. You can probably sell your property later for a profit.

You should purchase a home with a value of two to three times your annual household income, depending on your savings and debts. The financing rule of thumb used by lending institutions is that the monthly cost of buying and maintaining a home should not exceed 28 percent of gross (pretax) monthly income. For example, if your and your spouse's combined monthly gross income is $4,000 ...

$4,000 \times .28 = $1,120

You can probably qualify for a monthly mortgage payment of $1,120.

Other variables will affect where the $1,120 will be spent. Only some will go toward paying off the principal. The price you pay for borrowing money is the interest.

INTEREST AND INTEREST RATES

The mortgage market can fluctuate daily in accordance with any hiccups or adjustments by the Federal Reserve. The higher the interest rate, the more you pay for the same amount of money borrowed than if the rate was lower. Higher rates mean you can afford less house.

Mortgage rates are set by FNMA, FHLMC and the major mortgage banks. They are more likely affected by changes in Treasury Bills and the cost of funds at various Savings and Loan Associations.

Lenders and borrowers alike wait with bated breath whenever Alan Greenspan, Chairman of the Federal Reserve, announces any news about interest rates. Lower rates mean you can buy more house for your money.

Even though neither Alan Greenspan nor the Fed directly affects mortgage rates, as part of the money supply, mortgage rates are affected by changes in the economy including changes in the Prime Rate, Treasury Bill Rates, Savings Rate, and other sources of funds.

REAL ESTATE CONSULTANTS

The Mortgage Bankers Association of America (MBA), a Washington, D.C.–based association that represents 3,000 organizations related to real estate financing, suggests that first-time home buyers first talk with an accredited real estate loan officer.

Often, your broker, lawyer, or a friend can refer you to a loan officer they have worked with before and feel they can recommend. Also, a phone call or trip to any bank will put you in touch with a loan officer to help you.

The MBA's officers serve as consultants, answering questions and offering help and various plans. For more information on the process of finding a real estate loan officer in your area, call the MBA at 202-861-6500.

JUST A MINUTE

You should definitely go to more than one bank when beginning your search for the best mortgage rates. Also, check out the real estate sections in the newspapers, which can be very helpful when determining the best rates. Always read the fine print in the mortgage advertisements to determine the annual percentage rate and other costs of the loan, including limits and availability.

Another person to seek out is a mortgage broker. A mortgage broker acts as a "middleman" between the consumer, who wants to purchase a home, and the bank, which lends the money for the sale. According to one veteran of the mortgage industry who has served as both broker and lender throughout his 20-year career, mortgage brokers can often be more available to answer your basic questions than bankers. "The bank lender is there to make hundreds of loans a day and may not be able to come to the phone as often as a broker," he says. "The more the broker can be of help, the more money he or she makes."

Because the mortgage broker works for more than one bank, the broker makes money by charging a fee apart from bank fees, called an "origination fee."

If you are self-employed, most banks and mortgage companies can help you as well. Irregularities in income are usually overcome by averaging income over two or more years.

JUST A MINUTE

You and your lender will be working together on your home purchase for quite some time. Do some research; be sure there will be no extra or hidden fees. Keep in mind that banks, mortgage brokers, and companies that lend mortgage money are required to disclose all fees within three days of a written application.

FANNIE MAE, GINNIE MAE, AND FREDDIE MAC

These may sound like absurd characters out of the musical *Oklahoma*, but Fannie Mae, Ginnie Mae, and Freddie Mac each represent some of the largest sources of home-mortgage funds in the United States.

Fannie Mae is the lender that "backs" the loans made to consumers through banks. It is extremely helpful to lower-income and middle-class buyers who might otherwise not be able to afford a mortgage.

More specifically, Fannie Mae buys loans made by banks and sets the terms of these loans by standardizing them. Other banks buy these loans too, as investments that bring in interest. But because the major buyer is FNMA, the banks have adopted this standard. Thus the loan size, the points, the interest, and the form are all predetermined.

Freddie Mac is a stockholder-owned corporation chartered by Congress. It helps increase the supply of mortgage funds available for lenders to offer future homeowners.

Ginnie Mae is an agency run by HUD (Department of Housing and Urban Development) backed by the Federal Housing Administration. It helps work with Veterans Administration and government loans.

TIME SAVER

There's plenty of information about Fannie Mae, Freddie Mac, and Ginnie Mae loans on the Internet. You can access them at www.fanniemae.com or www. homepath.com. Check out www.freddiemac.com for information on Freddie Mac. Also try www.ginniemae.com for updates on Ginnie Mae loans.

FINDING THE RIGHT MORTGAGE FOR YOU

Let's talk about the various types of mortgage loans.

Before there was the wide array of mortgage choices that consumers have now, new homeowners could realistically choose between *fixed-rate* and *adjustable-rate* loans (explained in the following sections). Now, the well-researched consumer can consider an additional array of mortgage possibilities. One will be right for you.

If you feel you'll probably stay in one location for a long time, then the *30-year fixed-rate mortgage* is for you, as millions of Americans across the country have found. You pay a fixed rate for the 30 years of your mortgage.

Once your loan is paid off, the house is yours outright. Essentially, this means that the amount borrowed is charged a fixed rate of interest that will not change for the life of the loan. The fixed-rate mortgage is a traditional loan for consumers who don't want to have to be concerned with changing interest rates.

The *15-year fixed-rate mortgage* has a lower interest rate but higher monthly payments.

In an *adjustable-rate mortgage* (*ARM*), the interest rate is adjusted every year, every three years, every five years, or however the ARM is set up. The lender sets the rate for the first year, and the interest may go up or down at pre-established intervals. The most popular ARM adjusts annually depending on which index the lender uses to establish the interest rate.

Some of the indexes include Treasury Bill rates (T-Bill), Savings rates (COFI), the Prime Rate (PR), London Interbank rates (LIBOR), or any agreed-upon index that can be tracked. Most of these indexes are published daily in the financial sections of newspapers.

JUST A MINUTE

Ask your loan officer which index will be used for your ARM. How has this index performed in the past? Ask if you can obtain a copy, too, so you can stay on top of the rate.

With an annually adjusted ARM, the rate adjusts on the anniversary of the loan. There will be a *margin* used to calculate the interest for your loan. The margin is the amount the lender adds to the index rate to arrive at the interest rate charged on your loan. The margin amount remains constant, but the index rate changes every year. If you know the margin amount, you can combine it with the index rate to arrive at the totally adjusted rate.

HAVING A PRE-QUALIFICATION LETTER

Getting a pre-qualification letter can be the key to a smoother home purchase. Essentially, getting a pre-qualification letter means that a lender has reviewed your financial situation and is offering to loan you the money you need to buy your house. It's a good idea to try to get a pre-qualification letter before beginning your house-hunting, because you will have a better idea of what you can afford, and it will make you a stronger buyer when you make an offer on a house.

Try quicken.com and homeadvisor.com, which offer online pre-approval and pre-qualification services. The purpose of the pre-qualification letter is to advise the borrower, and sometimes the seller and real estate agent, just how much house he can afford.

First-Time Home Buyers

Some tips you might consider if you are a first-time buyer: If you have difficulty getting a mortgage you might consider getting a parent or other relative to co-sign. Also, many first-time buyers overbid on a house because they are so excited at the prospect of owning their own home. Don't let your enthusiasm cloud your assessment of the actual property value!

There are many special programs that can make getting a first mortgage easier. Some of the better-known national programs include the following.

Federal Housing Administration (FHA)

Federal Housing Administration loans are government-insured mortgages primarily for first-time home buyers. These loans allow you to buy a home with a lower down payment and come with guidelines that allow more people to qualify. They are available from most mortgage lenders. There may be specific benefits and restrictions to FHA loans in your area; be sure to ask your mortgage lender about specifics.

Low- to moderate-income families qualify for FHA loans. FHA publishes rates, terms, and loan limits in specified areas of the country. Again, an FHA lender will have these figures.

Veterans Administration (VA)

Some loans are available to veterans of the Armed Services, which can make it possible for these veterans to buy a home with no money down. Usually those currently on active duty or in the Reserves (or their spouses) can qualify as well.

The Veterans Association issues a qualification letter to those qualified for VA financing. The letter will address the amount and dates when VA financing is available.

RURAL HOUSING AND COMMUNITY DEVELOPMENT SERVICE (RHCDS)

Rural Housing and Community Development Service provides home financing to qualified borrowers who are unable to obtain home financing elsewhere. If you are a farmer or live in a rural area, see if you can qualify through your mortgage broker.

WHO CAN LEND YOU THE MONEY?

There are many different institutions that make mortgage loans. Some of them include …

- Banks
- Savings and Loans
- Credit Unions
- Mortgage companies
- Online mortgage companies

Whatever kind of mortgage broker or lender you go to, he or she will need some basic information to start the process and to see how much of a mortgage you can afford. Some of the items you should be sure to bring to the interview are …

- Your employment income (including salary and bonuses), and any other source of income for the past two years. Your W-2 forms should do the trick. If you are self-employed, you should bring your last two tax returns and a current-year profit-and-loss statement.
- The amount of any dividend and interest income you have received during the last two years.
- The amount of any other regular income you may receive, including alimony, child support, etc.

In addition, it is important to add up your personal assets and current credit and outstanding debts. Some elements to add up regarding your loan include …

- Current balances and recent statements for any bank accounts, including both checking and savings.
- Current market value of any investments you may have such as stocks, bonds, or CDs.
- Interest in retirement funds.

GO TO ▶ Refer to Hour 2, "Cleaning Up Clutter/Debt Repayment," to see methods of listing assets.

- Face amount and cash value of any life insurance policies.
- Value of any significant pieces of personal property, including automobiles.

Be sure to also add up the balances of your current loans and debts and bring the account numbers with you. These could include any car loans, credit card balances, or other outstanding loans.

WHAT TO DO IF YOUR MORTGAGE LOAN IS REJECTED

Your worst nightmare has come true. For some reason, your mortgage application has not been approved, even after all the work you have put into it. Following are some reasons why your loan may have been denied.

PROBLEM 1: INADEQUATE FUNDS

Because lenders have to take into account your work history and financial background, the lender may have determined that you do not have enough cash to make the down payment and/or cover closing costs. Of course, it will be your job in the future to be sure to have this amount of money on hand for future loan applications.

SOLUTION

There are several ways of developing a fund to cover your down payment: You might be able to borrow (or be given a gift from a relative) funds to help cover these costs. Another solution might include getting the seller to take back a second mortgage that would reduce the down payment requirement. Some enthusiastic sellers will sometimes cover closing costs, such as the origination fees.

Perhaps, too, this is a good time to reflect on whether or not the time is right to buy a house; you could correct the inadequate funds problem by waiting to buy your home until you have saved enough to cover the down payment and closing costs.

PROBLEM 2: APPRAISED VALUE TOO LOW

According to the MBA, one factor considered by the lender is the ratio of the loan amount to the sale price or the appraised value of the property, whichever is lower. If the appraisal on the property is substantially lower than the purchase price, the loan-to-value ratio, or LTV, may be higher than the lender will or can legally approve.

If you have applied for a maximum loan amount—90 to 97 percent of the purchase price—a low appraisal may make your requested loan too large. Your alternatives in this situation will depend upon the reasons for the low valuation.

SOLUTION

With the seller, you can try to renegotiate the price down to a level more in line with the market and one that the lender would accept in order to approve your loan.

One other solution is to accept a lower loan amount. Of course, this assumes that you have sufficient funds to cover the additional down payment.

PROBLEM 3: INSUFFICIENT INCOME

Because lenders look at your ability to repay the requested loan over time, they will look at your monthly income in relation to your proposed mortgage payments and in relation to all of your monthly debt and installment loan payments. This could be a stumbling block for some applicants.

SOLUTION

Your mortgage payment should not be more than 28 percent of your monthly gross income. Your total debt should not exceed 36 percent, including mortgage payments and other installment payments. Your lender may frown on less or not enough income to cover these overall expenses.

On the other hand, if you have had a long history of paying your rent or previous mortgage on time, the lender may look favorably on your mortgage application. When filling out any application, it is important to be truthful—in this case, it could work in your favor.

PROBLEM 4: TOO MANY DEBTS

Ouch. We've seen this problem before. Too much debt owed by an applicant can prevent him from qualifying for the loan.

SOLUTION

GO TO ▶
Refer to Hour 2 for more advice on debt repayment.

Start limiting your credit card use, begin paying off some of your accounts to bring down outstanding obligations, and make some headway in limiting the number of creditors you owe.

PROBLEM 5: UNSATISFACTORY CREDIT HISTORY

As most consumers know, your credit report is like your report card, but it follows you throughout your life and is given a heck of a lot of weight. If your credit report shows frequent late charges, past-due accounts, judgments, or bankruptcy, your loan approval chances become very slim. Lenders tend to have little tolerance for bad credit. Even low loan-to-value ratios and debt ratios cannot offset an unsatisfactory credit history.

SOLUTION

You may request a free copy of your credit report if you are turned down for a loan. (Again, see Hour 2 for more information on contacting the credit bureaus.) Take a close look at your report and see if it is correct and up to date. If there are errors, it is the credit bureau's duty to correct them.

Because many lenders look for two years' clean payment history (at least) to offset past credit problems, you need to start repaying outstanding balances on time in order to reestablish a solid and acceptable payment record.

REFINANCING

Refinancing the mortgage on your home can be beneficial. Refinancing your home is basically going through the entire mortgage process again, but with new closing costs, fees, and so on. Your goal this time is achieving a better rate of payment. The question is: Should you refinance?

Financing becomes worth your while if the current interest rate on your mortgage is at least two percentage points higher than the prevailing market rate, according to the MBA. This is a generally accepted safe margin when balancing the costs of refinancing a mortgage against the savings.

You might choose to refinance a loan that is only 1.5 percentage points higher than the current rate. You may even find that you could recoup the refinancing costs in a shorter time.

Think about how long you will be staying in the house that you want to refinance. Most sources say that it takes at least three years to fully realize the savings from a lower interest rate, given the costs of refinancing.

If you are a homeowner who was lucky enough to buy when mortgage rates were low, you may have no interest in refinancing your present loan. But perhaps you bought your home when rates were high. Or perhaps you have an adjustable-rate loan and would like to obtain different terms.

According to the MBA, refinancing can be a good idea for homeowners who ...

- Want to get out of a high-interest-rate loan to take advantage of lower rates. This is a good idea only if you intend to stay in the house long enough to make the additional fees worthwhile.

- Have an adjustable-rate mortgage (ARM) and want a fixed-rate loan to have the certainty of knowing exactly what the mortgage payment will be for the life of the loan.

- Want to build up equity more quickly by converting to a loan with a shorter term.

- Want to convert to an ARM with a lower interest rate or more protective features (such as a better rate and payment caps) than the ARM they currently have.

Refinancing is also recommended to afford large purchases, tuitions, emergencies, or vacations as indicated earlier.

ADDITIONAL COSTS FOR REFINANCING

Keep in mind that new costs for refinancing can include application fees, title search and title insurance, lender's attorney's review fees, loan origination fees and discount points, appraisal fees, prepayment penalties, and other miscellaneous items. A homeowner should plan on paying an average of 3 to 6 percent of the outstanding principal in refinancing costs, plus any prepayment penalties and the costs of paying off any second mortgages that may exist.

REFINANCING SAVINGS ON A $100,000 LOAN

Let's look at the benefits of refinancing a $100,000 loan. The savings can be very beneficial.

Present Mortgage Rate (%)	Current Monthly Payment	Monthly Payment at 8%	Monthly Savings at 8%	Annual Savings at 8%
14.0	$1,185	$734	$451	$5,412
13.5	$1,145		$411	$4,932
13.0	$1,106		$372	$4,464
12.5	$1,067		$333	$3,996
12.0	$1,029		$295	$3,540
11.5	$990		$256	$3,072
11.0	$952		$218	$2,616
10.5	$915		$181	$2,172
10.0	$878		$144	$1,728
9.5	$841		$107	$1,284
9.0	$805		$71	$852

From "A Consumer's Guide to Refinancing Your Mortgage," by the Mortgage Bankers Association of America.

ONLINE MORTGAGES

With online services evolving for buying everything from groceries to books, you knew it was just a matter of time before you could also buy a house (or at least get the mortgage approval) online as well. Online mortgage services are beginning to revolutionize the home-lending industry. According to the MBA, more than 3,000 lenders now offer mortgages on the Web, up from only 60 in 1996. The trade association estimates that by the year 2003, almost one out of every four loans will originate on the Internet.

When online, you can compare different lender sites with a touch of a button, which can save both time and money. There are more choices than ever, as the number of online lenders continues to grow.

Here are some sites of interest to online buyers:

- **www.eloan.com.** E-Loan Inc., a Palo Alto, California, online mortgage-brokerage firm, offers pre-qualification and pre-approval for home-equity loans as well as first mortgages and refinancing. It also features an icon that helps you check your loan status online as well as a link that helps you compare the values of different neighborhood homes. You can also program the site to send you e-mail when a particular interest rate becomes available.

- **www.homeadvisor.msn.com.** This cool site, created by the Microsoft Corporation, has only 11 lenders featured, but it has an easy-to-use, 10-step application process and helpful worksheets. If you don't qualify for the loan, the program suggests ways to meet your goal.

- **www.hsh.com.** If you're looking for purely objective data on interest rates and terms, this is a great site for you, because it does not make loans or accept lender advertising. The site surveys 2,500 lenders across the country and updates rates daily. It was created by the financial publishing company HSH Associates of Butler, New Jersey.

- **www.keystroke.com.** Keystroke Financial Inc., a mortgage brokerage firm based in Seattle, Washington, created this site three years ago and has built partnerships with 200 lenders in that time. The application process and fees involved are explained simply and without jargon.

- **www.iown.com.** I-own is a sharp, well-put-together site with information on shopping rates, finding a home and an agent, and the ability to apply online for your mortgage. I-own has 23 lender-partners, and you can get up to 10 lenders ranked by whatever aspect of the loan matters most to you—closing costs, interest rate, or monthly payment—and get a complete breakdown of closing costs and fees. Make a mental note, though, that I-own does charge a half-point fee for processing the loan. I-own also lists all of its state mortgage-brokerage license numbers.

- **www.mortgagelocator.com.** This site pales a bit in comparison to its brethren given earlier in this list. On this site, you don't look through a list of lenders' offers; instead you type in your particulars and interested lenders contact you. There is also a chat room where you can talk with lenders and real-estate agents.

- **www.quickenmortgage.com.** On this site you are asked to answer a list of time-consuming personal questions to pre-qualify for a loan. Once you've gone through this, a list of a dozen possible loans pop up, customized for you. You can apply instantly for one that appeals to you. Intuit Lender Services Inc. of Mountain View, California, handles the loans.

But there are pitfalls to online mortgages. Some consumers may find it hard to get information they need when they're not dealing face-to-face with a human being.

Try it yourself to see if an online mortgage is the way to go for you.

HOUR'S UP!

Try these questions to get up to speed on your knowledge of home buying:

1. True or false: Buying your own property helps you establish equity, which is really the money value of a property in excess of any debts that can be held against it.

2. True or false: When you make mortgage payments, you're paying the principal on your mortgage plus interest.

3. True or false: Mortgage interest payments on both first and second homes *cannot* be deducted from gross income on your tax return.

4. Your mortgage application has been rejected. Some of the reasons could include …
   a. Unsatisfactory credit history.
   b. Insufficient income.
   c. Too many debts.
   d. All of the above.

5. True or false: Refinancing is a good idea only if you intend to stay in the house long enough to make the additional fees worthwhile.

6. The financing rule of thumb used by lending institutions is that the monthly cost of buying and maintaining a home should not exceed what percent of your gross (pretax) monthly income?
   a. 26 percent
   b. 28 percent
   c. 30 percent

7. True or false: You can actually obtain an approved mortgage and pre-qualification letter over the Internet.

8. Fannie Mae is …
   a. The bank.
   b. The lender who "backs" the loans made to consumers through banks.
   c. The consumer.

9. True or false: New costs for refinancing can include application fees, title search and title insurance, lender's attorney's review fees, loan origination fees and discount points, appraisal fees, prepayment penalties, and other miscellaneous items.

10. True or false: Higher interest rates, as dictated by the Federal Reserve, mean that you end up getting more house for less money.

HOUR 17
Buying a Car

For many consumers, there are really two big-ticket items that loom large on the pocketbook: buying a home and buying a car. If you've already bought a home, you can give yourself a big pat on the back. Buying a home can be one of the best investments you can make for yourself and your family: it *appreciates* over time. That means it slowly increases in value over time.

However, what many people don't take into account is that a car, unlike a home, does not appreciate in value— in fact it *depreciates*. That means that with each passing year of use, a car will lose value.

So, that nice new car that you bought for $23,000 could potentially be worth thousands of dollars *less* the minute you drive it off the dealer's lot. By doing your homework ahead of time you can end up saving yourself several thousand dollars in value on your new purchase.

Some examples of depreciation can be found by looking at prices of the same model used car from two, three, or more years ago. See KBB.com and other Web sites for prices of used cars.

CHAPTER SUMMARY

LESSON PLAN:

In this chapter you will explore the ins and outs of buying a car. You will learn what you need to know before you buy and also how much you can get when you trade in your old car. You'll also learn how to:

- Budget for your car costs.
- Determine if leasing or buying is right for you.
- Negotiate for the best price.

Since buying a car can be a big decision, you need to ask yourself some important questions. It sounds simplistic, but it is definitely important to think through these basic questions before deciding which car you will buy.

Before going into your first car dealership, ask yourself the following questions:

- How well does my current car suit my needs? Is it too big or too small? Do I need a new car for family reasons? Work-related reasons? Vanity reasons? All of the above? What do I like or dislike about my present car?

- What is the car's resale value? What will I make back if I decide to sell or trade in?

- Is buying or leasing a car the better decision for me?

TIME SAVER

You can look up more information on a car's resale value at www.kbb.com.

Think through these questions carefully. Many consumers become disappointed or frustrated from not paying more attention to these really basic thoughts. There is always the potential of buying a car that looks great on the lot but doesn't suit your needs very well down the road. You may end up spending a lot more on more car when less car might do.

Also, with a trade-in you may be forced to sell or trade too early, which could set you up for bigger losses. Buying a car with poor resale value could mean paying for a car for years only to sell or trade in and find that you have little or no equity—or worse yet, still owe more than it's worth.

BUDGETING FOR YOUR CAR

Most people use some sort of financing in purchasing their car. (In other words, not many people have the handy $20,000 or more that it may take to purchase a new car off the lot!) Because using financing means you will have to take out a loan, which will include monthly installments, it is important to know well how much you can afford to spend each month.

Unfortunately, many consumers do it the opposite way. They will go to a showroom lot, fall in love with a new-model car, and somehow try to "fit" the payments for this car into their monthly budget rather than setting a reasonable payment and then picking the car. But if you reverse this process—by figuring out how much you can spend per month and then purchasing the car that fits that budget—you will come out ahead and with much more financial serenity.

CAR BUDGET CHART

One way to do this is to create a chart that will include the car payments you feel you can afford or want to spend per month, plus the average cost of insurance per month, average gas fill-ups, and repairs and maintenance.

For example, your chart could look something like this:

	Monthly Payment	Monthly Insurance	Average Gas	Repairs	Regular Maint.	Misc.
Jan	_____	_____	_____	_____	_____	_____
Feb	_____	_____	_____	_____	_____	_____
Mar	_____	_____	_____	_____	_____	_____
Apr	_____	_____	_____	_____	_____	_____
May	_____	_____	_____	_____	_____	_____
June	_____	_____	_____	_____	_____	_____
July	_____	_____	_____	_____	_____	_____
Aug	_____	_____	_____	_____	_____	_____
Sept	_____	_____	_____	_____	_____	_____
Oct	_____	_____	_____	_____	_____	_____
Nov	_____	_____	_____	_____	_____	_____
Dec	_____	_____	_____	_____	_____	_____
Total	_____	_____	_____	_____	_____	_____

GO TO ▶
Refer to Hour 3 to figure out where the car fits into your budget. Also, go to Hour 15, "Insurance," for more on different types of car insurance.

By examining your totals in a chart like this, you can fit them into your all-around budget that you created in both Hours 2, "Cleaning Up Clutter/Debt Repayment" and 3, "Budgeting Your Way to the Future."

DOWN PAYMENTS

After you figure out what you can spend each month, you need to think about how much you can use as a down payment. There are so many enticements out there not to put any money down. It feels like you'd be driving off the lot with a free car!

Not so. Keep in mind that even with so many ads enticing you to "Leave your checkbook at home" when you come to buy a car, don't do it. Even putting anything down is better than nothing.

Why? The more you can put down initially on your car, the less you will have to pay in higher interest rates. In the same way that a larger down payment on your house can result in less interest due over time, the same applies when buying a car.

Keep in mind that unless you own your trade-in outright (or have significant equity in it), you will want to use at least some cash as a down payment. Borrowing money can be very expensive. Down payments will lower your monthly payments, save you money on interest, and can sometimes earn you better rates on the money you do borrow.

LEASING A CAR

To consumers who like to own their cars, leasing can feel the same as renting your home rather than owning it. The only difference is that you can actually get the equivalent of the new car of your dreams without the depreciation of owning a car you'll later have to sell.

Keep in mind that leasing can be a great option if you are not planning to stay in an area for more than a year, or if you think you are going to use the car primarily for business reasons. Also, leasing gives you the flexibility of simply walking away from the deal at the end of the payment plan—no car, no hassles.

Many consumers like the leasing option because it gives them a new car every three years. If you were planning on buying a new car anyway, leasing could save you money. There are other incentives (sales, discounts, coupons) offered by the manufacturers and leasing companies to make leasing a practical alternative.

THE DRAWBACKS

There are also drawbacks to leasing a car, depending on your driving needs. There can be hidden charges for excess mileage that goes past the agreed-upon limit stated in your contract. Let's say, for example, that you are going to be driving the car more miles than the 36,000 allowed in your leasing contract. With a mileage charge of 20¢ for every mile over 36,000 miles, that could really add up.

Be sure to consider all aspects of this before signing on the dotted line.

How Long Are Car Leases?

The usual length of time to lease a car is three years, or 36 months. On the other hand, it may be cheaper to lease the car for less time, say for 24 or 12 months, according to Manhattan automobile dealer John Konyak. As long as you make the payments in full each month, or overpay them, you would have the option to "turn in" the car early toward the end of the period and actually "sell" it back to the dealer, thereby turning a profit!

Konyak explains, "If you have leased a car, you have the option to buy it at the end of the period. And you are the only individual with that option to buy. So, in effect, you can sell that option back to the dealer when you are ready to 'trade up.'"

Or another option is that you can sell your leased car yourself. You can put an advertisement in a newspaper. If you have leased a car for 36 months but have paid the lease back in full after 24 months, you're all done with it. You've made the extra payments, so you're all finished. (Even if you haven't, this technique still works.) If you notice that the sale price of your car is less than the market price, you could sell it.

Call your dealer and ask "What is the payoff on my leased car today? What would I have to pay today to buy it out?" He will look it up and can give you a number that works within a window of 30 days.

Then check the newspapers. If you see that you could actually sell it for more than the payoff price the dealer gave you, you can sell it and make a profit on it! You could collect your money first. Keep in mind that this often is the way car dealers do it.

Konyak explains again, "I got a big pat on the back from my company once because I sold a car this way. A guy brought in his leased car to me, a Chevy Blazer, and it sat in the back waiting for the finance company to pick it up. Sometimes the cars will sit back there for months!"

"Anyway, a guy walked in and wanted to buy a used Chevy Blazer, except we didn't have any in stock. I talked with my manager, and told him about the used Blazer in the back. The customer liked it—took a ride in it and loved it. In the meantime, my boss suggested we call GMAC for the payoff." (Keep in mind that dealers get a different payoff than regular customers.)

JUST A MINUTE

When negotiating a "buy-back" plan on a lease, try to get the dealer payoff rather than the regular customer payoff. You can save several hundred dollars in cost. To do this, you can generally call the leasing company for these figures.

Our friend the car dealer's boss ended up selling the used Blazer to the customer for the dealer cost plus "x" amount of dollars—many thousands above the regular cost! So the dealership made several thousands in profit on that deal.

Because it was a leased car, all the records were available, and the customer drove away very pleased. Remember: The car dealer has to lay out money to bring in cars to the lot.

BUYING A USED CAR

The cars typically found on a new-car lot are not going to be very old—that's why they're on a new-car lot vs. a used-car lot. Used cars sold on new-car lots tend to be three to six years old. It's a different kind of market for cars older than this—a good place to check is your local newspaper in the car advertisements or classifieds. Many local car owners will advertise their cars in this manner, and you can sometimes find many good deals this way.

In addition, cars of many varieties and costs can often be found in the classified advertisements and more recently by looking up "Cars" on the Internet. You can use any number of search engines, including www.yahoo.com and www.excite.com, for this purpose.

THE TRADE-IN

Trade-ins can be tricky. Trading in your car to a dealership is a test of wills: You think your car is worth "x" amount of dollars when you go to your dealer to negotiate a trade (you want the most money so you can use that toward your new car purchase or trade). Meanwhile, your dealer wants to give you "y" amount of dollars—usually much less than you anticipated. In fact, no matter what, it always seems that you get back less from your trade-in than you thought you would going in!

As mentioned at the beginning of this chapter, one of the many considerations to keep in mind when buying a car is its trade-in value. How much will the car be worth when you trade it in for a new car?

All of this can be deceiving. Dealers sometimes value your trade-in based on its "blue book" value, which is a commonly used digest of what each used car would be worth on the market. Not all dealers stick to the blue book value, though. Investigate the blue book value of your trade-in. The value of your trade-in and whatever amount you may still owe on it is one of the most important factors involved with buying a new car. Any equity that you have in your trade-in should add to your purchasing power, for example.

But it is also possible to have negative equity in a trade-in, as we will see later. It's easy for car dealers to confuse you when it comes to how your trade-in equity affects the deal, so we need to spend some time here and sort a few things out.

Many dealers play when it comes to your trade. To some dealers it is called the "trade-in allowance" game. What does that mean? For one thing, it is important to remember that the dealer is buying your car wholesale, which is always the case. On the other hand, it allows the dealer to tell you what you want to hear.

For example, some customers want a "big discount," and dealers can sense this. If that's the case, they will play the sale that way. On the other hand, some customers are more interested in seeing how much their trade-in is worth upon time of trading with the dealer. It is often up to the discretion of the dealer to present this in any way they want.

For instance, let's say you have brought in a used car for trade-in. The dealer can present the sale to you any way they like: a $1,000 discount and a $9,000 trade allowance still leaves you with a $10,000 trade difference. It's easy to become confused and frustrated.

The best advice? Don't involve your trade-in until after you get prices. Either way, knowledge is power and it is best to know the value of your trade and the car you want to purchase before you enter the dealership.

UNDERSTANDING YOUR TRADE

When you trade your car in to a dealer, you're selling it wholesale, whether you realize it or not. The wholesale value of your car is approximately what it would bring at a dealer auction and is hundreds or even thousands less than the going retail price.

In fact, some dealers completely disregard the blue book value. Speaking to a New York–based dealer, it became clear: Dealers are instructed to consider the auction price, not the blue book price, when making a deal with a customer.

In general, the auction price is the wholesale price—the price at which dealers will sell cars to each other. The retail price is the price the dealer will sell to a consumer.

SELLING YOUR CAR ON YOUR OWN

Of course, there is always the option of selling your car on your own, pocketing the money, and then going in with new monetary ammunition when buying your new or used car. As you know, though, this can bring up a whole lot of new headaches.

For instance, you must advertise your car and then field the calls that come in when customers are interested in your car. You have to make appointments, and you must be willing to let strangers take your car for test drives and accommodate scheduling appointments with their mechanics—only to have them haggle down the price you wanted for your car. And, in some cases, appointments you've made may never show up. Or worse, they might show up and be terrible drivers. You never know.

For these reasons, many consumers are dearly glad to be able to get their used car off their hands as a trade-in for driving a different car off the lot.

Consider also potential hassles with financing and timing. You may find someone to buy your car, but you may still owe money on it. This means they need to pay you first and then wait while your bank processes paperwork before getting the title to their new car. Not everyone will be willing to do that. Plus, after going through all the hassles already mentioned, you may need to wait for them to either sell their old car or get approved for financing their own. And so on and so on.

WHAT IS YOUR CAR WORTH?

So what is your car worth? Experts suggest knowing both the wholesale, actual cash value (ACV), and the retail value. Both prices can be found in a current edition of the *N.A.D.A. Used Car Guide* or *Kelley Blue Book* for your area. There are different regional issues that can be found at the library, bookstore, or on the Internet.

The automobile market can be as up and down as any Wall Street stock, so a number of factors can affect the value of your car positively or negatively. Some cars are notoriously "soft," which means they often bring less than book value, while other cars are "strong," and usually bring the book value or more. Some more "flashy" cars will always bring in a higher value than the less-flashy and more-predictable cars.

As a test, try to compare the book value to what cars similar to yours are selling for in your area. Once you have calculated the ACV, you need to deduct from it any balance that you still owe on the car. Be clear on this and call your bank to get an accurate payoff amount. To determine the amount left over (i.e., the equity in the car) calculate the following:

Cash value of trade-in	=	$14,000
Loan balance/payoff	=	$9,000
Your cash equity	=	$5,000

If you find yourself owing more on your car loan than your car is worth, first consider selling your car as a private sale to try to get more for it than its wholesale value. Also use your down payment or any other cash available to you to make up as much of the difference as you can.

If you still find yourself upside down, consider keeping your current car a little longer and continue paying it off. If all else fails, you can roll the negative equity into the new car. You are, in essence, financing your negative balance along with the cost of the new car. This is possible by paying full price (or perhaps more) for a car and using any discount you would have gotten to pay off the negative balance on your trade-in (remember the trade-in allowance game).

This should only be a last resort. Many people continually roll more and more negative equity into new purchases. Eventually this catches up with them because banks limit the amount they will lend on each car.

WHERE TO LOOK FOR USED CARS

You may have heard the old adage that buying a used car is like "buying another person's headache." That may be so in some circumstances. But chances are, if you do your homework, ask the right questions, and have an independent inspection done on any used car you're thinking of buying, you may just come out many dollars ahead.

As previously mentioned, driving a "new car" off the lot immediately reduces its resale value. It has already depreciated once it leaves the shop! A good used car, on the other hand, can have good value and can save you money over all. But also remember: caveat emptor! In other words, "Let the buyer beware."

Fortunately, most used-car dealers aren't exactly like the hucksters out there who want to sell you any old lemon off their lot. There are several national services that offer a wide selection of used cars in one huge outlet.

TIME SAVER

Check out AutoNation USA and CarMax, for example—two conglomerates that offer national representation for used cars. Both are also available by Internet.

There are several other ways of finding good used cars, including those auctioned off by the Department of Defense, the U.S. Marshall's Office, the IRS, U.S. Customs Service, police departments, and estate clearances. Many car rental companies have sales on their former fleet cars used for rental purposes. Oftentimes such cars have been well taken care of—as a result, don't be scared away just by high mileage numbers. You might just drive off with a very good deal on a car that has been well maintained.

TIME SAVER

The Internet can be a great research tool when looking up used cars. Check out www.edmunds.com, which provides reliability ratings and other information. Also take a look at www.carpoint.msn.com and www.autos.yahoo.com for more comparison shopping.

Here are some rule-of-thumb questions to ask yourself as you begin to check out used cars:

- How old is the car?
- How old are the parts in the car?
- Has any part of the car been rebuilt?
- What is its mileage? (According to some experts, the mileage should average between 10,000 and 15,000 miles per year.)

Here are some questions to ask about the car's condition:

- Are the sills, wheel arches, and door bottoms rusty?
- Is the paint work failing?
- Are the tires damaged or worn?
- Are the seat belts worn out? Do they have faulty mountings?
- Do door and window seals show signs of leaking?
- Are electronics faulty (lights, dashboard warning lights)?

Here are some questions to ask if you suspect that the car you are examining has been in an accident:

- Have the body panels been repaired?
- Is the color/texture of paint work patchy?
- Has welding been done on the engine/boot?
- Have repairs been done on the boot? (Check under carpet)

On the test drive—make sure you are insured for the test drive before you go out—be sure to consider the following:

- Are the brakes defective?
- Does the car pull to one side either when you steer or brake?
- Do the brakes squeal?
- Are there other unusual noises?
- Is the hand brake defective?
- Does the steering wheel shake or vibrate?
- Is changing gears difficult?
- Does the gear lever skip when you brake or accelerate?
- Does the clutch grab or slip?
- Does the engine sound different if the clutch is depressed when the car is idling?
- Is there a strong smell of oil?

Be sure to bring up any and all of these concerns with your dealer upon completion of the test drive. Also, keep a list to take to your independent mechanic to ask him or her about when you get the car checked.

TECHNICIAN'S CHECKLIST

Once you've decided on a car to test, take the car to a diagnostic center or repair facility for an overall inspection by a technician before you buy it. If the used-car dealer refuses to let you take the car to your technician for an inspection, look in the Yellow Pages of your local telephone book for a mobile diagnostic service so the car can be inspected on the car lot. If the dealer refuses to let the car off the lot, this might be a red flag that the dealer has not been completely honest about the car's history or driving performance.

The cost for a mobile diagnostic checkup varies, but the money you invest up front may save you many more dollars later. Ask for a written estimate of the costs to repair any problems the technician finds, and use that estimate as a bargaining tool if you make an offer for the car.

If you are unable to make any such arrangement for an inspection, you may want to consider taking your business to another dealer.

Some of the tests the technician should perform are ...

- An engine compression test.
- Check spark plugs and ignition system.
- A contamination diagnosis of oil and fluids.
- Check transmission fluid.
- Check fan and belts, charging system, power steering, and air conditioner.
- Check cooling system: radiator, heater, by-pass hose.
- Check braking system: lining, wheel and master cylinders, drums and front disks, hoses, bearings, grease seals.
- Check suspension: ball joints, tie rod end, idler arm.
- Remove differential plug and check lubricant.
- Test-drive the vehicle.

LEASING VS. BUYING COST COMPARISON CHART

Before you go into your dealer's showroom (and again once you're there), sit down with the following chart and fill out your options. This is a definite "reality check" you will thank yourself for down the road!

Comparison Chart

Leasing a Car	Buying a Car
Length of lease	Term of loan
Capital cost reduction (depreciation that you're paying for)	Down payment
Monthly payment (× number of months, plus tax)	Monthly payment (× number of months, plus tax)
Title/registration fees	Title/registration fees
Insurance premiums	Insurance premiums
Cost of early lease termination	
Total purchasing cost	Total leasing cost
	Net cost of car

Sometimes rebates, discounts, low-rate or interest-free financing, cap cost reduction allowances, etc. will help you decide whether to buy vs. lease, or finance vs. get a rebate. If the rebate is big enough, and you can get financing through your credit union, you could buy at a good price. Or, if the rate is low enough, financing would be recommended over taking the rebate. Some lease incentives are too good to pass up. Certain models of a car line may be offered at huge savings. Special sales and promotions are always a good reason to consider buying or leasing now.

GOOD LEASING SUGGESTIONS

Because leasing is really like a long-term rental of a car, it's important to ask yourself what your uses of the car will be. For some people who move to a new city, a leased car is perfect as they get settled into their new environment. Some people decide to lease a car at a low monthly rate and invest additional funds for a car they really want later. It's up to you.

DETERMINING IF LEASING IS FOR YOU

Be sure to consider some or all of the following before leasing your car:

- **Make sure the terms fit your needs.** As mentioned earlier in this chapter, sometimes it makes more sense to lease for less time than more, even if leasing for four years vs. three could stretch out the payments for you.

- **Double-check additional costs besides the monthly payment.** Often there will be leasing company charges or other fees.

- **Additional mileage fees.** Be sure to calculate these fees, especially if you think you might go over the limit as prescribed by your lease agreement.

- **Pick a car that you're comfortable with.** You'll be driving this vehicle for a couple of years at least, so be sure to choose wisely! Also, do your research on any car you're considering as if you were buying it. Remember: You (and possibly your family) are going to be behind that wheel, so safety is paramount!

- **Don't sign on a lease that you cannot commit to completely.** There's really no going back on a car lease. Sign wisely on the dotted line.

ONLINE WEB SITES

Here are some excellent car-related Web sites to surf:

- **www.autoweb.com.** A great site for buying, selling, or financing an automobile.

- **www.carfinance.com.** This site offers instant rate payments and analysis for auto loans.

- **www.careports.com.** This site offers up-to-the minute pricing information on all new cars available in the U.S. market by brand/make. It also offers an online library car loan calculator so you can easily figure out payments and other key numbers on any car loan you're considering.

- **www.1stopauto.com.** Also offers a rate and payment analysis calculator, with additional links to credit check sites.

- **www.kbb.com.** The Kelley Blue Book site. The site serves up all the pre-owned vehicle pricing information that Kelley has published for the past 20 years. New car prices are also freely available on the site in U.S. dollars for all the major international car makes. The KBB site also offers a "Lemon Checks" site for used car inventory.

JUST A MINUTE

Consumer Reports annually reviews both new and used cars. Your local library will carry the latest issue; if you can't find it, call their subscription number at 1-800-234-1645. For $24 a year, you can purchase their *Buying Guide,* which lists the latest information and a list of the most reliable used cars in prices ranging from $2,500 and up.

HOUR'S UP!

Without looking back, see if you can answer the following questions about finding a good financial advisor:

1. "Depreciation" is a term that could mean that …

   a. The new car you've just driven off the lot is instantly worth less than what you paid for it.

   b. Your car is a lemon.

   c. The car you've just bought will go up in value.

2. Creating a car budget can help you determine …

   a. Monthly payments.

   b. Monthly insurance payments.

   c. Your average gas bill.

   d. Repairs.

   e. All of the above.

3. True or false: It's better to put down a larger cash down payment on a car than to borrow more money over time.

4. True or false: Leasing can also be seen as "renting" a car for the long term.

5. ACV is an acronym for …

   a. American Cadillac vehicle

   b. American car value

   c. Actual cash value

6. True or false: If in fact you do lease a car for business reasons, you can deduct the amount of the lease on your tax return for that year.

7. The best lease period to choose for leasing your car is …

   a. 12 months.

   b. 24 months.

   c. 36 months.

8. You can find good used cars through auctions by …

   a. The Department of Defense.

   b. The U.S. Marshall's Office.

   c. U.S. Customs Service.

   d. Estate clearances.

   e. All of the above.

Quiz

HOUR 18
Estate Planning

CHAPTER SUMMARY

LESSON PLAN:

In this lesson, you will gain a clearer understanding of estate planning, wills, living trusts, and ways of carrying out your wishes for asset distribution upon your death. You'll also learn how to:

- Understand death and probate taxes.
- Avoid common court fees and other costs.
- Begin to create an estate plan.
- Make a worksheet to determine the value of your assets.

In this hour, we will be discussing estate planning, wills, and living trusts. Granted, this can be a touchy and very confusing topic for some. Many people do not want to give any thought to the fact that, yes, eventually, they will die; yet it will happen to each and every one of us.

For others, possibly people in their later years, the time may be right to begin getting clear on where their assets, money, and so on might end up when they are no longer around or able to make their own final decisions.

WHO NEEDS ESTATE PLANNING?

Two kinds of people should consider estate planning: (1) those who select and buy a burial plot ahead of time and decide to tie up any loose ends related to their estate planning *before* they die and (2) those who would rather not think about it at all and hope everything will turn out okay.

To that second group, keep in mind that by *not* making up your mind on crucial financial decisions about where you want your assets to go, your choice, in the long run, may wind up being harder on your survivors than you expect.

Rest assured: If you neglect your estate planning entirely, you will, in the end, be leaving much of the process tied up in the court system, with the IRS possibly becoming your biggest beneficiary. Subjecting your estate to probate (which we will discuss later in the hour) may mean additional costs and delays in transferring assets to your heirs. In the end, the courts may not have your best interests at heart.

You may be saying to yourself, "I have great kids and relatives who will only do what I tell them in my will!" Not necessarily. Too many times, lawyers have recanted tales of woe when relatives contested wills, drawing out painful distress among families. Creating an estate plan is not so much a matter of trust; rather, it is creating a sense of psychological serenity for you, your spouse, and your family, knowing that all you have worked so hard for in your lifetime will end up in the right hands.

PROCEED WITH CAUTION

Believe it or not, experts report that 70 percent of Americans have no written estate plan. Unfortunately, for the majority who have no plan in place, state law will dictate how their estate is to be distributed at death. Is that how you want your assets distributed after you die?

CREATING AN ESTATE PLAN

Estate planning forces you to face the financial consequences of death and take action to minimize the effects on your family after you're gone. It gives you a sense of control over how your estate will be distributed, plus over that final process.

When some people hear the words "estate planning," they get the (false) impression that they actually have to own a country "estate" with horses and servants to consider putting together a proper will or living trust. Not true!

You'd be surprised what your net assets could be worth by the age of retirement if you include your retirement plans, house equity, stocks, bonds, and so forth. Many consumers are astonished when they add up their total net worth and find it can be $500,000, $600,000, or more.

Estate planning is the creation of a definite plan for managing your wealth while you're alive and distributing it after your death. When we talk about an estate, we mean all assets of any value that you own, including …

- Real property.
- Business interests.
- Investments.

- Insurance proceeds.
- Personal property.
- Personal effects.
- Retirement accounts such as IRAs, 401(k) plans.

According to the American Academy of Estate Planning Attorneys, when people were asked to summarize their estate planning wishes, most would simply say that …

- They want their estate to be distributed to the people they choose according to their wishes.
- They want to avoid excessive attorney fees, court costs, and unnecessary delays in passing on their property.
- They want to avoid or at least minimize the payment of state and federal death taxes.

Let's take a look, then, at options available to you when planning how your estate will be divided after your death.

THE FOUR BASIC ESTATE PLANNING METHODS

What are the four basic methods you can use to plan your estate? You can …

- Do nothing.
- Create a will.
- Hold title to your assets in joint tenancy (explained later in the chapter).
- Establish a revocable living trust.

In addition, you will want to consider having a power of attorney (in case you become ill or hospitalized and are not capable of making decisions on your own) and a living will. The latter makes your wishes about life support known to doctors, who then take them into consideration. Setting up a durable power of attorney for healthcare helps enable you not only to put your feelings and wishes into effect, but to specify who will make the decision if you cannot.

As we've seen, doing "nothing" about your assets is a great prescription for a fall. So let's see about your other options.

CREATING A WILL

You think you know about what a will is, right? A will is a legal document that determines how your assets will be divided after your death. In some cases, drawing up a basic will might be the right option for you.

But, then again, all those courtroom scenes on *L.A. Law* and *Ally McBeal* come to mind with relatives contesting wills, lots of screaming and yelling, and, most important, assets not ending up in the proper hands—with the IRS taking the biggest cut. Is a basic will, then, really the best overall choice for your estate plan?

Let's take a closer look. There are several types of wills that can be drawn up. A simple will has assets distributed outright to the beneficiaries. A couple who draw up a will early in their marriage and bequeath everything to each other have what is sometimes called an "I love you" will.

But by creating such a will, you may have started an even more complicated process. Watch out for the IRS—they will be waiting to take what are called "death taxes" immediately. The will goes into probate—a given, after any death. As you'll see, that is something you definitely want to avoid.

More complicated wills may have testamentary trusts established to receive assets from the estate, or they may "pour over" (transfer) assets to a "pour over" trust created by another document.

It is important to have a professional estate planning counselor help you account for the various new situations that may arise throughout your lifetime. As you grow older and your assets continue to grow, your will should reflect this as your family situations change. A good example of this could be second marriages that include new children. Making an appointment with your estate planning counselor to be able to cover these new realities is key.

THE IRS AT THE DOOR

The IRS, as previously mentioned, looks forward to wills and probate, because this is where the biggest chunk of your estate can be taken. After your estate value reaches a certain amount, as much as 55 percent can be taken in taxes alone.

In 1999, that amount went up to $650,000. In 2,000, the amount has increased to $675,000. Essentially, this means that your estate can be valued at up to $675,000 before federal taxes will kick in. Presently, the exemption is

$675,000 with a planned gradual increase to $700,000 in 2002 and to $1,000,000 in 2006. In other words, as of 2006, the legislators in Washington will make it even easier for you and your spouse to give more of your assets to your family upon your passing, without giving a majority to the IRS.

The following is a list of the planned changes:

Year	Amount
2000	$675,000
2001	$675,000
2002	$700,000
2003	$700,000
2004	$850,000
2005	$950,000
2006	$1,000,000

By the time it gets to $1,000,000 ($2,000,000 for married couples) it will cover most people's estates.

But as of 1999, if your estate at the time of your death is less than the exemption—meaning if your estate is less than $650,000—there will be no federal estate taxes due. In deciding whether your estate is greater than or less than the exemption, the government includes everything you own—even the face value of your life insurance policies.

For people with assets below the $675,000 exemption, no further tax planning is necessary if the single person's assets are below the current exemption or a married couple have an estate plan that eliminates the estate tax by using both spouses' exemptions (or if their joint assets are below one exemption).

JUST A MINUTE

IRAs offer a way to claim a beneficiary that circumvents the probate process with the money going directly to the beneficiary. It is crucial to update the named beneficiaries of your IRAs to reflect changes in your life, such as divorce, remarriage, birth of children, etc.

With any changes such as divorce, remarriage, the birth of children, etc., it is crucial to seek expert help. The rules can become extremely technical, so it's important to have your bases covered.

STATE VS. FEDERAL TAX

In New York, the estate tax will be repealed February 1, 2000. It is replaced by an inheritance tax that is referred to as a "sponge tax" which means New York will only collect a tax if the Federal Estate Tax is applicable and then the New York tax will only be the amount that the Federal Tax allows as a credit for State tax and reduces the Federal tax dollar for dollar. In other words, if you don't pay it to New York the Federal tax will be higher, so New York says they will take whatever the credit is to reduce the Fed tax, but no more. So for states that have this kind of inheritance tax (most do), once the Fed tax is eliminated there is no tax at all.

The states that have the "sponge tax" vs. their own system as of about a year ago include Alabama, Alaska, Arizona, Arkansas, California, Colorado, Florida, Georgia, Hawaii, Idaho, Illinois, Kansas, Kentucky, Massachusetts, Michigan, Minnesota, Missouri, Montana, Nevada, New Hampshire, New Jersey, New Mexico, New York, North Dakota, Oregon, Rhode Island, South Carolina, Texas, Utah, Vermont, Virginia, Washington, West Virginia, Wisconsin, and Wyoming.

The states which do divvy their own taxes include Connecticut, Delaware, Indiana, Iowa, Louisiana, Maryland, Mississippi, Nebraska, North Carolina, Ohio, Oklahoma, Pennsylvania, South Dakota, and Tennessee.

JUST WHAT IS PROBATE, ANYWAY?

The probate process is usually terribly expensive and time-consuming. Ask any attorney worth her salt, and she will advise you to avoid living probate costs like the plague.

A will does not avoid probate—the legal process through which the court makes sure that your debts are paid and your property is distributed according to your will. It is because of this that the common belief that a will is the best way to plan one's estate is frequently not the case.

Probate costs, which must be paid from your estate before anything can go to your heirs, are estimated at 5 to 10 percent of your estate's gross value. This can be quite sizable, depending on your estate value. The probate process usually takes one or two years or longer in some states, and holds up your heirs receiving your assets.

According to the American Academy of Estate Planning Attorneys, the "evils" you potentially avoid when preparing your estate include …

- **Living probate.** The expensive court proceeding to manage your property if you are disabled.
- **Death probate.** The expensive court proceeding to manage and distribute your estate at your death.
- **Death taxes.** The taxes the government demands at your death. The federal tax starts at 37 percent and rises to 55 percent, depending on the value of your assets.

During probate, your family has no privacy or control of your estate. Probate files are open to the public, so anyone can see what you own and who you owe.

Jackie O Didn't Get It

For example, the most private of all public figures, Jacqueline Onassis, carefully guarded her own and her family's privacy throughout her life. But after her death, because she used a will to settle and distribute her assets, many of the details of her $200 million estate and the terms of her final wishes were made public. Anyone could go through it, since it became a public document.

On the other hand, years before famed entertainer Frank Sinatra died, he set up a living trust, so his wishes as to where his assets would be distributed never became public. An AP story recounted that, upon his death, Sinatra left much of his lucrative music catalog to his children and real estate to his widow. This information was made known through private sources, not through records of the living trust.

If you choose a basic will, the probate process—not your family—will end up taking control of the division of your estate. Your family will be left living within the restrictions and inconveniences that characterize the probate system, which can be long and costly.

Avoid Death Taxes Like the Plague

As the old saying goes, "Nothing is certain but death and taxes." And nothing is as certain as death taxes for estates over specific limits. Estate taxes begin at 37 percent for the first dollar over $675,000 and rise to a maximum of 55 percent for $3 million estates and greater.

The good news is that two tax breaks take some of the sting out of death taxes. The first is the *Unlimited Marital Deduction*. It allows a married taxpayer to pass his entire estate on to his surviving spouse, free of gift or estate taxes. (The full estate-tax bill comes due, however, when the couple's estate passes on to their ultimate heirs.)

The second tax break is the *Unified Credit*. As previously mentioned, the federal government provides a credit equal to the estate taxes due on the first $675,000 of a taxpayer's estate. You can bequeath $675,000 of your assets estate tax-free if you are single. Married couples can bequeath a combined $1.3 million of assets estate tax-free. But this tax break is only available to those who do their estate planning properly—and that means going beyond a simple will.

LIVING PROBATE

So far, we've discussed the probate proceedings that happen after you die. But, unfortunately, probate can also happen while you're living. It's often referred to as a "living probate," but it's technically called a "conservatorship" or "guardianship" proceeding.

For example, if you become mentally disabled before you die and you haven't designated a specific person to control your affairs, the court will appoint someone to take control of all your assets and personal affairs. These court-appointed agents must file strict annual accountings with the court. The entire procedure is expensive, time-consuming, and often humiliating.

As we will see later in the chapter, the revocable living trust is a good possible solution to this nightmare.

HOLDING ASSETS IN JOINT TENANCY

Two or more people holding title to an asset together is called joint-tenancy ownership. But unlike other forms of joint ownership, the entire interest passes automatically to the surviving joint tenants upon the death of one of the owners.

The problem here can lie in property ownership, for instance. Because a joint tenant's interest passes to the surviving joint tenants immediately at death, it's not controlled by the owner's will, according to the American Academy of Estate Planning Attorneys Plan for a Living Trust.

Let's say two good friends, Frank and Bob, own a piece of property as joint tenants. Frank dies, and his will states that upon his death all of his estate should go to his wife, Darla. What happens to his interest in the real property he owns with Bob? Because the title passes automatically at death to the surviving joint tenant, Bob will own the entire property, and Darla will get nothing.

This is only one of the unforeseen problems that joint-tenancy ownership can create. According to Gerald Dunworth, an estate planning attorney with Gibney, Anthony & Flaherty, LLP, in Manhattan and a member of the American Academy of Estate Planning Attorneys, other problems can include the following examples:

- Some people try to have equal joint accounts for their multiple heirs or beneficiaries. It is hard to keep everything straight and make sure everyone is being treated equally.

- If multiple children are joint owners of the accounts, they can all access the accounts. Many times parents do this out of love for their children, but this can be unsettling.

- A joint owner owns one-half of the account and thus his creditors can get the other owner's assets.

- If a child predeceases the parent, his or her share would not go to his or her children, but would go to the other joint owners.

- Transferring real estate and securities can get cumbersome when every joint owner's signature is required.

- Except for a joint account with a spouse, the IRS assumes that 100 percent of the account, co-op apartment, etc. was paid for by the decedent and therefore is 100 percent in the estate and taxable to the decedent. So if you can't trace the other person's contribution clearly, you might be paying estate tax on the half the survivor actually paid for.

THE LIVING REVOCABLE TRUST

All of the preceding discussion leads us to what is called a living revocable trust. This type of trust has saved many taxpayers hundreds of thousands of dollars in tax payments.

So what exactly is a living trust?

It is just another way for you to own your assets outright. Every living revocable trust is, first and foremost, a legal entity that can own and manage stocks, bonds, real estate, bank accounts, and whatever other properties are transferred to it.

This concept can be scary for people considering a living revocable trust, because it implies that by setting one up you lose control of your money. Not so!

The ownership of property by the trust is the essential feature that permits property to pass free of the costs and delays of probate at the death of the grantor. You still own everything and have control over all of your assets.

As we've noted, probate can be very costly and time-consuming. All the property you personally own, whether it passes by will or intestacy at your death, must go through the probate process of your state.

But property that you own through your living revocable trust during your life can pass to your designated beneficiaries free of all the costs and delays of probate.

A living trust can help reduce or eliminate estate taxes. It is difficult to contest. When you set up a living trust, you are simply transferring all of your property from your individual name to the name of your trust, which you control. In essence, you get to designate who controls the trust after you die.

MARITAL DEDUCTION

If you're married, you have the ability to transfer unlimited amounts of assets to your spouse without any tax. The concept is that there shouldn't be any tax until the money goes outside the marriage—to children, grandchildren, or other people.

Sounds simple, right? So why don't people just set up a living trust and be done with it? The IRS hopes people will do this—it's sort of a trap. That's where they collect—when one spouse's assets exceed the exemption amount.

According to Dunworth, setting up a living trust is "one of the ultimate selfless acts you can do. You are organizing the transfer of your assets to your heirs in a more efficient and easy method as opposed to having them deal with a bureaucratic nightmare."

Dunworth conducts seminars about financial planning in Manhattan and gives a variation on the following example in his talks:

Bob and Mary are a married couple in their 60s. They have two children, Lisa and Frank. When Bob and Mary add up their estate, meaning all of their assets, it turns out to be a sizable one: nearly $1,300,000 when including their home, stocks, etc.

If Bob and Mary did nothing and left all of their assets to each other, up to $675,000 of their assets would not be taxed, and (if Bob died first) Mary could keep these, fair and square. However, the remaining $675,000 would be taxed, resulting in an IRS gain of $258,500 in estate taxes.

However, if Bob and Mary had set up a living trust ahead of time, both Bob and Mary would have been named *trustors, trustees, and beneficiaries* of their trust, giving them full power over their assets. Bob's share could have gone into the living trust, which would have avoided any probate.

Again, Mary now has inherited $675,000 from her husband, which went to the family trust. Experts have said that surviving spouses live on average up to seven years longer after their spouse passes away. But let's say Mary lives 10 years after Bob passes away. Her assets can greatly increase in value the longer she lives. Financial planners say that her assets can at least double in value—up to $1.3 million.

When Mary passes away, how much of that $1.3 million estate will actually go to her heirs (her two children, Lisa and Frank), and how much will be taken out in probate and death taxes? If a living trust has been set up properly, there should be no probate on death, $1,300,000 can be passed estate tax-free, and this will also protect any grandchildren if Lisa or Frank dies.

Unfortunately, if Mary lives 10 years longer, she may get a debilitating illness such as Alzheimer's and have to go into a nursing home. Who would then pay her bills? And which child should take care of her?

Again, the living trust is quite specific on this. Mary can name a *successor trustee,* who can step in and manage her affairs without government interference and expense.

WHAT HAPPENS IF I DO NOTHING?

Without putting in place the proper channels, all of the preceding examples can become a nightmare for any and all of your family members concerned with your estate. It can become aggravating, and, especially where money is involved, can quickly turn into an expensive, time-consuming nightmare. Remember, the court proceeding will control the time.

With a living trust, much of this headache can be taken care of in advance.

GAY COUPLES

Dunworth says he and his firm also handle the estates of many clients who are gay. These are people in committed relationships who have the need to settle their affairs in case of one in the partnership dying even though they are denied the recognized right to marry in most states. Many times their families don't approve of their situation and may not agree with the deceased's choice of asset division. In order to probate a will, you have to get involved with the family.

Gay couples use living trusts for privacy and for keeping family members out of the process. Going through probate means requiring family members to be part of the process. Because in states like New York, a will cannot be probated unless all the next of kin (closest family members) receive official court notice and either sign a "waiver" of objections or cause the estate to go through a lengthy process of serving the relatives with process and then waiting the period of time for the hearing (about 30-60 days) to see if they are coming into court to file objections.

Often, gay couples have found that a disapproving family member can cause delays and aggravation. In addition to avoiding the probate process, the living trust means the one partner continues to own his or her assets and there is no gift or exposure to the other partner's creditors. The partner can always be a co-trustee and have access to the funds in the event the owner becomes incapacitated or dies. The living trust problem referred to above is the IRS presumption that 100% belonged to the decedent. You have to prove with documentation the contributions from the surviving joint owner. Sometimes people do not keep this documentation and proof is difficult so the survivor is faced with the IRS wanting to assess an estate tax on what is the survivor's one-half of the property.

SINGLE PEOPLE (OR SUDDENLY SINGLE PEOPLE)

Dunworth also says that 50 percent of his estate planning clientele are recently widowed or single, and most of them are older. The average age of his clients? Says Dunworth, "It used to be I'd see mainly older people. Now I am starting to see sort of yuppier people: baby boomers; late 40s, early 50s. But mostly, 60 or 70. They wake up and think, 'I've got to get this done!' Or they have a friend who has gone through it all and has mentioned the benefits of a living trust over a simple will."

For example, Harold and Bonnie are a typical married couple in their 60s. He is an architect. They have two kids but haven't done any specific planning. They have real estate, specifically houses, but they haven't arranged anything more specific for their estate division than an "I love you" will, leaving their remaining estate to their spouse. Everything is in both the husband's and wife's names.

If Harold passed away suddenly, Bonnie would inherit everything. She would have to go through the courts. Eventually, everything would end up in her name alone. She's then going to have more than the exemption amount, and her kids would then have to pay hundreds of thousands of dollars in taxes.

By setting up a living trust Harold and Bonnie could have avoided much of the post-death taxes.

IRREVOCABLE LIFE INSURANCE TRUSTS

As you can imagine, purchasing life insurance can be one of the smartest choices you can make in preparing your portfolio. For pennies on the dollar you are insuring that your loved ones will be taken care of in case of your (earlier than planned) death.

GO TO ▶
Refer to Hour 15, "Insurance," to read up on different types of insurance options.

The problem with people owning life insurance in their own names is that it is included in their estate when the government computes the estate tax liability.

Irrevocable life insurance trusts (ILIT) are basically life insurance policies purchased on individuals. The money to pay the premiums is contributed to the trust, which pays the insurance company.

When an ILIT is created, the ILIT, not the insurance owner, owns the life insurance policy. The policy's death benefit is no longer included in the estate. This, as a result, will lower the value of the estate and, correspondingly, the estate tax liability, if any.

Other insurance trusts (including grandchildren trusts) in which gifts are made to the trust that utilize up to the $10,000 per person gift exclusion for each beneficiary so that the premiums can be paid. You can stipulate how and when the money will be dispensed to the beneficiaries. It just must be irrevocable.

GIFTING

"Gifting" can include people with significant estates "giving" money away to get money out of their estate to bring the total value under $675,000. The generous relative giving away money can give up to $10,000 per year, tax-free, to whichever relative he chooses. In addition, if you are married, you can elect to split the gift amount with your spouse, raising the tax-free limit to $20,000.

Some people find this difficult to do, because they will watch their own assets become more depleted, relying on the trust that their children will take care of them in their older age. Trust plays a big factor here.

For clarity's sake, keep in mind that the Gift and Estate Tax is a "Unified System." In other words, it is a transfer tax on the transfer of wealth to the next generation. The same rules ($675,000 exemption, tax-free marital transfers) apply for transfers during lifetime (gifts) or transfers at death (inheritances). You only get one $675,000 exemption. If it is used for lifetime gifts, you do not get it again in your estate.

The additional rule for Gift Tax is something people have usually heard of, the ability to give $10,000 to someone each year without any Gift Tax. This is an administrative convenience rule. Married couples can each give their children the $10,000 annually. With $20,000 for each child, child's spouse, and grandchild, you can transfer a lot in a few years if you have a big family.

You can also establish irrevocable trusts to which you make annual gifts in the name of your children or grandchildren. The subsequent appreciation will not be counted in your estate. Again, a good estate attorney is needed here to create such a trust.

THE END OF WORK—HELLO SERENITY!

From our 20s to our 60s, we are trying to work and save and accumulate as much as we can. The way our economy works, when we retire—when we're past our earnings stage—we're going to (hopefully) live off what we have and then give away our estate to our heirs.

And this is what a proper estate plan can do for you.

EVALUATE YOUR ASSETS

Let's start at the very beginning. The first step in the process of estate planning is to evaluate any and all assets that you own, including real property, business interests, investments, insurance proceeds, personal property, and even personal effects.

In the same way that you listed all of what was due to your creditors, listing your assets, from life insurance policies to 401(k)s to stocks and bonds, will give you (and your spouse) a better picture of what you really are worth.

Before going in to consult with your estate planning attorney, you may want to create a will-planning worksheet like the following:

Will-Planning Worksheet

Names of executors (to administer the estate):

_____

_____

_____

_____

Names of guardians (and alternates) of minor children:

_____

_____

_____

_____

Provisions for payments of debts and taxes:

_____

_____

_____

_____

Specific requests of money and tangible property:

_____

_____

_____

_____

Name of person or organization: Amount or item:

_____

_____

_____

_____

Disposition of the remainder of property:

_____

_____

_____

_____

continues

Will-Planning Worksheet

Names of primary beneficiaries (including trusts):   Percent:

_____

_____

_____

_____

Names of contingent beneficiaries: Percent:

_____

_____

_____

_____

Assets:

_____

_____

_____

_____

_____

Insurance policies:

_____

_____

_____

_____

And, for a bit more incentive, the following is a fun chart that shows the benefits of *planning ahead.*

Estate Shrinkage of Famous People Who Failed to Plan*

Name	Gross Estate	Total Settlement	Net Estate	Percent Shrinkage
W.C. Fields	$884,680	$329,793	$554,887	37
Franklin D. Roosevelt	$1,940,999	$574,867	$1,366,132	30
Humphrey Bogart	$910,146	$274,234	$635,912	30
Clark Gable	$2,806,526	$1,101,038	$1,705,488	39
Gary Cooper	$4,948,985	$1,520,454	$3,428,531	31

Name	Gross Estate	Total Settlement	Net Estate	Percent Shrinkage
Marilyn Monroe	$819,176	$448,750	$370,426	55
Elvis Presley	$10,165,434	$7,374,635	$2,790,799	73
Walt Disney	$23,004,851	$6,811,943	$16,192,908	30
Dean Witter	$7,451,0 55	$1,830,717	$5,620,338	25

Used by permission of the American Academy of Estate Planning.

As you can see, with proper advice or instruction, many of our illustrious Hollywood and Wall Street notables—and their heirs—might also have benefited from estate planning.

FINDING A GOOD ESTATE PLANNER

The American Academy of Estate Planning Attorneys is an excellent place to start if you are considering creating a living revocable trust and don't know where to begin. They can help you find an estate planning attorney in your area. Contact them at 1-800-846-1555. Their Web site, www.aaepa.com, is filled with information, as well.

Your current attorney may be fine for your needs, and your will or living trust may be in good shape. But if you have questions and she is not up on current laws and the changes of the various exemptions, it may be worthwhile to investigate finding an attorney who is more versed in your various estate options.

MEDICARE AND MEDICAID

Finally, the hot-button topic of the 1990s and well into the future: healthcare. What will happen when or if they become disabled and must move into a nursing home is on the minds of many citizens today. The costs can be astronomical.

GO TO ▶
Refer to Hour 15 for various methods to pay for long-term healthcare.

Often, according to Dunworth, consumers sometimes think that setting up a revocable living trust is an easy way to bypass having to pay their long-term medical bills. Not so. "Setting up a living trust is not a Medicaid-planning device," says Dunworth. "It is not meant as a way to protect you in this way."

HOUR'S UP!

You know it's time to start thinking about your estate plan. Now you get to quiz yourself on your new knowledge! Try to answer the following without looking back in the hour.

1. Among the four methods given in this hour, which method should you use if you know your assets will exceed $675,000 at your death? You can …

   a. Do nothing.

   b. Create a will.

   c. Hold title to your assets in joint tenancy.

   d. Establish a revocable living trust.

2. True or False: Because Jackie Onassis did not use a living trust, her final wishes in her will became public.

3. True or false: The three "evils" that you can avoid when preparing your estate by preparing a living trust are living probate, death probate, and death taxes.

4. The tax break that exists allowing a married taxpayer to pass his or her entire estate on to the surviving spouse is called …

   a. Unlimited Marital Deduction.

   b. The 1998 Marital Insurance Act.

   c. Marital/Spouse Deduction Act.

5. True or false: Estate taxes begin at 37 percent for the first dollar over $675,000 and rise to a maximum of 55 percent for $3 million estates and greater.

6. Probate is something you definitely want to avoid because …

   a. Costs from probate can be estimated at 5 to 10 percent of an estate's gross value.

   b. The probate process can take up to one or two years or longer, holding up heirs from receiving assets.

   c. Your family has no privacy or control of your estate during probate.

   d. All of the above.

7. True or false: Regardless of questions 4 and 5, the full estate tax bill comes due when the couple's estate passes on to their ultimate heirs.

8. True or false: "Gifting" is a term meaning you can give away money. The amount that the government allows tax-free per taxpayer, per year is …

    a. $5,000.

    b. $10,000.

    c. $15,000.

9. True or false: Setting up a living trust is a way to bypass Medicaid.

10. According to the American Academy of Estate Planning Attorneys, upon his death, W.C. Fields' estate was reduced by 30 percent thanks to taxes and probate.

Quiz

PART V

Life's Changes and Growth

HOUR 19

Changing Goals, as You Age

CHAPTER SUMMARY

LESSON PLAN:

Because your financial goals change as you age, this chapter is devoted to outlining different financial choices you can make as you grow older and wiser about your money. You'll also learn how to:

- Teach your children practical money habits.
- Begin planning for college saving.
- Set goals with flexibility for retirement.

Financial freedom and serenity come from decisions you make through time and the financial goals you try to meet. No one has greater power to control your financial destiny than you. Not even the best, smartest, most thoughtful financial planner will be looking out so closely for you and your family.

That said, what are some of the ways that you can begin to plan your financial future?

THE STAGES OF YOUR FINANCIAL LIFE

Several things will change the way you invest: age, marital status, a new job, a lottery winning, even unemployment (you will have less money to invest). There are so many things that can happen in life that cause people to reevaluate their financial goals.

Let's take a look, then, at the five stages of your financial life. Each represents a different portion of the time that you were given on this earth to live your life, and grow financially as your financial knowledge continues to grow. If you have decided to begin a family, a new host of financial considerations and decisions need to be added to your financial equation. Once children are born and raised, they, too, will begin to have questions about financial matters, and may ask you for some financial guidance, as well, as we will discuss later in the chapter.

One technique you could use is to set up a time with yourself and your family every one, five, and 10 years to "check in" with yourself and to examine the state of your finances. There are so many changes in our lives, and we barely have time to reflect. By setting up a "family meeting," you can begin this process and make new goals for yourself.

INFANCY THROUGH CHILDHOOD THROUGH TEENAGE YEARS

As they say, there are no accidents in life. You were born at just the right time to the right parents for you. Even though many of your memories may not be truly "golden," your parents probably gave you the best advice they could at the time. Many of us still wrestle with the demons of childhood and the messages we were given—or not given. Because emotions can so often give way to poor financial choices, you must make a pact with yourself to put those messages aside and begin to make your own financial decisions as an adult.

Let's take a look at this from another perspective. Say you are a parent and you want to bring your children up with good money values. How can you do this?

GETTING YOUR KIDS OFF TO A GOOD FINANCIAL START

Think about it. Since the time your kids could reach up to the bathroom sink you've been teaching them to brush their teeth every day: every morning, before they go to school, and at night before they go to bed. You've also *tried* to get them to "clean up" and "put away" their toys before they go to sleep, instilling a good daily habit of orderliness and organization.

As your children grow up and become young adults, you try to keep up with their homework, their friends, what television shows they're watching. Why do you do it? It's simple. You're trying to instill good habits in your children, no matter what their age. Just as you teach them cleanliness and physical hygiene, you also want them to gain a sense of self-worth and self-confidence. Hopefully they will take these principles with them through their life into their own independence.

In the same way, you are also the caretaker of your children's financial health. The earlier you introduce good financial habits in your children, the better off they will be.

With that in mind, let's take a look at some good tips to help your kids plan their financial goals.

KIDS AND MONEY

Kids, overall, are fascinated by money. From a very young age, children can be presented with shiny round objects such as quarters, nickels, dimes, and pennies and will have a feeling of *ownership*. Later you can teach them the value of purchasing power by taking a trip to a store that carries items such as candy or small toys. Let your young children select and purchase their items with their own money. This can be a valuable lesson about decision-making and money.

Older children become very interested in board games that include money as a tool to use to win the game. Even though *play money* is used, oftentimes such *play* is a child's first introduction to *money* as a tool that can realize financial objectives and can be used to further their momentum toward ac-quiring personal *financial strength*.

Children can also be taught about investing, even at a young age. For exam-ple, how many children know that you can buy little pieces of companies like The Gap, McDonald's, Coca-Cola, and Disney for as little as $25 a month?

By asking your children what clothes and products interest them, you can help your kids establish their own stock accounts, letting them pick what stocks they want to follow. This will lead them to a better understanding of how markets work. Plus, they will be excited as they help *you* follow the ups and downs of the stock by reading *The Wall Street Journal* or the business section of a newspaper.

SHORT-TERM VS. LONG-TERM GOALS

This is also a great time to discuss short-term goals vs. long-term goals. Little Jimmy, age eight, who saves his allowance to make a raid on the local candy store every Friday, is contemplating a short-term goal. On the other hand, if he begins to save extra money toward a long-term purchase like a skate board a year from now, he would be planning a long-term goal. It's important to instill these principles early in kids because they often grow up thinking that they can get whatever they want from their over-generous parents.

Check out Linda Barbanel's excellent book, *Piggy Bank to Credit Card: Teach Your Child the Financial Facts of Life* (Crown Publishers, 1994). In it, she explores helping your children learn the nuts and bolts of money, savings, postponing gratification, and making financial decisions as they grow.

TIME IS ON THEIR SIDE

Your kids have something very important working for them: time. Billionaires have tons of money, but kids have tons of time. No matter what happens with the stock market, it gets better over time. Starting your infant child with a savings account that she can begin to manage when she's older, say eight or nine years old, can be a great way to start your child thinking wisely about money.

You can also begin to teach your kids about stocks, mutual funds, bonds, and portfolios. Even if they don't seem interested or attentive enough at first, keep at it. Start small and conservatively, perhaps advising your kids about mutual funds and then progress to actually buying stocks when they are old enough to understand the process.

For a terrific Web site for teaching kids about investing, check out the Stein Roe Young Investor Fund at www.steinroe.com, a five-star fund with a cool Web site geared toward kids. Another fun place to try is the "Fool's School" at the always-amusing www.fool.com, which has a section devoted to kids and money as well as www.fool.com/FamilyFool for more info on teens and investing.

BOYS VS. GIRLS?

There are still sometimes discrepancies between the information that girls get regarding money and the information boys get. If you are a mom, you may also remember not getting great financial advice when you were growing up. You can help rectify this if you have a daughter.

Thanks to *Girls, Incorporated,* a Manhattan-based think tank and policy group with a goal of financially empowering young women in their teenage years, here are several tips for raising financially savvy girls. Because daughters are often the ones who get "left behind" in the financial game, parents of daughters may want to make a special note:

1. **Make money moments.** Help your daughter understand that careful spending and financial planning are part of her everyday life. If you have a checkbook, balance it with your daughter. Clip coupons with her and talk about why you use them and how they can you can save money.

2. **Dollar and a dream.** Use the Sunday classified ads to talk about salaries, the cost of renting an apartment, or making a purchase such as furniture or a car. Create a scenario for your daughter to pick her favorite job. How much money would she make? Which apartment would she rent? Which furnishings or car could she afford to buy?

3. **Save for a rainy day.** Whenever your daughter gets money, whether it's 25¢ or $25, encourage her to save some of it to use at a later date. Ask her to pick a toy, book, CD, or any other item she would like to purchase. While she is saving her money, *visit* that item at the store to encourage her interest. Discuss her allowance and how to determine how much money to spend for things she wants now and how much to save for later.

4. **Take stock in America.** Pretend to buy a share of stock in your daughter's favorite company, toy store, or restaurant. Watch the company's commercials, advertisements, news articles, and the stock's growth and decline in the business section of your local paper or on television. If your daughter develops an interest in the stock, call the business for its annual report. The annual report describes the company and its holdings.

TIME SAVER

Check out the cool Web site www.MissMoney.com for more advice on teaching your daughter about investing. Also, check out www.girls-inc.org for more information about financially empowering your daughter for life.

5. **Adolescents and early adulthood.** A valuable item adolescents and people in their early 20s have before them is time. Your financial future is not exactly finished if you are 30 years old and just beginning to create an investment future, however. As you will see in the following sections, the gift of time can be used wisely to help you build your wealth. That's the beauty of compounded interest.

Just Let It Grow

One of the most fascinating tools at your disposal is compounded interest. Say you begin an IRA that compounds interest at a 10 percent rate at the age of 19. You continue to put in $2,000 each year until the age of 26 and do not put anything else in until your retirement age of 65. What happens? You will end up with an account balance of $1,035,148!

Now double-check and see what happens if you start the same IRA at 27 rather than at age 19. Notice you will have to continue putting in $2,000 a year for 38 years before you reach age 65. And even then, your total accumulation will be $805,185—far beneath the million+ dollars you would have earned if you had started this technique at age 19 and quit at age 26!

The Time Value of Money

The following chart will perhaps make a believer out of you, too:

Investor A: Investing at age 19.

Investor B: Investing at age 27.

Time Value of Money

Age	Investment	Total Value	Age	Investment	Total Value
19	$2,000	$2,200	19	0	0
20	$2,000	$4,620	20	0	0
21	$2,000	$7,282	21	0	0
22	$2,000	$10,210	22	0	0
23	$2,000	$13,431	23	0	0
24	$2,000	$16,974	24	0	0
25	$2,000	$20,871	25	0	0
26	$2,000	$25,158	26	0	0
27	0	$27,674	27	$2,000	$2,200
28	0	$30,442	28	$2,000	$4,620
29	0	$33,486	29	$2,000	$7,282
30	0	$36,834	30	$2,000	$10,210
31	0	$40,518	31	$2,000	$13,431
32	0	$44,570	32	$2,000	$16,974
33	0	$48,027	33	$2,000	$20,871
34	0	$53,929	34	$2,000	$25,158

Age	Investment	Total Value	Age	Investment	Total Value
35	0	$59,322	35	$2,000	$29,874
36	0	$65,256	36	$2,000	$35,072
37	0	$71,780	37	$2,000	$40,768
38	0	$78,958	38	$2,000	$47,045
39	0	$86,854	39	$2,000	$53,949
40	0	$95,540	40	$2,000	$61,544
41	0	$105,094	41	$2,000	$69,899
42	0	$115,603	42	$2,000	$79,089
43	0	$127,163	43	$2,000	$89,198
44	0	$130,880	44	$2,000	$100,318
45	0	$153,868	45	$2,000	$112,550
46	0	$169,255	46	$2,000	$126,005
47	0	$188,180	47	$2,000	$140,805
48	0	$204,798	48	$2,000	$157,086
49	0	$226,278	49	$2,000	$174,094
50	0	$247,806	50	$2,000	$194,694
51	0	$272,586	51	$2,000	$216,363
52	0	$299,845	52	$2,000	$240,199
53	0	$329,830	53	$2,000	$266,419
54	0	$362,813	54	$2,000	$295,261
55	0	$399,094	55	$2,000	$326,988
56	0	$439,003	56	$2,000	$361,886
57	0	$482,904	57	$2,000	$400,275
58	0	$531,194	58	$2,000	$442,503
59	0	$584,314	59	$2,000	$488,953
60	0	$642,745	60	$2,000	$540,048
61	0	$707,020	61	$2,000	$596,253
62	0	$777,722	62	$2,000	$658,078
63	0	$855,494	63	$2,000	$726,086
64	0	$941,043	64	$2,000	$800,895
65	0	$1,035,148	65	$2,000	$883,185

*All of the above based on a 10 percent compound rate with investment on January 2nd of each year.

That is a lot of money for such an early investment!

One couple who saw this visual was very surprised by the steep earning curve they could create for their child's future by starting and sticking to a simple investment discipline.

You Can Even Start at Age Two

One way you could build an investment like this is to merely begin saving $2,000 a year for your child even beginning at age two (assuming a conservative growth estimate of 10 percent per year). Think also of the benefits of putting the money in a custodial account, an IRA, or an annuity account. The custodial account is taxed less, a traditional IRA grows tax-deferred, and a Roth IRA grows tax-free. The annuity is also tax-deferred.

Don't feel that you're limited to $2,000, though; you could save more than this if you like and are able. Although you are limited to a $2,000-per-year investment if you have an IRA account, you can invest in other retirement accounts such as tax-deferred annuities in addition to this. Remember: time is on your side as you continue to save throughout your life.

College-Age Investors

Saving money is not exactly a first priority for college-age students. College is frequently a time when many students go into debt—buying books, meals out with friends, and paying for tuition. Your job in college is to try not to get into debt, by whatever means necessary. Also, if you have a work-study job or other job on or off campus, begin to put some of this money into savings.

Understandably, college can definitely be a tricky time to save. Keep in mind the "Time Value of Money" chart and how the numbers add up. If you can put aside $2,000 a year—or as much as you can afford—in an interest-bearing account (say a mutual fund that has done well over time), you may graduate college with a sizable "nest egg" to use in your retirement years.

Also, college is a great time to open an honest dialogue about money with your parents. Oftentimes, parents want to bail you out if you get into even severe money troubles—you're still their "baby," after all. As you become an adult, though, you will begin to realize that this is not always the right answer. Try to establish a balance with your parents about money and when you'll want or need them to bail you out. When you finally get out on your own, you don't want your parents meddling in your financial affairs!

You're out of College—Now What?

As we've mentioned, different events in your life will change the way you invest—age, marital status, a new job, winning the lottery, having children, unemployment (you will have less money to invest), and so on. There are so many things that can happen in your life that can cause you to reevaluate your financial goals.

No matter whether you are single, newly married, a professional living on your own for the first time, or still looking for post-college employment, you are going to want to keep your debt and your expenditures low. The more you can save at this point in your life, the better off you will be in the long run. (Refer to the "Time Value of Money" table if you need a reminder.)

GO TO ▶
Refer to Hour 20, "Financial Independence," for more insights on establishing yourself once out of college.

You will undoubtedly change jobs and move from one career to the next as you try out what works for you. If you accrued debt in college, you will be beginning a system of paying back what you now owe. Common types of college debts include student loans and any personal loans you may have had to take while finishing school. Just because you are out on your own does not mean you can forfeit on these debts! Even though your 20s are a time of experimentation and trying out new things—new jobs, new apartments, new friends, etc., they are also a time of responsibility—not infallibility.

But I Don't Make Enough to Save!

For the person who doesn't think he or she makes enough money to save, remember this: A portion of everything you ever make in life should always be yours to keep—and save. Why should you not be able to, with a bit more discipline in your personal spending and financial life, put away 10 percent of what you bring home?

GO TO ▶
Refer to Hour 2, "Cleaning Up Clutter/Debt Repayment," for any questions regarding your debt and debt repayment.

What if you'd like to invest but you're not making a lot of money, and you're living from paycheck to paycheck? You may not feel you have a substantial amount to invest. Even putting $2,000 a year into an IRA averages out to saving only $166 a month. Between what you spend on movies, going out to dinner, and your clothing budget, try to "pay yourself first" by sending your first $166 to your IRA. At age 65, you will be glad you did!

The Rule of 72

Let's say you hope to make 15 percent on your investments in any given year. Divide 15 into 72. The result tells you how many years it will take a lump sum of money to double when compounded annually. In this case, if you invest $2,000 in an IRA and do the math, it will take exactly 4.8 years for your money to double. If you have a specific monetary goal in mind, this formula helps you to practically approximate, assuming a given interest rate (but note that nothing can ever be truly assumed). But given an interest rate, you can have a better idea of how many years it will take for you to reach a certain financial goal.

Using these simple strategies over a lifetime, and given the way the market has averaged throughout history, everyone should be able to retire a millionaire if they begin investing prudently and early. Assuming that investment performance from years past can be replicated in the years ahead, if you start investing now, you could be well on your way to establishing a firm financial foothold.

Time for Marriage and Settling Down

Of course there comes a time in many people's lives when they decide they want to "settle down" and get married. One instant bonus that may come out of this decision is that if you and your future spouse are both working, your household income will greatly increase—seemingly overnight! By having two working spouses in one household, what was once an income for one becomes two incomes for two, eventually for three or more—if having children is one of your goals.

On the other hand, although most professional women tend to continue working while juggling kids and day care, there are many families where one spouse doesn't work or works part time. It is important for spouses to sit down together and rationally discuss the specifics of income before deciding on having a family. There can be a drastic cut in income if one of the married partners decides not to work or to reduce the number of hours worked.

The IRS gets involved, too. By getting married, the IRS gives you special deductions that you would not have if you filed as two single people, living together or otherwise.

How Can You Save?

Many newly married couples develop a strategy in which, if they're making enough money, one paycheck from one spouse helps pay for the daily expenses, while the other paycheck goes right into savings. One young

Manhattan couple—he a stockbroker, she a successful pianist—follow their finances closely along this route. Because their goal is to pay off their mortgage as soon as possible, they have elected to take on a 15-year mortgage and even "overpay" on that. The result? Their $180,000 condo is nearly half paid off—in just five or six years.

On the other hand, the same investor sees that he could also be putting this same money into savings if he chooses a 30-year mortgage plan. He sees the benefits of both: By paying off the mortgage early, he attains peace of mind; but, his money could be working "better" for him if invested properly rather than put toward paying off mortgage debt.

FAMILY GOALS

One way you may want to examine your goals as you age is to look at them as short-term, intermediate, and long-term goals. We have explored some of the following table in Hour 1, "Developing Your Financial Goals."

Short-Term Goals	Intermediate Goals	Long-Term Goals
Buy first home	Funding a major trip around the world	Comfortable retirement
Buy first car	Funding your kid's college education	Financial independence
Luxury items: nicer stereo, nicer TV	Purchasing a nicer home or a second home	Giving to relatives
Saving for a rainy-day purchase	Purchasing a boat	Giving to charity
	Starting a second business	Caring for an older relative
	Giving to charity	Funding a retirement vehicle
	Paying off a mortgage early	Funding long-term care
	Paying off debt	Luxury items

Again, many of your goals will change as you age. If you can plan out your own version of this chart—right now, as you read this—you will be on your way to examining how your financial goals have changed, say, since you were first starting out earning a living.

EVERY COUPLE IS DIFFERENT

Jerry, an attorney who didn't come from an overly privileged family background, made sure he worked during his summers as an undergraduate and then later defended cab drivers during his first, second, and third years of law school. In other words, he started working early and began saving and investing his money in his 20s.

He had some savings but no organized plan or master vision for the future. He was "just saving for the sake the saving, knowing that I'd need it somewhere and sometime. Back then I had no idea what I was going to do with it; I knew at some point it would come in handy."

During his third year of law school, Jerry's cab-driver-defense practice was growing, and he kept working steadily. His wife was working as an accountant. Basically, they only needed one of their incomes to live. The other they used to invest. This couple ended up owning a New York co-op together. Now they have three boys and live in a house they built on land they bought in Massachusetts.

Eventually, the husband built up quite a lot of real estate holdings that fluctuated greatly with the market's variations.

Says the attorney, "My goals changed quite a bit; mostly from senior year of college through law school there were a lot of changes. I got married after my first year of law school. When we bought the co-op in Manhattan, we were not even officially engaged. We just knew we didn't want to rent: We wanted to own something."

To make a long story short: Without a firm plan in mind, this attorney ended up having much of his money in real estate investments. This was not bad when the market was up, like in the mid- to late 1980s. But property values kept coming down with some of the fluctuations of the market, and he lost a lot when he reinvested and bought more property.

Jerry held relatively high-equity positions. So, fortunately, when things began to go sour, his holdings allowed him to breathe a bit easier about his situation. But because he had not diversified his holdings, he and his wife, in his own words, "hurt ourselves because we stayed within one sector. Now I am much more diversified in stocks and bonds. But back then, I put all of my eggs in one basket."

Again, a word to the wise: Begin saving early and have a plan to get where you want to go. If you're unsure, find a good, solid financial advisor and ask questions.

Having Kids: When?

Once you're in your 20s, 30s, and 40s, you may, like many couples do, consider having children. You may not be a part of a couple, but you still might want to have children. Having children, for most people, can be an overwhelmingly positive experience. But it is also one that you need to be financially prepared for.

GO TO ▶
Refer to Hours 1, "Developing Your Financial Goals," 5, "Investing Basics," and 13, "Finding the Right Financial Advisor," for more tips on saving early and making a financial plan.

One doctor, 38 and an Ivy League graduate, is finding that "one of the most financially overwhelming things that happens [in your life] is [when] you start thinking about your kids going to college. I'm starting to hear figures that by the time my kids start going, college could cost upwards of $275,000. You start to realize how much the expense of having kids is. When I told my father I was going to have a third child, he just began laughing since I was the one who was going to be paying for it!"

Granted, lots of grandparents love to dote on and give money to their grandkids; but in the end, the financial responsibility is all yours.

If you are newly married and are considering having a child, many financial calculators are available that can help you figure out what sort of savings you should begin if you want to have enough saved up by the time your child nears college age.

Let's imagine you're looking at spending a minimum of $50,000 a year on your kid's college expenses. You can plug in the amount you presently make, the present value of your account, how many years you have ahead until your little one, currently six months old, enters her first year of college, and the estimated return of the account you are considering.

Your chart may look like this:

Present value: 0

Number of years: 18

Interest rate: 8 percent monthly

Goal: $200,000

Letting the calculator do its magic, you would have to invest $5,340 a year—$445 a month—starting right now for every kid you want to send to college. To some parents, just saving half of their children's college costs is a major family financial goal.

There are dozens of college savings calculators out there, but try www.collegeboard.org/finaid/fastud/html/fincalc/fcintro.html for a standard calculator that can help you as you plug in the numbers that you are looking to project.

WHAT ABOUT WHEN YOU GET A RAISE?

Take the case of Mary and Bob Smith. Bob is an industrial engineer making $75,000. He just received a raise of $10,000 a year to pull in $85,000 annually. The raise of $10,000 a year adds $833 to Bob's paycheck a month. What should Bob do with this additional money? He's able to continue to pay off his mortgage, and he and his wife now have a surplus amount of $833 a month to play with. Do you think it would be in the Smith family's best interest to use that money as extra vacation money, use it as spending money, or to put it in a savings account earning just 2 percent interest?

GO TO ▶

Refer to Hour 13 for more tips on finding the right financial advisor for you.

According to one financial analyst, the Smiths should continue to add a portion of this extra money to their existing investments. Because this would be considered a life change, now would be a good time for Bob and Mary, or anyone in their situation, to reevaluate their goals and their investment discipline. This would also be a good time to reconnect with their financial advisor, or if they didn't already have one, to get one.

By all means, enjoy your life, and use your riches to do something nice for yourself and your family. When it comes down to it, though, remember that sometimes the greatest gift you can give your family is the gift of future savings. The Smiths could achieve a great deal by investing Bob's raise money for future growth potential.

PLANNING FOR RETIREMENT

Now, let's skip to the time so many people dream about: retirement. You want to have more time and money during your retirement years to do the things you want to do: see your grandkids, travel, and envision what you'd like to have or give away for the future. More than likely, as you approach retirement age, you have looked at your investments and perhaps have reallocated them to a more conservative investment strategy.

Many investment advisors advocate reallocating your investments from growth to income. Selling stocks and stock mutual fund holdings, or a portion of them, and allocating more heavily to bonds and bond mutual funds is one way to do this. You're much more protected from any fluctuations of the market this way.

What about your grandkids? Maybe you want to help establish a custodial account for them. You can give up to $10,000 (as of this current year) per year per child without incurring gift tax. If you are married, you and your spouse can give up to $20,000 per year without incurring gift tax.

One conservative way to approach this time of your life, according to one analyst, is to take your age and put a percentage next to it. If you're 40 years old, the percentage of your investments that should be in bonds is 40 percent. The rest of your investments should be in less conservative investments such as stocks. Logically, it follows that as you get older you get more conservative and less conscious of wealth-building than you are with wealth-preserving.

One example is a retiree who is 70 years old, who may very well have 70 percent invested in bonds. You may not be able to recoup that money at that age if you have your money in a more risky venture, say stocks. You need to preserve what you have.

All through life, you are going to be changing or altering your investment strategy. It's also not only your age, but your risk tolerance that will affect how and where you invest. Do you have a failsafe, or money socked away elsewhere? Will you mind taking risks when you are 60, 70, or 80 years old? These are questions that only you will be able to answer, in time.

CARING FOR YOUR AGING PARENTS AS YOU AGE

As you age, so do your parents. In a society such as today's when people are living longer, often into their 80s, 90s, and even 100s, you can expect longer life spans, and as a result, more needs to take care of with older adults.

GO TO ▶
Refer to Hour 18, "Estate Planning," for more information on taking care of your aging parents and yourself with long-term-care insurance.

Looking after the needs of growing children is hard enough. Add to that the demands of caring for aging parents, and the responsibilities of the so-called "sandwich generation" can be overwhelming—particularly when it comes to estate planning.

It is essential that adults with both young and old family members to care for address a number of estate planning issues. That way, no generation's happiness or well-being will be compromised at the expense of another's. And, because people are living longer, the chances of a family needing long-term care to help take care of its elderly has greatly increased.

HOUR'S UP!

Without looking back in the hour, see if you can answer the following questions about changing your financial goals as you age:

1. True or false: To achieve clarity on your financial goals as you age, schedule a "financial goals party" with yourself and your family every one, five, and 10 years to "check in" with yourself and your goals.

2. True or false: It is never too early to begin teaching your children about money, saving, and the stock market.

3. True or false: If you put $2,000 into a fund with a 10 percent interest rate each year between the ages of 19 and 26 and then put in $0 from ages 27 to 65, you would have greater resulting earnings than if you started at age 27 and put in $2,000 each year thereafter until 65.

4. The Rule of 72 is …

   a. A way of achieving your financial goals by age 72.

   b. A way of mathematically determining how many years it will take to double your investment.

   c. Calling 72 of your friends when you have an investment question.

5. What is the mathematical Rule of 72?

   A. You take the percentage of what you hope to make on your investments over a year and divide by 72, giving you the number of years it will take for your money compounded annually to double.

   b. $E = mc^2$

   c. 3.14

6. True or false: When you get married and begin to have two incomes in the family, don't worry about saving any of your spouse's check. Live it up and spend it all.

7. True or false: When contemplating having children, you may want to use a financial calculator or plan in making the decisions as to how much you want to put aside for their future college educations.

8. According to more conservative financial planners, if you are 50 years old and want to think conservatively about your portfolio, what percentage of your portfolio should be in bonds (the rest in stocks, mutual funds, and so on)?

   a. 40 percent

   b. 50 percent

   c. 60 percent

9. True or false: As you enter your retirement years, it is a good idea to reallocate your investments from growth to income to protect you from any fluctuations of the market.

10. True or false: No matter what your goals are as you age, it is also important to keep in mind the financial responsibilities of taking care of your parents, as they age.

Quiz

HOUR 20

Financial Independence

Let's face it. Being single and on your own with very few financial commitments can be a special time in your life—one of growth, exploration, and commitment to new challenges. Because you have fewer financial responsibilities than your married friends (for example, you don't have to plan for your kids' college educations yet), you can live with a kind of freedom that only youth (and singleness) can bring.

As your financial goals change and as you change, it is important to continue to be clear on your money flow and money goals. This is especially true as you leave college and enter the "real world" of paying bills, paying off loans, and starting a life on your own.

The earlier you begin planning for your future, the better off you will be. With various retirement plans and IRAs available, you would do better to save $2,000 a year for the 10 years during your 20s than if you started at 30 and put in $2,000 per year for the rest of your life. The more you plan for yourself financially—even in your early 20s and 30s—the more you will reap the benefits down the road of life.

YOU ARE RESPONSIBLE FOR YOU

As a single person, you are responsible for filing your own tax returns on time. Whereas once you might have relied on your parents for their tax benefits, once you are

CHAPTER SUMMARY

LESSON PLAN:

If you are single, your financial goals can differ greatly from a married couple's goals. You may be a single working person who makes a good salary and wants to figure out the best ways of making your money work for you. You'll also learn how to:

- Make a basic plan when you land your first job.
- Avoid debt and its pitfalls.
- Make a savings plan.
- Avoid or repair bad credit from a partner.

grown up and in the working world, that responsibility falls upon you. If you are single and are not claimed as a dependent on your parents' tax return, you must file a tax return if your adjusted gross income exceeds a certain amount as mandated by the government's most recent figures. This figure changes each year, so ask your accountant to double-check the figure for you if you have questions.

But the good news is that you don't have to do it alone. There are probably many good and reasonable accountants in your area. By looking through the Yellow Pages or asking friends who have had good success in working with one, you can find a decently priced accountant who can help you over the "hump" of transitioning into the real world.

GO TO ▶
Refer to Hour 14, "Taxes: Time to Get Clarity," to read more about filing correctly and filing on time.

Too often young people believe they can do "anything" and end up either not filing, not filing on time, or, if they do file properly, missing out on possible refunds or other benefits. Plus, there is definitely a peace of mind that comes from having another pair of eyes read through your tax information to make sure it is correct—at least the first time you file on your own.

A Young Story

This is the true story of a young woman in her early 20s. Lisa, a writer and a graduate of a prestigious Ivy League school, had always been told she was "special," that she was one of the "best and the brightest." Having gone to a top Ivy League school didn't help her when it came to responsibilities. For instance, she learned she could get extensions on papers, exams, and tests. Why not bills?

Lisa was determined to make her way to the big and bright lights of New York City. Even though she had been told how expensive and how dangerous it was to live there, she was determined to hold on to her dream of being a writer based in the Big Apple—Manhattan.

Of course, when she got there, she realized that she wasn't in college anymore. In fact, while Lisa had enjoyed her college experience, taking fine arts and English courses and writing for her college paper, she knew there was a much bigger world out there that she wanted to experience.

The only question was: How was she going to pay for it?

REALITY BITES

Here we get into a very important transition question for many just-out-of college young people who are making their first leaps into adulthood: How can you adjust your lifestyle so that you are enjoying your 20s but not going into debt doing it?

As you are well aware by now, credit cards are everywhere, with tempting offers of huge credit lines and low interest rates to unassuming college students—and people of any age.

Be well aware: Just because you are being offered credit at a young age does not mean that credit is good for you. In fact, you are probably at your most vulnerable at this time: Credit card agents know that you probably don't have tons of money floating around to pay off your credit cards on time. Thus, they get you by plying you with tons of interest charges while you can barely pay off the minimums.

WHERE DO PARENTS COME IN?

Parents of college-age and older children reading this might be nodding with recognition. What do you do when your fledgling daughter or son—a baby, really, in the real world—wants to "break free" and have a cool place of their own, but does not have the money to pay for it?

Many parents have had to put their own dreams on hold while they figure out ways of financing their children's college educations. This does not have to continue once your child has grown up enough to begin taking care of themselves.

ONE SOLUTION: POST-COLLEGE SAVINGS ACCOUNT

One solution you might consider is to begin thinking of starting a small "post-college" savings account for your progeny. Perhaps, too, your son or daughter could put money into this account from any work-study or off-campus jobs they might hold, as money toward the future.

This way, if your son or daughter needs to tap into this money to make their "transition" into the real world, let's say for a first-month, last-month, and security deposit situation on an apartment, they will be set without much of a financial hassle.

JUST A MINUTE

You don't want your children relying on you too much as they make their way into the world. The post-college savings account could save you a lot of headaches in this new financial time in your "grownup" child's life. By establishing this fund, you have democratically set up a fund that could even earn interest while your children begin to think about what they want to do with their lives.

GO TO ▶
Refer to Hour 24, "Your Future: Finding a Job Online," for more tips on easy job-searching skills.

Now, if you are a newly minted college grad reading this, remember that it is your responsibility not to get into debt after college and to keep working to bring in cash flow. Not sure yet what you want to do? There are many ways of bringing in money while you figure it out. One of the most popular ways of making money during this transition is temping, or working as a temporary employee in an office environment. Most college grads these days have a solid range of computer skills and can easily find themselves working in a variety of environments that use computer skills—and making good money, to boot.

NOT GETTING INTO DEBT

Getting back to Lisa, the writer just starting out in New York: After much phoning, sending resumés, and just plain walking around town, Lisa landed her first job at a magazine and found an apartment she shared with several roommates. In typical publishing fashion, she barely made enough to get by. But, again, she had her credit cards, which made life that much easier.

Eventually, Lisa was taking her Neiman Marcus card she received in college and treating herself to pricey lunches at Bergdorf Goodman on Fifth Avenue. Later, she'd take her Sears card with her to the big store and order a nice, pricey air conditioner, because it got hot in the summers in the city.

How did she pay for all of this? She couldn't—and she wouldn't. She'd skip payment dates, racking up more and more interest each month. And it wasn't all fun. Most of the time she spent racking her brain, wondering how she was going to stretch her measly magazine salary to cover each of her new bills as they came in. Telephone bills? Online costs? These she would neglect to pay. To her, her debt was a fog that would *someday* clear up. In fact, much of her life up to that point was in a fog.

By the time our friend Lisa caught up with herself, she was over $15,000 in debt, and was having to borrow massive amounts of funds from her parents semi-monthly just to pay the regular basic monthly bills. Her mother, in particular, was not happy with the situation, but what could she do?

The good news is, our friend Lisa found her way to an excellent 12-step program, Debtors Anonymous, which many people find has been incredibly helpful in stemming the root causes of compulsive debting and spending. Lisa slowly made progress in D.A. recovery. It wasn't easy, but now—over three years later—Lisa is committed to not debting a day at a time. She never debts and always pays her bills on time. She deals with her creditors in a timely fashion. In short, she became a "grownup" when it came to money issues. She realized she was no longer going to be able to rely on anyone else to get her out of her financial scrapes.

LANDING THAT FIRST JOB: NOW WHAT?

Not all stories are as drastic as Lisa's. Not everyone gets into a long-term debt situation. Take Stacy. She's a junior advertising assistant at a big firm on Madison Avenue. She makes a modest salary—the expected amount for a first-time job. She has credit cards, but she pays off her debt in full each month. She isn't making a lot now, but she envisions moving up the ladder and eventually getting her raises accordingly.

Stacy's background is a bit different from Lisa's. Her mother, an accountant, had Stacy help with looking through receipts and adding them up at tax time. Stacy was always prompt, paying her taxes on time or even a little before. Lisa was always vague about what exactly she should be filing when April 15 rolled around.

In short, Stacy was given a kind of overview about money from her parents, whereas Lisa was not.

When Stacy moved to New York, she found a decent and livable apartment that was reasonably priced to rent with three roommates. She interviewed and was hired at the advertising firm where she now works. She didn't have a lot of debt from student loans, and so she found she was able to begin saving some of her earnings each month.

WHAT CAN YOU DO ABOUT SAVING YOUR MONEY?

If you are in your early 20s, you have what a lot of people in their 50s and 60s don't have: time. From our example, Stacy, making $35,000 a year before taxes, was able to have a bit of nest-egg left over each month after paying her bills.

GO TO ▶
Refer to Hours 5, "Investing Basics," and 13, "Finding the Right Financial Advisor," for more on these topics.

John Leidy, a financial consultant at a major investment company in New York, says that, thanks to the law of compounded interest, it makes sense to begin investing as soon as you can. Say you invest $2,000 a year for 10 years from the time you're 22 until you're 32. Then you stop investing and let the money compound at 10 percent for 28 years until you're 59½, which, depending on the type of account, may be the earliest you can remove it without penalty. You'll have $505,629 after contributing a total of $20,000 and letting it compound.

On the other hand, if you wait until you're 32 to begin investing, and you put away $2,000 a year for 28 years until you're 59½, you'll only have $295,262, even though you'll have contributed a total of $56,000. Since money compounds more the longer you leave it in your account, it makes sense to start putting away as early as you can.

(Keep in mind that the above computations show only what is in your account and do not take into consideration the tax effects of your investments, which can vary greatly depending on whether you choose to make your fund contributions as tax-deferred contributions or to pay the tax up front.)

Says Leidy, "Time is on your side when you are a young investor. Start small. If all you can put into a mutual fund account is $50 a month, begin with that. It will all grow over time, due to compounded interest."

Your Goals

GO TO ▶
Refer to Hours 1, "Developing Your Financial Goals," and 2, "Cleaning Up Clutter/Debt Repayment," for foolproof techniques on focusing your goals.

The next step is to become clearer on your financial goals. Do you eventually want to own a house, either on your own or with a future spouse? Do you envision planning to take a special vacation trip around the world at the end of your work year, or perhaps the next summer? How much money do you want to have at your disposal?

These are all important goals to look at, and only you can know for sure what your goals are. Once they are categorized, you can begin to make mental arrangements for beginning to save toward each goal. Haphazard goal-setting will result in a lack of clarity about your money issues over time.

Debt expert Mary Hunt, in her book *Cheapskate Monthly Money Makeover,* advocates creating separate savings accounts for each of your various goals. Again, for your vacation account, you could put in an amount from each paycheck until you have saved what you need to take the trip. The same goes, say, for that new mountain bike you want to take with you when you go on your trip. Eventually, you will get into the habit of saving, and it will become a monthly habit rather than a burden.

SAVE WHAT YOU CAN EACH MONTH

To that end, a great strategy for growing your savings is to commit to investing a certain amount per month. If you can invest $100 a month, for example, and commit to increasing your monthly investment by the rate of inflation each year (so if the inflation rate is 4 percent, invest $100 a month the first year, $104 a month the second year, $108 the third year), your savings will add up quickly.

Be sure to find a good investment accountant who brings in a high rate of interest. You are young; you can afford a portfolio that is a bit on the riskier side than when you are say, 50 or 60 and have to be much more conservative about your investment choices.

As you send in your other bills, think of the $100 payment—or whatever amount you can afford—as a monthly expense like your phone or electric bill. Put the payment into a money-market account each month when you're paying your bills. If you invest $100 a month for five years and increase the monthly contribution by 10 percent a year, you'll have $9,278, assuming a 10 percent rate of return.

FIVE STEPS TO MAKING YOUR MONEY GROW

In short, here are five steps you can take to see the greatest return over time, according to Leidy:

- Start investing as early as you can.
- Get the highest interest rate or rate of return you can find.
- Be clear about your financial goals.
- Try to make the maximum allowable contribution every year, even if it's not tax-deductible.
- Leave your money in the account as long as you can after you've hit age 59½; your money will compound more the longer you let it sit.

WOMEN AND MONEY ISSUES

In decades past, women were often thought of as the second-place decision-maker in the family; the husband, the so-called "bread winner," was the one who would make the decisions about car buying, house buying, investing, etc. Not anymore! As times change, so has female buying power.

Nowhere was this more evident than in a recent *New York Times* article, "Castle First, Prince Later: Marketing to Ms." In this piece, author Julie V. Iovine examines some of the newest techniques that marketers are using to market home-building products to women, once the final province for men.

To quote Iovine, "Thanks to delayed marriages, profitable careers, higher divorce rates, and longer lives, the number of women living alone has increased by more than a third in the last 15 years to 30 million, according to the Census Bureau. Nearly 57 percent of single women now own their own homes, throwing cold dishwater on the accepted wisdom that homes are the exclusive territory of couples."

And, even though most homes are still purchased by couples, women who live alone or who are single heads of households increased as a share of total home buyers, from 10 percent in 1985 to 15 percent in 1997. That's some statistical jump!

Yes, women seem to be becoming proactive in handling their finances—much more than their mothers were a generation ago. Much of this stems from the overall baby-boomer generation entering its retirement years: There is now an overall new and vital interest in individual investing and retirement planning across the board.

Women have really begun to jump into the world of finance head on. More power to women investors!

TIME SAVER

 Several excellent money-related sites geared toward women and investing exist on the Internet. Check out www.ivillage.com, www.msmoney.com, www.womenconnect.com, and www.women.com for more financial information and ways of maintaining your personal portfolios and spending plans.

Let's Be Proactive

Proactively handling finances often seems a daunting task to many women because they don't understand the process.

According to Tiffany Bass, the founder and visionary behind an excellent new site for women exploring money issues called www.msmoney.com,

"Once women clear that mental block in their minds that associates money with difficulty, the doors to enlightenment will fly open and they will be ready to take responsibility for their financial destiny."

"Women only need to spend a little time learning about the financial world before they realize that it isn't so hard after all. And for single women, that can actually be a very empowering task."

One of the reasons Bass was compelled to create the MsMoney.com site grew out of personal experience. "I grew up in a neighborhood in Chicago where money was not prevalent. I saw too many people living paycheck to paycheck who were missing out on so much of life because they did not know the basics of money management."

"Those same people, if they put away a few dollars a week and eliminated their debt, could drastically change their whole lives. That is how simple it can be sometimes. Yet few people realize this, especially women."

She continues, by e-mail interview: "I realized that if you taught the woman of the household the financial management process (that same woman who makes 80 percent of all retail purchases), then you would teach the whole family. If [women] are the ones spending the money, then they should be the ones who know how much to spend and what to spend it on. It only makes sense, right?"

"Also, if you teach women something they are likely to not only teach their family the simple concepts, they also will be compelled to tell their community of friends."

THE FINANCIAL SERVICES SECTOR KNOWS

In the past, women felt that money and investing issues weren't for them. Their husbands, parents, or whoever were going to take care of all that! But all of that has changed. Banks and financial services firms especially have begun to realize the potential of women as investors. They are reaching out to women in more ways than ever before.

One way to learn more is to check out your local community college or seminar centers for classes on finance. Banks often offer mini-seminars in which you can walk right in and participate. Many of the big brokerage firms— sensing the opportunity that women present as smart, careful investors of the future—have set up in-house seminars that women can take if they are considering investing. It's never too early to start to learn. If you're a woman, there may have been too many reasons already why you've decided not to bite the bullet and invest in yourself!

According to the National Center for Women and Retirement Research Survey, 94 percent of women believe that they can be as capable as men at understanding money and investing. Eighty-eight percent are open to new investment opportunities; 78 percent actually prefer to be the family member making decisions.

PLANNING YOUR GOALS

You always hear about these "financial goals," but if you don't really sit down and write these goals down, the fact is you will not reach them. Financial goals can be as short-term as saving money to buy a new car or as forward-looking as planning for retirement. If you are a single young woman, say between 20 and 30, the time to start investing is now, as you have time on your hands.

Don't give up hope, though, if you are in your 30s, 40s, 50s, and up; once you begin taking financial power and using it to invest wisely, you will reap the benefits.

Clearly, it's never too early to begin planning for long-term goals. Keep these three rules in mind as you analyze your own goals:

- **Be specific.** Having "enough" money for retirement is not a goal. Retiring in 15 years with monthly income of $5,000 is a specific goal that you can reach.
- **Be realistic.** Realize that it will take time to achieve your goals. Financial planning is a long-term process.
- **Be patient and disciplined.** Pay yourself first, before your bills, and make regular saving a major part of your investment plan.

YOU ARE NOT YOUR MEMORIES

You are not your memories when it comes to finance. Too often, women dwell on the messages about money they were given as children or teenagers that stay with them for decades. Many link their personal successes or failures to money messages told to them by their fathers, mothers, or both.

Victoria, a successful book author, recently described a memory in her past about money: Her father, a successful businessman who divorced her mother when Victoria was young, used to say to her "Enjoy my money while you got it, because women don't make this kind of money."

If that weren't bad enough, Victoria's father began dating a woman named Glenda, who actually did have a successful career, lived in a luxurious apartment, and wore beautiful clothes. Since Glenda obviously made a lot of money, Victoria, age 12, asked her father about this discrepancy. Her father simply replied, "Well, Glenda is the exception."

How does that work? Many of our parents' generation also bring to the table the money messages they were given by their parents, and so on and so on. Laura, a successful advertising executive, remembers her mother trying to "cover up" the fact that their family was going through money problems by saying, "Oh, Laura—she'll never have to worry about money problems. She'll just get married."

To make a long story short: You are not your money messages, and you are not your money memories. Once you begin to own your possibilities and your knowledge about money, you gain back your confidence and self-reliance with money. You can be single and never married, in a committed relationship or marriage with someone, or divorced or widowed, and still have full knowledge of your money issues.

CREDIT PITFALL: WHAT TO DO WHEN YOU GET A DIVORCE

Unfortunately, not all marriages last. And unfortunately, where there was once love, trust, and commitment, a divorce can often lead to quarreling, distrust, and outright resentment when it comes to money issues. As a woman, it is important to protect yourself from falling into the possibility of losing your built-up worth in the marriage through a messy divorce. If you are not careful and do not have a good lawyer, you could get taken to the cleaners by your spouse. Sometimes it's not even money issues that lead to a marriage breakup, although money troubles can hide other problems for a while. Says Financial consultant Eileen Michaels, a powerhouse analyst at Legg Mason, married clients will often come to her in despair about their money issues.

Then they realize that their problems are really not all about the money. Says Michaels, "As soon as you clean up the money situation, they realize it's all about the other issues. I had two clients—with two therapists—who were sent to me by their therapists. As soon as they straightened out their finances,

GO TO ▶
Refer to Hour 21, "Marriage, Relationships, and Money," to explore the attitudes about money that develop in a marriage and to read more about prenuptial agreements, settlements, and so on.

they got divorced. It had been their cover-up for years. It wasn't the kids—the kids are grown. The dog is dead. The money's handled; now it's "I don't like you!" "Now I really know I don't like you—because it's not about the money anymore."

What If Your Spouse Has Bad Credit?

It can turn into a very sorry situation if you are suddenly made single through divorce or death, and your spouse has left you very much in debt and with high credit card charges. You don't technically need to be legally separated to free yourself of his blackened credit history.

The key to remember here is the concept of joint accounts. Any joint credit card accounts, mortgages, outstanding loans, or brokerage accounts that are held in both names will be reported to the credit bureaus in both names. Unfortunately, until laws are changed, this is how the system works.

If you want a clean slate on your debts, you will have to close out your joint accounts and open separate accounts. If you want to begin a separation process from your spouse, you must begin doing this before the divorce takes place.

In addition, before you separate from your spouse, it is important to establish your own credit record by having a credit card in your name alone. If you don't have one, apply for one immediately, before you consider separating, and make sure you pay off your balance each month regularly.

Your Own Storehouse of Nuts

As you will probably realize as you continue reading this hour, much of the way you regard money and your future with it is to realize that financial security and serenity really come through planning and forward-thinking, and not allowing someone else to help plan your financial life.

And keep in mind that you're not alone. According to the U.S. Department of Commerce, women make up 41.5 percent of all individuals with assets of $600,000 or more. And approximately 35 percent of the country's 51 million holders of common stock are women.

Debit Cards

Debit cards are also a godsend. Although not credit-related, using debit cards can be a great technique in keeping spending and debt down. They look just like credit cards, but your money is taken directly out of your checking account upon purchase. That way, you can make your purchase without dialing up any more credit card debt.

If you're in the midst of a messy divorce involving credit problems, both a debit card and a secured card (where you put money in advance into the secured card account with the bank who is issuing the card) can really come in handy.

Overall, women continue to make great strides in producing larger and larger incomes for their families and landing great and powerful jobs in an ever-changing world. Much progress has been made that would have been unthinkable 20, 30, or 40 years ago. As women consider new financial options and continue to reason things out for themselves, they continue to feel the freedom that comes from earning their own living and being able to make their own choices about the money they make.

HOUR'S UP!

Without looking back, see if you can answer the following questions about financial independence:

1. True or false: The sooner you begin saving—even if you're just in your early 20s—the better off you will be.

2. True or false: Feel free to fill out as many credit card applications as you can while in college; you can always figure out how to pay for them later, or maybe you can ask for your parents' help.

3. If you begin investing $2,000 a year for 10 years from the time you're 22 until you're 32, letting the money compound at 10 percent for 28 years, you will then have what amount at age 59½?

    a. None—if you keep taking some out every year.

    b. $200,000

    c. $400,000

    d. Over $500,000

4. True or false: A good rule of thumb is to save something every month and to make it a part of your bill-paying routine.

5. Getting a secured credit card is a prudent financial move because …

   a. You have pre-paid money into an account from which funds are drawn to pay for your purchases.

   b. It might be the only card you can get out of college.

   c. You want to stay away from accruing unsecured debt on regular credit cards.

   d. All of the above.

6. Thanks to delayed marriages, profitable careers, higher divorce rates, and longer lives, the number of women living alone has increased by more than one third in the last 15 years, to …

   a. 15 million.

   b. 30 million.

   c. 75 million.

7. True or false: The statistic given in the preceding question means that women are buying fewer houses, cars, and luxury items.

8. True or false: One way to save for your upcoming vacation is to create a separate savings account category for precisely this reason.

9. True or false: A good way to give your post-college-age child a solid financial footing after graduating is to have set up a post-college savings account.

10. True or false: If you are going through a divorce it is not important to help reestablish your credit rating because you can always wait until after the divorce is finalized.

QUIZ

HOUR 21

Marriage, Relationships, and Money

CHAPTER SUMMARY

LESSON PLAN:

In this chapter we will be exploring the ins and outs of marriage, relationships, and money. You'll also learn how to:

- Create a family spending record.
- Define and create a prenuptial agreement.
- Decide if joint accounts are right for you.
- Invest safely together.

Whether or not you've already gotten married, when you agreed to enter into the covenant of marriage, you took a pretty serious vow, indeed. It was to be committed to each other "for better or worse, in sickness and health, until death do you part." Sometimes it becomes "until divorce do you part."

To some couples, it seems that marriage can bring out both the best and the worst behavior between spouses when it comes to making financial decisions, causing many marriages to be thrown into turmoil, sometimes ending in separation or divorce.

Rest assured, money issues can be among the most emotionally challenging issues, especially to a married couple. On one hand, being able to sit down with your partner, hold hands, and discuss important financial decisions can be a decidedly "grown up" thing to do. When you two first met and fell in love, the financial picture was probably the last thing on your minds.

As the old adage says, "opposites attract"—and the worst-case scenario would be marrying your free-spirited husband only to later find out he is free-spirited with the checkbook, too.

You probably feel you knew everything there was to know about your future spouse when you decided to marry him or her. Keep in mind that a lack of communication about finances on a regular basis can bring the most solid of relationships into turmoil.

It's Not Just About Walking Down the Aisle

Take for example, a minister who recently married a young couple, describing the fact that very seldom do betrothed couples even look at the balance sheets before deciding to "get hitched." In one particular case of a young 20-something couple married on New York's Upper West Side, the groom was very much in debt, while the bride was not.

What does this tell us?

Perhaps it's time for newlyweds to take a much closer look at their finances before and after the actual "wedding ceremony." The wedding lasts one day; your financial health as partners together will last a lifetime.

Fewer people are seeking financial counseling before tying the knot, according to this minister, although doing so could truly prove beneficial in the long run.

JUST A MINUTE

 According to the National Study of the Changing Workforce conducted by the Families and Work Institute, 78 percent of married employees have working spouses, up from 66 percent in 1977.

"Married Debt" Can Rear Its Ugly Head

GO TO ▶
Refer to Hour 2, "Cleaning Up Clutter/Debt Repayment," for more information on getting clearer on your debts.

Debt that couples bring to a marriage can include anything from student loans to car payments to credit card bills. Will one spouse agree to help pay off his spouse's debts? Will it be split down the middle? Once married, depending on whether or not you combine accounts and/or credit cards, your credit rating could be very much affected by your spouse's past financial history.

Some experts recommend couples have a "let's get everything out on the table" money session well before getting hitched. This is definitely a good idea. Get everything out in the open: your income, what you owe, what you own, what savings you may have, or what investments you may own. Some experts even suggest swapping credit reports. Now there's an emotional button!

No doubt about it, opening your financial closets like this and exposing any skeletons takes guts and a lot of compassion. Money discussions bring up all kinds of emotions—be prepared for this purging and cleansing of any financial "secrets" you may harbor. If your spouse is truly compassionate and loving, she will forgive any past incongruities and can even help you figure out a way of cleaning up your debt.

A recent Census Bureau study found that 55 percent of new mothers return to the workforce within one year of giving birth, up from 31 percent in 1976.

HOW DOES THIS AFFECT OUR FINANCIAL GOALS?

While one spouse's pre-marriage debt or credit problems won't affect another's credit rating, it can hamper joint financial goals. For example, each partner's credit history will be scrutinized when they apply for a mortgage together. Once married, any joint credit accounts—including those for auto loans, credit cards, and mortgages—will show up on both spouses' credit reports.

In community property states (Arizona, California, Idaho, Louisiana, Nevada, New Mexico, Texas, Washington, and Wisconsin), all debts incurred during the marriage are considered joint debts even if a spouse applies for credit on his or her own. If a husband defaults on an auto loan, for example, the lending company can compel the wife to pay.

To some newlyweds, the financial picture is decidedly "backburner." For these reasons, as this chapter progresses, you will learn better techniques to keep your partnership—i.e., your marriage—as strong a financial partnership as possible.

The keys to financial success—and to future prosperity and harmony between partners in a committed marital relationship—lie in compassion and communication between the couple.

PLANNING A MONTHLY BUSINESS MEETING

So, you wonder, how do we do this? For instance, let's say you have a successful marriage, kids, a mortgage, and some savings, but are never sure what's coming in and going out. Or, perhaps, one of you in the couple is a spendthrift (i.e., someone who spends too much) and the other is a hoarder/saver (i.e., someone who never spends a dime on themselves, thinking that everything has to be saved for a "rainy day."

What do you do?

One good answer: You plan a monthly Family Business meeting.

CEOs do it. Why not you?

For example, if you were running a corporation, you would arrange monthly, semi-monthly, or perhaps quarterly business meetings with your managers, your stockholders, and so on. Company CEOs do this as a way to keep pertinent information about the running of the business in the forefront of the company's mind. Stock reports are often issued as a result of such business meetings and can influence the value of the stock as a result.

In the same way, you and your spouse, on the road to financial health and serenity, can and should schedule a monthly business meeting to encompass any new financial changes within the household, new education expenses that may have arisen regarding your children, and so on. Couples often find themselves at wit's end arguing about the ups and downs of their financial picture, whereas scheduling these official "meetings" can better organize thoughts and "clear the way" for smoother conversations about money.

STARTING A FAMILY SPENDING RECORD

If you think back to Hour 2, you began to create a spending plan for yourself. This way, you were able to track exactly what was coming in and going out of your budget each month.

In the same way, we are going to set up a spending record for you both, as a couple, to clarify your finances and to discuss, modify, and examine every month.

LET'S START AT THE BEGINNING

Couples vary in what they designate to be "shared" expenses as opposed to "personal" expenses. So, too, decisions are made on having separate vs. joint checking and savings accounts. The first task of your meeting is to list all of the household's expenses. Utilities, for example, usually fall under "household expenses." Your designer bag is your expense; his collectors set of baseball cards is his expense.

Start listing in your mind other expenses that you might consider to be the "household's." They may include:

- Car costs
- Children's expenses
- Gas/electricity costs
- Groceries for household

- Home furnishings
- Home repair/maintenance
- Housecleaning (maid service)
- Investments
- Life insurance
- Medical insurance
- Property taxes
- Rent/mortgage
- Telephone
- Vacation/travel
- Other miscellaneous

There will certainly be others; you may modify this list and add to it as you wish.

What must now occur is a meeting of minds: How many of the preceding categories should be taken out of a combined "household" fund? And how should this fund be created—what should each spouse put into it on a monthly basis without either spouse feeling "taken advantage of"?

A FORMULA THAT WORKS

Take, for example, a two-income family: Jane makes $100,000 a year, and Jim makes $50,000. Together, though, they have worked through the categories that make up their "household expenses" and have agreed that they want to begin a "household expense" account in order to pay for these various expenses.

One solution is that Jim will not have to fork over as much of his personal paycheck as Jane since she makes twice as much as he does. They might just as easily have one person pay all the expenses and the other make investments, or one person may pay the household bills one month, and the other the next. Often, couples put all their available cash into one account and all the bills are paid from that account.

Along with your spouse, as in this Jane and Jim example, add up all your joint expenses—the rent or mortgage, telephone, food, utilities, etc. Let's say Jane's and Jim's joint expenses add up to $4,000 a month. If Jane's take-home pay is $6,000, and Jim's is $3,600, then the two checks together come to $9,600. Now, if you divide the total of the joint expenses ($4,000) by the total of your joint take-home checks ($9,600) you'll have .4166, or 42 percent. This percentage is what both Jane and Jim need to contribute from their take-home pay to the joint account each month. In Jane's case, 42 percent of $6,000 is $2,520. Jim, on the other hand, has to pay 42 percent of $3,600, or $1,512. Add up both figures and you get $4,032, which is slightly over the projected monthly amount.

COMMUNICATING WITH YOUR SPOUSE

But, you might say, my spouse won't sit down with me long enough to discuss these things! She hates talking about money and always leaves it up to me to belabor over!

If this rings familiar with you, take a deep breath and collect your thoughts. There are ways to communicate with your partner that are nonthreatening. To many, exploring finances taps into very deep-seated psychological issues that cause some "grownups" to revert back to their "childhood" images of themselves.

Consider some of the following thoughts when putting together a dialogue with your spouse:

- **Agree on a mutually agreeable appointment time to set up your "business meeting."** Don't lean too much on your spouse; take out your calendars and decide on a time when you are both free of children, household, or other family duties and can concentrate on the task at hand.

- **Select a time when you both have the energy to explore the task at hand.** If you are more of a morning person but your spouse thrives in the evening hours, pick a time when you both can focus and not feel frustrated.

- **Find a quiet spot—with no distractions.** If necessary, turn off the television and unplug the telephone. This is your time—make the most of it! Have the kids play at a friend's house that afternoon or evening, giving you parents some "alone" time.

- **Position yourselves in a comfortable position, preferably facing one another.** This technique helps both spouses feel that they are part of the process; one is not looking down at the other.

- **Agree to the technique of taking turns to be heard.** If you each begin to interrupt each other or attempt to solve the other person's problem, tempers can flare and you each can get burned as a result.

In some cases, using a timekeeping device can aid the process. Have one spouse watch a clock while the other person speaks for five minutes. After four minutes are up, issue a "one-minute warning," in which the partner speaking must wrap up. During this time, the timekeeper may not interrupt his or her spouse.

- **Stick to one issue at a time.** Don't become too courageous and try to get in everything at once. Have a systematic list ready to go through each issue as it comes up.

COUNSELING COUPLES ON MONEY ISSUES

At some points in a marriage, even with the best of intentions, communication about money can break down, sometimes with dire consequences. At these times, a couple with serious money problems might seek out an experienced counselor who deals mainly in money issues. Noted Brooklyn-based money therapist Judith Gruber is one such counselor who counsels individuals, couples, and groups (as well as writes a column for MsMoney.com and facilitates Money and Self-Empowerment workshops in New York). When she works with couples and their money issues, it is sometimes as a last resort to help save their marriage.

Says Gruber, "When you have a man who is thrifty with money, for example, and a wife who is a spender, that combination can create tremendous friction. Usually the one who has the most "charge" on their money habits will control the money dynamic between them. Usually, the one who has the most power will run the game. The other one ends up taking a submissive role, which creates underlying anger and resentment. Consequently, it comes out in other ways in their marriage and thus creates more friction."

And, ironically, the person who feels most in control is not always the one who actually earns the money.

Gruber explains. "You could have someone who makes a lot of money and the wife still stays home. She's at heart a very big spender. Many times couples have a co-dependent relationship which is usually an unspoken contract between them. This keeps each person blind to what they really feel because they're so busy trying to keep the other one happy. A negative vicious cycle is created whereby each person is trying to attend to the other's needs while being in denial of their own. Thus, their individuality is compromised which in turn unconsciously compromises their self-esteem and self-respect. When asked if newlyweds speak enough about money before marriage, Gruber—who has seen hundreds of couples through her practice of money therapy—says, "I think most people don't plan it out well enough. No matter how aware they think they are about each other's habits, the money issues are often not one of the things they deal with."

Another noted psychologist and author, Linda Barbanel, M.S.W., C.S.W., notes that with more autonomous financial power, women have gained more self-respect and more respect within their relationships.

"The autonomy aspect is important," says Barbanel. "Women need to have their own discretionary money, their own investments, as well as their own checking. Women are really getting into finance, because they have more money to manage—they are really getting more independent! They can support themselves more independently. They're doing okay!"

In her groundbreaking book, *Sex, Money and Power: Smart Ways to Resolve Money Conflicts and Keep Them from Sabotaging Your Closest Relationships* (Macmillan Spectrum Books, 1996), Barbanel describes several tips to deal with spendthrifts, i.e., those spouses who might be too quick to draw out their wallet and spend without thinking. Some tips include:

- Can he or she afford his or her expenses?
- Does he seem upset with his spending habits?
- Do you notice that he buys things that he never uses?

Talk to him or her about your concerns and ask about his or hers; make it clear that you care for him as a person, independent of financial issues.

Bring his attention to all the clues he's left for you. Make your case by referring to specific examples. Tell him there is a serious issue here, one that makes you uncomfortable and has to be addressed.

GO TO ▶
Refer to Hour 2 for more information and addresses on how to contact Debtors Anonymous and various credit-counseling services.

Getting to the point of accepting help can take a while, but when he or she is ready, psychotherapy, self-help groups, Debtors Anonymous, and credit-counseling services can be of help.

On the other hand, your spouse may be of the "cheap" variety, meaning he watches every penny to the point of being "anorexic" about spending. These are not terms to be thrown around lightly; however, they better emphasize the problems found with many couples trying to find serenity with their money issues.

If you find that your spouse would rather pinch pennies than live the more full life that you'd like, keep in mind the following illuminations (taken from Linda Barbanel's book, *Sex, Money, and Power: Smart Ways to Resolve*

Money Conflicts and Keep Them from Sabotaging Your Closest Relationships): "Be aware that 'cheap' or 'tightwad' spouses are often trying to make up for not getting enough love, attention, or money during their childhood."

Know that super-cheapness is the result of guilt for real or perceived aggressiveness early in life. Staying in control and still, in an odd way, being aggressive is what stinginess is. Help your partner to find better ways to get what he or she needs instead of using money.

Help your partner figure out his issues of guilt, insecurity, and control around money by encouraging him to talk about such things as how he learned about money when he was growing up. Many of the ideas he learned from his childhood may be outdated and outmoded. If he can hear what he's saying, perhaps the chances are better that he'll see how "funny" his ideas are and will try to change.

Buying into a partnership with a self-denying individual who puts himself at the bottom of every priority list will find you there, too.

JOINT CHECKING AND SAVINGS?

Now you need to determine whether or not you need separate accounts. Most couples don't think twice as they merge their money into a joint checking or savings account when they get married. Some remember their parents' checks with both names printed in the upper-left corner. If it worked for our parents, goes the standard reasoning, why won't it work for us in the twenty-first century?

More practical reasons to combine accounts vary from being able to keep better tabs on the cash flow to creating a sense of "oneness" with your partner in marriage and finance.

But think twice about making this financial decision automatically and without discussion. Some experts say the decision to take joint accounts shouldn't be so cut and dried because each person brings a different set of money habits to the relationship. Some married partners swear by the idea of having separate accounts—with their own money to "play with" while having a third "joint" account to handle everyday household expenses.

One prosperous New York couple, married nearly 15 years—he for the second time, she for the first—swear by the idea of having separate accounts. "It has kept us from so much frustration," says the wife, Theresa. "We each have our own money to deal with, but when it comes to taking care of the household expenses, we have a third account from which to take out any money we may need to cover expenses as they come up."

With one joint checking account, both paychecks are deposited into it and all bills are paid from it. This way, both people know where they stand financially as a couple, and it's often easier to be budget-conscious, say some marriage counselors. In addition, bookkeeping and accounting costs may be kept to a minimum because of the higher, combined balance.

There are generally three different financial scenarios for couples:

- One joint checking account in both names
- Two personal checking accounts
- One joint account and two personal accounts

Some couples may feel restricted by having just one joint account because neither has his or her own money. While it's easier to manage the joint account by using just one checkbook, bad feelings or mistrust concerning money issues may be alleviated if the couple uses two checkbooks.

A couple who choose to have two separate checking accounts may decide to use one checkbook from either of the accounts if expenses are divided right down the middle.

A couple may also opt to have one joint checking account and two separate checking accounts. The majority of money can go into the joint account to pay daily living expenses. The remainder is divided between two personal accounts. The positive side to this arrangement is that you have your own money to control, as well as joint cash.

JUST A MINUTE

Watch that little word "and." According to the Federal Deposit Insurance Corp., by listing a joint checking account as, say, Jane or Jim Doe as the primary holder the account automatically will go to the surviving spouse in the case of divorce or death. But by listing the account as Jane and Jim Doe, the money in that account may be subject to seizure by any of the deceased spouse's heirs.

NEW INSURANCE ISSUES

Another area that couples need to be aware of is how much of the money in a joint account is insured. The FDIC Board changed the deposit insurance rules in March, 1999 to a simple, one-step process for determining the coverage of joint accounts. Under the new standard, a person is insured up to $100,000 in total for his or her share of any joint accounts at an insured bank or savings institution, even if one of those accounts has a balance of more than $100,000.

For example, under the revised rules, if two people own a joint account with a balance of $200,000 and they have no other joint accounts at the same insured institution, each person would be insured for $100,000 on the joint account.

A couple should also decide who would receive the money in a joint checking or savings account should either person die. These payable-on-death accounts, as the FDIC calls them, are those in which the depositor indicates in the account records that upon his or her death the money will be payable to one or more named beneficiaries. The FDIC extended the list to include the account holder's parents and siblings in addition to the spouse, children, and grandchildren.

PREMARITAL AGREEMENTS

Even though you may hate the sound of it, no chapter on "Marriage, Relationships, and Money" would be complete without an overview of prenuptial and premarital agreements.

You might be saying, "My future spouse and I love each other. We have love and respect for each other. There is no reason to doubt our love, or our mutual respect for each other's money."

Fair enough. But because you are both grownups, and getting married is for the long haul, it is important to plan for whatever the future may bring, bad and good. Keep in mind, too, that even if you are not bringing large amounts to the table when you enter the marriage, you may want to protect future earnings, stock purchases, and so on down the road.

SECOND AND THIRD MARRIAGES

Some couples may have been down this road before and have seen what can happen when marriage and money go wrong. Couples may want to protect assets from previous marriages from going into hands other than their children's. As an alternative to prenuptial agreements, living trusts can also help specify where money from previous marriages should go.

GO TO ▶
Refer to Hour 18, "Estate Planning," for more information on divvying up your estate to your heirs.

A premarital or prenuptial agreement is essentially a legal contract you enter into before marriage. It states how you and your spouse want your assets and debts divided in a way that is acceptable to both parties in case of a divorce.

There are other variations on this theme, too. You can enter into a *marital agreement* while you are married, or while you are living together enter into a cohabitation agreement.

What is one of the most public prenuptial agreements you've heard of? Donald Trump comes to mind. Before he married his second wife, Marla Maples, he wisely had a prenuptial agreement drawn up to which she agreed. If they split up (which they later did) she was awarded some $2 million total for her trouble.

Prenuptial agreements need to be put in writing and signed by both parties. Each future spouse should retain an individual attorney to review the contract in order to advise them about its implications before signing. In most courts of law, property includes everything from your mother's piano to your retirement funds. Also included are your debts, patents, car, furniture, jewelry, and so forth. When going through your itemized list of assets, be sure to expand your thinking and include everything.

SEPARATE PROPERTY

Property that was acquired before your marriage is known as separate property. As long as you keep this property in your name alone, it remains separate. I recommend having a good lawyer who can instruct you well when figuring out what constitutes your own property and shared property with your future spouse.

SPOUSAL IRAS

What are some of the ways that you and your spouse can invest together? One is an IRA called a Spousal IRA. One New York–based financial advisor opened a Spousal IRA for one of his clients who wanted expressly to benefit from this special savings option.

Essentially, a Spousal IRA can be opened by a spouse to benefit the other spouse who doesn't work. Normally, IRAs are for people who are working with an income. The Spousal IRA is an after-tax item—up to $2,000 can be contributed, even if you have a spouse who is not working.

Eligibility: Even if your spouse has no personal income, or income less than $2,000—you (on behalf of your spouse) can make an IRA contribution. If you file a joint income tax return, you can make an IRA contribution for any tax year prior to that spouse becoming 70½. Your spouse's compensation, if any, must be less than yours.

The best time to make contributions is after January 1, and keep in mind that spousal deductibility is eligible up to a joint income of $150,000 to 160,000. As with other IRAs, Spousal IRAs do have some restrictions that you should be aware of before you start one. Generally, you may not withdraw any money from the account before you reach the age of 59½ without paying a 10 percent penalty on top of the income tax due on the money withdrawn. This is not the case with contributions that weren't tax deductible in the first place. Nor are there penalties on money withdrawn to pay certain medical expenses.

INVESTING TOGETHER

Here's an update of that old saying, namely "The family that invests together stays together." For example, you may be averse to taking big risks with your family's investments, while your spouse may enjoy the ups and downs of following the volatile stock market.

It's best to sit down together—perhaps at a special "business meeting" devoted to just this topic—and discuss what exact type of risk you'd like to see with your combined investments. Some couples enjoy investing their own money separately; however, in many cases it makes much more sense to combine assets and savings and create a combined portfolio that benefits you both.

However, one spouse may feel her needs are not being considered if the other spouse feels it is his right to spend and invest their joint money together as he sees fit. One recent and sad example of this was seen in the case of the day trader in Atlanta, Georgia, who, having racked up hundreds of thousands in debts through persistent day trading (obviously without the knowledge or consent of his wife), managed to go through his family's entire life savings in the course of a week.

As a result, he sadly went on a rampage, killing many of the people who worked at the two day-trading facilities who facilitated the trades, and then later killing his family and himself.

This is, of course, an extreme example. But a surprising percentage of couples are in the dark when it comes to their investments. The more each couple knows about their combined assets, the better off they will be.

HOUR'S UP!

Let's now test your new knowledge about "Marriage, Relationships, and Money." Try to answer the following without looking back in the hour for the answers:

1. Before a couple decides to get married, they should ...

   a. Do nothing about their finances.

   b. Ask each other to share their complete financial histories, including debt, income, and assets.

   c. Decide that it's too early to really consider their financial options; they can wait for a year or two to see how things work out.

2. The percentage of married employees with both spouses working in 1999 was ...

   a. 70 percent.

   b. 78 percent.

   c. 90 percent.

3. True or false: In community property states (Arizona, California, Idaho, Louisiana, Nevada, New Mexico, Texas, Washington, and Wisconsin), all debts incurred during the marriage are considered joint debts even if a spouse applies for credit on his or her own.

4. True or false: The keys to financial success—and to future prosperity and harmony between partners in a committed marital relationship—lie in compassion and communication between the couple.

5. True or false: A recent Census Bureau study found that 75 percent of new mothers return to the workforce within one year of giving birth, up from 31 percent in 1976.

6. The best time to schedule a monthly "business meeting" is when ...

   a. Both partners are hungry and tired after work.

   b. On a Sunday when one spouse wants to go golfing.

   c. When both partners are fresh and have the energy to focus on their mutual financial goals and desires.

7. True or false: A Spousal IRA allows one spouse who does not work outside of the home to put aside up to $2,000 a year on a tax-deferred basis.

8. Spousal deductibility on a Spousal IRA is eligible up to a joint income of ...

   a. $90,000.

   b. $110,000.

   c. $150,000 to 160,000.

9. True or false: A premarital or prenuptial agreement is essentially a legal contract you enter into before marriage, stating how you and your spouse want your assets and debts divided in a way that is fair and reasonable to both parties in case of a divorce.

10. You should only consider a prenuptial agreement if ...

   a. You're Donald Trump.

   b. You're Elizabeth Taylor.

   c. You seriously want to consider the financial ramifications to your life and the lives of your heirs if your current marriage does not last.

Quiz

HOUR 22

Potential Financial Pitfalls—and How to Avoid Them

CHAPTER SUMMARY

LESSON PLAN:

In this chapter, we will explore potential financial pitfalls you should try to avoid. These include credit card debt, bankruptcy, day trading, taking out home-equity loans if you're not in good financial shape, and more. You'll also learn how to:

- Avoid making a mistake that could effect your credit rating forever.
- Have a secure financial future.
- Plan for a rainy day — or a big emergency.
- Protect yourself in a divorce.

You might think that bankruptcy could be the "quick fix" for you. But rest assured—bankruptcy must really only be declared as a last resort. The results of bankruptcy can stay on your credit rating for 10 years.

PITFALL #1: THINKING BANKRUPTCY IS THE "EASY WAY OUT"

Bankruptcy is certainly a word that carries much less of the social "stigma" today than it did back in the 1950s and earlier, when "declaring bankruptcy" could signal the end to a person's business career (or life!). There are those today who think "If I get into any more debt, I can always just declare bankruptcy."

Bankruptcy is often called a 10-year mistake because a notation that you filed for bankruptcy will remain on your credit bureau file for up to 10 years from the date you filed. This notation can prevent you from getting credit or from getting favorable terms if you do get credit. Until 10 years have passed, you will continue to have the stigma of bankruptcy follow you.

Keep in mind, too, that for the rest of your life, you will always have to check off whether you've ever filed for bankruptcy on any mortgage application, car loan, or personal financial statement. This could have a negative bearing on whether or not you end up receiving a loan.

The two main types of bankruptcy filings are Chapter 7 and Chapter 13. Chapter 7 is designed for debtors in financial difficulty who do not have the ability to pay their existing debts. The purpose of Chapter 7 is to obtain a discharge of your existing debts. Under Chapter 7, a trustee takes possession of all your property. You may claim certain property as exempt under governing law. The trustee then liquidates nonexempt property and uses the proceeds to pay your creditors according to priorities of the Bankruptcy Code.

When you file for bankruptcy, some property may be claimed as exempt, such as your home, your car, or assets used in the production of income. This exemption varies from state to state. Most states will allow you to use Federal exemptions, while 15-25 states have their own exemptions, which can vary greatly. For instance, Florida and Texas each have a Homestead Exemption, which allows you to protect the property where you live from creditors. The equity in your home in this example would be exempt. It is important to check out these exemptions with a bankruptcy lawyer or advisor who can clarify which exemption might or might not work for you in your state.

Chapter 13 is designed for individuals with regular income who are temporarily unable to pay their debts but would like to pay them in installments over a period of time. You are only eligible for Chapter 13 if your debts do not exceed certain dollar amounts set forth in the Bankruptcy Code. Under Chapter 13, you must file a plan with the courts to repay your creditors all or part of the money that you owe, using your future earnings. Usually the period allowed by the courts to repay your debts will be not more than five years. The courts must approve your plan before it can take effect. Chapter 13 is mainly used to stop a foreclosure action.

As you can see, filing for either Chapter 7 or Chapter 13 is not something to be taken lightly.

JUST A MINUTE

Any responsible bankruptcy lawyer will not choose Chapter 7 as an option for you unless your assets are exempt. Be sure to ask your lawyer about this.

After 10 years, the credit-reporting agencies should automatically remove the bankruptcy notation from your file. To be sure the notation has been removed after the 10 years has gone by, call any of the primary credit-reporting agencies (CRAs) to get a copy of your credit bureau file. If you see the bankruptcy notation is still on your file, you will need to contact the CRAs yourself and demand they remove this notation.

The three primary credit-reporting agencies are …

- **Experian.** 1-800-643-3334; www.experian.com.
- **Equifax.** 1-800-685-1111; www.equifax.com.
- **Trans Union.** 1-800-916-8800; www.transunion.com.

For an excellent Web site on debt repayment vs. bankruptcy options, check out www.debtworkout.com. This site has links to various sites dealing with mortgage loans, bankruptcy information, and ways of working yourself *out* of debt once and for all.

PITFALL #2: IGNORING YOUR FINANCIAL FUTURE BY NOT PLANNING FOR RETIREMENT

Some people feel that deadlines and planning their financial future is like death—it takes all the fun out of living. To this, we say, start planning! As long as you continue to procrastinate, you are missing out on all kinds of ways to start building your nest egg for the future.

Even the IRS offers extensions—for a price. Not so with saving your money!

Many people, once they begin to see the benefits of sitting down and sketching out a five-, 10-, or 20-year plan, can see more clearly how their lives can turn out if they manage their money responsibly. By not planning carefully, you might end up paying higher taxes while also missing out on savings opportunities. Financial confusion can also lead to overpaying for financial services that you may or may not need. If you don't feel you're up to the task, choose a good financial planner you can trust to help you handle the load. Bring in your spouse to the planning session so he or she will be a part of the strategy session with you.

Even if all you can save is $50 per month in a mutual fund, do it. The rule of compounded interest guarantees that over time, this seemingly small monthly deposit can bring you big returns.

Also, when considering whether or not to take the full deduction out of your paycheck each month for your 401(k) plan, DO IT! Too many times employees think they can't live on the take-home pay in their bimonthly checks as it is and pass up on one of the best deals the government offers: tax-free savings removed in the guise of a 401(k) or similar plan. "Max" out this offering. Have as much removed from your paycheck each pay period as the

GO TO ▶
Check out Hour 13, "Finding the Right Financial Advisor," for more details on finding the right advisor for you. Also, Hour 21, "Marriage, Relationships, and Money," can help you and your spouse find a good way to agree upon your money issues.

company will allow; many companies will match this contribution. Check with your financial advisor about which IRA is right for you. Both the traditional IRA and the Roth IRA offer certain advantages for the investor over time.

Having the intention to start saving is all well and good. But unless you begin even a simple system—say, saving $50 a month in an IRA, retirement fund, or mutual fund and building from there—you will turn around and be 65 without any type of savings to live on. Don't let this happen to you!

PITFALL #3: MISUSE OF CREDIT CARDS

GO TO ►
Refer to Hour 2, "Cleaning Up Clutter/Debt Repayment," for more information on cleaning up your credit problems.

Oftentimes consumers run into that dreaded syndrome of robbing Peter to pay Paul. If you are using credit cards to pay minimum payments on other credit cards, realize that this is a major sign of financial trouble. If, for instance, you have $15,000 in credit card debt and a new credit card issues you a line of credit of $10,000, and you try to pay off the first card, where does that leave you? Still massively in debt.

If you are trying to "rob Peter to pay Paul" because you are unable to pay your credit card bills and are looking for a universal "Band Aid" solution to fix things, DON'T DO IT. You could, over time, end up digging yourself into an even bigger financial hole.

The upside of using one card to pay off another is that you can typically arrange for a lower interest rate, thus reducing your overall payment. These days, competing credit card companies want your business and will offer you competitive, lowered interest rates to get you to switch cards. Rule of thumb: If you generally DO NOT have problems paying your minimums on your credit card bills on time and can responsibly switch to a lower-interest-rate card, then by all means do so.

According to debt-repayment lawyer Mory Brenner, misusing credit cards this way is similar to the following medical scenario:

Let's say you have a pain on the left side of your body and numbness in your left arm. What would you do? You'd get yourself to the emergency room to have it examined, wouldn't you? In the case of opening up a credit card bill and seeing that you've maxed out your card again—for the sixth time this year, perhaps—you could also recognize this type of debt as part of a much bigger problem and get yourself checked out.

Another thing that will help is to stop getting more credit cards. Even though credit offers seem to be available all the time, this does not necessarily mean that getting 15 credit cards is a good thing. People seem to think that if someone gives them a credit card, the company seems to have some kind of magical insight into their self-worth. "Oh, yes! I must be important if I just got an Ultima/Optima/Diamond card!"

You do not need every card that comes to you in the mail! Throw each of these new credit card offers straight into the trash. You are not your credit. That is not your identity. If you're one of those consumers who likes to keep accepting each of 15 cards—just for emergencies, say, or for something you really need—forget it. Get rid of this extra credit that you don't need.

Too many times, according to Brenner, clients will arrive in his office in debt to the tune of $100,000 or more in credit card debt and have no idea how they got there. Don't be like this! Stick to a good credit diet, and you will happier—and more financially healthy—for it.

PITFALL #4: THE OSTRICH EFFECT: IGNORING YOUR SHORT-TERM FUTURE

Do you tend to stick your head in the sand, especially when it comes to taking a realistic picture of your current finances?

Are you in debt but don't really want to face it?

Maybe you lost a well-paying job recently but still want to have the same outflow, spending the same amount of money on high-priced dinners out, vacations you can't afford, extra presents at holiday time, and so on? Even though you're behind in mortgage payments, do you still want to "put on a good face" and pay the entire amount for your son's wedding so he can have the "best wedding ever" while you put yourself into financial jeopardy?

If so, you may be exhibiting "The Ostrich Effect."

Remember: You cannot become financially clear and "above ground" unless you get your head out of the sand. To get more clear about your finances, reread Hour 1 on developing your financial goals (and fill out the charts on how to plan for those goals) as well as Hour 2, which can help you get a true picture of your overall debt.

Only when you take your head out of the sand can you really take control of your financial life!

PITFALL #5: IMPROPER CASH-FLOW ALLOCATION

"When people have cash-flow problems, they compound their problems by not allocating their cash properly. Debtors will decide they cannot pay all of their bills and conclude that the next best thing is to pay as many bills as they can. That's a terrible mistake."

"They will lay out their 15 or so bills on the kitchen table. They can't pay everyone, so they think that if they pay 14 out of 15 debts, that's the proper and responsible thing to do. What they most often leave behind is the mortgage payment."

Brenner continues, "People quite often pay the second mortgage instead of the first mortgage, even though by not paying the first mortgage they'll lose the house. If the first is going to foreclose, then paying the second means nothing."

The result from not paying your mortgage? You could end up losing your house.

Only when you truly know what you're dealing with can you understand the possibilities for your financial future.

WHICH COMES FIRST: YOUR DEBT OR YOUR HOUSE?

Brenner explains, "If you asked someone, 'Would you rather lose your credit cards or your house?' almost everybody says they'll keep their house. Would you rather have a roof over your head or your credit cards?"

If you knew your car was going to be repossessed tomorrow, would you buy four brand-new tires for it today? That's what paying your second mortgage instead of the first is like.

You should pay your first mortgage first, even if it means that you're paying one bill out of 15. If the best you can do is pay your mortgage and utilities, begin there; there are ways of dealing with your creditors that will not mean forfeiting your house.

If you are preparing a financial plan on your own, and are worried about your house going into foreclosure, it is important to contact ALL of your creditors and let them know that you are having some major debt trouble, including losing your house to foreclosure. You can ask if they will give you a payment moratorium. This can vary, according to what the nature of your foreclosure is. Some creditors will give you a 1- to 4-month moratorium if circumstances are explained.

Communication is very important.

According to Brenner, "Many people's tendencies are to clam up and hide when they can't pay. Creditors are MUCH more willing to work with you if you keep the lines of communication open."

Which creditors get your money when everyone can't be paid must be a decision you make based on your own situation, not who calls you the most or who you owe what.

TAKE A LOOK AT THE CASH FLOW

Brenner recommends:

1. Figure out how much you saved or spent from savings in the last month. This number should be a hard fact. Either you added to an account or needed to borrow from savings, friends, or relatives to make ends meet. Write this number down and put it aside.

GO TO ▶
Refer to Hour 2 for a way of keeping good records of your monthly spending habits.

2. Make a list of all your available income for the month. Use the regular net income of both spouses, and do not include inconsistent items such as occasional overtime, tax refunds, or gift proceeds.

   Are working children or other adults living in the home who could contribute funds? This subject sometimes meets with a lot of resistance, but when the only other option may be losing the house, it must be examined!

3. Make a list of extra income available. What savings can be used? Do you have available credit lines or available cash advances from credit cards? Can you borrow money from friends or relatives?

   Look under the sofa cushions or any other sources that may be unique for you—a 401(k) plan or whole-life insurance policy, perhaps.

4. Make a list of all monthly expenses.

Only after going through many of the preceding questions can you get the breakthrough clarity you will need to begin to get your finances in order.

PITFALL #6: NOT HAVING LONG-TERM-CARE AND DISABILITY INSURANCE

You may not think bankruptcy can happen to you, but it can. By not planning out your long-term future with regards to healthcare for your family, you might just be setting yourself up for a very big financial fall, complete with the possibility of losing many of the assets you have built up for your family just when you need them most.

Medicaid is changing fast. In the past, wealthier folks used to think up ways of shifting assets around so that Medicaid would end up paying for their long-term care. It's getting much more difficult to do this.

There is nothing you can do when an unexpected illness hits, but you can take steps today to be sure that your loved ones are financially protected in the future. That is where long-term-care insurance (LTC) comes in.

Suze Orman, financial guru and author of *The Nine Steps to Financial Freedom,* suggests that the best age to purchase a LTC policy is around age 54. Experts can disagree on that figure, with some arguing that 54 is too early to be dealing with this. You may have additional financial burdens at that time such as college tuition payments for your children, and other costs.

Nonetheless, it is important to consider such an option around this time in your life. If you carry a LTC policy and have to go to a nursing home one day, you will almost certainly pay less for all your LTC insurance payments combined than you would for one year in that nursing home.

Long-term-care premiums are based on how old you are when you purchase the policy, and are projected to stay stable at that amount for the lifetime of the policy. For instance, it will cost you less if you purchase your policy at 55 than if you purchase it at 65. The premiums are expected to remain stable during the life of the policy, so check with your financial planner and/or your insurance agent before committing to one forever.

If you are under 65, your odds of becoming disabled are much greater than the odds of dying, so make sure you are adequately insured for disability, and not so much for life insurance. Long-term disability (LTD) insurance can protect you if a catastrophe happens that prevents you from being able to earn a living. Certain chronic illnesses, injury, or other conditions could keep you from being able to work.

But wait, you say. I'm covered for disability through my workers' compensation at work. Yes, that's true, but you would have to be injured while on the job in order for workers' comp to pick up the bill. LTD helps insure you whether you are injured on the job or on vacation.

PITFALL #7: NOT HAVING ENOUGH MONEY FOR MEDICAL EMERGENCIES

It is important to keep an extra pocket of savings set aside to cover deductibles, "the unforseeables," and especially catastrophic situations. Most medical treatments will be covered by your medical insurance plan issued by your employer. But by having extra cash set aside, you will be covering yourself and your family in the event of an uninsured or catastrophic emergency not covered by your existing plan.

One Florida couple has a one-year-old son with leukemia, and his medical expenses have broken their bank account. Even with insurance, experimental procedures like the drug Zophran they needed in order to get him to eat during his chemotherapy treatments were $450 a day. The boy is in remission, but the family is broke and considering bankruptcy. For such reasons, it's most important to have extra funds in your bank account.

PITFALL #8: BORROWING CASH ADVANCES FOR YOUR BUSINESS

Suppose you've been working in the corporate world for most of your working life, and you want to try to break off and start a business of your own. Fine plan. The only caveat: Don't borrow from your credit cards to finance your small business. It can only cause headaches later on as you try to sort out your personal financial costs vs. your business' costs. You also run the real risk of getting yourself into a large debt/financial crisis down the road.

It's better to begin having a positive cash flow with real cash and assets. This may mean not expanding as quickly as you'd like, or maybe not buying or renting the prime real estate you envisioned for your business when you first started out.

Be especially wary of this pitfall. It is one of the most common and can end up being the biggest nightmare.

PITFALL #9: HOME-EQUITY LOANS

Is taking out a home-equity loan on your house a good thing? Rarely. If you're thinking of taking out this kind of loan to pay off other debts—perhaps to take that dream vacation you've always wanted—stop the fantasy in its tracks. Home-equity loans can be real trouble down the road.

According to our expert attorney Mory Brenner, there is seldom a good time to get a home-equity loan, "unless you've built up your credit cards for a strange and singular purpose, let's say a horrible surgery. Perhaps there was a one-time event such as this and you were uninsured. Now you have to pay back these medical bills. That might be one of the few times to consider taking out an equity loan on your house."

Don't use your home equity for any purpose unless you understand you are putting your house at risk and are confident that there is just never going to be an issue. If you are wrong you will lose your house.

In this particular example, two clients, owning two businesses, plenty of credit cards, and several parcels of undeveloped, raw land saw their debt continue to increase. At one point, they thought it would be nice to wrap together all of their debt into one big package. They thought it would be less hassle, like taking out a second mortgage. Unfortunately, things did not turn out so nicely. This hard-working young couple came very close to losing their house because they took out the "easy" second mortgage on their home, and were unable to pay these much larger payments. It happens every day.

JUST A MINUTE

When faced with such a dilemma as whether or not to take on a second mortgage, definitely seek out a financial counselor or attorney who specializes in debt options. He can help you sort out your financial plan.

PITFALL #10: DIVORCE

GO TO ▶
Refer to Hour 21 for more information on prenuptial agreements, keeping joint savings and checking accounts with your spouse, and so on.

Not that you can always avoid getting a divorce when you feel your marriage is "over," but definitely try to protect your financial situations, especially during this tough emotional battle. Often people can "give ground" to an ex-spouse in order to get the divorce finalized quickly. In some cases this is effective. But in the long run, take a look at your financial life with your ex-spouse and figure out an equitable way for assets to be shared accordingly.

You probably have friends who have lost it all in these expensive battles of the heart. Keep your wallet out of the arguments if you can.

PITFALL #11: DAY TRADING

The explosion in popularity of day trading throughout the country does not mean that you have to become a part of this addictive craze in our country. Be wary.

The definition of a "day trader" is an active stock trader who holds positions for a very short time and makes several trades each day. This gives the day trader the incentive to trade more, not less.

Because he or she is gambling with the "big boys" of Wall Street (those analysts who have the bucks and the resources at their firms to research stocks correctly), day trading becomes more of a lifestyle for those who participate. You have to spend more and more time online "trading" than you do actually living your life.

Day trading comes quite close to legalized gambling. You may remember the recent (and tragic) story of a day trader in Atlanta, Georgia, who, losing all of his money to the tune of $150,000, walked into an office he used to day trade with a loaded shotgun. He shot many of the people working there that day before shooting himself. It was later found that he had killed his wife and kids beforehand.

Of course this is a very extreme and tragic story of someone out of their league when it came to financial trading. No doubt about it, it's fun to be able to track your stocks at the touch of a button. People with Internet access can now get what's called "real-time" quotes just by logging on to the Internet.

But researching and seeking knowledge of stocks is much different than trading them constantly online all day. If you feel you must become a day trader, definitely discuss your financial decisions and actions with your spouse or partner. Be sure that he or she is in agreement on these financial decisions and that you are not just "playing in the dark."

The last thing you want is to not be accountable for your life savings after a day of "trading" stocks. Only trade with money you can afford to lose.

GOOD TIPS TO REMEMBER

The following tips are good enough to paste up on your refrigerator next to this week's shopping list. Make a mental note to follow up on some of the financial pitfalls you may be headed for without realizing it:

- If you want to save your home, pay your mortgage first. If you are already behind on bill payments, formulate a way to catch up. Then call your bank and tell them your plan and why it will work. Do the same for all mortgages or rent.

- Communicate with your creditors. Don't wait until you get in trouble. Before you miss a payment, give them a call and let them know you need help and why.

- Never waste money. No lottery, no gambling, no get-rich-quick schemes. Be very wary of scam artists; they will be out to get you.

- If your credit has already turned sour, don't try to rebuild it until the current problems have been resolved.

- Paying more than the minimum payments on credit cards does not give you a better credit rating.

- Don't become emotionally attached to any asset. Reevaluate all of your possessions, and don't be afraid to give them up. Should you be driving that Lexus or would you be better off in an Escort for a while? Maybe necessity dictates moving to a smaller house or a less-affluent neighborhood.

- Identify the cash drains and plug them up. This may mean closing a business or losing an income property.

- Don't make arrangements you won't be able to keep. Tell creditors what you can really do, not what you think they want you to say.

- Do not spend money on house repairs if you may be losing your house.

- Explore all options, but be ready for the worst, including an exploration of the rental market.

- Formulate a plan as soon as you see the first sign of trouble. Do not wait!

- If home foreclosure looms above you, ignore the collection agencies from the unsecured creditors. You have more important things to worry about. Don't let them bully you into giving them anything. You may need every cent to save your home.

- Don't waste money or flaunt your spending. For instance, keep in mind the story of the debtor who had almost completed negotiations with a bank for a deeply discounted settlement. When the loan officer called to finalize the plan she was told the debtor was vacationing in the Caribbean. She figured if he could afford the trip, he could afford to pay her in full, and the deal was off.

- Don't file for bankruptcy unless it's really the right thing to do. It's not the only option. If your attorney doesn't explain the other options, get a new attorney. If the bankruptcy option works the best for your situation, don't be afraid or ashamed to do it.

- Find the time to deal with your money problems. If your house matters to you, this is more important than almost anything else. If you hate the house anyway, don't pour money in to save it; explore other residence options.

- You will not be put in jail for falling behind on your payments. You will not be shunned by the whole community. Most people will never know about your situation unless you tell them. Yes, this even goes for small towns with legal notices in the paper. Those who do find out will soon forget.

- Don't pour money into black holes. If your situation has taken a permanent downturn to the point that an asset will ultimately be lost, stop wasting savings or current income just to delay the inevitable. You will need that money for other things, such as finding a rental after a foreclosure.

- Don't spend money on big gifts or celebrations. Your daughter would surely rather have a smaller wedding than homeless parents.

- Once in the foreclosure process, call a lawyer before paying anything. When you've reached this stage, little time remains. You'll need someone familiar with all legal options.

- If you really want to keep the house, be prepared to work for it. This may mean cutting items you thought were essential like cable TV, or getting a second job.

- Think twice before not paying income taxes or your employees withholding or FICA match. These will probably not be dischargeable in bankruptcy.

- Once you know you will be filing a bankruptcy do not run up a bill or credit card subject to discharge. This would be fraud, not to mention nondischargeable.

(Courtesy of www.debtworkout.com and Mory Brenner, Esq.)

In most bankruptcy cases the creditor receiving top priority will be the first mortgage holder on your home. This obligation likely represents a debtor's largest payment.

Human tendency evidences payment to smaller creditors when money gets tight. Often, credit cards and second mortgages may be paid in full once first mortgage payments cease. This results in a short-sighted solution. Soon your credit becomes blemished anyway, and foreclosure on your home follows.

Negotiating with first mortgage holders can be more difficult than with other creditors.

Perhaps the most important: Don't lose hope, and don't give up. No matter what pitfall you may have fallen into, there is always help, guidance, and assistance out there from someone who has already been there and can help you, too.

HOUR'S UP!

As a quiz on your newfound knowledge of the amazing financial pitfalls you could find yourself in if you are not careful and don't read this book, try to answer the following questions without referring back to the hour:

1. True or false: The sooner you begin creating a financial plan the more money and financial serenity you can build for your future.

2. True or false: It is best to be foggy about your net worth; that way, you never know how much you can really save.

3. The length of time a bankruptcy stays on your credit report will be …

    a. 5 years.

    b. 10 years.

    c. 15 years.

4. The best item you could supply for your family is LTC insurance. This stands for …

    a. Long-term-care insurance.

    b. Loving tender care insurance.

    c. Living trust care insurance.

5. True or false: Credit card companies understand when you have to pay off one creditor with another credit line because they can always offer you another card.

6. True or false: If you only have the money to pay 14 of your 15 creditors each month, it's wise to skip your mortgage payment and pay everyone else off.

7. True or false: Under Chapter 13, you must file a plan with the courts to repay your creditors all or part of the money you owe using your future earnings.

8. True or false: If you do decide to day trade, it is important to keep your spouse abreast of what is occurring to the savings that you share.

9. When considering taking advantage of a 401(k) plan at work, it's usually best to …

    a. Only have the minimum allowed amount deducted from your check.

    b. Have the maximum amount allowed deducted from your check.

    c. Have nothing deducted from your check.

10. True or false: When considering marriage, it is important to consider the financial ramifications of this decision as well. In many cases, a prenuptial agreement may be in order.

Quiz

HOUR 23

Financial Serenity—It's Not All About the Money

CHAPTER SUMMARY

LESSON PLAN:

In this chapter we will be exploring ways of developing financial "serenity" about your money issues. You'll also learn how to:

- Be happy with what you have.
- Understand how money is right for your future.
- Get your bill paying on track.

"Our lives are hell not because money is so important to us, because it is not important enough."

—Jacob Needleman, *Money and the Meaning of Life*

Think about that for a second. Money really does play an important role in our lives. Some people wake up, instantly begin to calculate how much cash flow is coming in and going out, and begin their day with worry that somehow the bills aren't going to get paid this month, that they don't have enough invested in their future, and so on. Planning for your financial future is definitely important. But so is planning just for today.

When you think about abundance, do you think of all the things you want sometime in the future? Or do you think about and give thanks for the abundance you have right now? Therein lies a prosperity consciousness.

Until you develop a healthy, peaceful serenity (yes, serenity) about money issues, your money (or lack of money) will control you. You will not control it. Thus begins a true "relationship."

A LIFETIME RELATIONSHIP

Let's look at it a different way: Say you've begun a relationship with someone new. Being with that person gives you joy, pleasure, and love. But what if that relationship one day turns sour? No longer are you in love with your significant other. The joyous days turn to sorrowful ones. You can't really remember how you two ever hooked up in the first place.

In this sad circumstance, you have several options. You can part—friends, or otherwise—or you can call it a day. You are free to go your own two separate ways.

Now, think about this. In this lifetime, you will *always* have a relationship with money. Always. Period. For the rest of your life. It's not something you can just walk away from. Money will always be your partner, through good and bad, thick or thin. How you feel about money will result in how prosperous or unprosperous you end up being.

THE MONEY TEST FOR THE REST OF YOUR LIFE

Now comes the fun part. How are you going to think about money for the rest of your life? Are you going to think of it as a burden? Something that has to be earned at a job you hate for 70 hours a week? Or are you going to think of it as an energy source? Something to be accumulated and something to be given away? Something to be feared? Something to be treasured and nurtured?

As with anything in life, your thoughts are up to you. It's your relationship with money, over your lifetime. You get to decide if the money messages given to you as a child were good, bad, ineffective, or nonexistent. You get to decide, as an adult, whether you are going to want to instill good and beneficial financial habits in your children. It's all up to you to decide. And your prosperity consciousness can get you there.

THE SHIP IS SAILING

What happens if you've become debt-free but you still don't feel like you're prospering? To paraphrase Brooklyn-based money psychologist and therapist Judith Gruber, you are what you sail.

"Let's say your ship is you, and you find that you have 'plugged up the holes' (your debt). Now what? How do you sail away?"

One woman living on New York's Upper West Side had several plants on her windowsill. They were beautiful, full, pink, purple, and white geraniums when she brought them home from the plant store, and they continued to grow nicely. She watered them, gave the soil fertilizer, and watched them grow.

Over time, though, the lovely plants began to lose some of their luster. They started to droop and lost their vitality. The woman kept watering them and doing all of the same things she usually did to enrich them. No luck.

Finally, she considered repotting the plants. She removed them from their too-small pots and replanted them in much larger pots with more soil around the edges. The roots that had been pushed against the sides of the pots now had a chance to really thrive and expand.

HOW BIG DO YOU WANT YOUR POT TO BE?

In the same way, if you think about it, your thoughts are your plants. What you think and how you nurture these thoughts is how you will grow. As you begin to "repot" your feelings about money, you will begin to see changes. If thinking about money always brings up fear and resentment with your past and how your parents felt about money, begin to rethink through these thoughts and "repot" them. Try adding a bit of "prosperity consciousness" as your fertilizer.

As you "water" your thoughts with this new kind of awareness about abundance, not only will you develop a new and wonderful way of looking at money, but your relationship with your thoughts about money will also expand, bringing in new possibilities, opportunities, and abundance.

In addition, with today's information technologies, more pure information is available about various money options. As we begin the new millennium, many people are becoming more obsessed with where their money is going to take them than where they are right now with their money.

Know that you mean more than your money. You control your money. Your money does not control you.

LET'S TAKE A DEEP BREATH

If you could only take the time out, take a deep breath, and really explore the importance of how you feel about money, your life would change. As in any growth experience, it takes time to really figure out what role money plays in your life. As Needleman suggests earlier in his quote, if money were *more* important to us, we would try to better understand its impact in our lives and how it influences nearly every decision about how we live our lives.

But does life get any easier? And will we always be worrying about money along the way?

It's all in how you think about it. Are you going to let money rule your life, or are you going to begin to focus on serenity around money issues first, and accumulation of money second?

ALREADY ON THE RIGHT TRACK

As an intelligent, interested reader of this book, you have already read and taken quizzes on topics such as investing basics, stocks, mutual funds, retirement plans, finding a good financial advisor, and so on. In just the space of 24 hours you have begun to grow and nurture your sensibilities about money and how to work with it in your life.

Perhaps when you first considered the idea of financial goal-planning or investing for retirement it seemed out-of-sight and unlikely. But by gathering information, reading good financial books, and talking to people who knew more than you, you gained confidence. Suddenly, the idea of investing didn't seem so frightening anymore.

Once some people begin to get a better hold on their finances, they find that nurturing a healthy financial life doesn't seem so intimidating. It can be fun and empowering, in fact.

JUST A MINUTE

Women, especially, are becoming more and more empowered with their money issues. Where once a woman had to rely on others—her husband or her parents—to take care of her financially, now more women are able to earn a living, support themselves and their families, and invest their money wisely.

IT CAN ALSO GET YOU DOWN

Money continues to be a volatile and complicated issue between couples, family members, siblings, and even among friends. Many relationships have been lost or made more complicated over money. Families have been torn apart by mismanaged funds or ill-advised financial decisions.

Many people were also given misleading financial advice—or no advice—from well-meaning parents who may well have been still growing themselves and learning about money. One topic still to be explored at length is the mother-daughter money connection.

As you grow older, raise families, lose jobs, apply for new jobs, and plan for retirement, you hopefully learn a thing or two. Where once keeping a checkbook balanced seemed difficult or impossible, with some focus and "keeping the eye on the ball" you are able to get better at the financial aspect of your life.

LET'S SEE HOW YOU FEEL ABOUT MONEY

As you grow and continue to develop through life, you must also develop, expand, and determine your financial pathways and explore your deep-seated emotions and feelings about money.

Your money choices are all around you. What kinds of things do you like to have in your house? Do you like to buy fine, expensive items or would you rather keep that nice big bank account with lots of zeros in it and not spend a lot of it? Do you feel you sometimes sabotage your feeling of well-being by underearning, in some way debting against yourself and your possibilities?

Needleman says it best: "Think of your relationship to nature, to ideas, to pleasure. Think of your sense of self-identity and self-respect; think of where you live and with what things you surround yourself; think of all your impulses to help others or serve a larger cause; where you go, how you travel, with whom you associate—or just think of what you were doing yesterday, or what you will be doing tomorrow, or in an hour. Think of what you want or what you dream of, for now, or next year, or for the rest of your life. It will take money, a certain, definite amount."

Good food for thought.

BILL-PAYING: NOT NECESSARILY EVIL

You may sigh while looking at your calendar, seeing that the first of the month is right around the corner and rent will soon be due. You can either make this a stressful time in your life or a serene one. Either way, no matter where you go or what you do in your life, rest assured that you are always going to have bills to pay. Always. Even lottery winners have bills to pay, and they do not always come out the happiest of bill payers.

In any case, think of your bills as necessary friends. If you are keeping solvent and not debting a day at a time, you can feel a definite sense of accomplishment by meeting your needs and paying your bills on time without late payments or interest charges. Try it for a month and see if you can catch up with all of your bills and send payments on time.

Then, the next time around, try moving back your payment week by an additional seven days. You're repotting your plant. You're giving yourself some room to breath and experimenting in how that feels to you. Imagine the serenity you can feel if you plan out your bill-paying month, set a "date" with yourself, and then turn on soothing music, light a candle, pour your favorite juice into a wine glass, and sit back and pay your bills. Not only will you feel a sense of serenity, but you also will know that your cash flow is happening within a schedule of "flow" you have set; not from a place of "stuck energy," fear, and sorrow.

ONE GREAT TIP: MONEY ORDERS

At first you might think, money orders? Those are only for people who aren't doing well in their lives. People who can't "make it." People you just don't want to do business with.

Well, think again. To many people in this country, bounced checks continue to be a problem. Banks charge upward of $20 per returned check ($30 at some banks in New York), which does not include what the retailer might also charge for a returned check. If you have had or continue to have problems bouncing checks, i.e., writing phantom checks when there's not enough actual money to cover these purchases, consider using money orders instead to pay off each of your bills.

Suzie, a singer/songwriter in New York, found herself bouncing checks to the tune of three or more each month. At the rate of $30 per check, she was accumulating "over-the-limit" fees of $90 per month. If you multiply that figure by 12 months, she was paying the bank $360 a year just to cover her bounced-check fees. That's a lot of music paper she could have bought instead to write music on. Or, a trip that she could have taken.

She found out that if she prepared her list of bills, creditors, and so on, she could buy money orders to pay her bills at her local post office. She could pay for the money orders using her debit card, which would take the funds right out of her account. It took maybe 10 minutes to fill out each money order, lick and stamp each envelope, and she was done. It no longer mattered when each proprietor received her check; it didn't matter when they cashed them.

In essence, her "money flow" was in good shape: She never had to "sweat it" again like she did in the old days when she was never sure when a check was going to clear—or bounce. This way, she knew exactly how much money was left in her account for her to use and how much was needed to pay her bills. She kept copies of all receipts and carbons for her records. She saw amazing progress in her prosperity.

FIND THE SYSTEM THAT WORKS FOR YOU

Buying money orders at the post office may not work for you, however. Maybe you can't get to a post office within their 9-to-5 hours, for example. See if that excuse might be coming from a place of fear or resentment rather than "money flow." You have to experiment and see what money techniques work for you. Various prosperous people have different methods that helped them become that way. It's up to you to find the right method for you.

TITHING: SPIRITUAL INVESTING

The thought of tithing may leave a bad taste in your mouth. "I barely have enough to get by on as it is. Why should I have to tithe? And, who am I supposed to tithe to?" Whether or not you are a religious person, examine the thought of tithing. Does it come from a place of prosperity and abundance? Or does it come from a place of poverty-consciousness and fear?

It is true that if you think often enough it will come true. If you tell yourself over and over again that you don't have any extra money for things such as tithing, then you'll probably not have any extra money to tithe with, now will you? You might also find yourself without extra money for yourself or for your family. And you deserve to treat yourself once in a while to something that makes your heart tick!

Our thoughts are our lives. Whether you attend a church, a synagogue, or ashram, go to daily yoga classes, or meditate, it comes down to asking yourself, "What kinds of thoughts am I going to let into my life today? Good or bad?"

Perhaps a second thought would be, "How much and to whom would I like to tithe to this month?"

OPENING YOUR MIND TO PROSPERITY

Catherine Ponder, in her infinitely insightful book *Open Your Mind to Prosperity,* explains the origin of the idea of tithing. She says that as "the ancients knew it, they practiced [tithing] as '10, the magic number of increase.' The ancients invoked the number of increase through systematic tithing or returning to their gods one tenth of their game, crops, and other channels of income."

In fact, the word *tithe* means "tenth," and ten was a sort of magic number for increase used by many different civilizations including the ancient Egyptians, Babylonians, Persians, Arabians, Greeks, Romans, and Chinese, according to Ponder. So if you begin a nice ritual of tithing 10 percent of your income, you'd be in good company with all of those good people who came before you!

BUT, IT'S THE TWENTY-FIRST CENTURY!

Okay, I see you rolling your eyes. Or, maybe you're clucking your tongue, saying, "We live in the twenty-first century. We don't need to tithe. We're above all of that type of superstition. We've got the Internet, IPOs, and Bill Gates. Who needs *tithing* anyway?"

Well, think about it. Bill Gates, the wealthiest man in the world, has recently increased his tithing to such a degree that he now has become the wealthiest philanthropist in the world as well. Love him or hate him, realize that he is definitely putting back into the universe some of the wealth that came into his life.

On the other hand, you may not be quite sure who to tithe *to*. For example, one successful writer living in the mid-west posed this question over coffee during a recent book tour in New York: "What if I don't feel connected to the idea of just giving money to my organized church? Can I turn around and just 'tithe' the money to my daughter whom I love dearly and want to be happy? Does it have to be outside of our family?"

There are no answers to this question.

One approach might be to examine your thoughts in a different way. Rather than figuring out where and how much personal satisfaction you are going to get out of giving first, just choose a charity that means something to you or those you are close to. In the case of the writer, she and her daughter could pick a charity that they both were interested in and felt a "calling" toward, say, a literacy project.

In short, tithing should be about money flow: to send out a portion of the abundance that comes your way each month, without fear or resentment. If you can "clear the way" as part of your monthly spending plan, the abundance will follow. "Stuck" energy equals "stuck money flow."

If you were raised in an overly religious family, however, where tithing to a church or a different organized religion was not only expected but demanded—if you were judged upon whether and how much you gave—remember that as an adult you can now decide to feel differently about money than the way you did as a child. If giving to an organized church or synagogue is not comfortable for you, give instead to a charity, organization, or other group that interests you and that you feel good about giving to.

Only you can decide the right place to give to. Only you can decide the right amount to give. But, in time, tithing will feel as good as breathing, brushing your teeth, and eating a good, nourishing meal. In a way, you're taking care of your financial health by giving some of it away and, in turn, feeling solid and "taken care of" by the universe.

All that you need you have right now, as you're reading this. Why not give back some of this abundance? Try tithing 10 percent of your salary for six months, and see what kinds of abundances come back to you.

In any case, tithing should become a part of your life. If at first you feel resentment towards giving, try to make a place on your spending plan for a small percentage per month. Start small, say, 5 percent of your income and work up to 10 percent.

SPIRITUALITY AND FINANCE

So where does spirituality fit into all this? Just the word "spirituality" might make you go screaming for the hills. You may not even consider yourself a spiritual person, and you're just trying to make a living, not get into any more debt, and live life with abundance of spirit. Okay. Whatever life you'd like to have, it's out there if you can envision it. Say to yourself, "One day at a time, by being grateful for what I have today, I will someday achieve my goals and dreams."

One person who was able to incorporate his spirituality with his financial goals was Sir John Templeton, the father of the mutual fund.

Brad Bannon, a New York–based independent investor who advises clients of all age groups—from college age to retirement age—also travels throughout the country giving seminars on the life of Templeton.

Templeton came from England originally, and he was raised in a poor but hard-working family. He got married right out of college, and never borrowed a dime from anyone. He actually never even had a mortgage!

The Templetons developed a system of tithing that worked well for them. They decided to tithe 10 percent of their income and 10 percent of their time. They would tithe either to their church or to charities, and it didn't have to be anything organized. The Templetons lived off 40 percent of their income and saved the remaining 50 percent, which is pretty hard to do.

GO TO ▶
Refer to Hours 4, "How Can I Keep Track?" and 13, "Finding the Right Financial Advisor," for more tips on keeping track of your money and finding a financial advisor to help you.

It's terrific if you can do such a large savings plan. However, this may be unrealistic. Check with a financial planner about creating a realistic savings plan for you and your family.

The Templetons invested in stocks and bonds, which led to much of Sir Templeton's success. Templeton also created a list of Rules of Personal Finance, which is the basis for Brad Bannon's seminars, eight of which appear here:

RULE 1: PESSIMISM IS NOT A VIRTUE

This rule speaks for itself. If you think about it, pessimism is the opposite of the whole principle behind investing. Be optimistic about the future.

RULE 2: COUNT YOUR BLESSINGS

Count your blessings to enrich yourself and your neighbors first spiritually and then perhaps financially.

RULE 3: INVEST IN YOUR FUTURE

GO TO ▶
Refer to Hour 2, "Cleaning Up Clutter/Debt Repayment," for more tips on keeping your debt in check.

Debt, whether personal or collective, should not keep you from investing in your future. Because there is a whole spectrum of debt, keep in mind that no debt is best. But it is most important to be consistent, once you begin investing; set up and implement an investment or debt-payment system that works for you.

JUST A MINUTE

When beginning an investment plan, the key is consistency. Set up a plan that you can afford and make it demanding yet obtainable, whether in a 401(k), IRA, etc. Check out Hour 5, "Investing Basics," to get you started on firming up your investment options.

One Biblical passage that captures this rule is Ecclesiastes 11:4: "Whoever watches the wind will not plant; whoever looks at the clouds will not reap."

According to Bannon, everyone should be saving around 10 percent of their salary for their retirement funds. Setting up another savings account for your future kids is also part of Bannon's savings plan, even though he currently does not have children. "You don't have to have a big salary to be a millionaire," says Bannon, "You just need time. If you don't start early, you run out of time real soon."

RULE 4: UNDERSTANDING COLLECTIVE DEBT

Debt seems to be everywhere in this country, and according to Bannon, it is usually met with a negative connotation. "Looking at our national debt, it's mostly in Treasury bills and Treasury bonds that are owed to the small-town investors like Aunt Loula in Idaho who's living off of the interest from the bonds. That's not a bad debt."

According to Templeton, each American citizen, in effect, owns an acre of Alaska. To continue that thinking, every man, woman, and child has an ounce of gold in Fort Knox, one mile of interstate highway, part of an air-force base, and about 20 books in a public library. As taxpayers, we pay for all of these things.

Says Bannon, "No matter what kind of debt, other than credit card, that you might have, you should be investing that money, and investing it early. Don't keep putting it off, as if you have something else to do with it. Just get started."

According to Bannon, a good rule of thumb to use to chart a good percentage for investing is to use your age as a percentage. If you're 20 years old, for example, invest 80 percent in stock, 20 percent in bonds. If you're 40, invest 40 percent in stock, 60 percent in bonds. As you age, you will want to choose less-risky choices because you want to protect your assets.

RULE 5: MONEY SHOULD DO MORE THAN SIMPLY REPRODUCE ITSELF

Peter 4:10 says the following: "Each one should use whatever gift he has received to serve others, faithfully administering God's grace in its various forms." Templeton was of this path. He said, essentially, that we should not just be reproducing money, but that we should be putting it someplace where it will do some good.

Even if you do not believe in this idea, the principle stands on its own. Whatever gifts you have been given, whether you are a writer, Wall Street financial analyst, chemical engineer, or ice skater, if you can give back some of the abundance you earn through your talents, you are, in fact, helping the universe continue to grow and expand.

RULE 6: NEVER FORGET THE SECRET OF CREATING RICHES FOR YOURSELF IS CREATING RICHES FOR OTHERS

Again, tithing comes in here! Tithing 10 percent of your money and 10 percent of your time is again an excellent rule of thumb.

RULE 7: LOOKING OUT FOR NUMBER ONE DOESN'T MAKE YOU NUMBER ONE

What is "unseen" is eternal. What is here today could be gone tomorrow. Be sure that your ego is secondary in your search for prosperity and abundance.

RULE 8: MEASURE SUCCESS ON A SINGLE WORD: LOVE

This too, speaks for itself.

HOUR'S UP!

Let's now test your new knowledge about "financial serenity." Try to answer the following without looking back in the hour for the answers:

1. True or false: Your money "relationship" can change throughout your life. What you were told about money when you were young does not necessarily still apply when you're an adult.

2. True or false: You must always hoard your money because you may lose it all one day. Then where would you be?

3. A good amount to tithe every month is how much of your salary?

    a. 5 percent

    b. 10 percent

    c. 20 percent

4. According to Sir John Templeton, how much of your time should you tithe each month?

    a. 10 percent

    b. 20 percent

    c. 30 percent

5. True or false: If you are someone who has a problem with bouncing checks and vagueness over your money, using money orders can be a good replacement tool in place of writing checks.

6. The best time to pay your bills is …

    a. Once a month.

    b. Twice a month.

    c. Never.

7. True or false: When sitting down to pay your bills, put on some nice music in the background, light a candle, and create a ritual out of taking this action.

8. True or false: It is important to be consistent when investing your money; start small but keep putting regular amounts into your savings or retirement account on a monthly basis.

9. True or false: It is important to diversify investments because of the inherent risk involved in keeping all your money in one type of investment.

10. True or false: John Templeton's philosophy is that no debt is best.

Quiz

Hour 24

Your Future: Finding a Job Online

CHAPTER SUMMARY

LESSON PLAN:

In this chapter we will be exploring ways of conducting a job search online, using the newest Internet technologies to help research salary, job placement, and finding a new career. You'll also learn how to:

- Secure your future with the right job and career.
- Use the Internet to find out how much you're really worth.

With the words "Silicon Valley," "IPOs," and "Internet millionaires" on the tips of everyone's tongues these days, you can't do business or look for a job without knowing how to use the Internet. Back in the early 1980s, no one could have predicted how important personal computers and Internet technology would become in our daily lives.

Because of the competitiveness in our modern society, if you don't have home or business Internet access—or don't have a way of getting access—you may be at a real disadvantage when competing for jobs and looking for salary information.

At the same time that more information is available at our fingertips, the nature of careers and job searching is changing at a more rapid pace than ever. Once upon a time an employee could be hired at 18, retire at 65 from the same company, and get a gold watch. These days, some workers will change jobs every two to five years—if not sooner!

For example, do you realize that you might change jobs at least seven times in your working life? Sound improbable? Not really, if you think about it. If you grew up in the early days of the Internet age, you know that job security is really a thing of the past. It is job flexibility that is becoming the name of the job-search game.

WHO'S THE COMPETITION, ANYWAY?

GO TO ▶
Refer to Hours 5, "Investing Basics," and 9, "Retirement Plans," for more information on your investment and retirement goals.

With you and approximately 149 million of your counterparts getting up and going to work in the new millennium, you can see that your competition will continue to be fierce. The good news is that even though the labor force continues to grow and add new laborers at a steady pace, it will be at a slower pace than in the previous 30 years when baby boomers were first entering the world of work.

Like the financial bubble baby boomers created when they were first born, this key population statistic will create the new trends of the early part of the twenty-first. We are already beginning to see the outcome of such trends in the growth in popularity of personal financial and retirement knowledge.

The Fastest-Growing Job Markets

Out of the 10 fastest-growing occupations, six are in the health-services fields and four are computer-related. Trends show that the computer industries will continue to need smart, trained people who know computer programming in its various languages. In addition, as our population continues to age, trained health-care professionals are needed to help take care of our elderly. Web designers and planners are another hot industry.

**Top-Ten Fastest-Growing Occupations
(1996 to 2006 Numbers in Thousands of Jobs)**

Occupation	Employment Change Number	1996 to 2006 Percent
Database administrators, computer support specialists	249	118
Computer engineers	235	109
Systems analysts	520	103
Personal and home-care aides	171	85
Physical- and corrective-therapy assistants and aides	66	79
Home health aides	378	76
Medical assistants	166	74
Desktop publishing specialists	22	74
Physical therapists	81	71
Occupational therapy assistants and aides	11	69

Source: Bureau of Labor Statistics

JUST A MINUTE

If you are deciding on a new or different career path, the Bureau of Labor Statistics has an invaluable Web site at www.bls.gov that describes in detail jobs available in the United States, the pay scale, and future outlook. Click on the 1999 to 2000 Occupational Outlook Handbook for up-to-date stats.

HEALTHCARE, ANYONE?

As you can guess, the health-care industry continues to expand into the twenty-first century. As people age, healthcare will continue to account for the largest increase of new jobs—about three million in the year 2000. Because of shifts from hospital care to outpatient facilities, nursing homes, and so on, more attendant care and physical aides are going to be needed.

JUST A MINUTE

Want to try to find a job in healthcare online instantly? Go to www.ask.com and type in a question such as, "How can I find jobs in the health-care industry?" This site allows you type in full sentences, reducing the risk of linking you to the wrong site. Also, go to www.monster.com and type in "health-care industry jobs."

COMPUTER WORLD

As you may have noticed already, the computer world is expanding at an incredible rate. By the time you have finished this chapter, some young Internet entrepreneur in Palo Alto, Iowa, New York, or Alaska may well have set up the next new Internet company that will rake in the next $500 million IPO. You, too, can be part of this ever-expanding, seemingly unending web of computer-linked possibilities.

To that end, keep in mind that you can't fail to help yourself by continuing to update your computer skills. The so-called Internet explosion has brought us new careers, new career titles, and new programming languages in the space of 15 or so years. It is important to have some technical skills these days if you are exploring a career in the computer industry.

Keep this in mind: Try to accumulate as much computer knowledge as possible as you go through your work life, no matter what career you are in. You'll find this knowledge will help you in many ways.

JUST A MINUTE

Check out www.mediainfo.com, a Web site that has thousands of links to on-line newspapers and help-wanted ads. Scanning this site frequently can help you keep up with career opportunities and industry trends.

The Internet—How It Can Help You

No matter what career field you are in or aspire to, the Internet should go hand in hand with your job search.

What is simply amazing is the scope of the Internet and the information it offers. There was a time when you might have picked up your local paper, circled some listings in the employment section, made some phone calls, sent in a resumé, and hoped for the best. Now by just getting online you have access not only to your local paper's online job listings but also those of hundreds of newspapers across the country.

In addition, there are some mega-job-search sites that have sprung up on the Internet that encompass whatever type of job you're looking for. Suppose you're looking in the entertainment industry. You can go online, go to a search engine, and type in "entertainment and employment." Or, perhaps you're in retail in New York, and you want to see if there are similar job openings available in San Francisco. You can go online and instantly find out what's out there.

The Monster Mega Sites

As you begin your search, keep in mind that there are some really terrific sites on the Internet. This chapter will presuppose that you have at least a working knowledge of "searching" for items on the Web. If not, there are many computer books out there that can help you. Also, most libraries now have public access to the Internet, and librarians are available to help you with your search.

Searching on the Web can be really easy. Simply go to your "gateway" software to the Web (several of the most popular include America Online, CompuServe, and Mindspring), point and click on the Web feature, and then type in any of the following Web sites. Once up and running, you can then type in whichever categories of employment you are looking for.

Some of the main "mega sites" include …

- **America's Job Bank.** www.ajb.dni.us
- **CareerMosaic.** careermosaic.com
- **CareerPath.com.** www.careerpath.com
- **E.span.** www.espan.com
- **Headhunter.net.** www.HeadHunter.net
- **Monster.com.** www.monster.com
- **Online Career Center.** www.onlinecareercenter.com
- *The Wall Street Journal*'s **Career page.** www.careers.wsj.com/
- **Yahoo! Classifieds.** classifieds.yahoo.com/employment.html

Two other terrific sites are "meta sites," which make use of the resources of most of the other sites. One is Myjobsearch (www.myjobsearch.com), which has detailed reviews of just about every job-search site out there. The other is Careershop.com (www.careershop.com), which will enable you to search for jobs using the databases of up to 40 other sites at once.

According to Gary Susman, writer, editor, and New York–based Web-surfer extraordinaire, all of these sites have the "McLuhanesque" property of being best suited for people looking for computer jobs (the medium is indeed the message), though they're not bad for people looking for most other kinds of jobs, too.

OFF-BEAT SITES

Some other general employment sites that you may not have considered but are worth looking at are …

- **CareerCast.** www.careercast.com
- **NationJob Network.** www.nationjob.com
- **Net-Temps.** www.net-temps.com

OTHER REFERENCE TOOLS

There are also some super-quick reference tools out there if you are researching a certain company's background. Some of these include …

- **Ready Reference** at **www.ipl.org/ref/RR.** A good site for finding reference material quickly
- **BigBook** at **www.bigbook.com.** An Internet Yellow Pages–type directory

- **HotSheet** at **www.hotsheet.com.** A one-stop shop for finding other quick-reference sites

For company information, you also can't beat the following:

- **Hoover's Online** at **www.hoover.com.** Provides sources for company profiles
- **BizWeb Business Guide to the Web** at **www.bizweb.com.** An online guide to over 40,000 companies
- **Companies Online** at **www.companiesonline.com.** You can search for companies by name, city, state, ticker symbol, or industry at this site. This is a site produced by Dun & Bradstreet, a recognized name in providing company information.

HOW MUCH ARE YOU REALLY WORTH?

Perhaps you are thinking of changing jobs. Or perhaps you're thinking of relocating from one city to another and are not sure how much your cost of living will be in the new city. Many sites are available to help you in figuring out just how much you are worth, such as …

- **JobSmart** at **www.jobsmart.org.** Offers a directory of more than 300 salary surveys, in fields such as accounting, human resources, law, and marketing. This link also offers interesting advice on negotiating a better salary. For a direct link to salary information, go to http://www. jobsmart.org/tools/salary/index.htm.
- **Wageweb** at **www.wageweb.com.** Specializes in providing salary information on low- to mid-level positions in areas including finance, information management, sales and marketing, engineering, and healthcare.
- **Yahoo! City Comparison** at **verticals.yahoo.com/salary.**
- **Homebuyer's Fair Salary Calculator** at **www2.homefair.com/calc/ salcalc.html.**

These sites are useful if you're planning a move within the United States and want to research the salary you would need to maintain your current standard of living. For example, if your salary is $40,000 in Phoenix, Arizona, you'll need about $60,000 in New York City.

RESUMÉS—TO E-MAIL, FAX, OR SEND?

In the old days, a letter of reference worked as an entrée into the world of work. As times changed, and technology changed with them, the resumé—in short, the chronology of one's work history detailing dates and places of employment, and education history—became the employer's document of choice and an addition to the job seeker's portfolio.

Needless to say, there still remain many ways of obtaining a job without a resumé. The best job searches are created out of finding a goal and reaching it using whatever tools or networking necessary to achieve it. That said, a resumé in 9 times out of 10 is going to be needed when conducting a proper job search.

In today's information age, two questions remain:

- What is the communication tool to express one's interest in a job?
- What is the best way of communicating that interest?

Years ago there was only one choice: You mailed in your cover letter and resumé to a future employer and hoped for the best. But now we have evolved into a technological age where "snail mail" is just one of several methods of getting your resumé to the person who can hire you.

When you submit your resumé, your short-term goal is to make sure it gets noticed. Period. If it doesn't, you don't have a chance of ever landing the job. Because there are many excellent resource guides on creating the right resumé for you that will get you noticed, this chapter will not deal thoroughly with this issue. Suffice it to say, your goal is to get the clearest, sharpest, and most direct resumé to the employer or human resources person who can best reward your job search.

So, how can you do this in the age of the Internet? Let's take a look at the options.

CONSTRUCTING AN ELECTRONIC RESUMÉ

Fortunately or unfortunately, the growth of a new medium like the Internet brings with it a whole set of new rules. Where five or so years ago you could have managed a complete job search without worrying about electronic resumés, these days it's a whole new ballgame. It's important to get up to speed with these new parameters of telling your work history in a way that Internet-savvy employers want to hear.

Basically, it comes down to this: You are going to need two resumés: a scannable paper resumé and a plain-text electronic one. If you have to make a choice, know that the order of preference given to types of resumés is as follows:

- **E-mailed plain-text resumés.**
- **Scannable resumés** that are printed out on white paper and mailed via postal mail.
- **Faxed resumés that are scannable** are usually an employer's last choice and should be yours, too. When an employer puts an advertisement in a Sunday paper and gets deluged with fax responses, yours may be somewhere in a stack of hundreds. That's not the best way to get to the employer who can hire you.

Keep in mind, too, that you will need to know how to e-mail an electronic resumé to an employment database, to an employer's Web site, or to an individual's e-mail address.

PLAIN-TEXT RESUMÉS

Plain-text resumés are just that: plain. No fancy frills to attract attention, just text. Normally a plain-text resumé contains no italics, underlining, bold fonts, or any other formatting to make it prettier. Another name for a plain-text resumé is an ASCII resumé. This is because ASCII (American Standard Code for Information Exchange) is a very simple form of text that almost all computers can read and understand.

Without a doubt, the clearer you can make your resumé, the better it is going to work for you.

According to Pam Dixon's excellent book *Job Searching Online for Dummies* (IDG Books, 1998), you should choose a plain-text or ASCII resumé when …

- You e-mail a resumé to an employer.
- You post your resumé on online employment sites and databases.
- You send a resumé to a corporate Web site.
- A contact asks you to e-mail a resumé.
- A job advertisement lists an e-mail address.

The plain-text resumé is your default resumé to use when you are not 100 percent sure the employer you are trying to reach will be able to open a resumé in the type of format you are using on your computer.

JOB POSTINGS IN THE NEWSPAPER

Sometimes you may use a formatted electronic resumé. This type of resumé would be a normally formatted resumé using one of many word-processing programs such as Microsoft Word. Sometimes a job advertisement will indicate that you can send a Word document online. That means that if you have Microsoft Word and have formatted your resumé with it, you can send it as an attachment to the e-mail address given in the ad.

Some online job sites allow candidates to post Microsoft Word resumés for potential employers to read. Two large sites that offer this service are Net-Temps and E.span. In this case, you can send your Word resumé via e-mail to the employment site's contact address.

FOLLOW UP

Definitely be sure to follow up by making a phone call after sending your resumé to a company via the Internet. Even though it may appear that the resumé was sent properly from your computer system, there is always a chance that it will not get to the employer's system correctly. A well-timed phone call allows you to follow up your e-mailed resumé while also making your first personal contact with the company.

As per the usual job search routine, be sure to be courteous with whomever you have reached by phone; if the only person you are able to reach is a secretary, be as courteous and respectful to him or her as you would be to the CEO! You would be surprised how much a good secretary can tell you about the inner workings of the company: who is "in," who is "out," and so on. The best executive secretaries can literally be the boss's "eyes and ears."

JUST A MINUTE

To look at some excellent sample resumés on the Web, check out www. resweb.com. You can search resumés by key word or look at a resumé index categorized by profession. Looking at resumés is free, but you must pay to post one. Also, Yahoo! Classifieds has an excellent giant open resumé database at classifieds.yahoo.com/employment.html (click the Resume Bank button). And check out Resumania at www.umn.edu/ohr/ecep/resume.

BUILDING AND USING AN ELECTRONIC COVER LETTER

Another very important and fundamental element to the online job search is the electronic cover letter. In the old days, you could send a full-page, three-paragraph cover letter, written with address, date, "Sincerely yours," and so forth.

If you are using snail mail as one of the processes of your job search, the traditional cover letter continues to apply. However, there's a whole new world out there when it comes to electronic cover letters. Keep in mind that some employers don't even keep cover letters, only the resumés!

Because of new resumé-tracking software, many cover letters are seen *after* the resumés now. This means that some electronic tracking systems take a picture of the cover letter and store it in a file for employers. So some employers never even see the cover letter until after they have seen the resumé.

THREE CHANCES TO SHINE

In e-mail correspondence, there are really three ways that you can shine when contacting a potential employer. Remember that the employer looking to hire new employees may not have a lot of time to sift through and read long cover letters—that is, if he sees them at all! Keep in mind that brevity is the spice of life, and keep your cover letters short.

THE ELECTRONIC PARAGRAPH—THE 30-SECOND PITCH

Because your potential employer may only have 30 seconds to read your e-mail cover letter, make it short, strong, and to the point. Generally, you don't need to make your cover letter any longer than a salutation, one or two paragraphs, and closing remark. And be sure to have your "pitch" wrapped up in 30 seconds!

The following is an example of a good "30-second" cover letter:

Dear Beth Greenberg:

I saw the position of Senior Programmer with Fuzzbot Communications advertised on Monster Board. (Requisition #456789). Although I am currently employed by one of your competitors, I am considering excellent opportunities such as yours. Attached please find my resumé.

I will e-mail you this week to see if we can arrange a meeting to discuss this opportunity.

Best,

Howard Miller
212-555-1234
Hmiller@lookingforjob.com

As you can see, this job seeker gets right to the point; he draws the parallel between the advertised job and his current position, and he ends with a good follow-up suggestion, which he will then hopefully turn into an interview.

THE LONGER COVER LETTER

Another technique is to use a longer, but still e-mailable, cover letter. This type of cover letter may give a bit more information about yourself than would a more traditional cover letter. Be specific, though, and make every paragraph count. This technique should be used by more higher-level professionals, or if a recruiter contacts you for more information.

DIGITAL COVER LETTER

The third type of cover letter is a basic digital cover letter. This is your basic parallel to a typical snail-mail letter of the past, but it has been formatted to be attached to your resumé. Usually, the digital cover letter will follow the standard format of date, name, address, salutation, three to five paragraphs, and closing remark. These can also be used in response to advertisements, if a certain format is described for communication.

YOUR OWN E-MAIL ADDRESS

Keep in mind, too, that employers these days expect you to have your own e-mail address. In the same way that everyone has a telephone and can be contacted in that form, most employers expect to be able to contact you via e-mail. You can be dated immediately by your response to the following question: "What's your e-mail address?" If you answer, mumbling, "Uh, I don't know—I don't have one," it's time to get one. Most Internet gateway companies have come down in price, so being online is not as expensive as it once was.

Plus, employers expect to be able to see your e-mail address on any resumé sent via snail mail or e-mail. So, get cracking, get online, and get going!

THINGS TO AVOID IN YOUR E-MAIL SEARCH

Keep in mind that you can definitely turn off an employer as easily as you can get her excited about hiring you. Again, your job is to be able to make contact and get the interview without bugging your prospective employer too much!

E-Mail Clutter

Never e-mail a resumé to an employer again and again without specific instructions from the employer to do so.

You would think this is common sense, but many people make this mistake over and over again. Yes, e-mail is much more convenient for employers to read and consider. But too many e-mails are only "clutter" on their system. If you must e-mail an employer again after making initial contact, first re-contact this person by phone.

As some experts agree, if after several months you have not heard back from the company that you are interested in working for, you may then go ahead and e-mail your resumé again without it seeming bad form. Use your best judgment with this.

Never Send Negative E-Mail!

Negative e-mail is a big mistake. You never know where your e-mail might end up or where it might get forwarded. Never make a paper trail of negative e-mails. It will only come back to haunt you, and it can't possibly help you.

Do Not Use Your Work Address as Your E-Mail

Yes, that's right. The first red flag an employer will think is: If you have e-mailed him looking for a new job from your current work or office computer, what's to keep you from doing that six months, a year, or five years down the road from your new job?

Not only is e-mailing from your current job bad form, if you think about it, you are, in fact, stealing from your current employer. You are taking company time (or if after hours, it's still company computer time) and using it for your own benefit to find a new job. Not smart. Don't make this mistake!

A Few Words on Privacy

Believe it or not, the Internet, in all its vast glory, has also brought out some new—and very serious—issues about personal privacy in the computer age. With companies of all kinds selling products from the Internet with access to your credit card information, a new type of computer piracy has sprung up in many niches of the Web. It is of the utmost importance that you consider privacy issues before you begin your online job search.

JUST A MINUTE

Check out a couple of great sites on computer privacy issues: www.epic.org (Electronic Privacy Information Center), www.eff.org (Electronic Frontier Foundation's Web page), and www.privacyrights.org (Privacy Rights Clearinghouse).

IT'S YOUR WORLD OUT THERE: GO FOR IT!

Without a doubt, there really is no better time to start looking for a new job than now. The computer revolution and the invention of the Internet have expanded your opportunities beyond your wildest dreams. Expand your horizons, go for your dreams, and research your way into your future by going online. You're worth it, and with a little fun and "elbow grease" (or should that be "cyber-grease"?), you can plan your destiny with just a touch of a button.

See you in cyberspace and in the new millennium!

HOUR'S UP!

Let's now test your new knowledge about finding a job online. Try to answer the following without looking back in the chapter for the answers:

1. True or false: Job security is no longer the number-one item to consider in your job search. Job flexibility has become the wave of the future in finding a job in the new millennium.

2. The number of workers who will be working in the new millennium hovers near …
   a. 100 million.
   b. 149 million.
   c. 200 million.

3. True or false: The average worker will be changing jobs at least seven times over the course of her working life.

4. The fastest-growing job sectors over the next five years will be …
   a. Teachers.
   b. Computer professionals and health-care workers.
   c. Police officers.

Quiz

5. True or false: When you use a search engine such as www.yahoo.com or www.hotbot.com, you can type in "employment" and "_____" (fill in the blank) for whichever industry you're interested in to find the fastest results.

6. True or false: It's not important to consider the salary differences between cities that you may be moving to as part of your job search; you can always earn more later.

7. True or false: There are three types of good e-mail cover letters to use, with the rule of thumb being "short and to the point."

8. True or false: It is considered bad form—and detrimental to your job search—to e-mail a future employer from a current work e-mail address.

9. True or false: It's always fine to e-mail a future employer as many times as you want—they may never have received your resumé and so it's okay to re-send a dozen times.

10. True or false: When using the Internet, posting an online resumé, or sending e-mail, it is always important to investigate your privacy rights.

Appendixes

APPENDIX A
20 Minute Recap

HOUR 1

In Hour 1 you learned many of the fundamentals needed to decide upon your financial goals in life. Because your life will change as you grow older, your financial goals will also change. By having a clear blueprint in place, the financial aspirations for your family and your retirement plans can and will come true. In this hour you learned how to assess your net worth and set financial goals.

HOUR 2

In Hour 2 we found that the better understanding you have of how you earn and spend your money, the sooner you can begin to imagine a financial life free of debt. Investing for your future, saving with serenity, spending money that you know you have earned, and enjoying your financial life in general are just a few of the benefits. As you read through this guide, you saw how important it is to create a foundation on which you can build clear and abundant goals for yourself and your family.

HOUR 3

In Hour 3 you learned the secrets of budgeting, getting organized, filing the paperwork, and keeping good records. You learned to distinguish the fixed expenses from the variable expenses to allow for flexibility, and proceeded to calculate the true costs of achieving your financial goals.

Hour 4

Trying to track the details of your financial life can feel a little like hunting for dinosaur eggs: time-consuming and fruitless. If you pay for most of your purchases with cash, it just adds to the confusion. It's a lot easier with the help of technology, such as personal finance software, online tools, and Web sites.

Hour 5

In Hour 5 you learned that investing really means putting your money to work for you and that you need to set some goals, figure out your time horizon, and determine your risk comfort level before you start to invest. You also decided on your investment strategy and learned what common mistakes to avoid.

Hour 6

Investing in the stock market is an ideal way to make sure your dollar will outpace inflation. In Hour 6 you learned what the many forces are that influence the stock market and the price of a stock. You also learned about the several varieties of stock, such as blue chip and cyclical, and how to track their daily performance in published stock tables.

Hour 7

Mutual funds are a convenient way for an investor to have a diverse portfolio without having to buy one stock, bond, or Treasury bill at a time. They can be purchased directly from the company and offer professional management, choice, and liquidity.

Hour 8

In Hour 8 you learned what bonds are and how they are issued. You also looked at the different types of bond categories available: government, corporate, and municipal. You know how to calculate a bond's current yield and know the three things to look at when thinking about buying a bond: the par value, coupon rate, and maturity date. While bonds are considered safe investments, the rating will tell you what level of risk is involved in buying a particular bond.

Hour 9

A retirement plan may seem like the last thing you need when you're struggling to meet today's bills. Imagine yourself still struggling to make ends meet 20 years from now. Even if you plan to rely on Social Security, it won't pay all your expenses. With the benefits of tax-free compounding available through retirement plans, a little saved every month now will mean a lot to you in your golden years.

Hour 10

Keeping your money in the bank is not only safe, it's a great way to keep track of your finances. Most banks are federally insured and regulated on a state and federal level. With careful research and comparison shopping, you can find accounts to suit your banking needs and save on excess fees.

Hour 11

There is a lot of information out there today, some very valuable and some not worth your time. In Hour 11 you learned how to hone your research skills to avoid wasting time on the losers. You also found a myriad of sources to turn to when you need information and advice, both online and off. Finally, you learned the Internet addresses of some complete Web sites and directories to help you manage your personal finances.

Hour 12

In Hour 12 you discovered that the risks of taking your money into cyberspace are not much different than taking it to a city street. You just need to be Web-ready and aware. You also learned about the many transactions that can be done online to help make money management easier and more convenient. From tax planning to buying a home, you can find a Web site with advice and information.

Hour 13

In Hour 13 you learned the basic questions to ask yourself before beginning to look for a financial planner and once found, the categories to work with to begin creating a financial plan for yourself. In addition, you learned more about the different ways that financial planners charge for their services and how brokers differ from financial advisors.

Hour 14

In Hour 14 we found that the more clarity you get with your taxes and your earned income, the sooner you can begin to envision a more serene life when it comes to money. Clearly, one of the best steps forward you can take is to come to terms with the IRS if you are still owing back taxes. Being up to date on the different kinds of exemptions you qualify for is extremely important. In addition, having an excellent CPA or tax planner on your side can give you the confidence to find this clarity and move on to your investments.

Hour 15

As we have seen, buying insurance can be confusing. But in Hour 15 you learned about the five main types of insurance: life, homeowner's, auto, health, and disability. You learned about the differences between term, whole life, and variable universal insurance and how best to pick the right policy for you. We also explored automobile insurance, long-term-policy insurance, and various Internet sites to explore for online insurance coverage.

Hour 16

In this hour you learned more about the advantages of investing in real estate, how to figure out how much you can afford to spend on property, and how to apply for a mortgage. In addition, you learned more about the types of lenders and loans available to homeowners, including Fannie Mae, Freddie Mac, and Ginnie Mae loans. You also got the chance to explore new online mortgage capabilities and the differences between mortgage brokers and lenders.

Hour 17

Buying a car doesn't have to be a big deal, as you learned in Hour 17. This hour gave you certain basic questions to ask yourself before beginning your new- or used-car search. You also learned what you need to know before you buy, and where and how you can determine what you might get when you trade in your old car. You also determined whether buying or leasing is for you, as well as how to negotiate with dealers for the best price.

HOUR 18

In Hour 18 we found that the sooner you begin exploring your asset-planning options, the more clear you become on making decisions about where your assets should go after you die. By not making a decision on your finances, you are essentially allowing the court system to make it for you, which has the potential to result in much expense and aggravation for your heirs.

In addition, by taking a closer look at probate and death taxes, you can see that setting up a living trust can often be an excellent option, depending on your assets and financial situation. By creating an inventory of assets and beneficiaries, a clearer picture evolves of what you actually own, which will give you greater peace of mind when it comes to deciding who you'd like to possess your worldly possessions once you're gone.

HOUR 19

As you learned in Hour 19, your financial goals will definitely change as you age. With each financial turn, whether it is getting married, having children, getting fired from a job, or saving money for retirement, you are constantly faced with new choices about how your money should be used wisely. Hour 19 also explored ways you can teach your kids good money habits (so they can start planning financial goals as *they* age), plan wisely toward saving for college, and be flexible with your goals as you go into your retirement years.

HOUR 20

Being single can be great fun. Your financial responsibilities and goals will differ from your married friends, and you may have more liquidity. But even if you are a single working person living alone and bringing in a good salary, it makes good business sense to begin a good savings plan for your future. In Hour 20 you learned more about savings plan options if you are single, a recent college grad, or recently divorced. In addition, you saw that many more psychological issues can pop up during and after a divorce, especially around money issues.

HOUR 21

In Hour 21 you learned about the harmony and financial security that can result from two married partners exploring their finances openly and honestly.

By taking a look at some of the common and realistic experiences that can arise when a committed couple plans and experiences a life, you can help chart the course of your financial life more clearly and truthfully. This hour also included a section on becoming clear about your expenses with your spouse, defining and creating prenuptial agreements, and deciding whether joint accounts are for you. The financial harmony and sanity that results from a committed marital partnership can only benefit both partners in the long run and can create a healthy financial space in which to grow and prosper.

Hour 22

In Hour 22 we explored some of the many financial pitfalls to avoid as you begin creating financial abundance in your life. Some of these potential traps include credit card debt, bankruptcy, day trading, and taking out home equity loans if you're not in good financial shape. You also learned to focus on making the right decisions on medical care and insurance for your family as you get older. By keeping these tips in mind, you can avoid making ill-informed choices in your financial life.

Hour 23

The term *financial serenity* can mean different things to different people. Even though you must always go through life developing, expanding, and determining your financial pathways, you may also begin to deeply explore your feelings about money. In this chapter you learned that many of your fears or dread about money come from the thoughts you allow into your mind. Some of these thoughts come from the past as you take them into your present. Rethinking through your thoughts about money, you can make room for new abundant thoughts about money based on a prosperity consciousness rather than a poverty consciousness. Only then will you begin to find serenity in your everyday life. In the end, you'll find that it's truly "not all about the money."

Hour 24

As we head into the new millennium, the Internet continues to change the way we conduct job searches. In Hour 24 you learned ways of conducting a job search online, using the Internet as a valuable resource in researching salary levels, job placement, and growth industries. Also, you learned new ways of creating sharp and focused e-mail resumés, cover letters, and good e-mail etiquette, along with remembering to protect yourself with Internet privacy.

APPENDIX B

Further Readings

There are many sources of information available for further reading on personal finance. For a complete listing of magazines and Web sites, refer to Hours 11, "Guide to Online Research," and 12, "Online Money Management."

DEBT, CREDIT CARDS, AND SPENDING HABITS

Detweiler, Gerri. *The Ultimate Credit Handbook.* New York: Plume, 1997.

Hunt, Mary. *The Cheapskate Monthly Makeover.* New York: St. Martins Press, 1995.

Mundis, Jerrold. *How to Get Out of Debt, Stay Out of Debt and Live Prosperously.* New York: Bantam Books, 1995.

———. *Earn What You Deserve.* New York: Bantam Books, 1995.

———. *Making Peace with Money.* New York: HarperCollins, 1999.

INVESTING

Bigham Bernstel, Janet, and Christy Heady. *The Complete Idiot's Guide to Making Money in the New Millennium.* New York: Alpha Books, 1999.

Gardner, Tom, and Dave Gardner. *You Have More Than You Think: The Foolish Guide to Investing What You Have.* New York: Simon & Schuster, 1998.

Lavine, Alan, and Gail Liberman. *The Complete Idiot's Guide to Making Money in Mutual Funds.* New York: Alpha Books, 1998.

Morris, Kenneth M., and Virginia B. Morris. *The Wall Street Journal Guide to Understanding Money & Investing.* New York: Simon & Schuster, 1999.

Walden, Gene. *The 100 Best Stocks to Own in America.* Illinois: Dearborn Financial Publishing, 1999.

BUDGETS

Burket, Larry. *Family Budgets That Work: A Pocket Guide.* Illinois: Tyndale House Publishers, 1988.

———. *The Financial Planning Workbook.* Illinois: Moody Press, 1991.

Wycoff, Malia McCawlay, and Mary Snyder. *You Can Afford to Stay Home With the Kids: A Step-by-Step Guide for Converting Two Incomes to One.* Ontario: Career Press, Inc., 1999.

OTHER RECOMMENDED BOOKS

Bach, David. *Smart Women Finish Rich.* New York: Broadway Books, 1999.

Barbanel, Linda, M.S.W. *Piggy Bank to Credit Card: Teach Your Child the Financial Facts of Life.* New York: Crown, 1994.

———. *Sex, Money and Power: Smart Ways to Resolve Money Conflicts and Keep Them from Sabotaging Your Closest Relationships.* New York: Macmillan, 1996.

Berger, Esther M. *Money Smart: Take the Fear Out of Financial Planning.* New York: Avon, 1993.

Blue, Ron. *Master Your Money.* Nashville: Thomas Nelson Publishers, 1993.

Bryan, Mark, and Julia Cameron. *Money Drunk, Money Sober: 90 Days to Financial Freedom.* New York: Ballantine, 1999.

Carlson, Richard. *Don't Worry, Make Money: Spiritual and Practical Ways to Create Abundance and More Fun in Your Life.* New York: Hyperion, 1998.

Dixon, Pam. *Job Searching Online for Dummies.* Foster City, California: IDG Books, 1998.

Ealy, C Diane, and Kay Lesh. *Our Money Ourselves: Redesigning Your Relationship with Money.* New York: American Management Association, 1998.

Fisher, Mark. *The Millionaire's Secrets: Life Lessons in Wisdom and Wealth.* New York: Fireside, 1996.

Gillies, Jerry. *Money-Love: How to Get the Money You Deserve for Whatever You Want.* New York: Warner, 1978.

Hayden, Ruth. *How to Turn your Money Life Around: The Money Book for Women.* Deerfield Beach: Health Communications, 1991.

Kaye, Yvonne, Ph.D. *Credit, Cash and Co-Dependency: The Money Connection.* Deerfield Beach: Health Communications, 1991.

Mellan, Olivia. *Money Harmony: Resolving Money Conflicts in Your Life and Relationships.* New York: Walker and Company, 1994.

Michaels, Eileen. *When Are You Entitled to New Underwear and Other Major Financial Decisions: Making Your Money Dreams Come True.* New York: Scribner, 1997.

Needleman, Jacob. *Money and the Meaning of Life.* New York: Currency: 1991.

Ponder, Catherine. *Open Your Mind to Prosperity.* DeVorss Publications, 1971.

Stanley, Thomas J., and William D. Danko. *The Millionaire Next Door: The Surprising Secrets of America's Wealthy.* New York: HB/DJ, 1996.

FURTHER RESEARCH

Here are some highly recommended books for further research:

Dominguez, Joe, and Vicki Robin. *Your Money or Your Life: Transforming Your Relationship with Money and Achieving Financial Independence.* New York: Penguin Books, 1992.

Kobliner, Beth. *Get a Financial Life: Personal Finance in Your Twenties and Thirties.* New York: Fireside Books, 1996.

Laut, Phil. *Money Is My Friend.* New York: Ballantine, 1989.

Orman, Suze. *The Nine Steps to Financial Freedom: Practical and Spiritual Steps So You Can Stop Worrying.* New York: Crown Publishers, 1997.

———. *The Courage to Be Rich.* New York: Crown Publishers, 1999.

Stanny, Barbara. *Prince Charming Isn't Coming: How Women Get Smart About Money.* New York: Viking, 1997.

APPENDIX C
Glossary

12b-1 Fee expenses are paid by shareholders in a mutual fund to cover costs such as advertising and public relations.

account minimum The minimum initial investment amount to open a mutual fund account, normally between $1,000 and $10,000.

all or none An order to sell *all* of your stock, not a few shares pieced out to different traders.

annuity A tax-deferred investment (non-FDIC-insured) underwritten by an insurance company. Annuities provide payments for a specified period, sometimes for life.

asset Something you own that has value.

compounding When money you save or invest earns interest and that interest begins earning interest as well.

dividends A share of the profits earned in a specified period, usually paid to the shareholder in the form of money or stock.

electronic commerce The business of buying and selling goods and services over the Internet.

encryption codes Encryption codes transform data into unreadable formats while it's being transferred from one point to another.

expense ratio The computation in percentage form of total assets used to pay for fund expenses.

fill or kill Sometimes confused with "all or none," this means you want to sell all your stock immediately or sell none.

firewall An electronic security system made up of software and hardware designed to keep unauthorized users, especially Internet users, from accessing private networks connected to the Internet.

fund assets Amount of assets, or holdings, contained in one fund.

GTC or Good 'Til Canceled An order to keep your stock bid or offer live for the next 90 days or until you cancel the order.

hedge   A strategy used to offset risk. A hedge against inflation attempts to keep inflation from eroding the purchasing power of your savings.

hyperlink   An electronic link that takes you from one marked place in a Web page to another in the same or a different document.

inflation   The rise in the prices of goods and services.

limit order   An order that limits your purchase to a certain price.

management fee   An annual fee charged for the management of a mutual fund or for administration services for shareholders.

margin   When you trade on margin, you borrow cash, with interest terms, from your brokerage firm to buy securities.

market order   You tell the broker that you will buy or sell a stock at whatever price the floor trader sets.

no-load fund   A mutual fund that you buy directly from the mutual fund company, eliminating brokerage commission fees.

offering prospectus   A formal written offer to sell securities that should provide key information for the potential investor.

performance   A mutual fund's rate of return for a particular year.

portfolio   The array of investment and savings products you own.

principal   A capital sum of money.

rate-of-return   The change, up or down, in the value of money you invest.

redemption fee   The fee for selling shares of your index fund.

risk   The possibility that money you invest will perform poorly or be lost.

search engine   A Web-based indexing system used for finding information, much like a card catalogue is used in a library.

stop order   A red flag signaling when you want to sell your stock.

symbol   The ticker symbol used to identify a security on the market exchanges.

unsecured debt   Debt, such as credit card debt, that is not supported by collateral.

volatility   Frequent and dramatic rises or drops in value in the stock market.

Web crawlers, spiders, and robots   Programs that roam the Internet, searching all of the available content and providing you with the Internet address of the page you're looking for.

Web 'zine   An electronic magazine.

APPENDIX D

Answers to Quiz Questions

HOUR 1

1. True
2. False
3. False
4. False
5. False
6. b
7. True
8. True
9. d
10. False

HOUR 2

1. False
2. d
3. True
4. True
5. False
6. d
7. False
8. False
9. d
10. False

HOUR 3

1. d
2. c
3. a
4. c
5. a & b
6. True
7. d
8. d
9. d
10. c

HOUR 4

1. True
2. d
3. True
4. True
5. d
6. d
7. True
8. False
9. a
10. True

Hour 5

1. True
2. False
3. False
4. True
5. c
6. True
7. True
8. c
9. c
10. True

Hour 6

1. c
2. d
3. True
4. False
5. c
6. c
7. c
8. True
9. b
10. True

Hour 7

1. b
2. False
3. b
4. c
5. a

6. True
7. True
8. b
9. True
10. True

Hour 8

1. b
2. c
3. b
4. a
5. b
6. b
7. c
8. b
9. c
10. False

Hour 9

1. c
2. c
3. c
4. c
5. d
6. b
7. True
8. True
9. True
10. False

Hour 10

1. d
2. a
3. True
4. b
5. b
6. d
7. False
8. c
9. b
10. b

Hour 11

1. c
2. True
3. True
4. b
5. b
6. c
7. False
8. d
9. True
10. c

HOUR 12

1. d
2. True
3. d
4. c
5. a
6. False
7. True
8. True
9. d
10. d

HOUR 13

1. True
2. b
3. False
4. False
5. True
6. True
7. True
8. d
9. d
10. True

HOUR 14

1. True
2. b
3. d

4. b
5. True
6. True
7. False
8. d
9. True
10. True

HOUR 15

1. True
2. False
3. True
4. False
5. b
6. True
7. True
8. b
9. True
10. b

HOUR 16

1. True
2. True
3. False
4. d
5. True
6. b
7. True
8. b

HOUR 17

1. a
2. e
3. True
4. True
5. c
6. True
7. b
8. e

HOUR 18

1. d
2. True
3. True
4. a
5. True
6. d
7. True
8. b
9. False
10. True

HOUR 19

1. True
2. True
3. False
4. b
5. a
6. False

7. True
8. b
9. True
10. True

Hour 20

1. True
2. False
3. d
4. True
5. d
6. b
7. False
8. True
9. True
10. False

Hour 21

1. b
2. b
3. True
4. True
5. False
6. c
7. True
8. c

9. True
10. c

Hour 22

1. True
2. False
3. b
4. a
5. False
6. False
7. True
8. True
9. b
10. True

Hour 23

1. True
2. False
3. b
4. a
5. True
6. a
7. True
8. True
9. True
10. True

Hour 24

1. True
2. b
3. True
4. b
5. True
6. False
7. True
8. True
9. False
10. True

Index